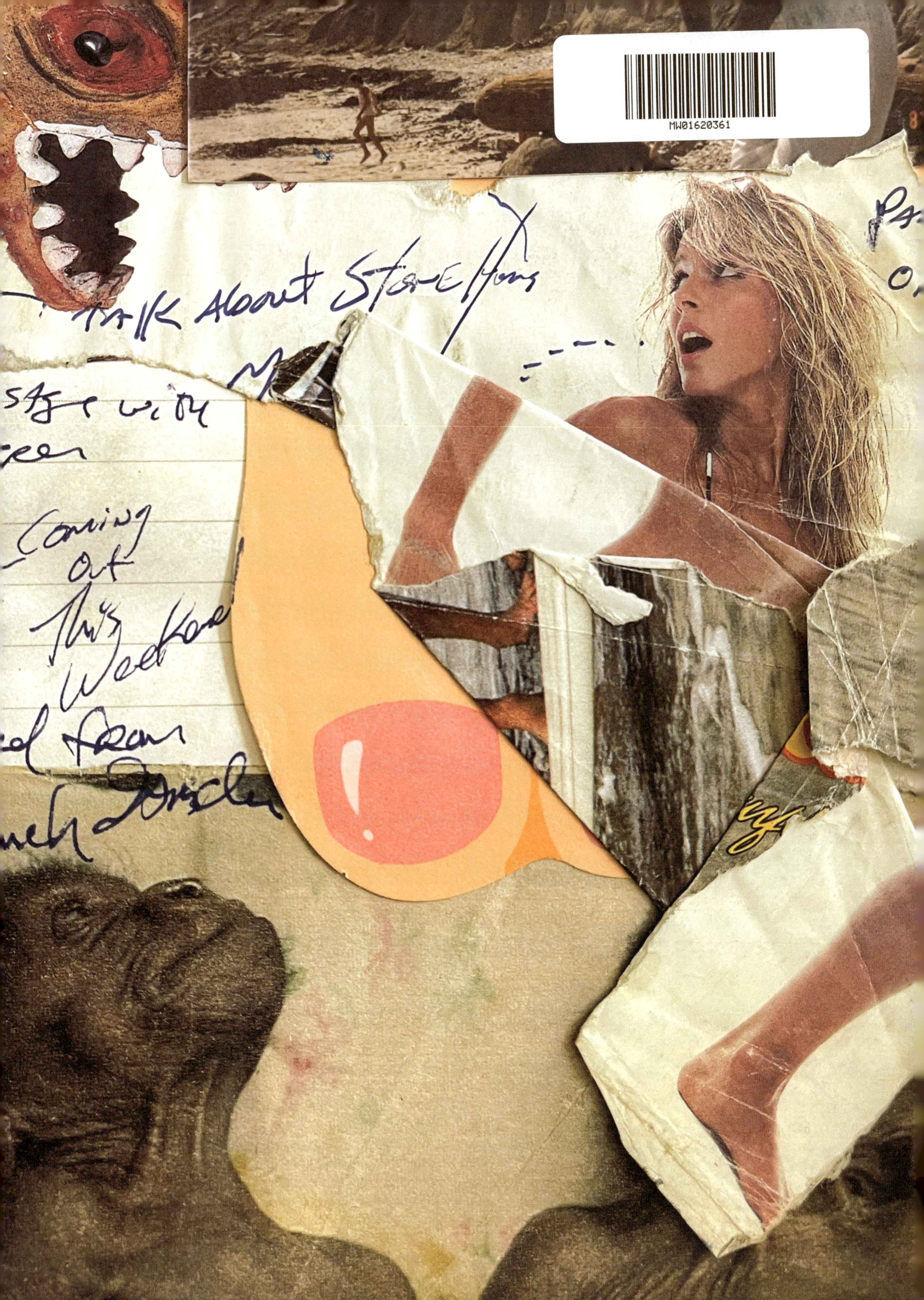
MW01620361
Talk About
Coming
Out
This
Weekend

DEDICATED TO

ALLAN WEISBECKER

PETER BEARD

JIMMY BUFFETT

GREG NOLL

RICK RASMUSSEN

RUSTY DRUMM

PATRICK ABRAMS AKA

'CAPTAIN ZERO'

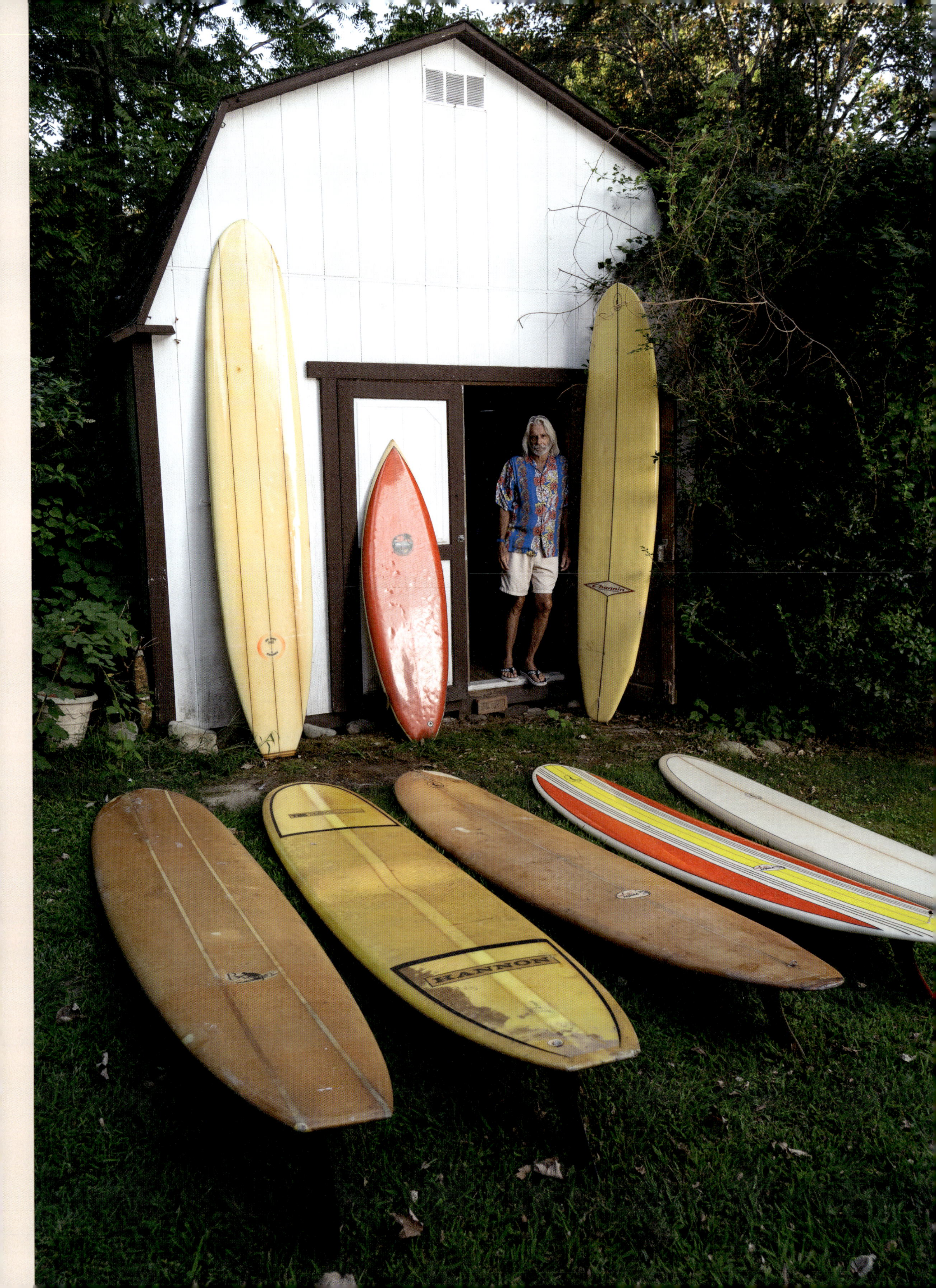
Channin
HANNON

INTRODUCTION

By Zack Raffin

In 2001, Tony Caramanico pushed me into my first wave.

Little did I know that at four years old my life had become forever changed by a man I had met 15 minutes earlier in the parking lot of Ditch Plains in Montauk. Many people have surf instructors, but in Tony, I found so much more: a friend, father figure, coach, and inspiration. Jeff Bridges may be 'The Dude,' but in my eyes Tony was unequivocally 'The Man.'

Born in 1950 into a big Italian family in Amityville, New York, Tony caught his first wave at 13 years old at Gilgo Beach. Like the strike of a match, that wave kicked off a 60-year love affair with everything surfing. He got a job at Beachcomber Surf Shop at age 14 and could be found in his 16-foot wooden Thompson ripping through the canals of upper Long Island to get to the beach at even the slightest hint of waves.

Make no mistake; surfers are addicts, just as hooked by their endeavor as one can be a contemporary substance. Modern addictions are rooted in behavior. Input = output, their effect on biology tried and tested. Meanwhile, surfers are chasing a more mythical dragon: the indescribable sensation of wave riding. A feeling that exists solely in the mind and soul of those firmly grasped within its claws.

While Gilgo Beach is where Tony fell in love with surfing, Montauk is where he said, 'I do.' Tony's first trip to Montauk came in 1965, a journey that he still remembers to this day: "My friend Bobby Schneider's dad had a big sport fisherman boat. We left Amityville on the south shore and went through Shinnecock Inlet and into Montauk. The Californians had Baja, but for us Montauk was 100 miles away. We could have been anywhere. I remember coming in over big rolling waves and going, 'wow.'"

After graduating college in 1969, Tony settled in Montauk and eventually moved in with renowned artist Peter Beard in 1978. Living on the Beard property came with much hoopla, and Beard had one simple request: keep a journal.

Thankfully for us, he did just that.

What began as simple notes on the day's waves slowly evolved. A printout of a surf article here, a business card there. By 1980, the journals had taken on a whole new life. Opening up one of these duct tape-bound, 18-inch thick binders invites one on a mind-numbing journey of colorful exotica through the lens of surf culture. Layered with pop cultural moments from old Tylenol and bikini ads to the Iran hostage crisis and Clinton's impeachment, the journals act not only as a ledger of Tony's immense surfing life but a life well lived through four decades of profound cultural evolution. And that's all before we mention the travel. Morocco. Indonesia. Egypt. Tobago. Jamaica. Kenya. France. Japan. China. All in pursuit of that same mythical feeling he first achieved at age 13.

By the time you read this, Tony will have completed well over 16,000 journals. From 1978 to present, he has yet to miss a single day. It's important to note that until 2000, Tony didn't display his journals as art. This was a purely creative endeavor, reflexive in every way, or as Tony would say, "like having a coffee in the morning."

The journals depict a thrilling existence, one that goes far beyond the modern world and into a time we too easily forget. While you dive into 4 decades of art, love, and life below, remember: Tony Caramanico is many things. A historian. An accomplished competitive surfer. An artist. A devoted husband. A quintessential Italian New Yorker with the mustache to boot. And while all true, Tony Caramanico is, first and foremost, a lifelong surf-obsessed kid from Amityville, New York, who still gets up and checks the waves every single day.

I'll always be honored to call Tony Caramanico my friend.

DECEMBER 1978

4 MONDAY
Early Morning love
With Folly. She leaves
Breakfast with Patrick, Mt Irvine
* Waves 3-5' good with Tom+Patrick
Good things

Folly leaves

5 TUESDAY
~~Sarah Beth leaves~~
Mushroom with Tom
Beach bar barbacue
lots of Thinking
Feel good about Things
Surfed 2-3'
Think about Folly?

6 WEDNESDAY
Mushroom's with Ray
had nice surf session 2-4'
evening dinner MonSori
and Turtle beach
Start work on story
about Surfing.
Ran & Surf

DECEMBER 1978

THURSDAY 7
Mushroom's Tom
Ran, tryed to work on story
Waves 2-3' stayed in
at night and wrote letter
to Folly

FRIDAY 8
Hilton Hotel Trinadad
Rental car Flew from Tobago
Breakfast MT Irvine
great dinner at Hilton
1st class
Ralf leaves
small waves

SATURDAY 9
Bob Marley Concert in Trinadad
Hilton Hotel dinner drove around
countryside in Trinaded
also Market Place No Waves

SUNDAY 10
Back to Tobago
dinner Mt Irvine with Tom Brad
No Waves today

CUT HERE

First Journal. 1978

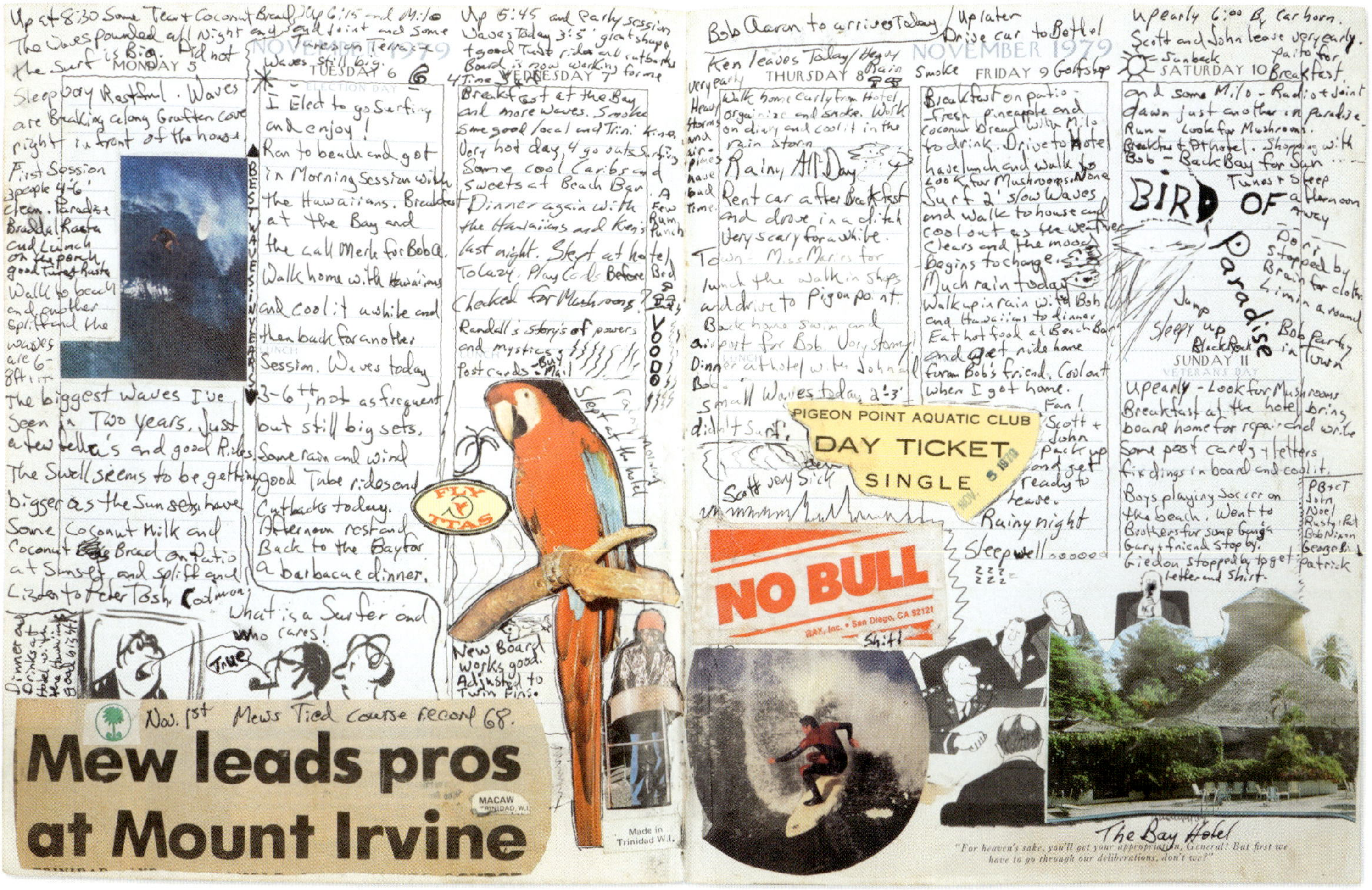

NOVEMBER 1979

MONDAY 5

Up at 8:30 Some Tea + Coconut Bread. The waves pounded all night and the Surf is Big. Did not Sleep Very Restful. Waves are Breaking along Grafton cove right in front of the house.

First Session people 4-6'. Clean. Paradise Bread + Rasta and Lunch on the porch good times. Walk to beach and another spliff and the waves are 6-8ft. The biggest waves I've seen in Two years. Just a few rollers and good Rides. The Swell seems to be getting bigger as the Sun sets. have Some Coconut Milk and Coconut Bread on Patio at Sunset, and spliff and Listen to Peter Tosh

TUESDAY 6

ELECTION DAY

Up 6:15 and Milo and small joint and some waves still big.

I Elect to go Surfing and enjoy! Ran to beach and got in Morning Session with the Hawaiians. Breakfast at the Bay and the call Merle for Bobo. Walk home with Hawaiians and cool it awhile and then back for another Session. Waves today 3-6 ft, not as frequent but still big sets. Some rain and wind. Good Tube rides and Cutbacks today. Afternoon rest and Back to the Bay for a barbacue dinner.

BEST WAVES IN YEARS

What is a Surfer and who cares!

TRUE

WEDNESDAY 7

Up 5:45 and Early session. Waves today 3'-5' great shape. Board is now working for me. Breakfast at the Bay and more waves. Smoke Some good local and Trini. Very hot day 4 go out Surfing. Some cool Caribs and sweets at Beach Bar. Dinner again with the Hawaiians and Kevin last night. Start at hotel. Today. Play Cool. Before Bed Checked for Mushrooms.

Randall's story's of powers and mystics. Post cards. Mail.

VOODOO

FLY TTAS

New Board works good. Adjusted to Twin Fin.

Nov. 1st Mews Tied course record 68.

Mew leads pros at Mount Irvine

MACAW

Made in Trinidad W.I.

THURSDAY 8

Bob Aaron to arrive Today. Ken leaves Today. Heavy Rain.

Walk home early from Hotel, organize and smoke. Walk on diary and cool it in the rain storm.

Rainy All Day

Rent car after Breakfast and drove in a ditch. Very scary for a while.

Town. Miss Marie's for lunch. Then walk in shops and drive to Pigeon Point. Back home. Swim and airport for Bob. Very stormy. Dinner at hotel with John and Bob.

Small Waves today 2-3'. didn't Surf.

Scott very Sick

FRIDAY 9

Up later. Drive car to Bethel. Smoke. Golf shop.

Breakfast on patio - Fresh pineapple and coconut bread with Milo to drink. Drive to Hotel have lunch and walk to look for Mushrooms. None. Surf 2' slow waves and walk to house and cool out as the weather Clears and the mood begins to change. Much rain today. Walk up in rain with Bob and Hawaiians to dinner. Eat hot food at Beach Bar and get ride home from Bob's friend. Cool out when I got home.

Fan! Scott + John pack up and get ready to leave.

Rainy night. Sleep well

PIGEON POINT AQUATIC CLUB

DAY TICKET

SINGLE

NOV. 5 1979

NO BULL

San Diego, CA 92121

Shit!

SATURDAY 10

Up early 6:00 By Car horn. Scott and John leave very early. Sunback. Patio for Breakfast and some Milo - Radio + Joint. dawn just another in paradise. Run - Look for Mushrooms. Breakfast at hotel. Shopping with Bob - Back Bay for Sun. Tunes + Sleep afternoon.

BIRD OF Paradise

Dori stopped by. Brain for clothes.

Jump. Sleep up. Blackrock. Bob Party in town

SUNDAY 11

VETERANS DAY

Up early - Look for Mushrooms. Breakfast at the hotel. bring board home for repair and write some post cards + letters. Fix dings in board and cool it. Boys playing soccer on the beach. Went to Brothers for some Ganja. Gary + friends stop by. Giedon stopped by to get letter and Shirt.

PB+T John Noel Rusty Pat Brennan George B. Patrick

The Bay Hotel

"For heaven's sake, you'll get your appropriation, General! But first we have to go through our deliberations, don't we?"

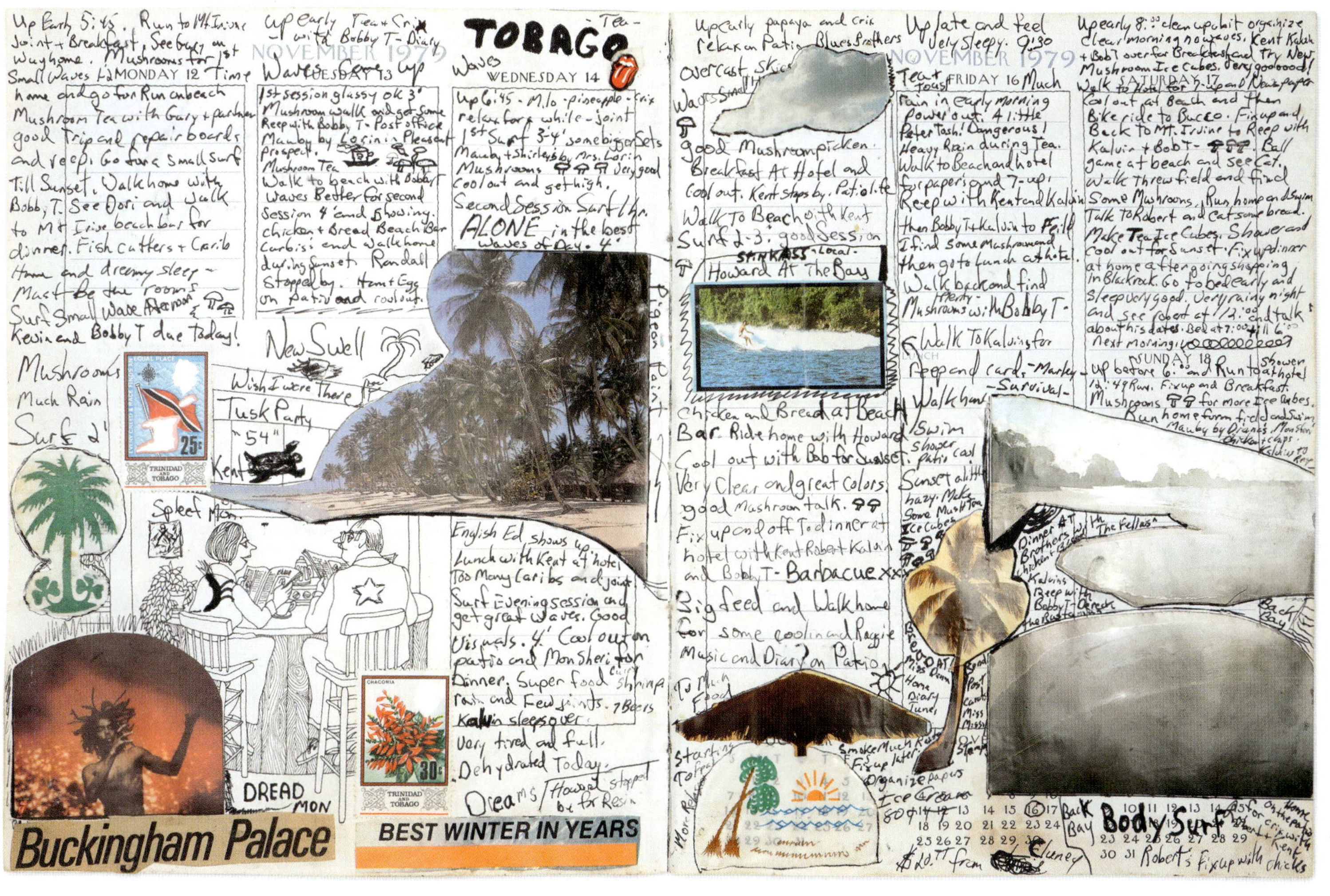

NOVEMBER 1979

MONDAY 12

Up Early 5:45. Run to Mt. Irvine. Joint + Breakfast. See Gary on way home. Mushrooms for 1st time. Small Waves. Take home and go for Run on beach. Mushroom Tea with Gary + partner. good Trip and repair boards and rest. Go for a small surf Till Sunset. Walk home with Bobby T. See Dori and walk to Mt Irvine beach bar for dinner. Fish cutters + Carib. Home and dreamy sleep. Must be the rooms. Surf Small Wave Afternoon. Kevin and Bobby T due today!

Mushrooms. Much Rain. Surf 2'

TUESDAY 13

Up early. Tea + Cris with Bobby T - Diary. Waves Come up.

1st session glassy ok 3'. Mushroom walk and get some. Keep with Bobby T. Post office. Mauby by Lorin. Pleasant prospect. Mushroom Tea. Walk to beach with Bobby T. Waves Better for second session 4' and showing. Chicken + Bread Beach Bar. Carbs and walk home during sunset. Randall stopped by. Ham + Eggs on patio and cool out.

New Swell

Wish I were there

Tusk Party "54"

Kent

Spleef Mon

WEDNESDAY 14

TOBAGO

Tea - Waves

Up 6:45 - Milo - pineapple - Tea relax for a while - Joint. 1st Surf 3-4' some bigger sets. Mauby + Shirley by Mrs. Lorin. Mushrooms very good. Cool out and get high. Second Session Surf 1hr. ALONE in the best Waves of Day. 4'

Pigeon Point

English Ed shows up. Lunch with Kent at hotel. Too Many Caribs and joint. Surf Evening session and get great Waves. Good Visuals. 4' Cool out on patio and Mon Sheri for Dinner. Super food. Shrimp rice and Feed joints. 7 Beers. Kalvin sleeps over. Very tired and full. Dehydrated Today.

Dreams / Howard stopped by for Rest

DREAD MON

TRINIDAD AND TOBAGO 25c

TRINIDAD AND TOBAGO 30c

Buckingham Palace

BEST WINTER IN YEARS

THURSDAY 15

Up early papaya and Cris. Relax on Patio. Blues Brothers. Overcast Skies. Waves Small.

good Mushroom picken. Breakfast At Hotel and Cool out. Kent stops by. Patio life. Walk To Beach with Kent. Surf 2-3' good Session.

STARKASS - Local. Howard At The Bay

Chicken and Bread at Beach Bar. Ride home with Howard. Cool out with Bob for Sunset. Very Clear and great colors. good Mushroom talk. Fix up and off To dinner at hotel with Kent, Robert, Kalvin and Bobby T - Barbacue. Big feed and Walk home for some cooling and Reggie Music and Diary on Patio.

FRIDAY 16

Up late and feel very sleepy. 9:30 Tea + toast. Much Rain in early morning. Power out. A little Peter Tosh! Dangerous! Heavy Rain during Tea. Walk to Beach and hotel for papers and 7-up. Keep with Kent and Kalvin then Bobby T + Kalvin to Field. Find some Mushrooms and then go to lunch at hotel. Walk back and find Plenty Mushrooms with Bobby T.

Walk To Kalvin's for Reep and cards - Marley - Survival -

Walk home. Swim. Shower. Patio. Cool. Sunset a little hazy. Make Some Mush Tea. Ice Cubes.

SATURDAY 17

Up early 8:30 clean up a bit, organize. Clear morning, no waves. Kent, Kalvin + Bob T over for Breakfast and Try New Mushroom Ice Cubes. Very good! Walk to Hotel for papers. Cool out at Beach and then Bike ride to Bucco. Fix up and Back to Mt. Irvine to Keep with Kalvin + Bob T. Ball game at beach and see Cat. Walk thru field and find Some Mushrooms. Run home and Swim. Talk to Robert and eat some bread. Make Tea Ice Cubes. Shower and Cool out for Sunset. Fix up dinner at home after going shopping in Blackrock. Go to bed early and Sleep very good. Very rainy night and see Robert at 12:00 and talk about this dates. Bed at 7:00 till 6:30. Next morning.

SUNDAY 18

Up before 6. and Run to hotel. Shower. 1/2 49 Run. Fix up and Breakfast. Mushrooms for more Ice Cubes. Run home from field and Swim. Mauby by Dianne's Monshiri.

Dinner At Brothers with chicken. Kalvins. Keep with Bobby T. The Fellas.

Back Bay

Body Surf

Robert's Fixup with chicks

13 14 15 16 17
18 19 20 21 22 23 24
25 26 27 28 29 30

10 11 12 13 14 15
23 24 25 26 27 28 29
30 31

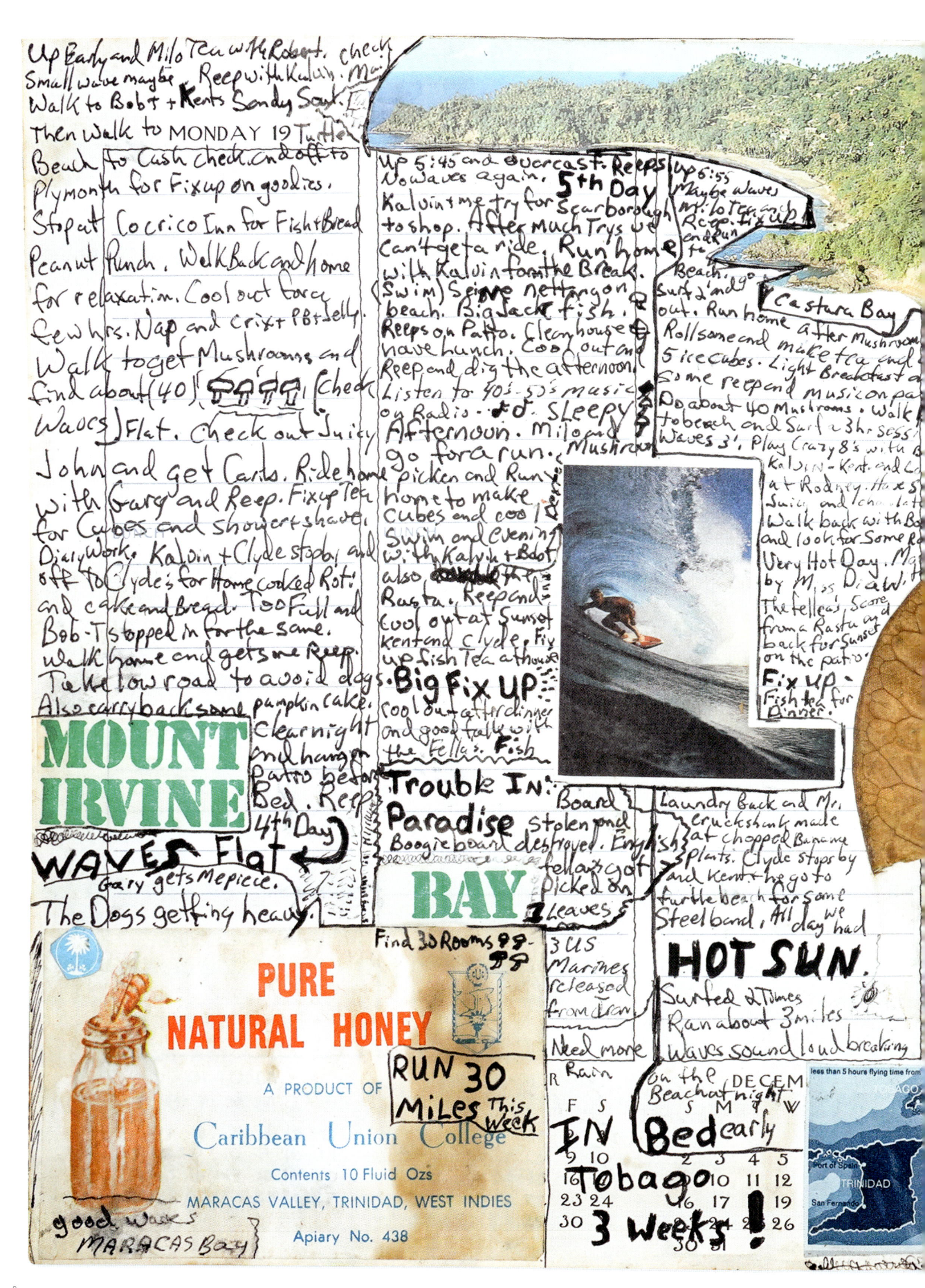
Up Early and Milo Tea with Robert. Check
Small wave maybe. Reep with Kalvin. M
Walk to Bob T + Kent's Sandy Spot.
Then walk to MONDAY 19 Turtle
Beach to Cash check and off to
Plymouth for Fixup on goodies.
Stop at Cocrico Inn for Fish + Bread
Peanut Punch. Walk Back and home
for relaxation. Cool out for a
few hrs. Nap and crix + PB + Jelly.
Walk to get Mushrooms and
find about (40). Check
Waves) Flat. Check out Juicy
John and get Cards. Ride home
with Gary and Reep. Fixup Tea
for Cubes and shower + shave.
Diary Work. Kalvin + Clyde stop by and
off to Clyde's for Home cooked Roti
and cake and Bread. Too Full and
Bob-T stopped in for the same.
Walk home and get some Reep.
Take low road to avoid dogs.
Also carry back some pumpkin cake.
Clear night and hang on Patio before Bed. Reep
4th Day
MOUNT IRVINE
WAVES Flat
Gary gets Me piece.
The Dogs getting heavy.
Up 5:45 and overcast. Reeps
No waves again. 5th Day
Kalvin + me try for Scarborough
to shop. After much Trys we
can't get a ride. Run home
with Kalvin for the Break.
(Swim) Seine net on
beach. Big Jack fish.
Reeps on Patio. Clean house &
have Lunch. Cool out and
Reep and dig the afternoon.
Listen to 40's-50's music
on Radio. Sleepy
Afternoon. Milo and
go for a run. Mushroom
picken and Run
home to make
cubes and cool
Swim and evening
with Kalvin + Bob T
also the
Rasta. Reep and
cool out at Sunset
Kent and Clyde. Fix
up fish Tea at house
Big Fix up.
Cool out after dinner
and good talk with
the Fellas. Fish
Trouble In Paradise
Board stolen and
Boogie board destroyed. English
fellas got
picked on
Leaves
BAY
Find 30 Rooms
3 US Marines released from Iran
Need more Rain
Up 6:55
Maybe waves
Milo Tea and
Reep. Fix up
and Run to
Beach.
Surf 2 and
out. Run home
Castara Bay
after Mushroom
Roll some and make tea and
5 ice cubes. Light Breakfast
Some Reep and music on pa
Do about 40 Mushrooms. Walk
to beach and Surf a 3 hr sess
Waves 3'. Play Crazy 8's with
Kalvin - Kent and
at Rodney
Juicy and chocolate
Walk back with Bo
and look for some
Very Hot Day.
by Miss Diaw.
The fellas Score
from a Rasta and
back for Sunset
on the patio.
Fix up
Fish tea for
Dinner.
Laundry Back and Mr.
Cruickshank made
at chopped Banana
Plants. Clyde stops by
and Kent + he go to
turtle beach for some
Steel band. All day we had
HOT SUN.
Surfed 2 Times
Ran about 3 miles
Waves sound loud breaking
on the Beach at night
In Bed early
IN Tobago 3 weeks!
DECEM
F S S M T W
9 10 2 3 4 5
16 10 11 12
23 24 16 17 19
30 26
30 31
PURE NATURAL HONEY
A PRODUCT OF
Caribbean Union College
Contents 10 Fluid Ozs
MARACAS VALLEY, TRINIDAD, WEST INDIES
Apiary No. 438
RUN 30 MILES This week
good waves
MARACAS Bay
less than 5 hours flying time from
TOBAGO
Port of Spain
TRINIDAD
San Fernando

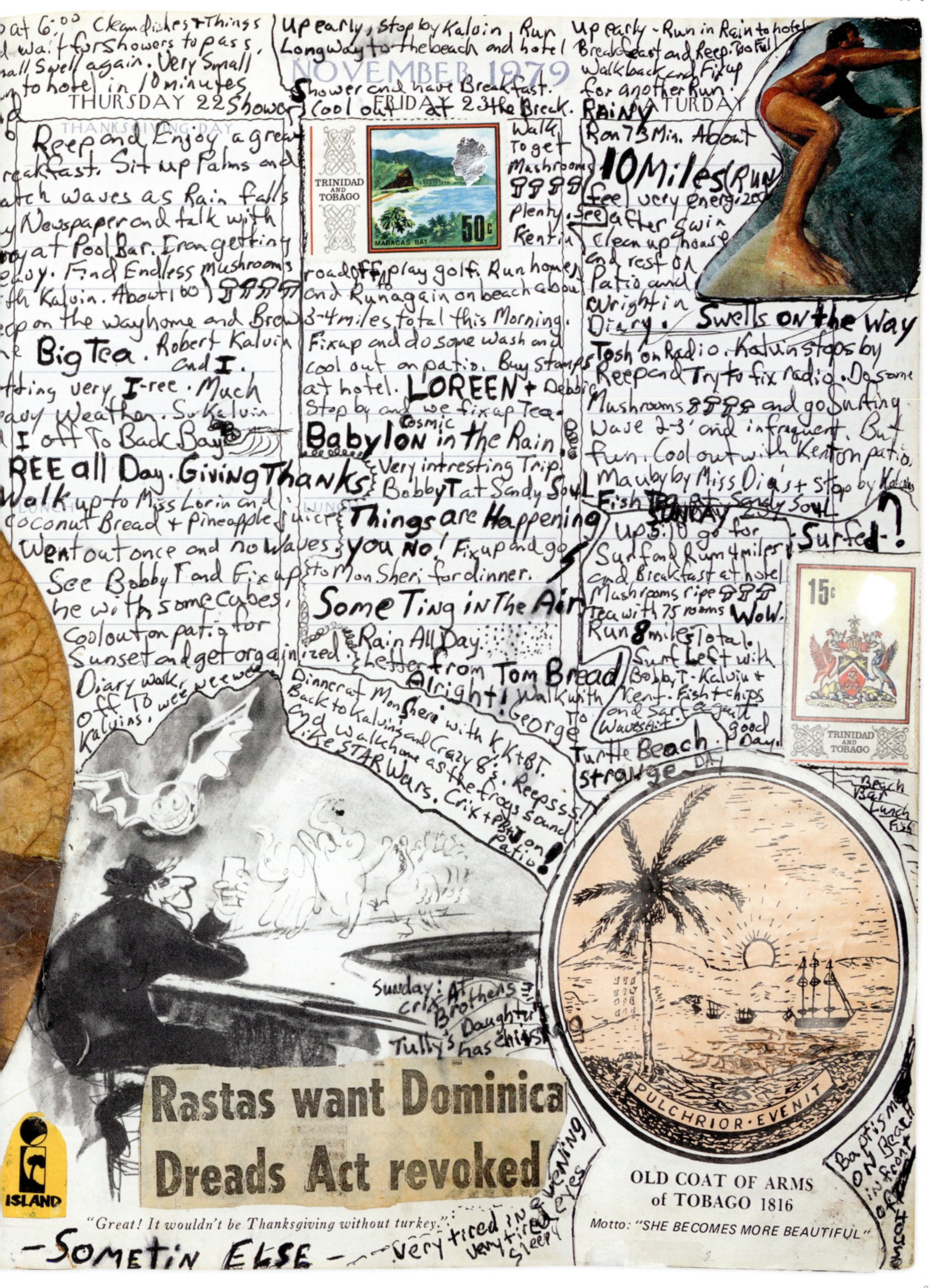
NOVEMBER 1979
THURSDAY 22
THANKSGIVING DAY
FRIDAY 23
SATURDAY
SUNDAY
TRINIDAD AND TOBAGO
MARACAS BAY
50c
15c
TRINIDAD AND TOBAGO
LOREEN + Debbie
Babylon in the Rain
Things are Happening
Some Ting in The Air
10 Miles
Swells on the way
Surfed
Rastas want Dominica
Dreads Act revoked
ISLAND
PULCHRIOR EVENIT
OLD COAT OF ARMS
of TOBAGO 1816
Motto: "SHE BECOMES MORE BEAUTIFUL"
"Great! It wouldn't be Thanksgiving without turkey."
-SOMETIN ELSE-

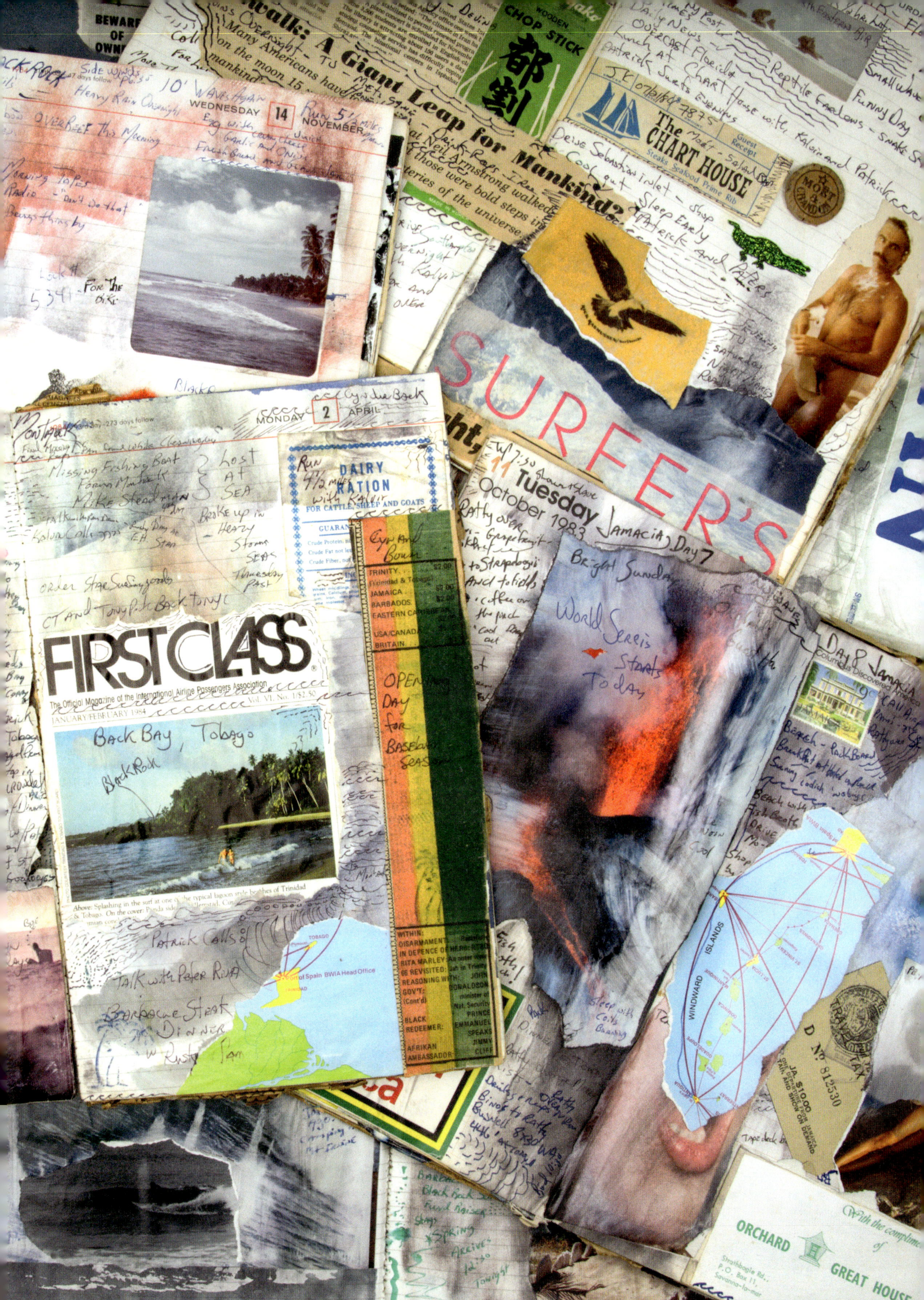

walk: A Giant Leap for Mankind?
WEDNESDAY 14 NOVEMBER
MONDAY 2 APRIL
DAIRY RATION
FOR CATTLE, SHEEP AND GOATS
The CHART HOUSE
Steaks Seafood Prime Rib
SURFER'S
Tuesday
October 1983
FIRSTCLASS
The Official Magazine of the International Airline Passengers Association
JANUARY/FEBRUARY 1984
Back Bay, Tobago
TRINIDAD
JAMAICA
BARBADOS
EASTERN CARIBBEAN
USA/CANADA
BRITAIN
WINDWARD ISLANDS
ORCHARD GREAT HOUSE
With the compliments of

JOURNALS

1980s

The story of Tony's journals begins in 1970 when a wide-eyed 20-year-old moves to Montauk to start a business with his two childhood friends, Dave Williams and Lee Bieler. For $35,000, they bought an A-frame in town, started a surf shop, and built a restaurant they named Albatross.

Tony was both proprietor and cook, living in the store's upstairs studio while manning the grill for what was the consensus best breakfast in town. They say all good things come to an end, and after a successful seven year run, the trio closed the business.

Enter Peter Beard.

World-renowned artist and infamous playboy, Peter's wildlife photography, mixed media journals, and collaborations with Warhol, Salvador Dali, and The Stones made him far and away Montauk's most prominent resident. The larger-than-life personality split time between Kenya, New York City, and Montauk, where he was known to hire locals to help with odd jobs on Thunderbolt Ranch, a sprawling 6-acre beachfront property that was famously the closest house to the tip of Long Island, or as he would tell visitors, "the last house on the right." Upon the sale of his business, Tony bought a trailer within the Ditch Plains trailer park, which sat in front of the most consistent wave in town. With plans to call that home, Tony was set, that is until a chance run-in with Peter at Shagwong Tavern where, after explaining his situation, Peter lovingly chimed that he should pull the trailer up to Thunderbolt Ranch and live with him.

While Ditch Plains was good, Peter's house sat directly in front of a series of long, right-hand point breaks that, on their day, are considered to be some of the best waves on the East Coast. For a surf-obsessed 27-year-old, this was a no-brainer. He ditched the trailer and jotted up the road where he took root within one of Peter's guesthouses.

Tony's move to Thunderbolt Ranch marked the beginning of his journaling journey. He began keeping daily notes in 1978, then graduated in 1979 to a larger format journal gifted to him by Beard's then-girlfriend, model Cheryl Tieg. In '79, the Beard influence can be seen creeping into the pages of Tony's journal via additions of newspaper clippings, surf photo cutouts, and whimsical cartoons. But if '79 was the appetizer, '80 was the filet.

With two years of journals under his belt, 1980 marks a stark evolution in the depth and artistry Tony brought to the page. This is in no small part because Tony and Peter began working collaboratively on their journals via a process they called 'rubbing.' Using a since discontinued toxic industrial cleaner called Afta Cleaning Fluid, they would pull choice imagery from newspapers and magazines, place the photos onto pages of their journals and rub the page with a fluid soaked rag, transferring the image in an abstract, illustrative way. Staged in the basement of Beard's house, these rubbing sessions most often took the form of substance-infused all-nighters where they would prep dozens of pages at a time.

There's a reason Afta Cleaning Fluid is no longer on the market. The cleaner was so toxic that Tony's throat would burn as he emerged from each and every rubbing session. Eventually valuing their health over their journals, they inevitably stopped their rubbings in the late '80s. Long term health aside, the colorful rubbings provided a unique texture with which Tony laid his work upon.

While the rubbings are one reason for the journal's developments, Tony's professional growth played a big role as well. An around-the-world trip to produce the first surfing-based episode of ABC's American Sportsmen provided Tony with a breadth of new material and infused within him a new, creative light.

New waves in far-off tropical lands are any surfer's dream, and in 1980, Tony invites us to live that dream through his unique lens. Once he got going, he never looked back, and while the '80s journals offer a wide use of rubbings, color, and sensational surf and pop cultural imagery, they also depict the experience of transitioning from your late '20s into your '30s with love, loss and everything in between. Trips to Beard's Hog Ranch in Kenya, where his tent was visted at dawn by a curious giraffe, long nights at Studio 54, stints on his beloved Tobago, the endless days of phenomenal waves on the East End, and so much more.

A visual thrill ride in full color. Go deep!

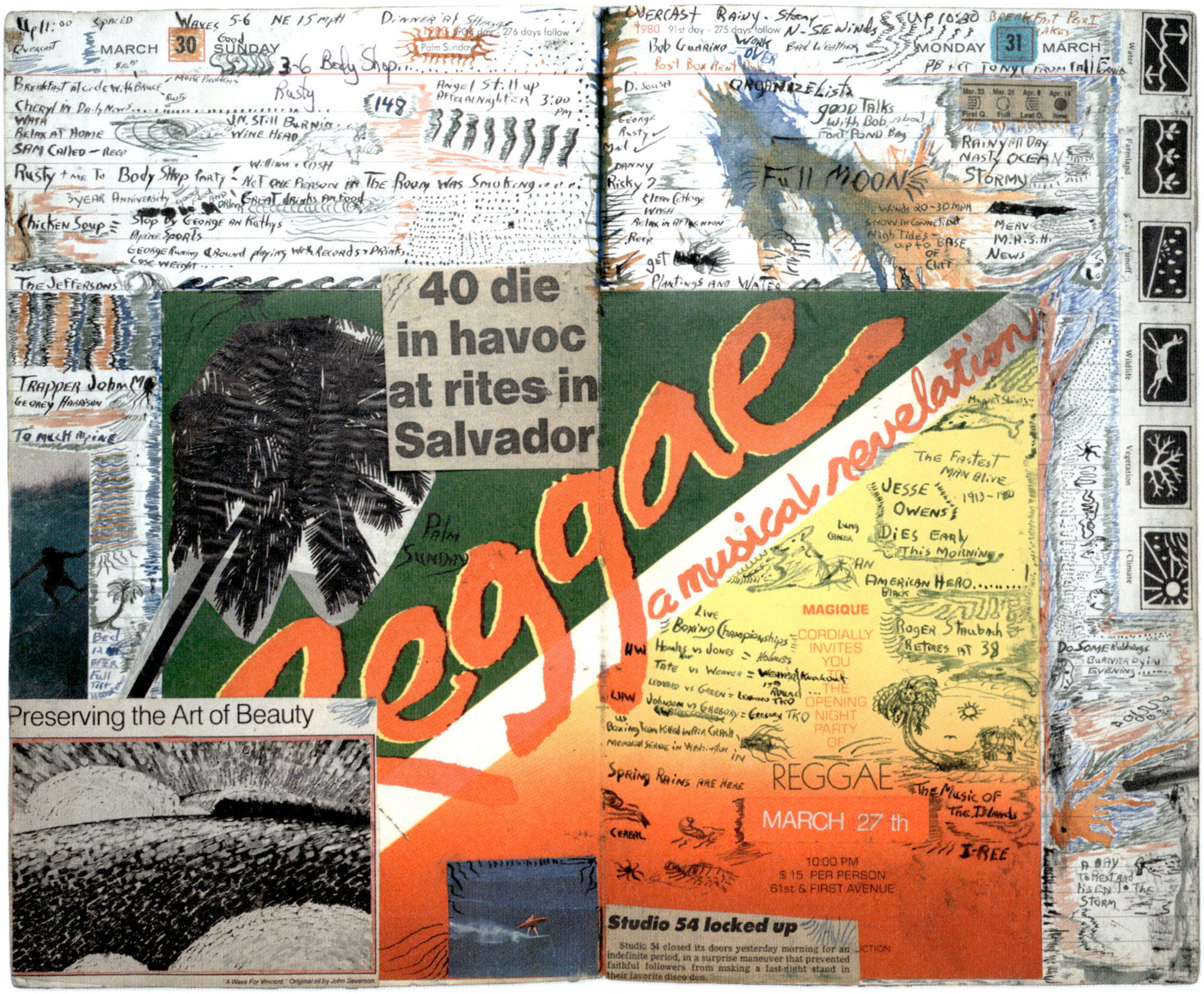

MARCH 30 SUNDAY
Palm Sunday
276 days follow

1980 91st day – 275 days follow
MONDAY 31 MARCH

40 die in havoc at rites in Salvador

Reggae
a musical revelation

MAGIQUE
CORDIALLY INVITES YOU TO THE OPENING NIGHT PARTY OF
REGGAE
MARCH 27 th
10:00 PM
$ 15 PER PERSON
61st & FIRST AVENUE

Preserving the Art of Beauty

"A Wave For Vincent." Original oil by John Severson.

Studio 54 locked up

Studio 54 closed its doors yesterday morning for an ...iction indefinite period, in a surprise maneuver that prevented faithful followers from making a last-night stand in their favorite disco den.

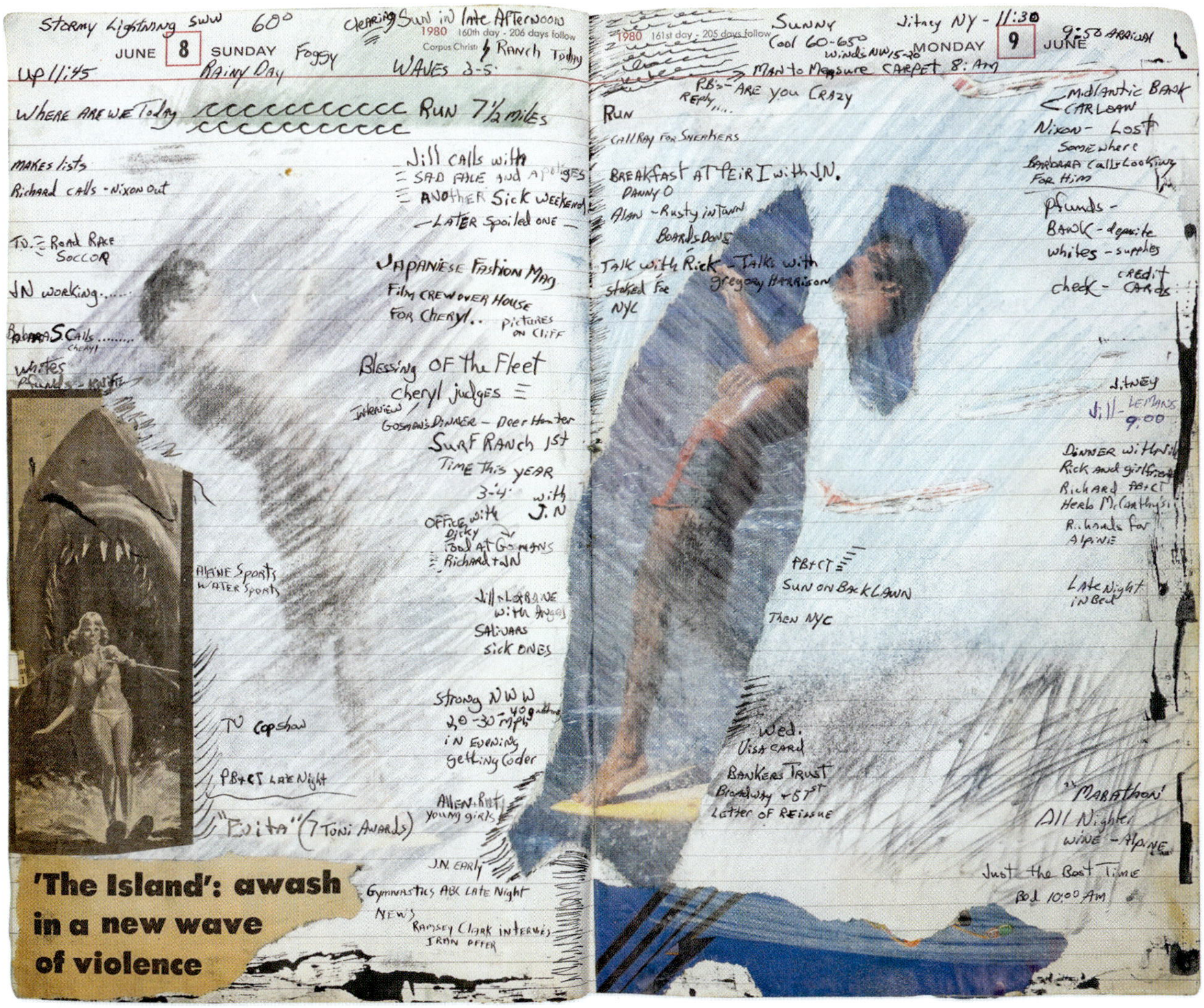

JUNE 8 SUNDAY
1980 160th day – 206 days follow
Corpus Christi

1980 161st day – 205 days follow
MONDAY 9 JUNE

'The Island': awash in a new wave of violence

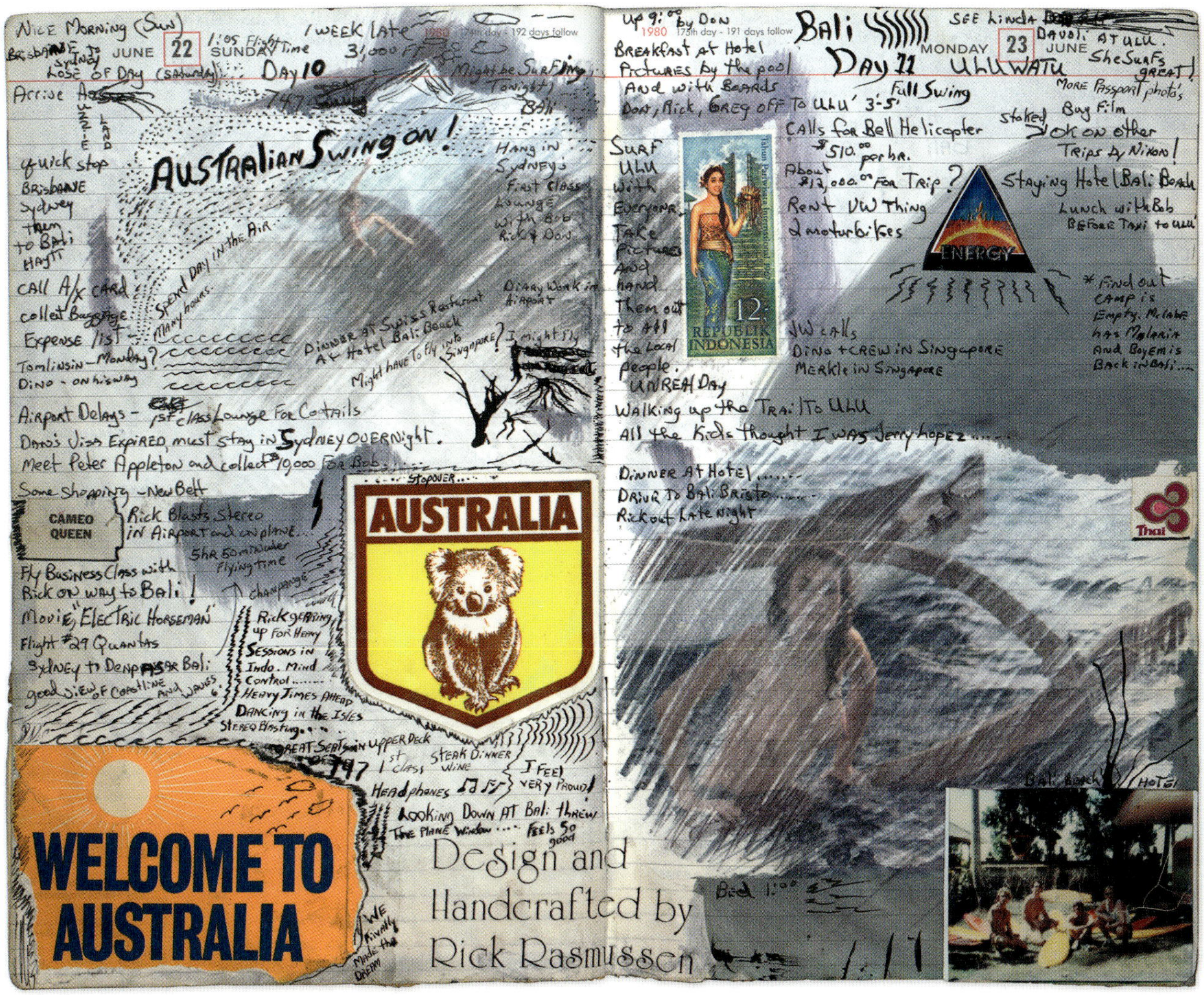

Nice Morning (Sun)
JUNE 22 SUNDAY
1 week late
Day 10
Australian Swing on!
Quick stop Brisbane Sydney then to Bali
Call A/x card
collect Baggage
Airport Delays - 1st class Lounge for Cocktails
Dino's Visa Expired, must stay in Sydney overnight.
Meet Peter Appleton and collect $19,000 for Bob.
Some Shopping - New Belt
CAMEO QUEEN
Rick Blasts Stereo in Airport and on plane.
Fly Business Class with Rick on way to Bali!
Movie, "Electric Horseman"
Flight #29 Quantas
Sydney to Denpasar Bali:
good view of Coastline and waves
AUSTRALIA
WELCOME TO AUSTRALIA
Looking Down At Bali through the Plane window... Feels so good

Design and Handcrafted by Rick Rasmussen

Up 9:00 by Don
Bali
MONDAY 23 JUNE
Day 11
Uluwatu
Breakfast at Hotel
Pictures by the pool
And with Boards
Don, Rick, Greg off to Ulu 3-5' Full Swing
Calls for Bell Helicopter $510.00 per hr.
About $12,000.00 For Trip?
Rent VW Thing
2 motorbikes
Staying Hotel Bali Beach
Lunch with Bob Before Taxi to Ulu
ENERGY
REPUBLIK INDONESIA
Surf Ulu with Everyone. Take Pictures And hand them out to All the Local people.
UNREAL Day
Walking up the Trail to Ulu
All the kids thought I was Jerry Lopez......
Dinner At Hotel......
Drive To Bali Bristo......
Rick out Late night
Thai
Bed 1:00

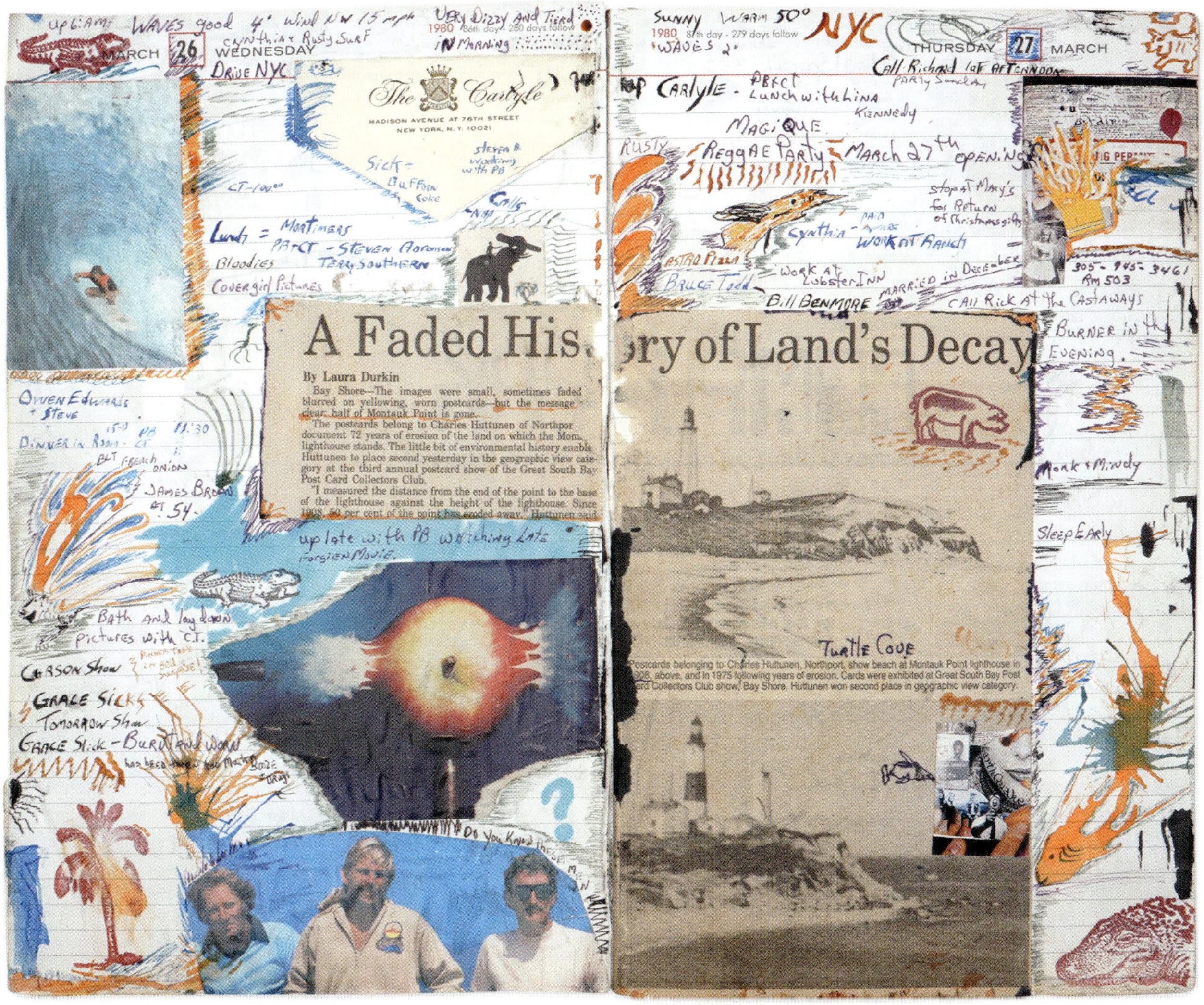

Up 6 AM Waves good 4' wind NW 15 mph
1980 Very Dizzy And Tired in Morning
MARCH 26 WEDNESDAY
Drive NYC
The Carlyle
MADISON AVENUE AT 76TH STREET
NEW YORK, N. Y. 10021
Lunch = Mortimers
PB + CT - Steven Aaronson
Terry Southern
Bloodies
Covergirl Pictures

A Faded History of Land's Decay

By Laura Durkin

Bay Shore—The images were small, sometimes faded blurred on yellowing, worn postcards—but the message clear: half of Montauk Point is gone.

The postcards belong to Charles Huttunen of Northpor document 72 years of erosion of the land on which the Mon lighthouse stands. The little bit of environmental history enable Huttunen to place second yesterday in the geographic view category at the third annual postcard show of the Great South Bay Post Card Collectors Club.

"I measured the distance from the end of the point to the base of the lighthouse against the height of the lighthouse. Since 1908, 50 per cent of the point has eroded away," Huttunen said

up late with PB watching Late forgien Movie.
Bath And lay down
Pictures with C.T.
Carson Show
Grace Slick
Tomorrow Show

Sunny Warm 50°
1980 Waves 2'
NYC
THURSDAY 27 MARCH
Carlyle
Reggae Party March 27th opening
Cynthia - Work at Ranch
Astro Pizza
Bruce Todd - Work at Lobster Inn
Married in December
Bill Benmore
Call Rick At the Castaways
Burner in the Evening
Mark + Mindy
Sleep Early
Turtle Cove

Postcards belonging to Charles Huttunen, Northport, show beach at Montauk Point lighthouse in 1908, above, and in 1975 following years of erosion. Cards were exhibited at Great South Bay Post Card Collectors Club show, Bay Shore. Huttunen won second place in geographic view category.

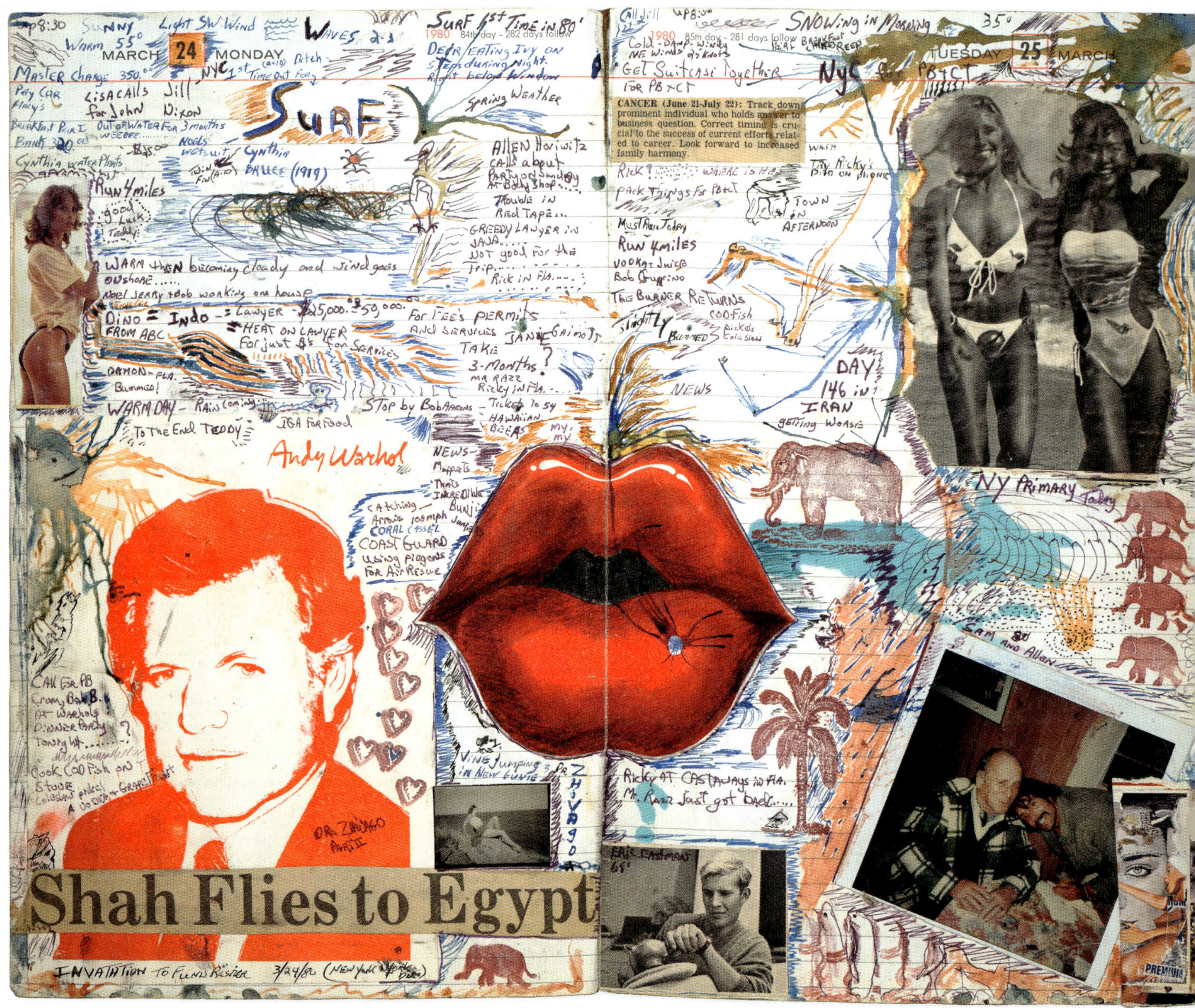
24 MARCH MONDAY
1980 84th day - 282 days follow
SURF
1980 85th day - 281 days follow
TUESDAY 25 MARCH
CANCER (June 21-July 22): Track down prominent individual who holds answer to business question. Correct timing is crucial to the success of current efforts related to career. Look forward to increased family harmony.
Andy Warhol
Shah Flies to Egypt
NY Primary Today
DAY 146 in IRAN

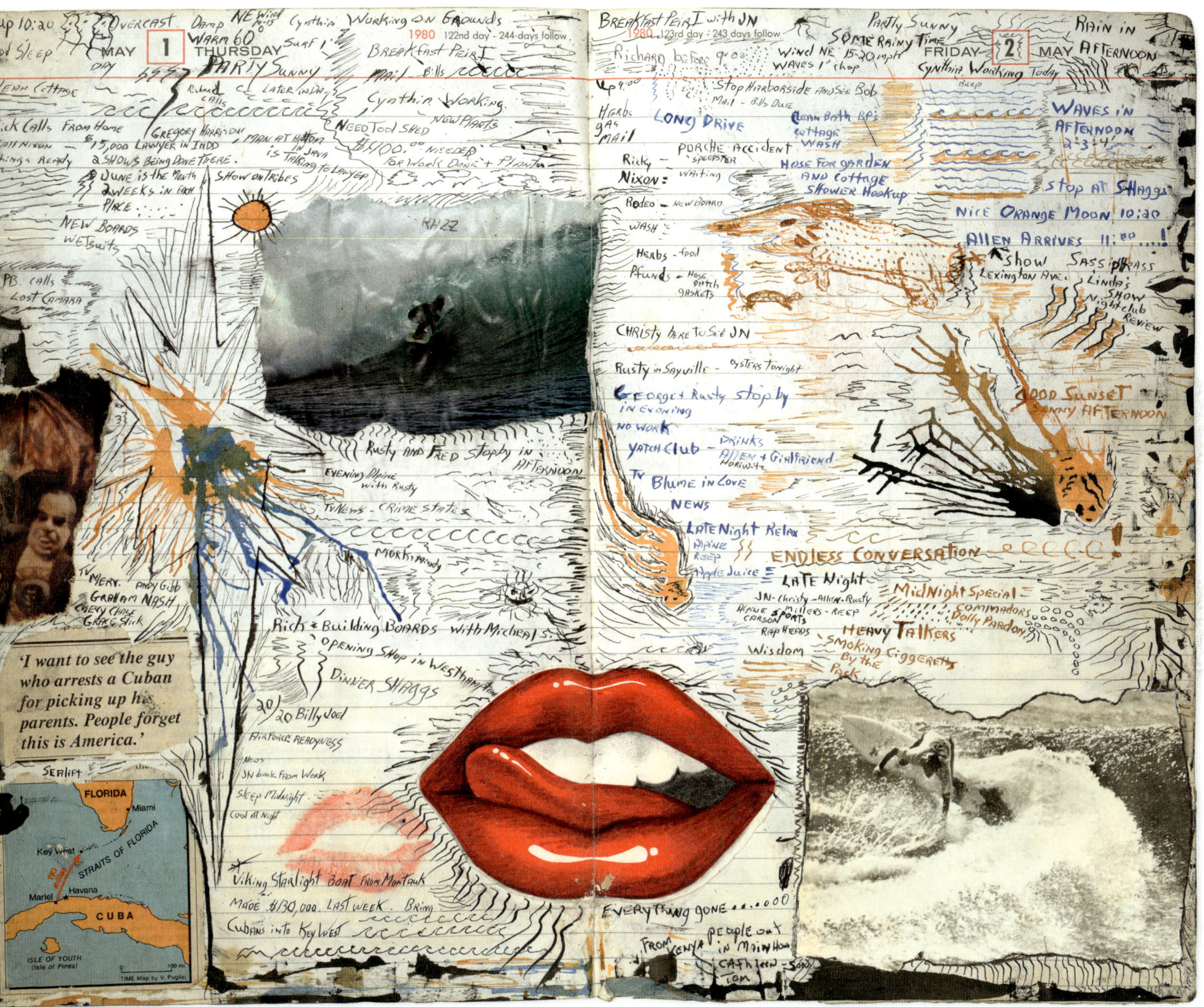
MAY 1 THURSDAY
1980 122nd day - 244 days follow
OVERCAST
PARTY SUNNY
Cynthia Working ON Grounds
BREAKFast PeirI
Cynthia Working
NEW PLANTS
NEED Tool SHED
GREGORY HARRISON
June is the Month
NEW BOARDS
WETsuits
P.B. calls
Lost Camara
Rusty AND FRED Stop by in AFTERNOON
EVENING Alpine with Rusty
TV News - CRIME states
TV MERV. ANDY Gibb GRAHAM NASH CHEVY CHASE GRACE Slick
'I want to see the guy who arrests a Cuban for picking up his parents. People forget this is America.'
FLORIDA
Miami
Key West
STRAITS OF FLORIDA
Mariel
Havana
CUBA
ISLE OF YOUTH
(Isle of Pines)
TIME Map by V. Puglisi
Rick + Building BOARDS with Micheal S.
OPENING Shop in Westhampton
DINNER SHAGGS
20/20 Billy Joel
AIR FORCE READYNESS
JN back From Work
Sleep Midnight
Cool At Night
Viking Starlight Boat From Montauk
MADE $130,000. LAST WEEK. Bring Cubans into Key West
BREAKfast PeirI with JN
1980 123rd day - 243 days follow
Partly Sunny
SOME RAiny Time
FRIDAY 2 MAY
RAIN IN AFTERNOON
Wind NE 15-20 mph
WAVES 1' chop
Cynthia Working Today
Stop Harborside AND See Bob
LONG DRIVE
Clean Bath BP's
Cottage WASH
PORCHE ACCIDENT
HOSE FOR GARDEN AND Cottage SHOWER Hookup
WAVES IN AFTERNOON
Stop At SHAggs
NICE ORANGE MOON 10:30
ALLEN ARRIVES 11:00
CHRISTY here to See JN
Rusty in Sayville - Oysters Tonight
George + Rusty stop by IN EVENING
NO WORK
YATCH Club - DRINKS ALLEN + Girlfriend
TV Blume in Love
NEWS
LATE Night Relax
ENDLESS CONVERSATION
LATE Night
MidNight Special
HEAVY TALKERS
Wisdom
GOOD SUNSET
SUNNY AFTERNOON
Everything gone
people out in Main House

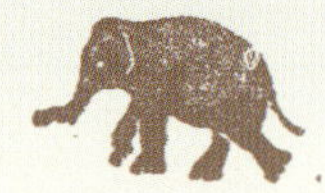

"BEING AROUND BEARD WAS A LITTLE INFECTIOUS. HE WAS A GOOD TIME, A CREATIVE SPIRIT, EXTREMELY CONNECTED. IT WAS A LOT OF FUN. PARTIES AND PEOPLE. I WASN'T A PHOTOGRAPHER OR INTO WILDLIFE, I WASN'T THIS PLAYBOY KIND OF DUDE, BUT I WAS A SURFER. I HAD SOMETHING GOING ON. I WANTED THE JOURNALS TO BE A RECORD OF MY LIFE THROUGH SURFING. I TOOK OFF IN THAT DIRECTION AND THAT VERY SAME YEAR I PUT TOGETHER AN EPISODE OF THE TV SHOW AMERICAN SPORTSMEN WITH RICKY RAZZ THAT WON AN EMMY. WE WENT AROUND THE WORLD IN 30 DAYS AND THAT HELPED JUMPSTART THE JOURNALS IN A BIG WAY."

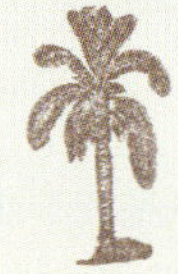

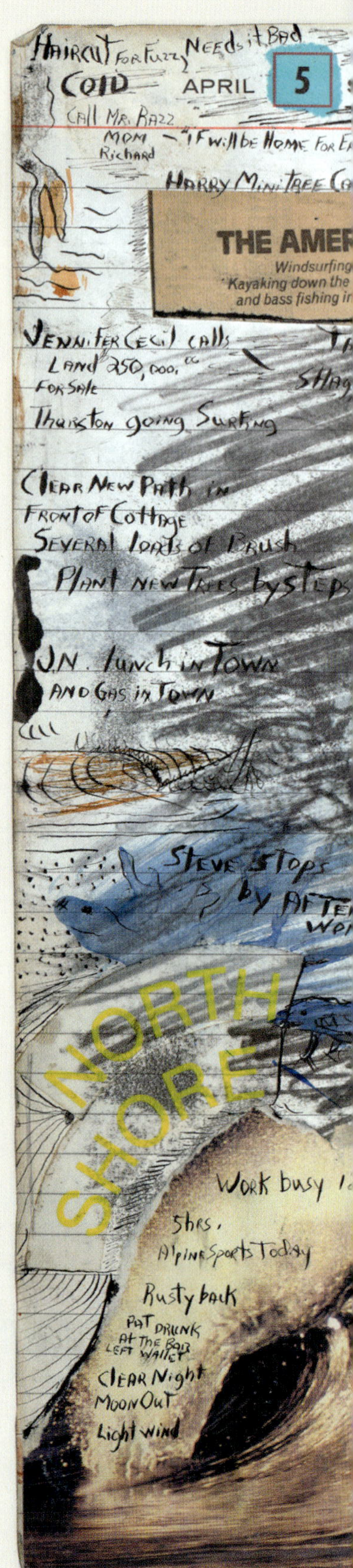

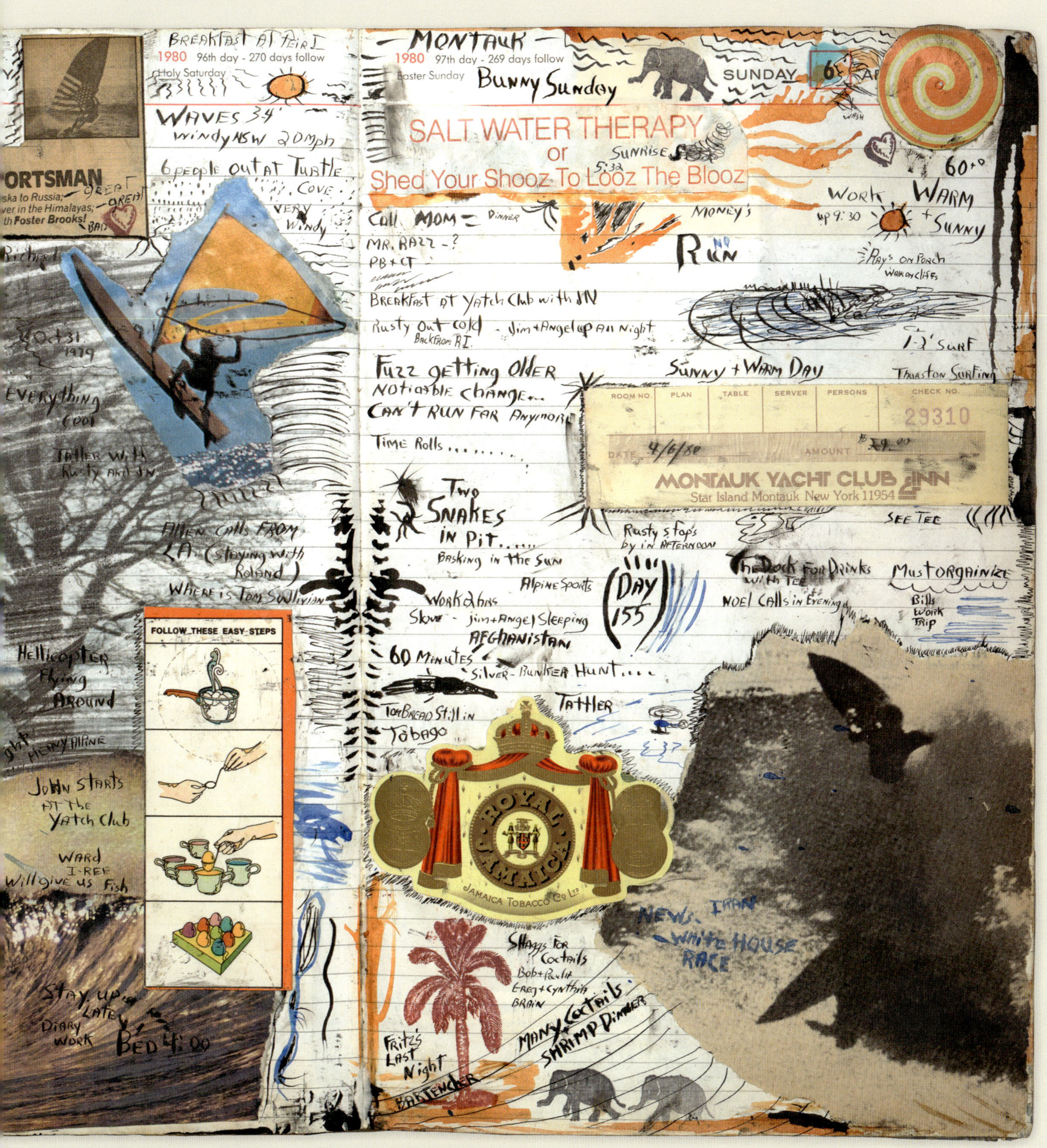

Breakfast At Peir I
1980 96th day - 270 days follow
Holy Saturday
Waves 3-4'
windy NW 20mph
6 people out at Turtle Cove
Very Windy
SPORTSMAN
Alaska to Russia;
over in the Himalayas;
with Foster Brooks!
Great
Oct 31 1979
Everything Cool
Taller with Rusty and JN
Allen Calls From LA (Staying with Roland)
Where is Tom Sullivan
FOLLOW THESE EASY STEPS
Hellicopter Flying Around
John Starts at the Yatch Club
Ward I-REF Will give us Fish
Stay up Late
Diary Work
Bed 4:00
Montauk
1980 97th day - 269 days follow
Easter Sunday
Bunny Sunday
SUNDAY
SALT WATER THERAPY
or
Shed Your Shooz To Looz The Blooz
Sunrise 5:32
60+°
Call Mom - Dinner
Mr. Razz - ?
PB+CT
Money's
Run
Work
Warm + Sunny
up 9:30
Rays on Porch
Walk on cliffs
Breakfast at Yatch Club with JN
Rusty Out Cold Back From R.I.
Jim + Angel up All Night
1-2' Surf
Fuzz getting Older
Noticable change...
Can't Run Far Anymore
Sunny + Warm Day
Thurston Surfing
Time Rolls.......
ROOM NO.
PLAN
TABLE
SERVER
PERSONS
CHECK NO.
29310
DATE 4/6/80
AMOUNT
MONTAUK YACHT CLUB INN
Star Island Montauk New York 11954
Two Snakes in Pit.....
Basking in the Sun
Rusty stops by in Afternoon
See Tee
The Dock For Drinks with Tee
Noel Calls in Evening
Must Orgainize
Bills
Work
Trip
Alpine Sports
Day 155
Work 2 hrs
Slow - Jim + Angel Sleeping
Afghanistan
60 Minutes
Silver - Bunker Hunt....
Tattler
Too Bread Still in Tobago
ROYAL JAMAICA
JAMAICA TOBACCO CO LTD
News. Iran
White House Race
Shaggs for Coctails
Bob + Paulit
Greg + Cynthia
Brain
Many Coctails
Shrimp Dinner
Fritz's Last Night
Bartender

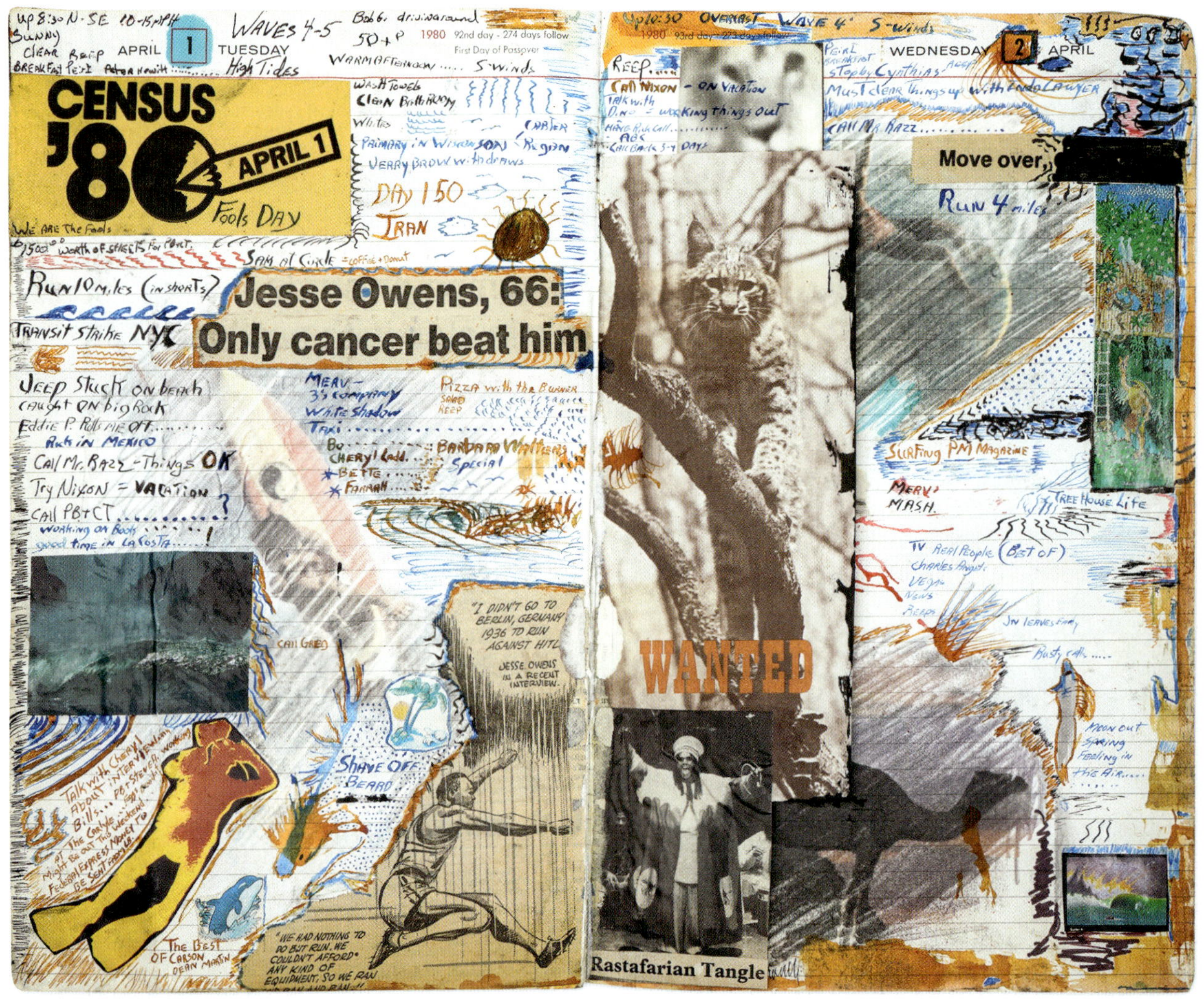
APRIL 1 TUESDAY
1980 92nd day - 274 days follow
First Day of Passover
WAVES 4-5
CENSUS '80
APRIL 1
Fools Day
Jesse Owens, 66:
Only cancer beat him
Run 10 miles (in shorts)
Transit Strike NYC
Jeep Stuck on beach
Call Mr. Razz - Things OK
Try Nixon = VACATION
DAY 150
IRAN
"I DIDN'T GO TO BERLIN, GERMANY, IN 1936 TO RUN AGAINST HITLER" JESSE OWENS IN A RECENT INTERVIEW.
"WE HAD NOTHING TO DO BUT RUN. WE COULDN'T AFFORD ANY KIND OF EQUIPMENT, SO WE RAN"
Shave OFF Beard
The Best OF CARSON
WEDNESDAY 2 APRIL
1980 93rd day
WAVE 4' S-winds
Call Nixon - ON VACATION
Move over,
Run 4 miles
WANTED
Rastafarian Tangle
SURFING PM MAGAZINE
MERV - MASH
TREE HOUSE LIFE
TV Real People (Best OF)

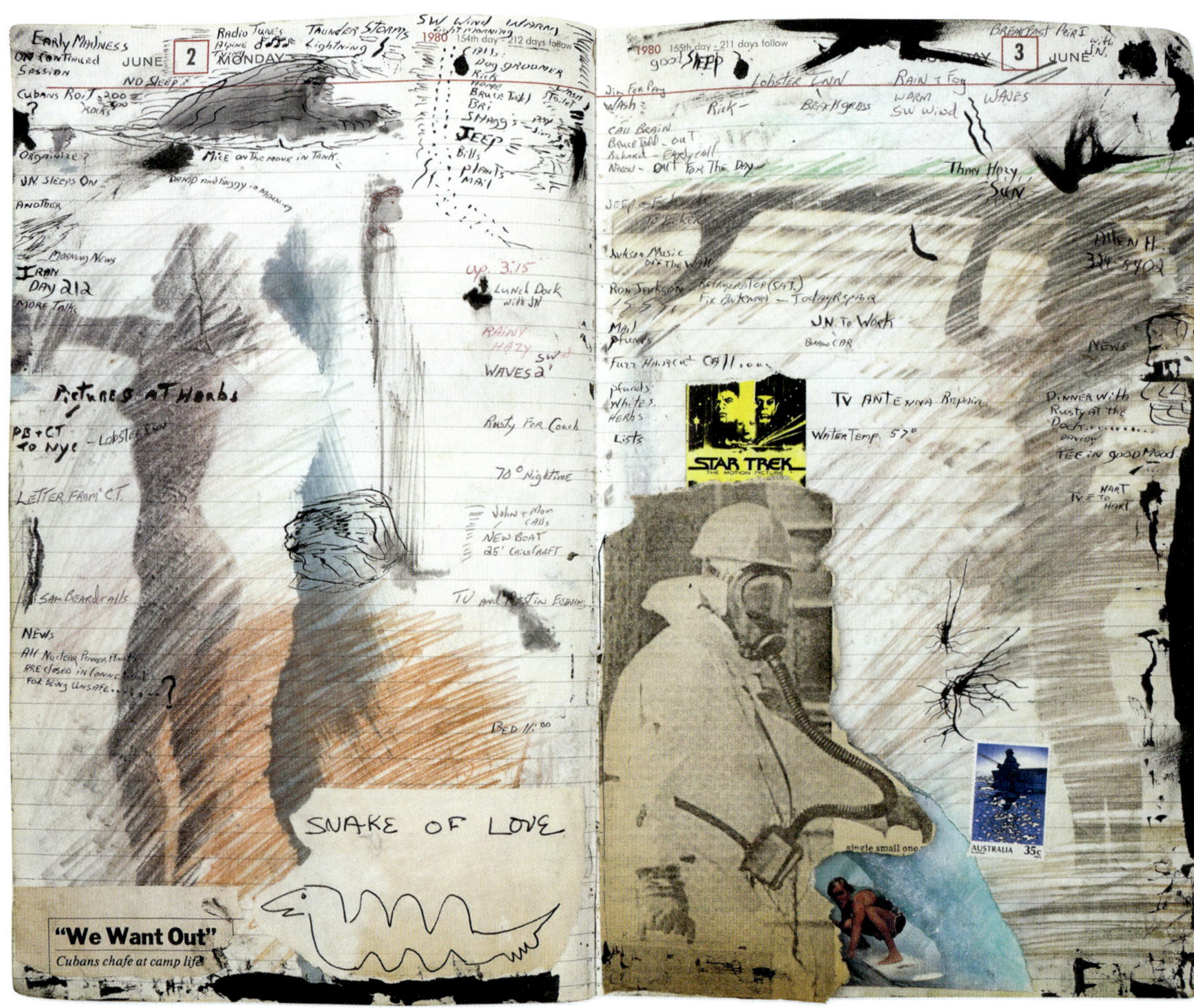
JUNE 2 MONDAY
1980 154th day - 212 days follow
Early Madness
Thunder Storms
SW Wind
IRAN DAY 212
Pictures at Herbs
Letter From CT
up 3:15
Waves 2'
70° Nightime
Bed 11:30
SNAKE OF LOVE
"We Want Out"
Cubans chafe at camp life
1980 155th day - 211 days follow
JUNE 3
Breakfast Perl
good SLEEP
Rain & Fog
WAVES
Thin Hazy SUN
TV ANTENNA Repair
Water Temp 57°
STAR TREK THE MOTION PICTURE
single small one
AUSTRALIA 35c

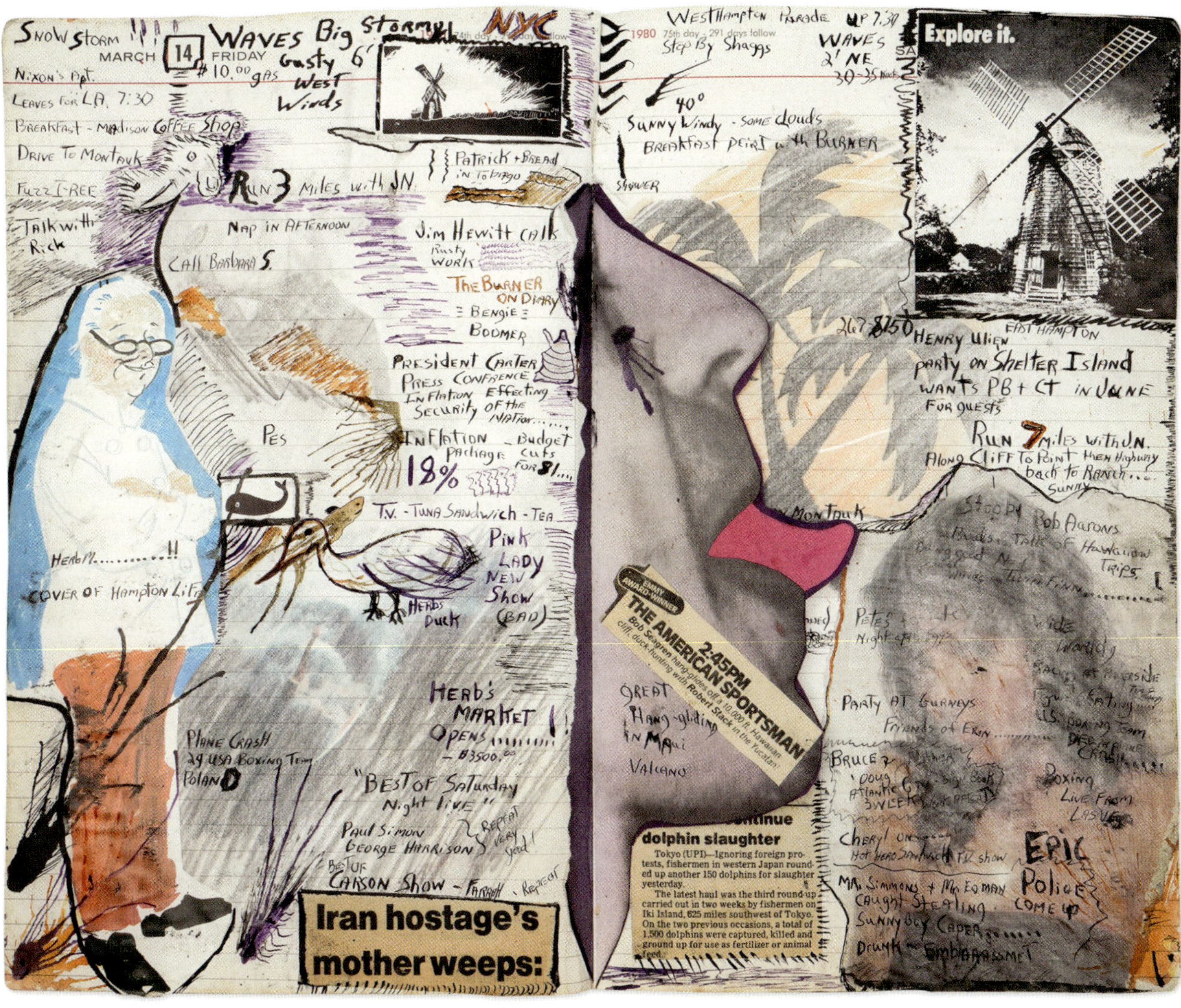
Snow Storm
MARCH 14 FRIDAY
Waves Big Stormy
Gusty 6'
West Winds
NYC
Nixon's Apt. Leaves For L.A. 7:30
Breakfast - Madison Coffee Shop
Drive To Montauk
Run 3 miles with J.N.
Nap in Afternoon
Call Barbara S.
Jim Hewitt Calls
The Burner on Diary
President Carter Press Conference
Inflation - Budget package cuts
18%
T.V. - Tuna Sandwich - Tea
Pink Lady New Show (Bad)
Herb's Duck
Cover of Hampton Life
Herb's Market Opens
Plane Crash 29 USA Boxing Team Poland
"Best of Saturday Night Live"
Paul Simon George Harrison
Best of Carson Show
Iran hostage's mother weeps:
1980
Westhampton Parade
Waves 2' NE
40°
Sunny Windy - Some clouds
Breakfast Point with Burner
Explore it.
Henry Ulien
party on Shelter Island
Run 7 miles with J.N.
Montauk
2:45PM THE AMERICAN SPORTSMAN
Great Hang-gliding in Maui Valcano
Party at Gurneys
dolphin slaughter
Boxing Live From Las Vegas
Epic Police Come Up
Drunk - Embarrassment

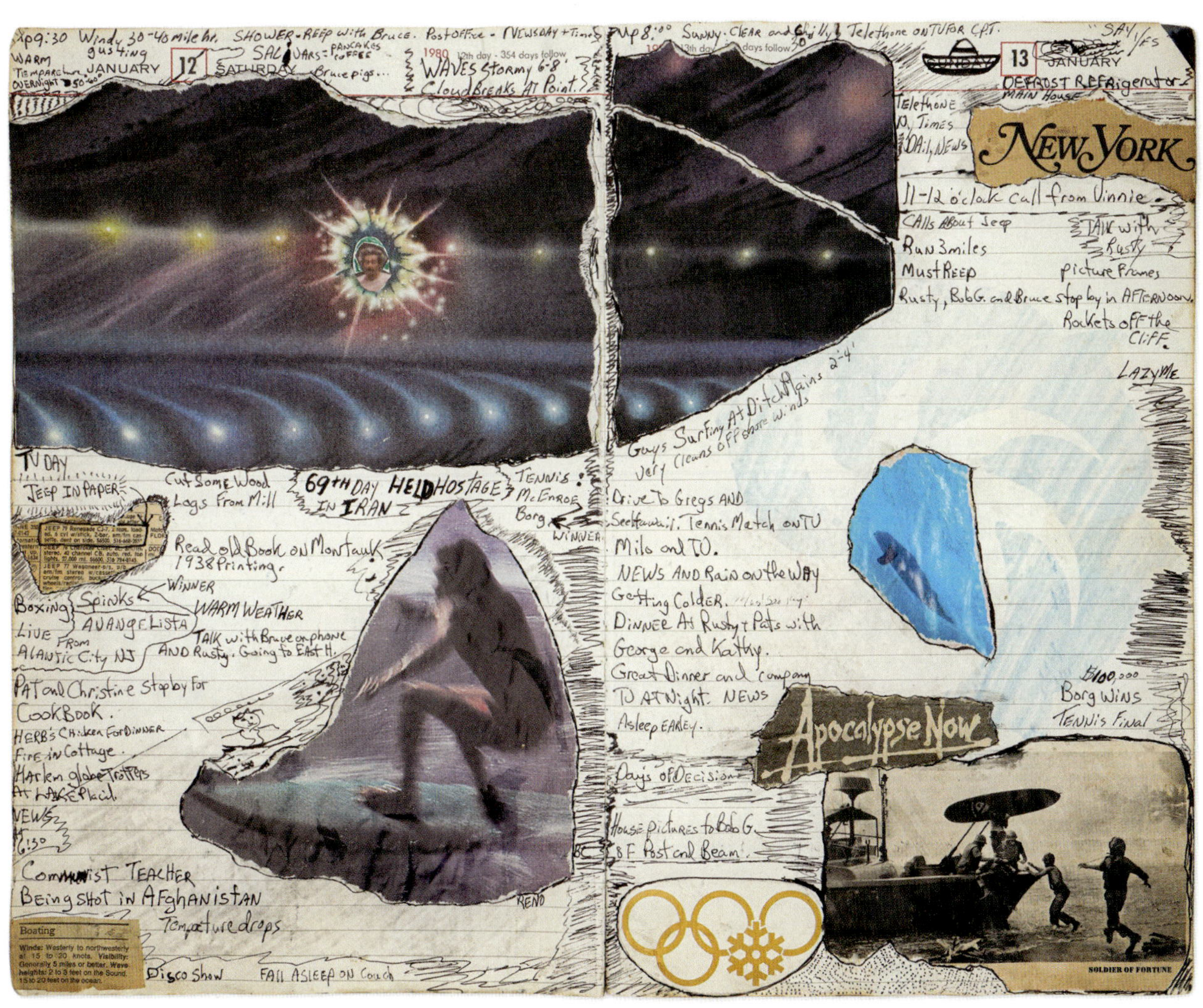
Windy 30-40 mile hr.
JANUARY 12 SATURDAY
1980
Waves Stormy 6-8'
Cloud Breaks At Point
TV DAY
Jeep in Paper
Cut Some Wood Logs From Mill
69th DAY HELD HOSTAGE IN IRAN
Tennis: McEnroe Borg
Read old Book on Montauk 1938 Printing.
Boxing Spinks
Warm Weather
Live From Atlantic City NJ
Pat and Christine Stop by For CookBook.
Communist Teacher Being Shot in Afghanistan
Disco Show
Fall Asleep on Couch
Boating
13 JANUARY
Defrost Refrigerator
NEW YORK
11-12 o'clock Call from Vinnie
Run 3 miles
Must Reep
Picture Frames
Rockets off the Cliff.
Guys Surfing At Ditch Plains 2-4'
Drive To Gregs And Seefountains Tennis Match on TV
News And Rain on the Way
Getting Colder.
Dinner At Rusty + Pats with George and Kathy.
Great Dinner and company
TV At Night. News
Asleep Early.
Apocalypse Now
Days of Decision
$100,000 Borg Wins Tennis Final
SOLDIER OF FORTUNE

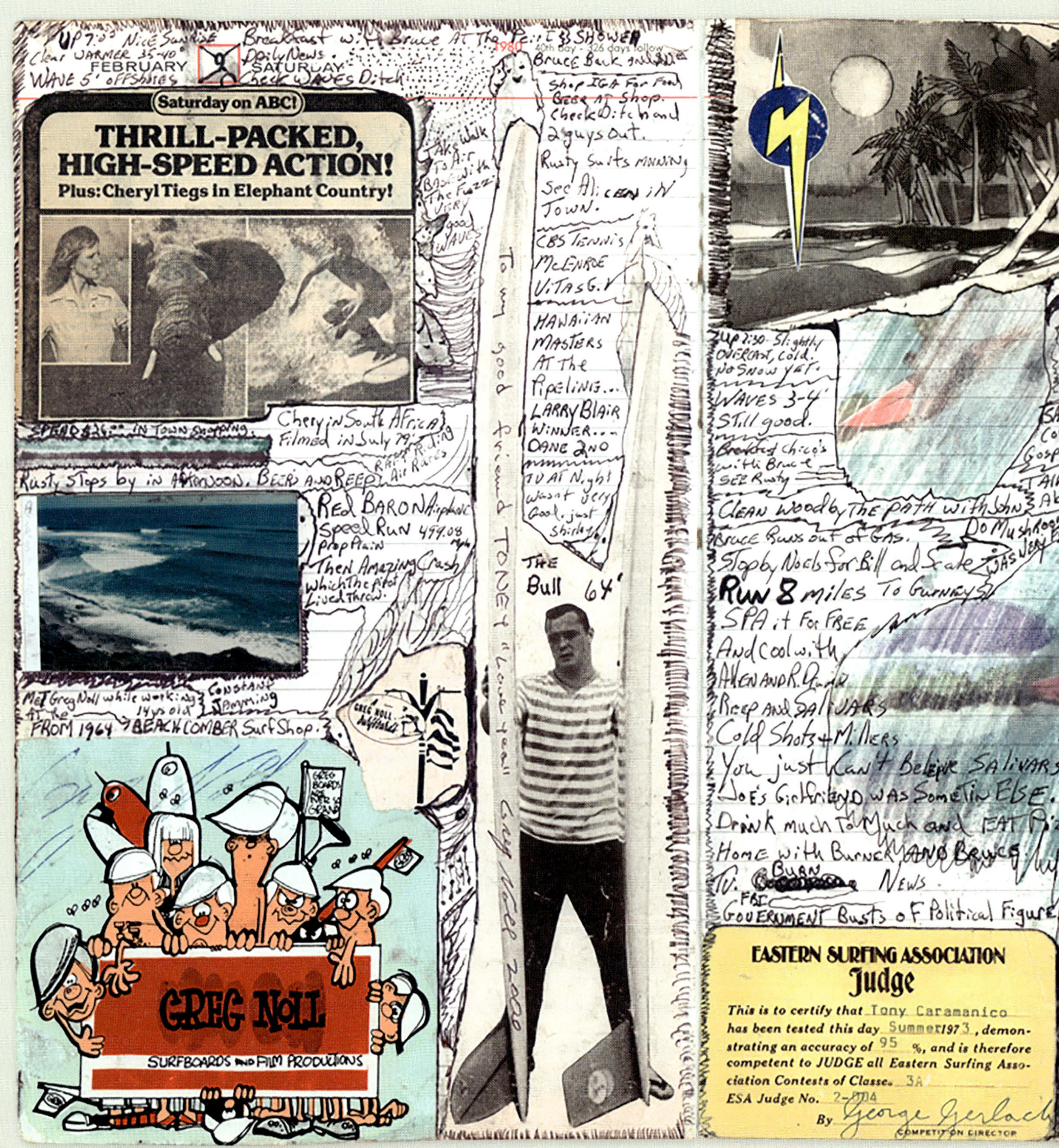
UP 7:00 Nice Sunrise
Clear Warmer 35-40°
Wave 5' offshores
FEBRUARY
SATURDAY
Breakfast with Bruce At The Pier & Shower
Daily News
Check Waves Ditch
40th day - 326 days follow
Saturday on ABC!
THRILL-PACKED, HIGH-SPEED ACTION!
Plus: Cheryl Tiegs in Elephant Country!
Cheryl in South Africa
Filmed in July 79
Spend $26.00 in town shopping
Rusty Stops by in Afternoon. Beers and Reefs
Red BARON Airplane Speed Run 499.08 mph
Then Amazing Crash Which The Pilot Lived Threw.
Met Greg Noll while working at the Beachcomber Surf Shop.
14 yrs old
FROM 1964
Constant Jamming
Bruce Back and ...
Shop IGA For Food
Beer At Shop.
Check Ditch and 2 guys out.
Rusty Surfs Morning
See Alice in Town.
CBS Tennis McEnroe Vitas G.
Hawaiian Masters At the Pipeline...
Larry Blair Winner...
Dane 2nd
TV At Night wasn't very Good, just Shirley
To my good friend TONEY! Love you! Greg Noll 2000
THE Bull 6'4"
GREG NOLL
SURFBOARDS AND FILM PRODUCTIONS
Up 7:30 Slightly Overcast, Cold. No Snow Yet.
Waves 3-4' Still good.
Breakfast Chico's with Bruce
See Rusty
Clean wood by The Path with John
Bruce Runs out of Gas.
Stop by Noel's for Bill and Scate
Run 8 miles To Gurney's
SPA it For FREE
And cool with Allen and R.
Reef and Salivars
Cold Shots + Millers
You just Can't Believe Salivars
Joe's Girlfriend was Sometin Else.
Drink much To Much and EAT Pizza
Home with Burney and Bruce
TV. News
FBI Government Busts of Political Figure
EASTERN SURFING ASSOCIATION
Judge
This is to certify that Tony Caramanico
has been tested this day Summer 1973, demonstrating an accuracy of 95 %, and is therefore competent to JUDGE all Eastern Surfing Association Contests of Class 3A
ESA Judge No. 2-004
By George Gerlach
COMPETITION DIRECTOR

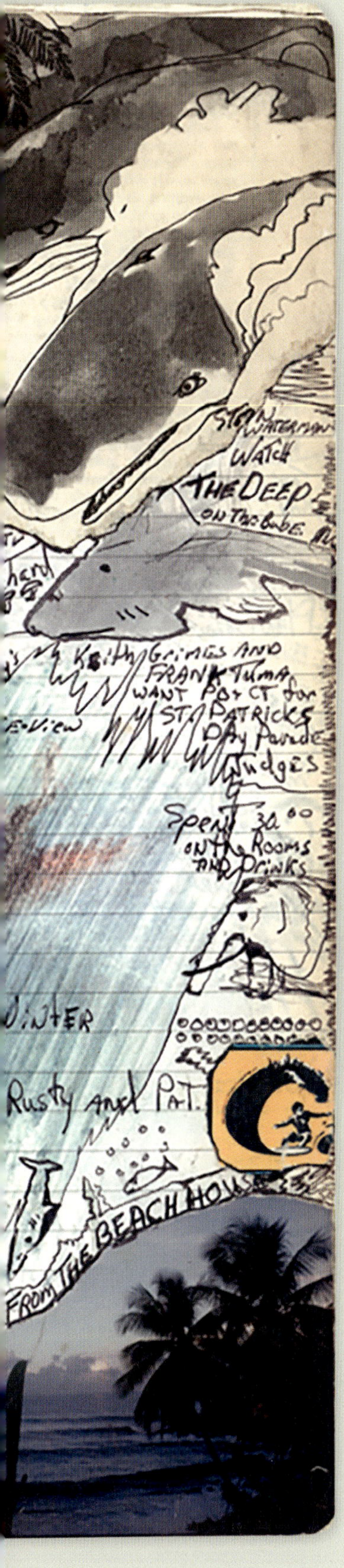

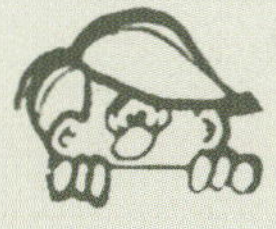

IN THE SUMMER OF '64 I GOT A JOB AT BEACHCOMBER SURF SHOP. I WAS JUST A LITTLE SHOP RAT. WE SOLD ALL THE GREAT SURFBOARD BRANDS, WEBERS, BINGS, GREG NOLLS. I WAS SITTING AT THE SHOP WATCHING THE STORE AND ALL OF A SUDDEN A BIG BLACK JAGUAR PULLED UP AND OUT POPS GREG NOLL. AT THE TIME HE WAS THE GUY IN SURFING. HE CAME WALKING IN AND SAW I WAS A LITTLE KIDDER. WE HAD DECALS AND HE SIGNED THE GREG NOLL DECAL AND GAVE IT TO ME. THAT'S THE SAME DECAL THAT'S IN THE JOURNAL. THAT BECAME THE GREG NOLL PAGE 20 YEARS LATER. TO BE ABLE TO THEN WORK WITH HIM AND HAVE MY OWN MODEL WITH HIM 30 YEARS LATER WAS TRULY SOMETHING SPECIAL.

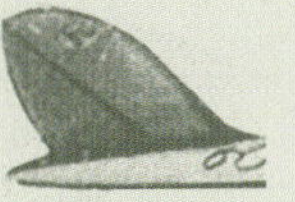

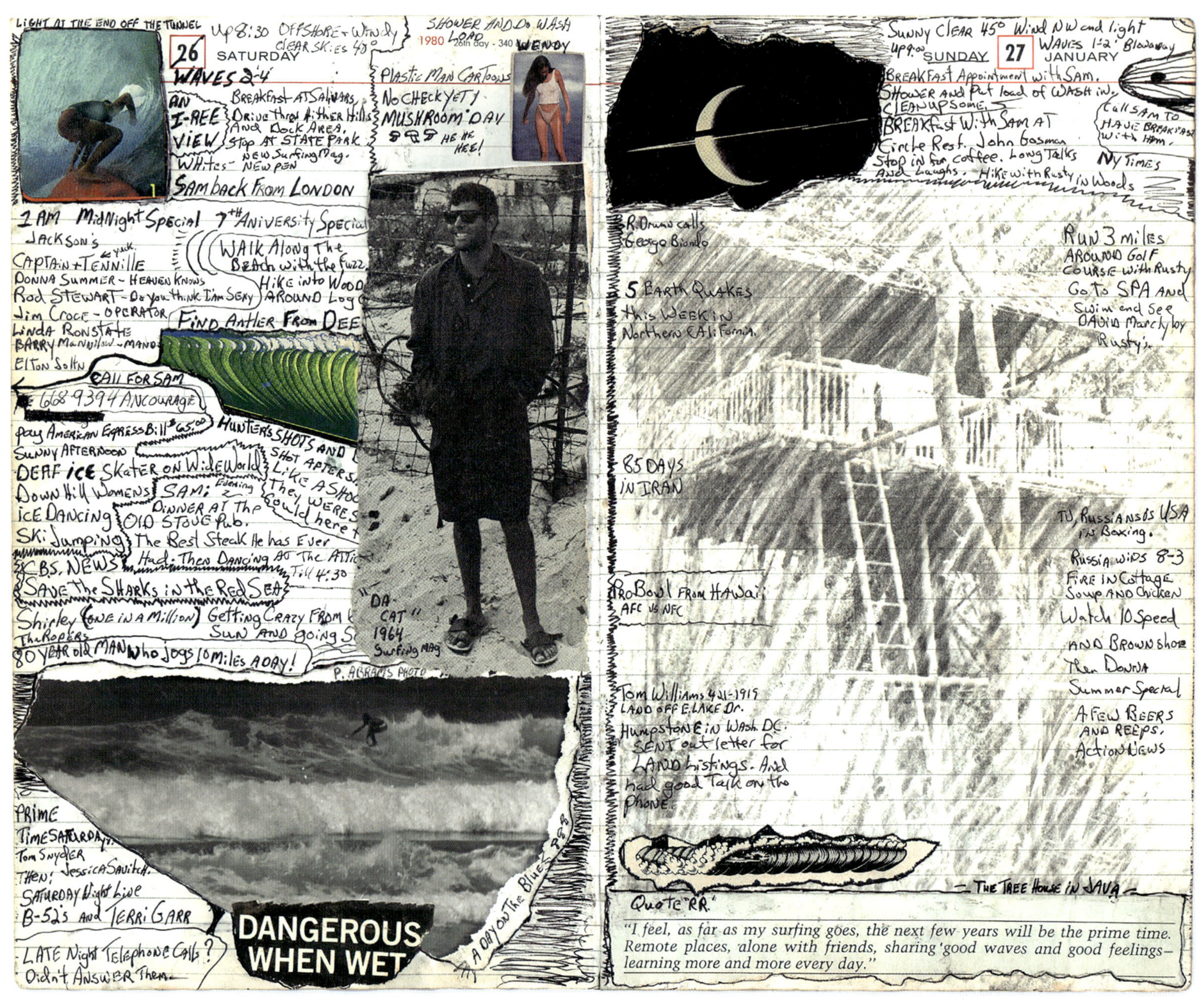

LIGHT AT THE END OFF THE TUNNEL
26
SATURDAY
1980 26th day - 340
WAVES 2-4'
SHOWER AND DO WASH LOAD
WENDY
Plastic Man Cartoons
No CHECK YET
MUSHROOM DAY
Sam back From LONDON
1 AM MidNight Special 7th Aniversity Special
WALK Along The Beach with the Fuzz
FIND Antler From DEER
CALL FOR SAM
DEAF ICE Skater ON WideWorld
SAVE The SHARKS in the Red SEA
80 YEAR old MAN Who Jogs 10 Miles A DAY!
"DA CAT" 1964 Surfing Mag
P. ABRAMS PHOTO
DANGEROUS WHEN WET
A DAY ON The BLUES
LATE Night Telephone Calls? Didn't Answer Them.
SUNDAY
27
JANUARY
BREAKFast Appointment with Sam.
5 EARTH QUAKES this WEEK in Northern CALifornia
85 DAYS IN IRAN
Run 3 miles
ProBowl From HAWAII
AFC vs NFC
Quote "RR."
THE TREE HOUSE in JAVA
"I feel, as far as my surfing goes, the next few years will be the prime time. Remote places, alone with friends, sharing good waves and good feelings–learning more and more every day."

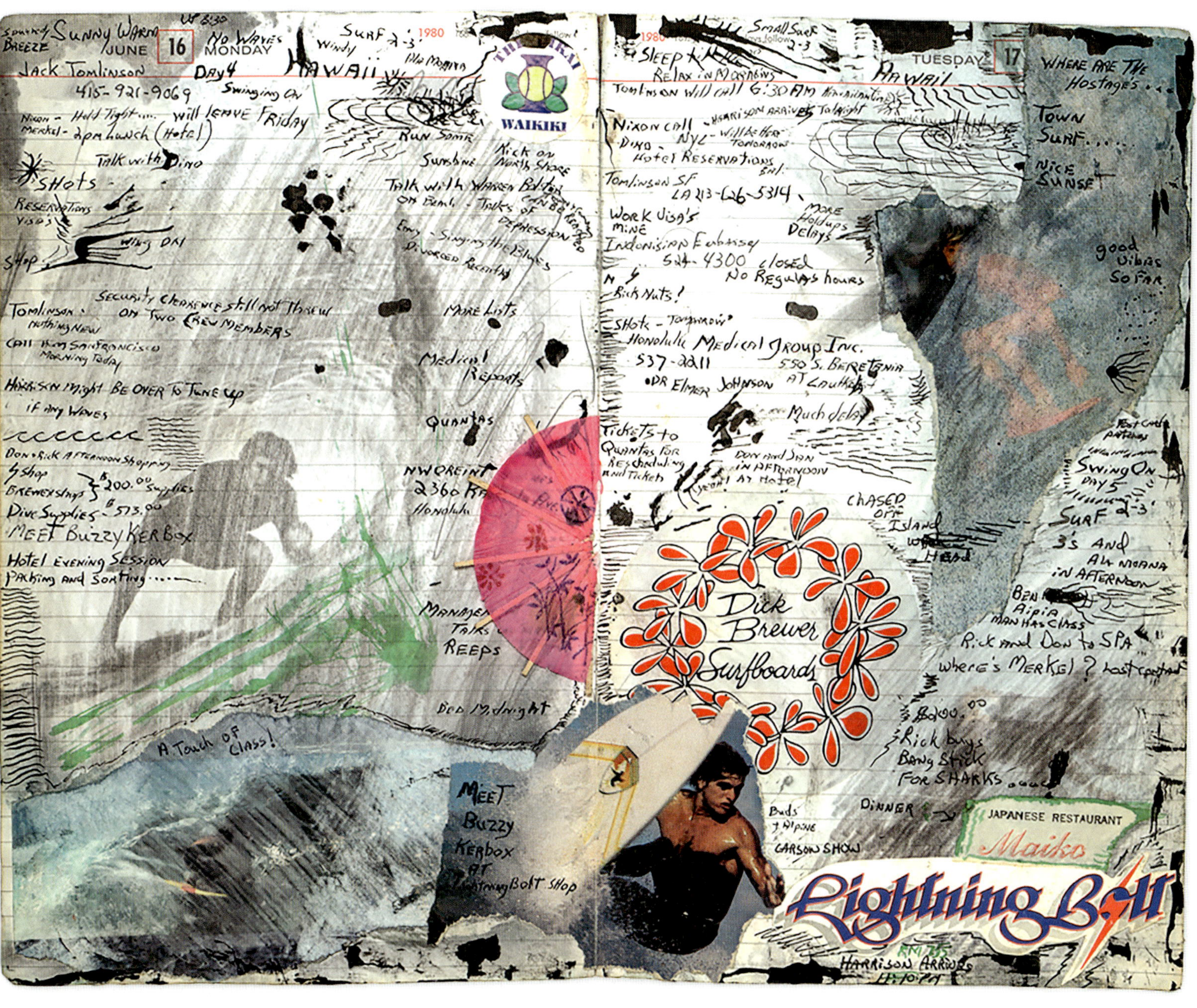
Sunny Warm
JUNE
16
MONDAY
No Waves
Surf 2-3
1980
Jack Tomlinson
Day 4
HAWAII
415-921-9069
Swinging On
will leave Friday
Talk with Dino
Shots
Reservations
Visa's
Shop
WAIKIKI
Run Some
Sunshine
Kick on North Shore
Talk with Warren Bolster
Divorced Recently
Security Clearance still not threw on two crew members
Tomlinson: nothing new
Harrison might be over to tune up if any waves
More Lists
Medical Reports
Quantas
Hotel evening session
Packing and sorting.....
Meet Buzzy Kerbox
Manager Talks Reeps
Bed Midnight
A Touch of Class!
Meet Buzzy Kerbox at Lightning Bolt Shop
1980
Small Surf 2-3
Sleep
Relax in Mornings
TUESDAY
17
HAWAII
Where are the Hostages.....
Nixon call
Hotel Reservations
Tomlinson SF
LA 213-626-5314
Work Visa's
Indonisian Embassy
524-4300 closed
No Regular hours
More Holdups Delays
Rick Nuts!
Honolulu Medical Group Inc.
537-2211
550 S. Beretania
DR Elmer Johnson
Much delay
Tickets to Quantas for Rescheduling
Town Surf.....
Nice Sunset
good vibes so far
Swing On Day 5
Surf 2-3
3's and Ala Moana in afternoon
Rick and Don to SPA
where's Merkel? lost
Rick buys Bang Stick for Sharks
Dinner
Carson Show
Dick Brewer Surfboards
JAPANESE RESTAURANT
Maiko
Lightning Bolt
Harrison Arrives

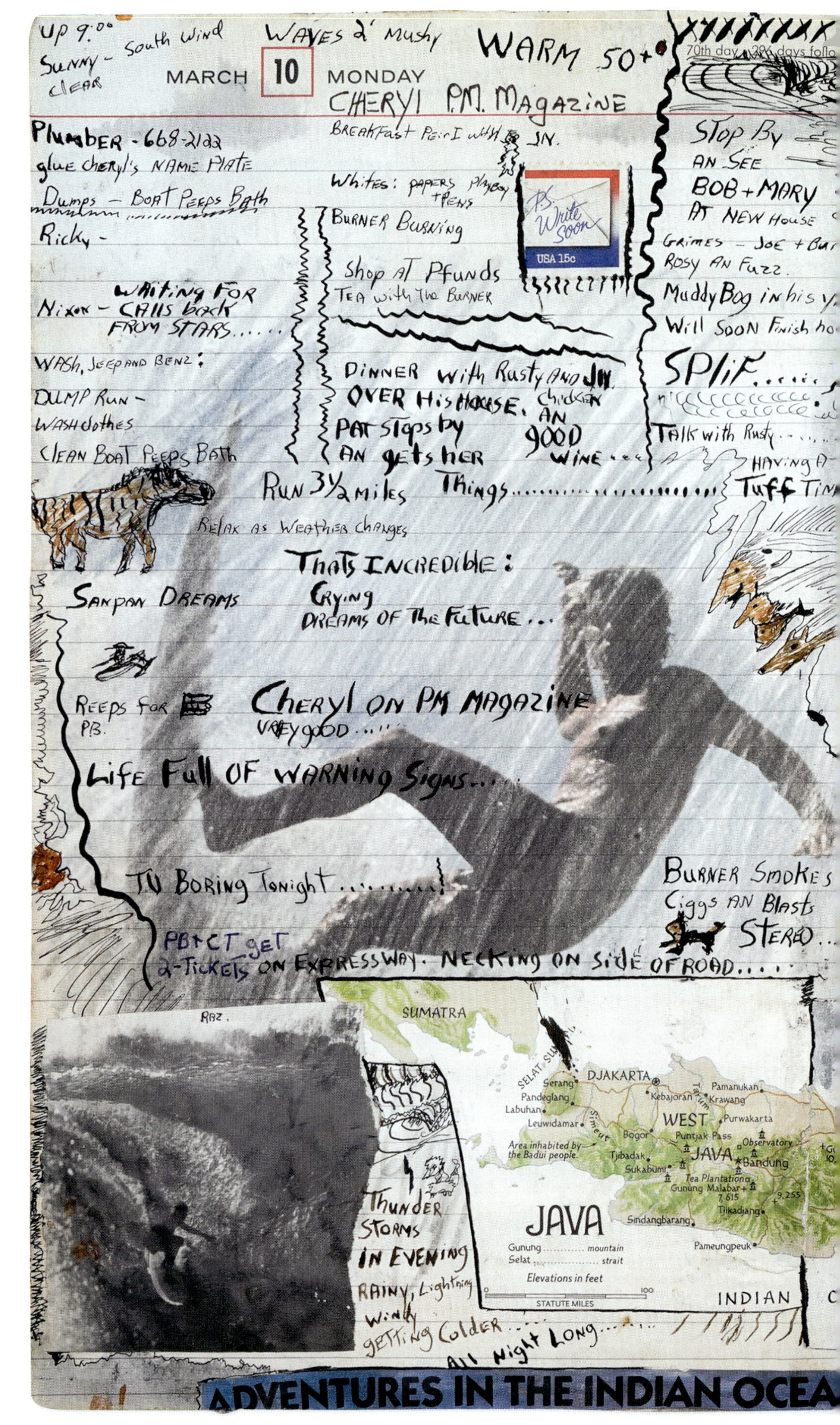

Up 9:00
Sunny - South Wind
clear
Waves 2' Mushy
WARM 50+°
MARCH
10
MONDAY
Cheryl P.M. Magazine
Plumber - 668-2122
glue cheryl's NAME PLATE
Dumps - Boat Peeps Bath
Ricky -
Breakfast Pe.r.I with JW.
Whites: papers playboy +pens
Burner Burning
P.S. Write Soon
USA 15c
Shop At Pfunds
Tea with The Burner
Stop By
An See
BOB + MARY
At New House
Grimes - Joe + Bu
Rosy An Fuzz.
Muddy Bog in his
Will Soon Finish ho
Nixon - Waiting For Calls back From Stars.....
WASh, Jeep And Benz:
Dump Run -
WASH clothes
Clean Boat Peeps Bath
Dinner with Rusty And JW.
Over His House. Chicken
An
Pat Stops by
good
An gets her
wine...
Things.....
SPLIF.....
Talk with Rusty.....
Having A
Tuff Tim
Run 3½ miles
Relax as Weather changes
Thats Incredible:
Crying
Dreams of The Future...
Sanpan Dreams
Reeps For
PB.
Cheryl on PM Magazine
Very good.....
Life Full of Warning Signs...
TV Boring Tonight.........
Burner Smokes
Ciggs An Blasts
Stereo...
PB+CT get 2-Tickets on Expressway. Necking on side of road....
Thunder
Storms
In Evening
Rainy, Lightning
Windy
Getting Colder...
All Night Long.......
SUMATRA
SELAT SU
Serang
Pandeglang
Labuhan
Leuwidamar
Area inhabited by the Badui people.
DJAKARTA
Kebajoran
Pamanukan
Krawang
WEST
Purwakarta
Bogor
Puntjak Pass
Observatory
Tjibadak
Sukabumi
JAVA
Bandung
Tea Plantations
Gunung Malabar
Tjikadjang
Sindangbarang
Pameungpeuk
JAVA
Gunung .... mountain
Selat .... strait
Elevations in feet
STATUTE MILES
INDIAN
ADVENTURES IN THE INDIAN OCEA

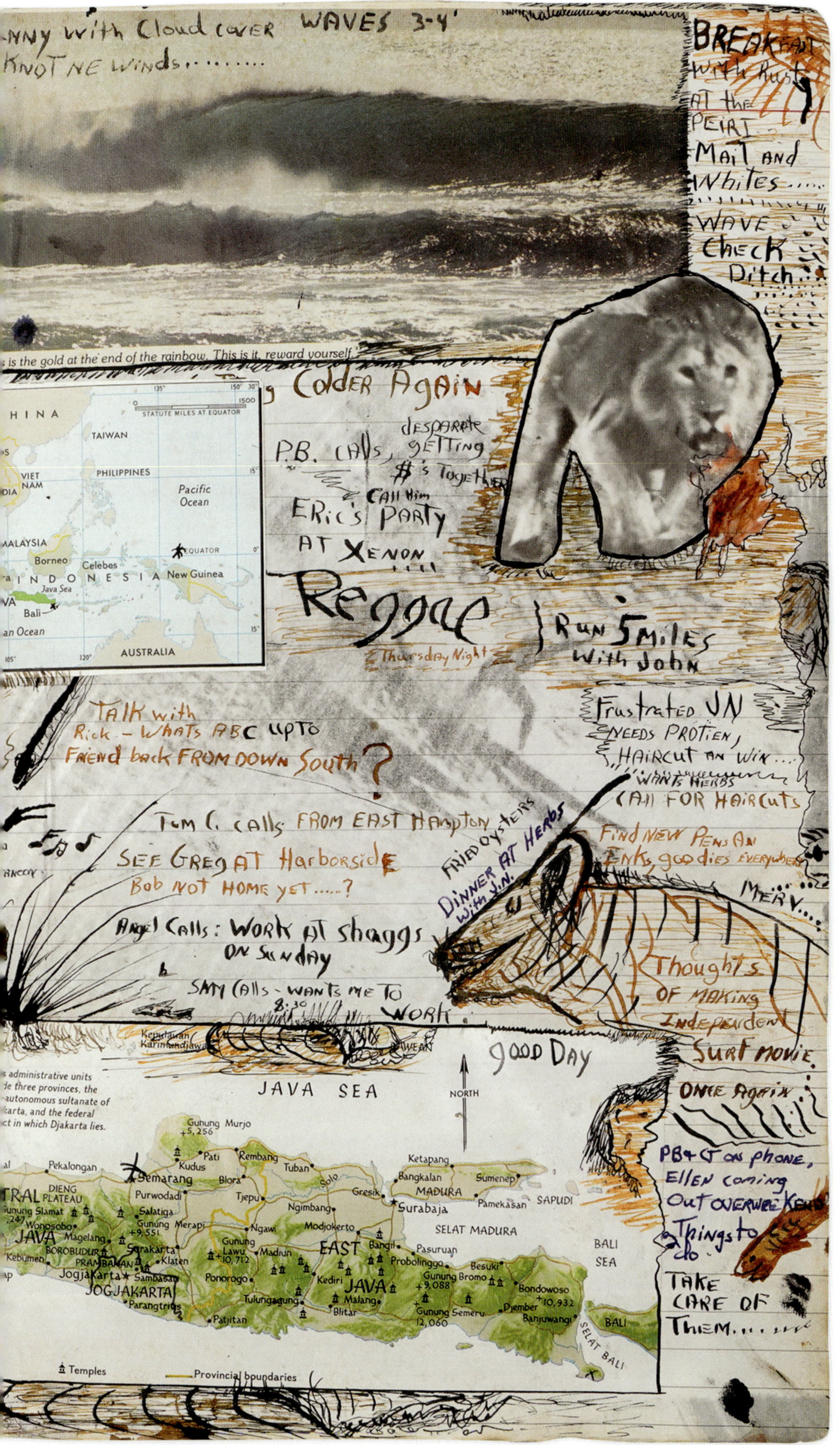

WAVES 3-4'
Breakfast with Rusty at the Peir
Mail and Whites.....
Wave Check Ditch
s is the gold at the end of the rainbow. This is it, reward yourself.
Colder Again
P.B. calls, desparate getting $'s Together
Call Him
Eric's Party at Xenon
Reggae
Thursday Night
Run 5 Miles with John
Pacific Ocean
TAIWAN
PHILIPPINES
Borneo
Celebes
New Guinea
Java Sea
Bali
AUSTRALIA
EQUATOR
STATUTE MILES AT EQUATOR
Frustrated VN needs protien, haircut an win...
Wants Herbs
Call for Haircuts
Talk with Rick - Whats ABC upto
Friend back from down South?
Tom C. calls from East Hampton
See Greg at Harborside
Bob not home yet.....?
Fried oysters
Dinner at Herbs with V.N.
Find New Pens an Inks, goodies everywhere
Angel Calls: Work at shaggs on Sunday
Sam calls - wants me to work
Thoughts of making Independent Surf movie
Good Day
Once Again
JAVA SEA
NORTH
Surabaja
MADURA
SELAT MADURA
BALI SEA
BALI
SELAT BALI
JOGJAKARTA
Temples
Provincial boundaries
PB+G on phone, Ellen coming out overweekend
Things to do
Take care of them.....

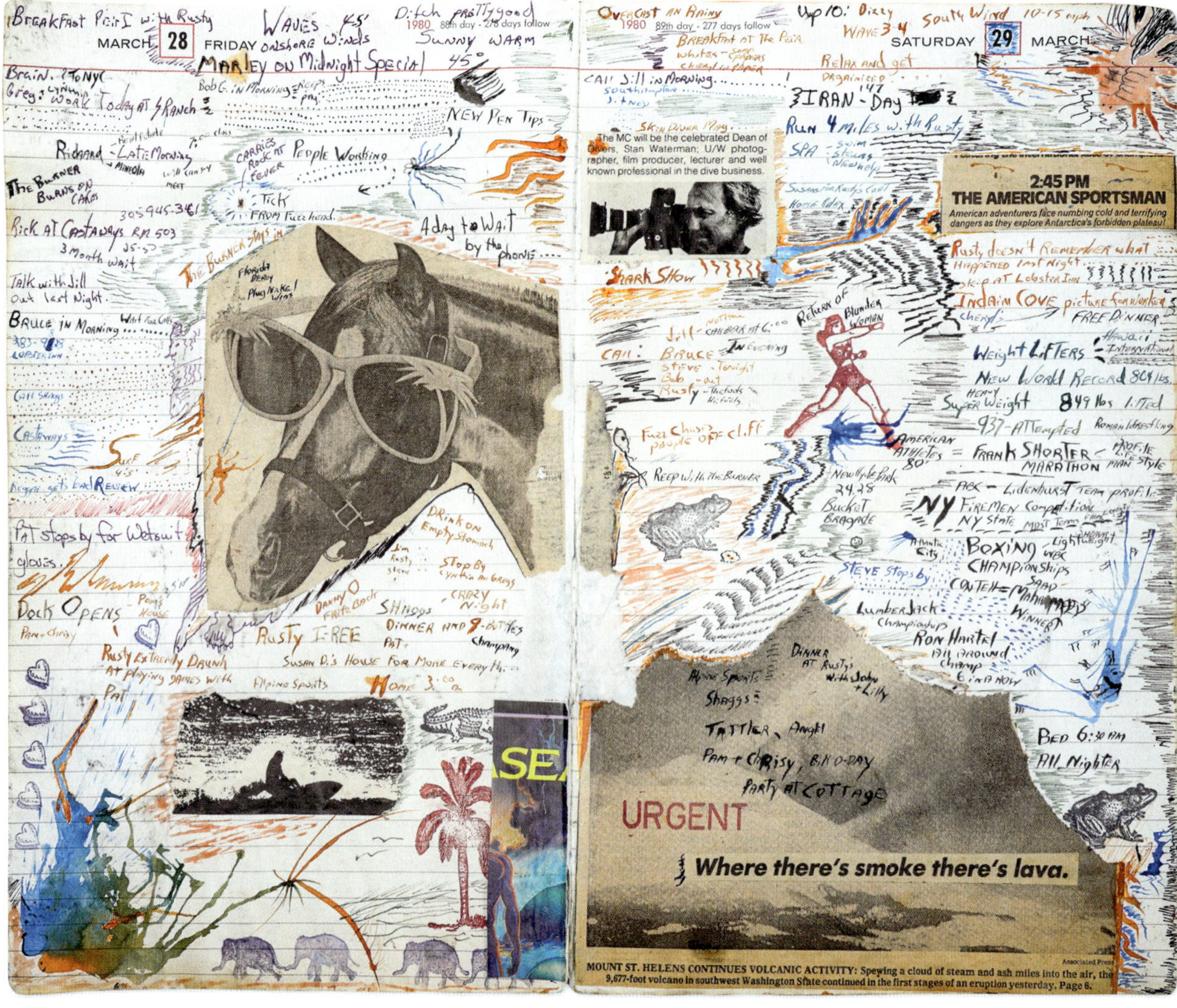
MARCH 28 FRIDAY
1980 88th day - 278 days follow
SATURDAY 29 MARCH
1980 89th day - 277 days follow
The MC will be the celebrated Dean of Divers, Stan Waterman; U/W photographer, film producer, lecturer and well known professional in the dive business.
2:45 PM
THE AMERICAN SPORTSMAN
American adventurers face numbing cold and terrifying dangers as they explore Antarctica's forbidden plateau!
URGENT
Where there's smoke there's lava.
Associated Press
MOUNT ST. HELENS CONTINUES VOLCANIC ACTIVITY: Spewing a cloud of steam and ash miles into the air, the 9,677-foot volcano in southwest Washington State continued in the first stages of an eruption yesterday. Page 6.

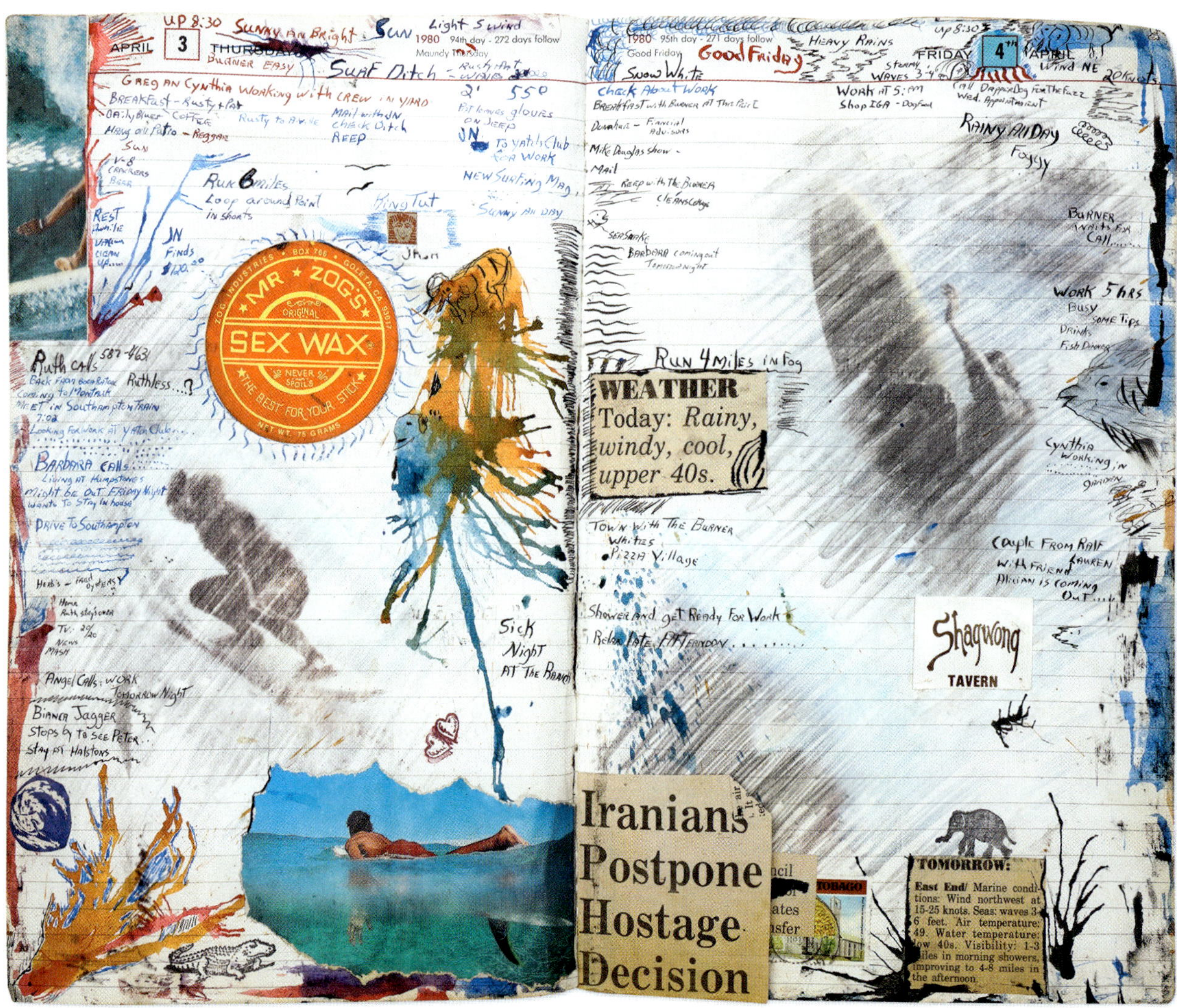
APRIL 3 THURSDAY
1980 94th day - 272 days follow
Maundy Thursday
MR. ZOG'S
ORIGINAL
SEX WAX
NEVER SPOILS
THE BEST FOR YOUR STICK
NET WT. 75 GRAMS
1980 95th day - 271 days follow
Good Friday
FRIDAY 4 APRIL
WEATHER
Today: Rainy, windy, cool, upper 40s.
Shagwong
TAVERN
Iranians Postpone Hostage Decision
TOMORROW:
East End/ Marine conditions: Wind northwest at 15-25 knots. Seas: waves 3-6 feet. Air temperature: 49. Water temperature: low 40s. Visibility: 1-3 miles in morning showers, improving to 4-8 miles in the afternoon.

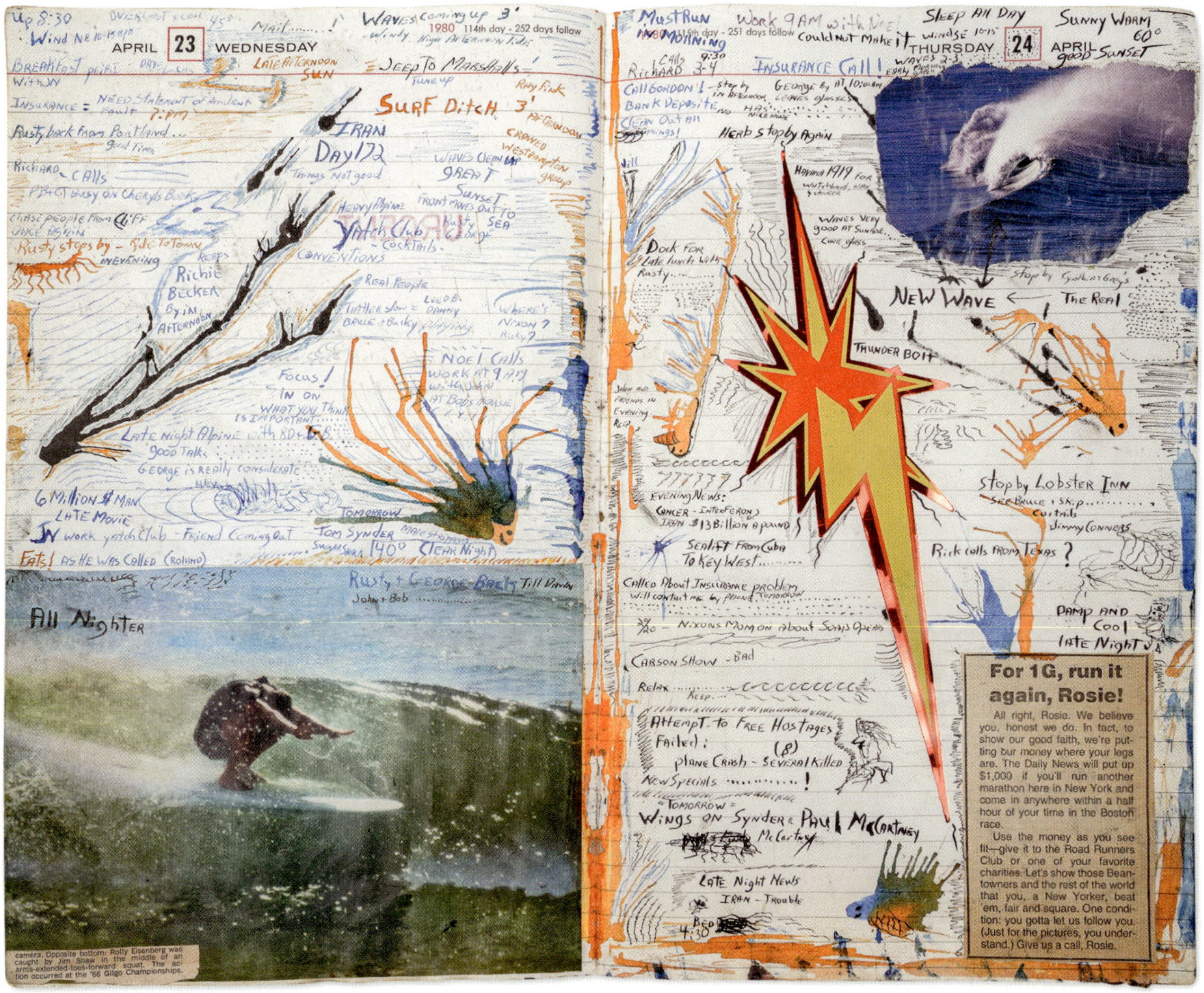

Up 8:30
Wind NE
APRIL 23 WEDNESDAY
1980 114th day - 252 days follow
Waves Coming up 3'
Late Afternoon Sun
Jeep To Marshall's
Surf Ditch 3'
Rusty back from Portland ...
IRAN Day 172
Richard Calls
Yatch Club
Rusty stops by
Richie Becker
Noel Calls Work at 9 AM
Late Night Alone with AD
6 Million $ Man Late Movie
Tomorrow
Tom Synder
Clear Night
Rusty + George - Back Till Dawn
All Nighter

camera. Opposite bottom: Rolly Eisenberg was caught by Jim Shaw in the middle of an arms-extended-toes-forward squat. The action occurred at the '66 Gilgo Championships.

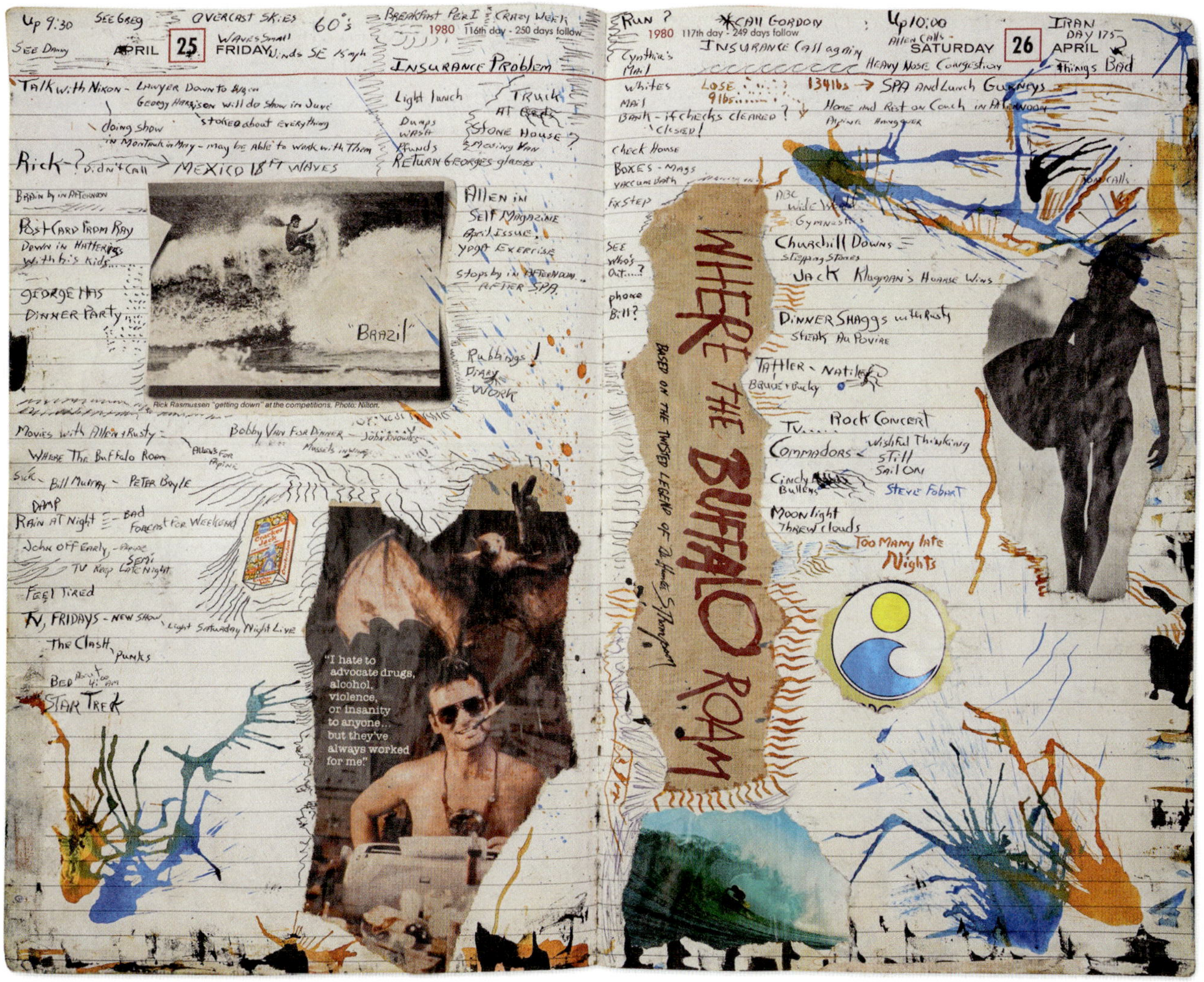

Must Run
Work 9 AM with Noel
1980 115th day - 251 days follow
Sleep All Day
Sunny Warm 60°
THURSDAY 24 APRIL
Good Sunset
Richard Calls
Insurance Call!
Herb stops by Again
New Wave
The Real
Thunder Bolt
Evening News:
Stop by Lobster Inn
Rick Calls From Texas ?
Damp and Cool
Late Night
Carson Show - Bad
Relax
Attempt to Free Hostages Failed;
Plane Crash - Several Killed (8)
New Specials ...
Tomorrow
Wings on Synder - Paul McCartney
Late Night News
Iran - Trouble
Bed 4:30

For 1G, run it again, Rosie!

All right, Rosie. We believe you, honest we do. In fact, to show our good faith, we're putting our money where your legs are. The Daily News will put up $1,000 if you'll run another marathon here in New York and come in anywhere within a half hour of your time in the Boston race.

Use the money as you see fit—give it to the Road Runners Club or one of your favorite charities. Let's show those Beantowners and the rest of the world that you, a New Yorker, beat 'em, fair and square. One condition: you gotta let us follow you. (Just for the pictures, you understand.) Give us a call, Rosie.

Up 9:30
See Greg
Overcast Skies 60's
1980 116th day - 250 days follow
APRIL 25 FRIDAY
Insurance Problem
Talk with Nixon
Rick ?
Mexico 18 FT Waves
Post Card From Ray Down in Hatteras with his kids
George Has Dinner Party
Allen in Self Magazine
"Brazil"

Rick Rasmussen "getting down" at the competitions. Photo: Nilton.

Movies with Allen + Rusty
Where The Buffalo Roam
Bobby Van For Dinner
Peter Boyle
Damp
Rain At Night - Bad
Feel Tired
TV, Fridays - New Show
The Clash, Punks
Bed
Star Trek

"I hate to advocate drugs, alcohol, violence, or insanity to anyone... but they've always worked for me."

Run ?
1980 117th day - 249 days follow
Call Gordon
Up 10:00
IRAN DAY 175
SATURDAY 26 APRIL
Things Bad
Insurance Call again
Heavy Nose Congestion
SPA and Lunch
Check House
WHERE THE BUFFALO ROAM
BASED ON THE TWISTED LEGEND OF Dr. Hunter S. Thompson
Churchill Downs
Dinner Shaggs with Rusty
Rock Concert
Commadors
Steve Forbert
Moonlight
Too Many late Nights

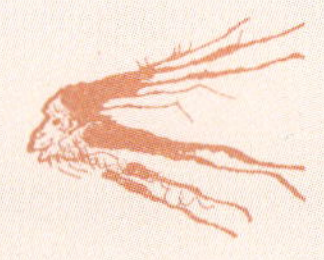

“I WAS HELPING ABC PRODUCE A PROGRAM ON ORANGUTANS AT A RESEARCH CAMP IN BORNEO. I WAS THERE FOR A LITTLE BIT AND GOT KIND OF RESTLESS. IN MY JOURNAL I HAD A TAB OF MR. NATURAL LSD. I WAS INTO RUNNING THEN, THATS WHEN I WAS DOING MARATHONS. I TOOK IT AND IT GAVE ME A LITTLE BUZZ, SO OFF I GO RUNNING INTO THE JUNGLE. YOU’RE A MILLION MILES FROM NOWHERE. I’M RUNNING AND I’M PROBABLY ABOUT 45 MINUTES INTO THE JUNGLE AND I HEAR RUFFLING AND GO ‘SHIT’. I SEE SOMETHING, AND BORNEO HAS SOME BIG CATS. I TOOK OFF “PEEEEEWWWW” LIKE THE ROAD RUNNER. I’VE NEVER RUN SO FAST IN MY LIFE.”

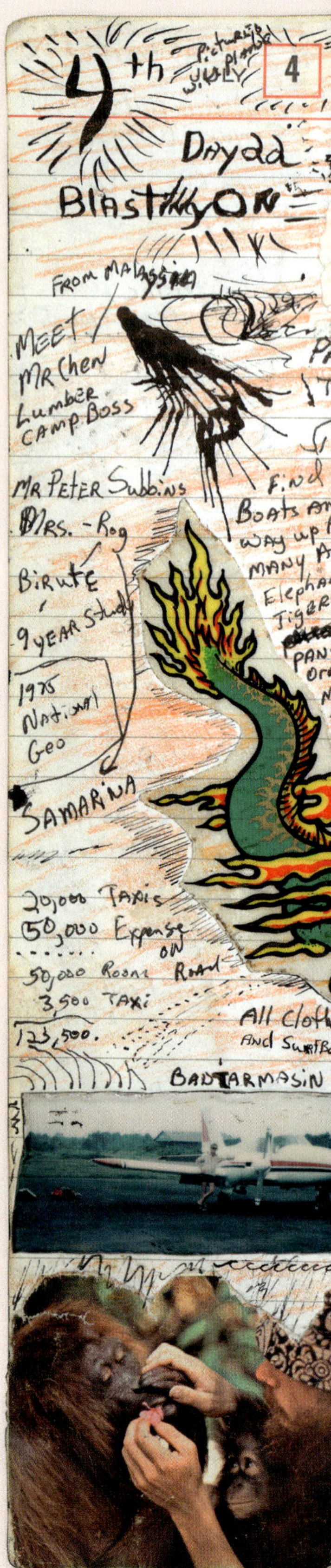

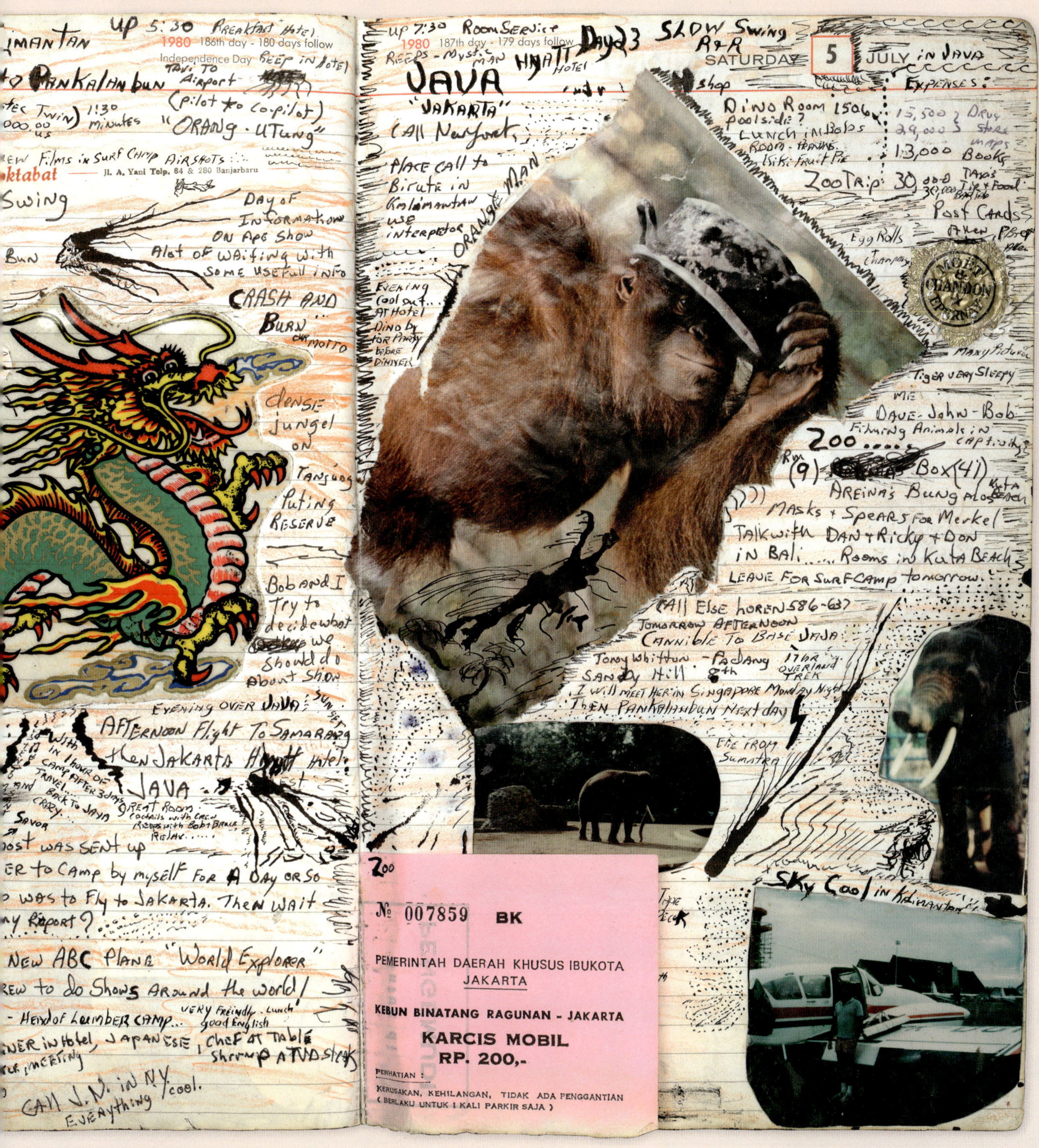
1980 186th day - 180 days follow
Independence Day
Jl. A. Yani Telp. 84 & 280 Banjarbaru
1980 187th day - 179 days follow
SATURDAY 5 JULY
MOET & CHANDON EPERNAY
№ 007859 BK
PEMERINTAH DAERAH KHUSUS IBUKOTA JAKARTA
KEBUN BINATANG RAGUNAN - JAKARTA
KARCIS MOBIL
RP. 200,-
PERHATIAN :
KERUSAKAN, KEHILANGAN, TIDAK ADA PENGGANTIAN
(BERLAKU UNTUK 1 KALI PARKIR SAJA)

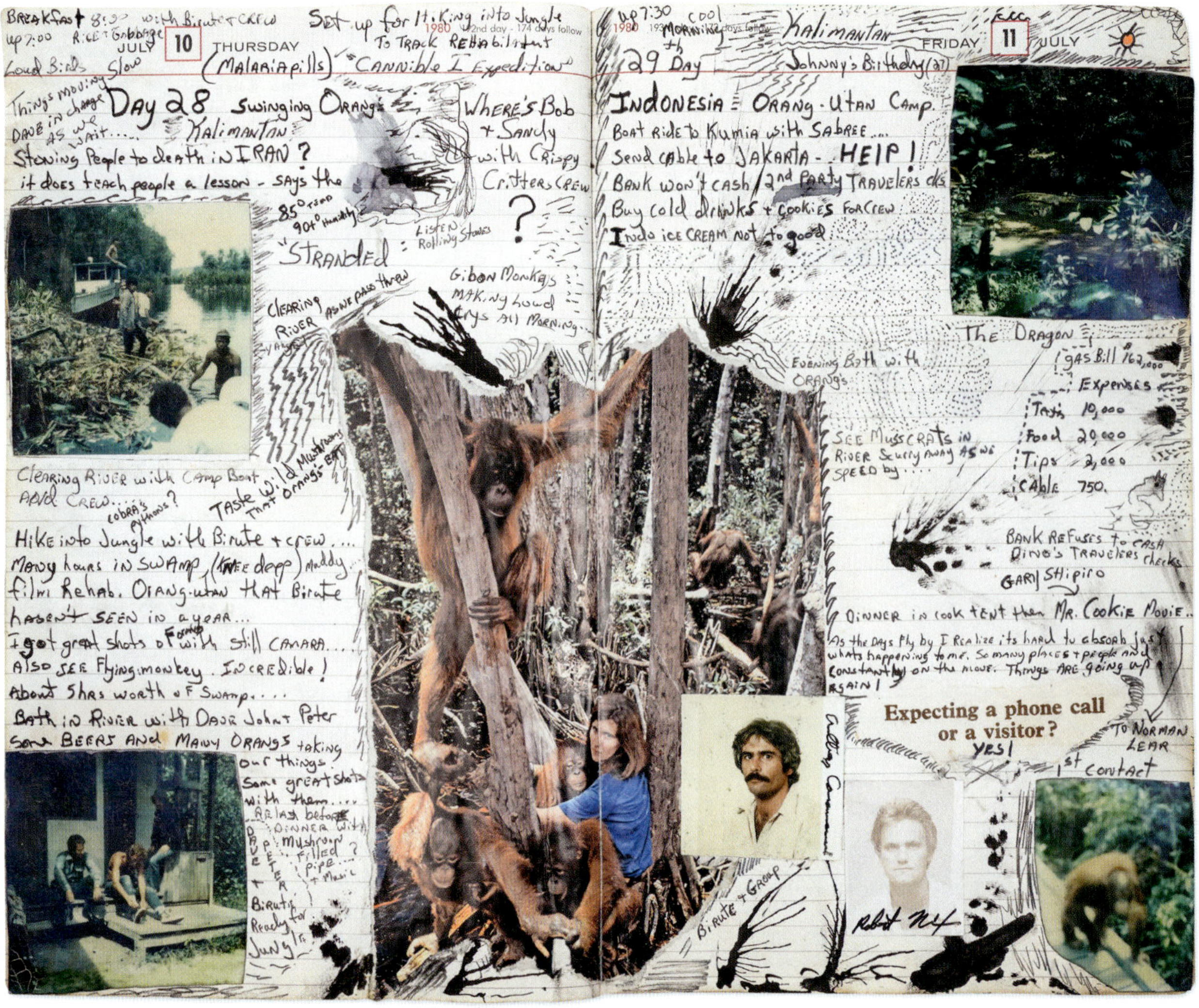

BREAKfast 8:30 with Birute + CREW
up 7:00 Rice + Gabbage
Loud Birds Slow

JULY 10 THURSDAY

Set up for Hiking into Jungle To Track Rehabilitant
1980 192nd day - 174 days follow
(MalariA pills) "Cannible I Expedition"

Things moving Dave in charge as we wait....

Day 28 Swinging Orang's
Kalimantan

Stoning People to death in IRAN?
it does teach people a lesson - says the

Where's Bob + Sandy with Crispy Critters Crew ?

85° temp
90+° Humidity

Listen Rolling Stones

"STRANDED"

Gibon Monkeys making loud crys All Morning...

Clearing River as we pass threw

Clearing River with Camp Boat and Crew.... cobra's pythons?

Taste Wild Mushrooms That Orang's Eat

Hike into Jungle with Birute + crew....
Many hours in swamp, (knee deep) muddy...
film Rehab. Orang-utan that Birute
hasen't seen in a year...
I got great shots of Fomo with still camara....
Also see Flying monkey. Incredible!
About 5hrs worth of Swamp....
Bath in River with Dave John + Peter
Some Beers and Many Orangs taking our things.
Some great shots with them....
Relax before Dinner with mushroom filled ? pipe... + Music
Dave + Peter + Birute Ready for Jungle

up 7:30 cool Morning
1980 193rd day - 173 days follow
29th Day

Kalimantan

FRIDAY 11 JULY

Johnny's Birthday (27)

Indonesia = Orang-Utan Camp.
Boat ride to Kumia with Sabree....
Send cable to Jakarta... HELP!
Bank won't cash / 2nd Party Travelers cks
Buy cold drinks + cookies for Crew
Indo ice cream not to good

Evening Bath with Orangs

The Dragon

gas Bill 162,000

Expenses
Taxis 10,000
Food 20,000
Tips 2,000
Cable 750.

See Musscrats in River Scurry Away as we speed by....

Bank Refuses to cash Dino's Travelers checks
Gary Shipiro

Dinner in cook tent then Mr. Cookie Movie..
As the days fly by I realize its hard to absorb just whats happening to me. So many places + people and constantly on the move. Things are going up again!

Expecting a phone call
or a visitor?
YES!

To Norman Lear
1st contact

Birute + Group

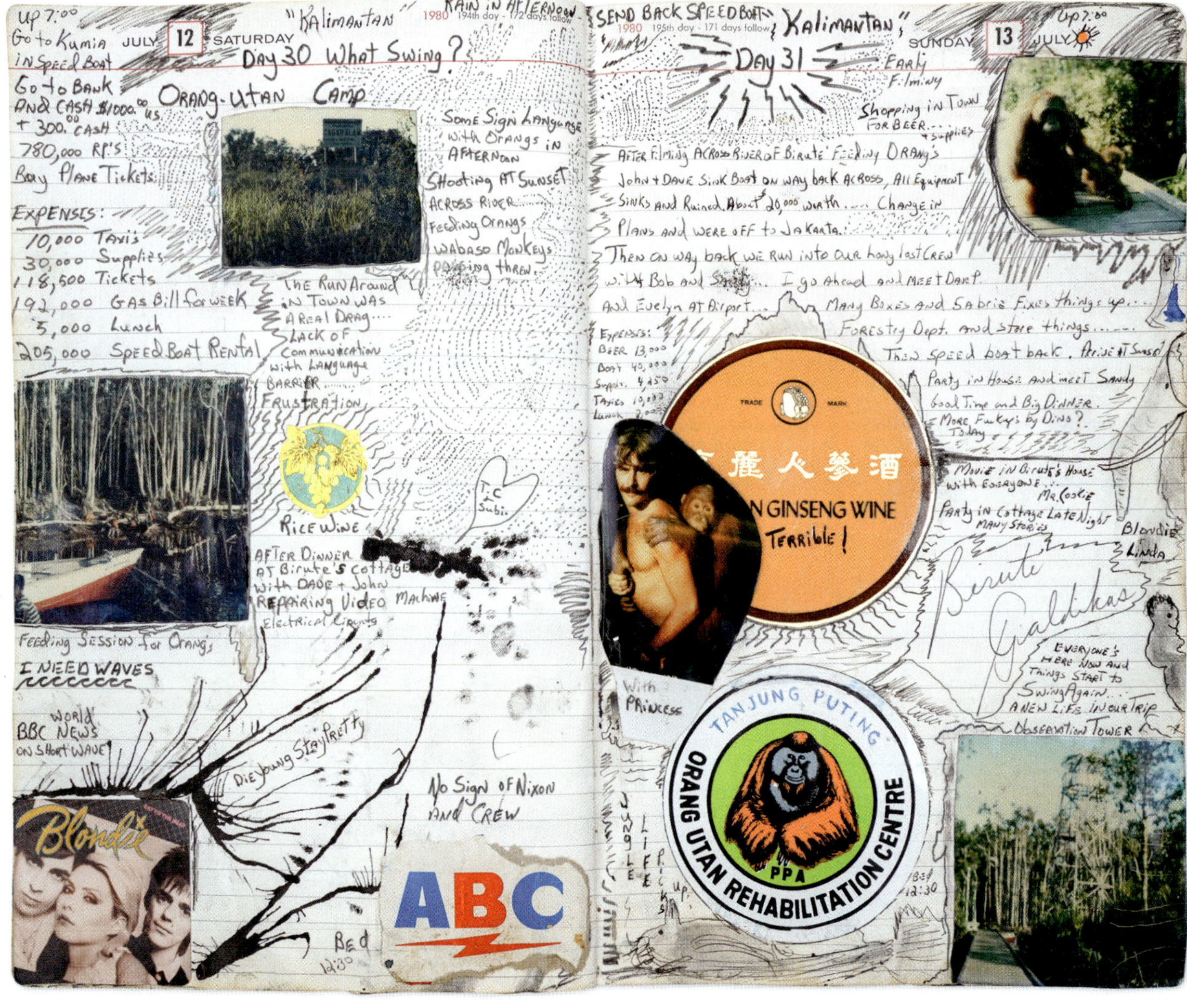

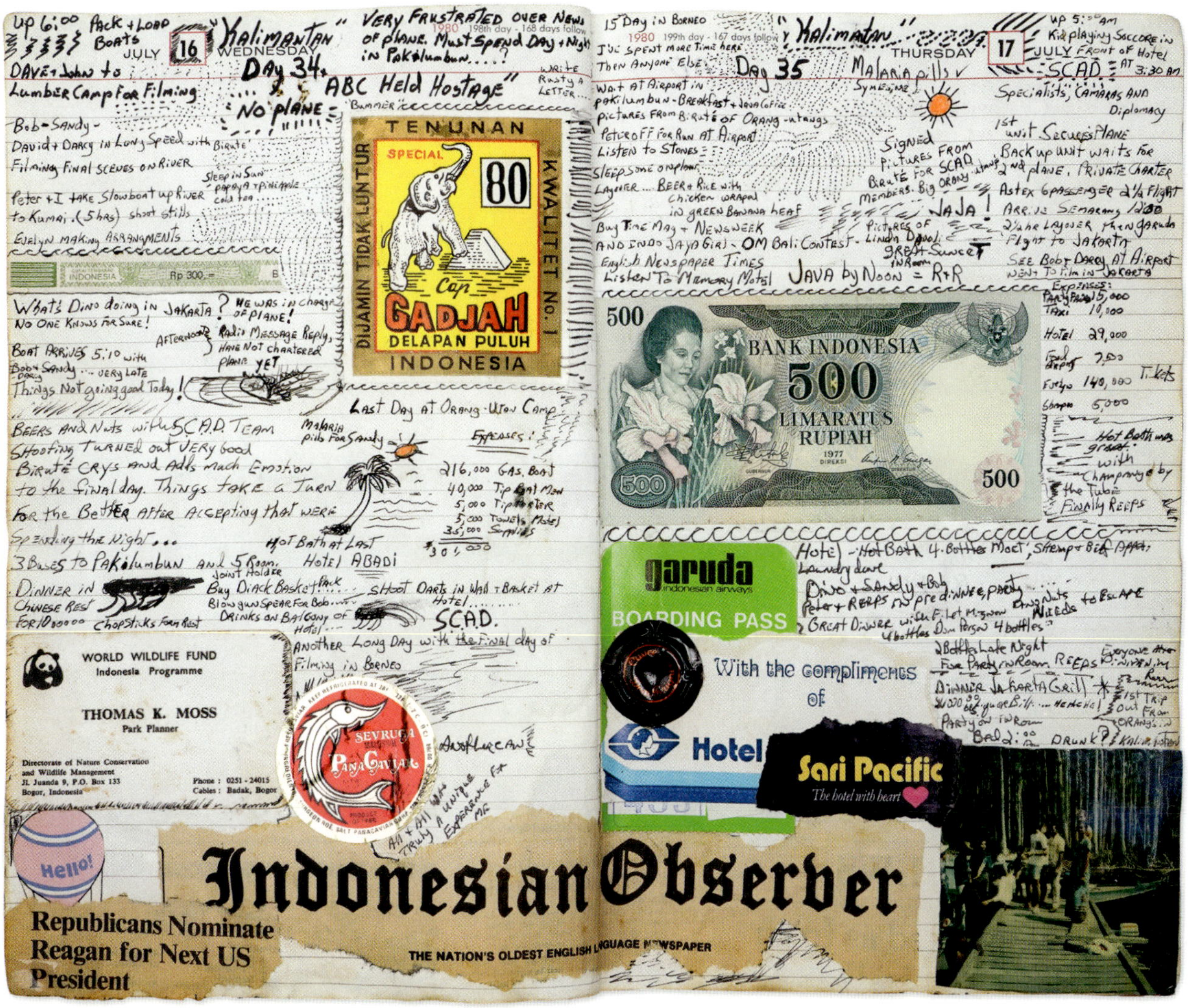

Kalimantan
JULY 16 WEDNESDAY
1980 198th day - 168 days follow
Day 34
"ABC Held Hostage"
No plane

TENUNAN
SPECIAL 80
Cap GADJAH
DELAPAN PULUH
DIJAMIN TIDAK LUNTUR
KWALITET No. 1
INDONESIA

Kalimantan
THURSDAY 17
1980 199th day - 167 days follow
Day 35

BANK INDONESIA
500
LIMARATUS RUPIAH
1977

garuda
indonesian airways
BOARDING PASS

With the compliments of
Hotel
Sari Pacific
The hotel with heart

WORLD WILDLIFE FUND
Indonesia Programme
THOMAS K. MOSS
Park Planner
Directorate of Nature Conservation and Wildlife Management
Jl. Juanda 9, P.O. Box 133
Bogor, Indonesia
Phone: 0251 - 24015
Cables: Badak, Bogor

SEVRUGA
Hello!

Indonesian Observer
THE NATION'S OLDEST ENGLISH LANGUAGE NEWSPAPER
Republicans Nominate Reagan for Next US President

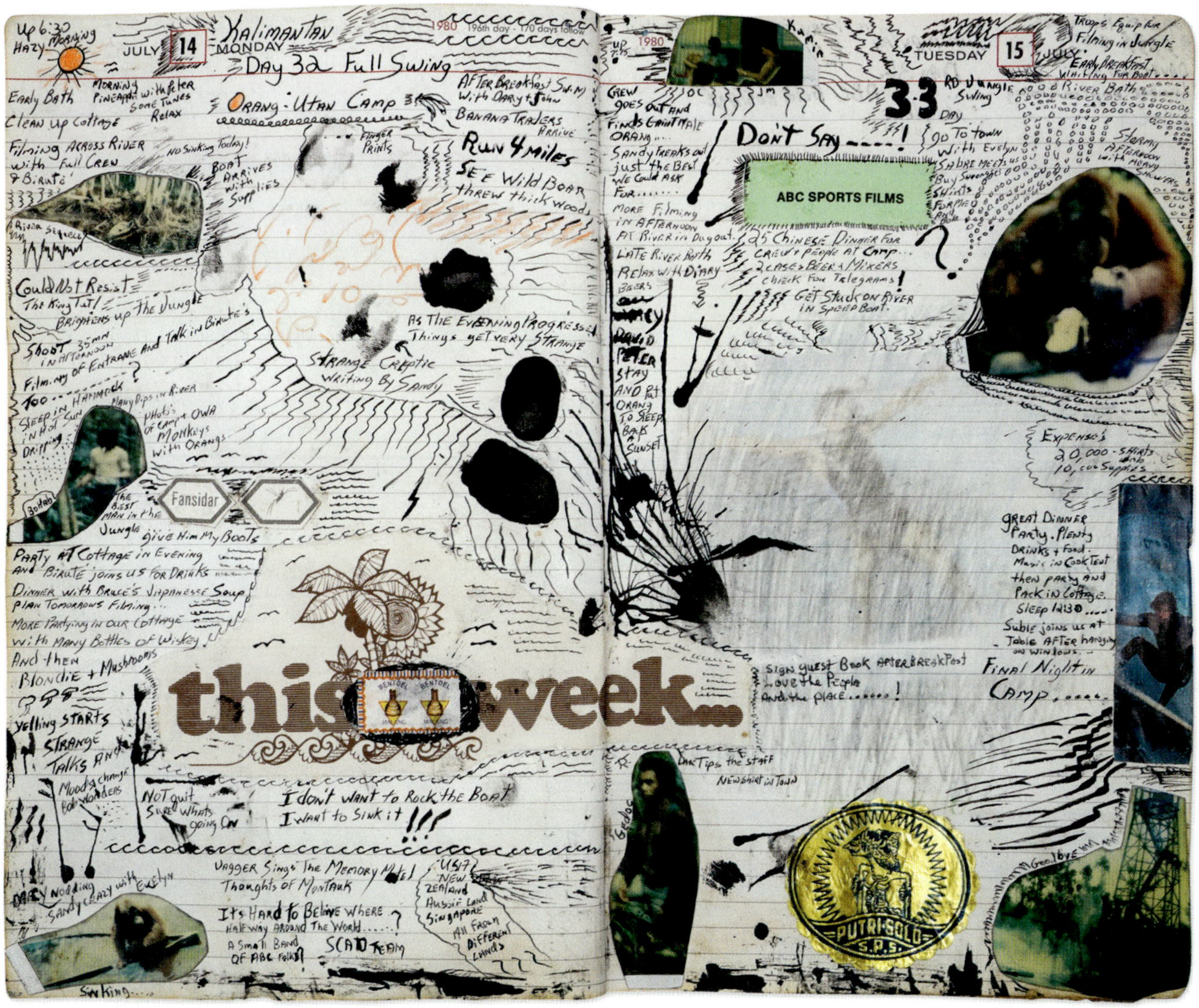

Kalimantan
JULY 14 MONDAY
1980 196th day - 170 days follow
Day 32 Full Swing
Orang-Utan Camp

TUESDAY 15
Day 33
Don't Say
ABC SPORTS FILMS
Fansidar
PUTRI GOLD

this week..

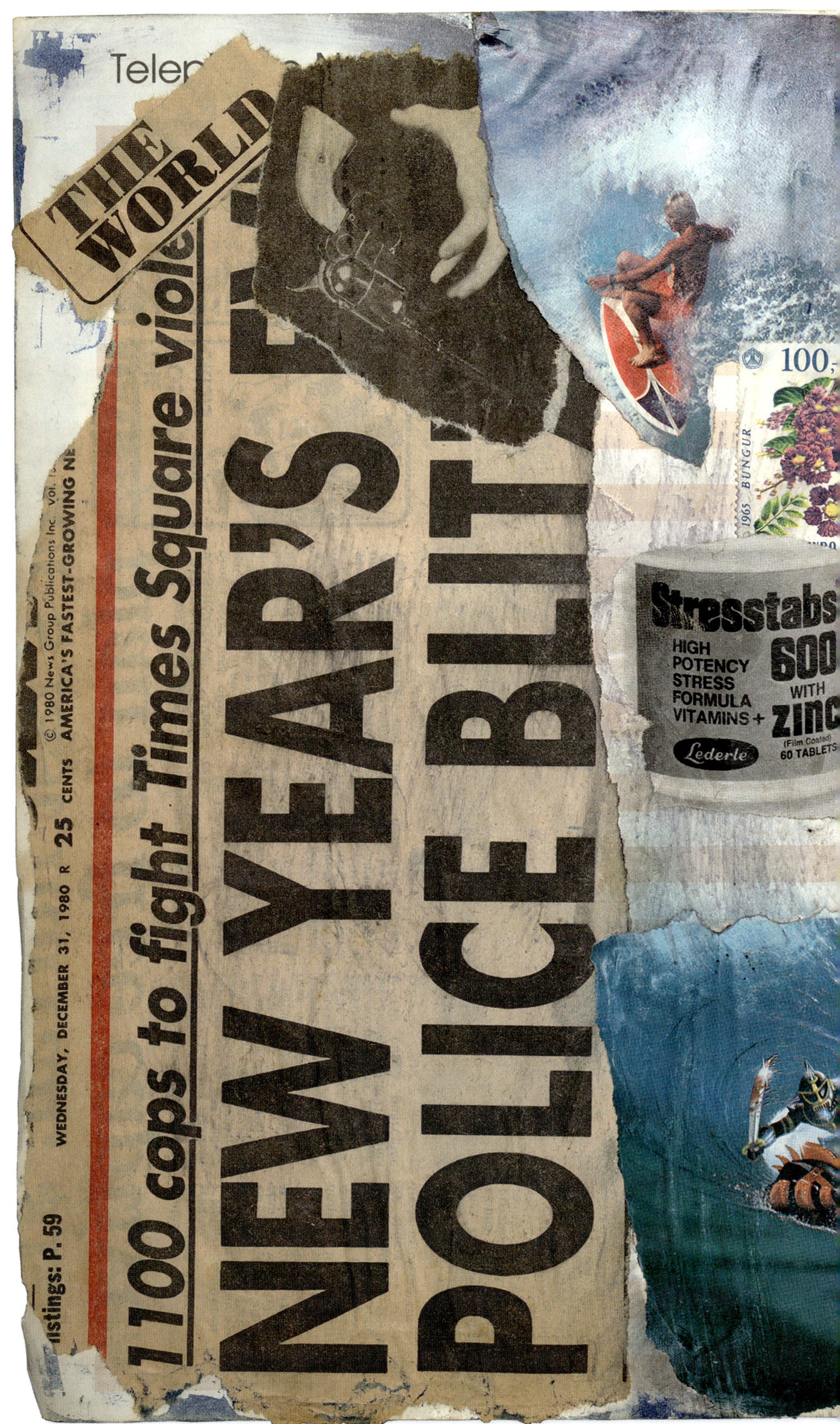
THE WORLD
1100 cops to fight Times Square viole
NEW YEAR'S
POLICE BLIT
WEDNESDAY, DECEMBER 31, 1980 R 25 CENTS
© 1980 News Group Publications Inc.
AMERICA'S FASTEST-GROWING NE
listings: P. 59
Stresstabs
HIGH POTENCY STRESS FORMULA VITAMINS +
600
WITH
ZINC
(Film Coated)
60 TABLETS
Lederle
1965 BUNGUR
100,

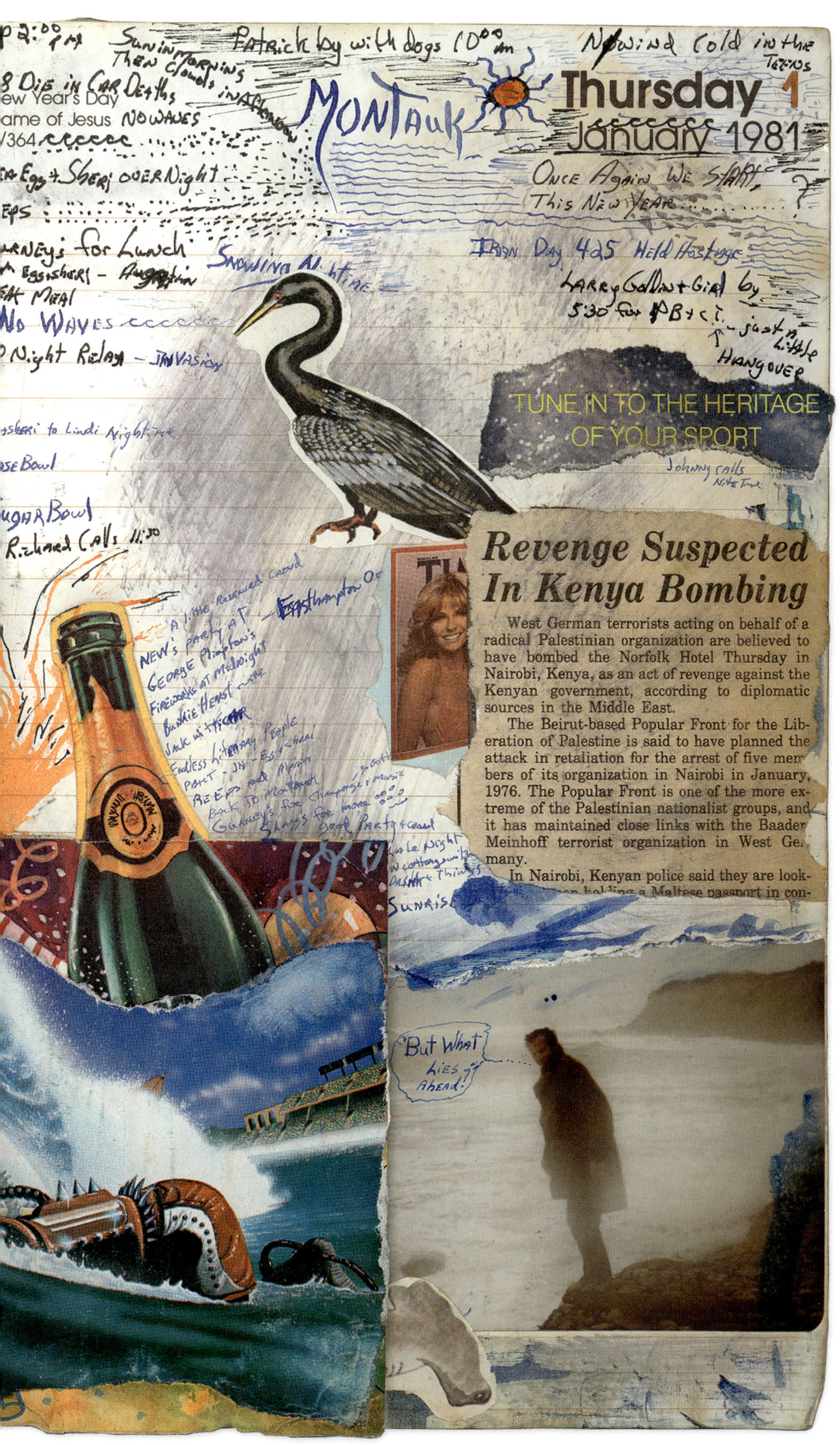

Revenge Suspected In Kenya Bombing

West German terrorists acting on behalf of a radical Palestinian organization are believed to have bombed the Norfolk Hotel Thursday in Nairobi, Kenya, as an act of revenge against the Kenyan government, according to diplomatic sources in the Middle East.

The Beirut-based Popular Front for the Liberation of Palestine is said to have planned the attack in retaliation for the arrest of five members of its organization in Nairobi in January, 1976. The Popular Front is one of the more extreme of the Palestinian nationalist groups, and it has maintained close links with the Baader Meinhoff terrorist organization in West Germany.

In Nairobi, Kenyan police said they are look-

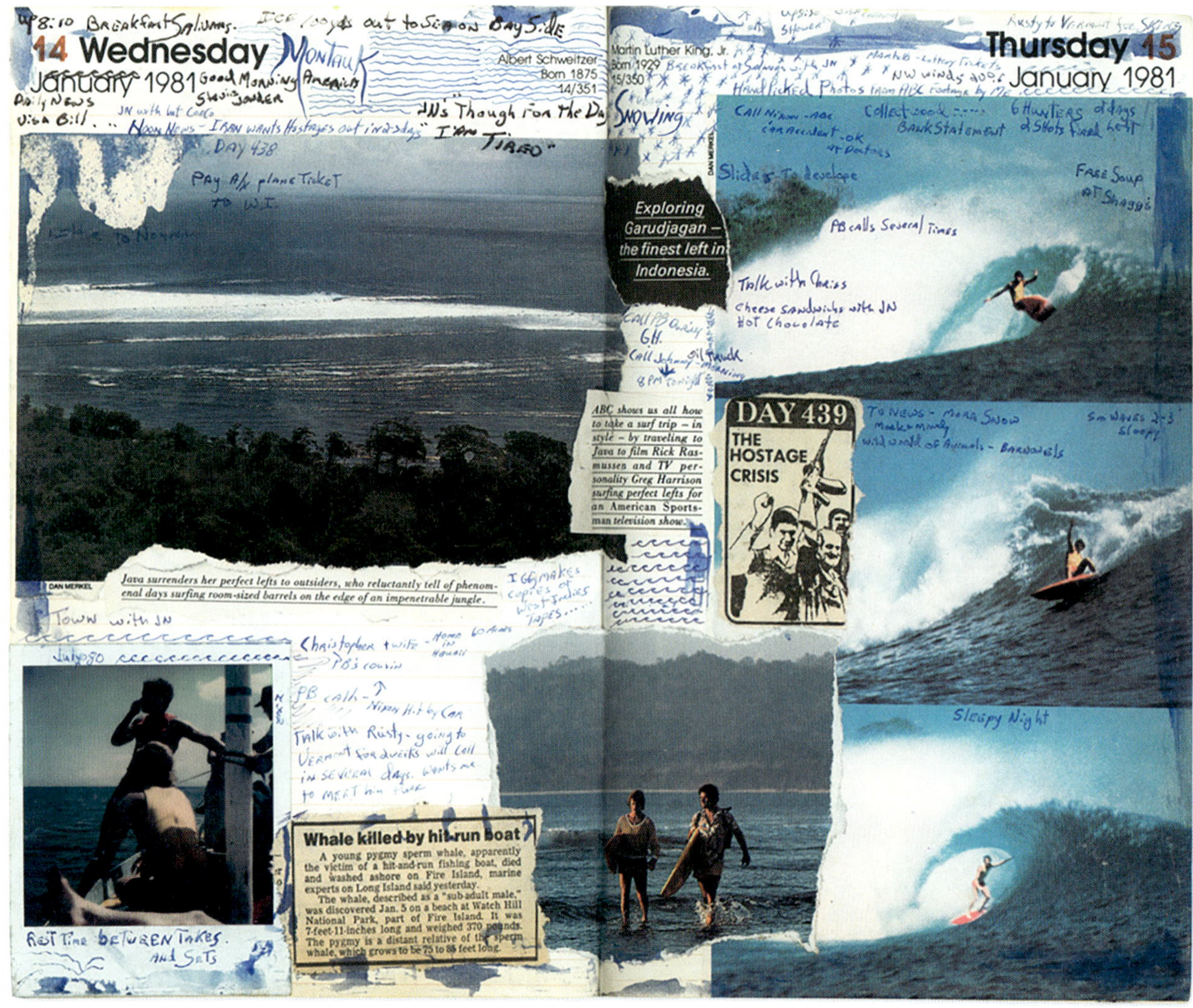
14 Wednesday
January 1981
Albert Schweitzer
Born 1875
14/351
Montauk
Day 438
Martin Luther King, Jr.
Born 1929
15/350
Thursday 15
January 1981
Snowing
Exploring Garudjagan – the finest left in Indonesia.
ABC shows us all how to take a surf trip – in style – by traveling to Java to film Rick Rasmussen and TV personality Greg Harrison surfing perfect lefts for an American Sportsman television show.
DAN MERKEL
Java surrenders her perfect lefts to outsiders, who reluctantly tell of phenomenal days surfing room-sized barrels on the edge of an impenetrable jungle.
DAY 439
THE HOSTAGE CRISIS
Whale killed by hit-run boat
A young pygmy sperm whale, apparently the victim of a hit-and-run fishing boat, died and washed ashore on Fire Island, marine experts on Long Island said yesterday.
The whale, described as a "sub-adult male," was discovered Jan. 5 on a beach at Watch Hill National Park, part of Fire Island. It was 7-feet-11-inches long and weighed 370 pounds. The pygmy is a distant relative of the sperm whale, which grows to be 75 to 85 feet long.
Sleepy Night
Rest Time between Takes and Sets

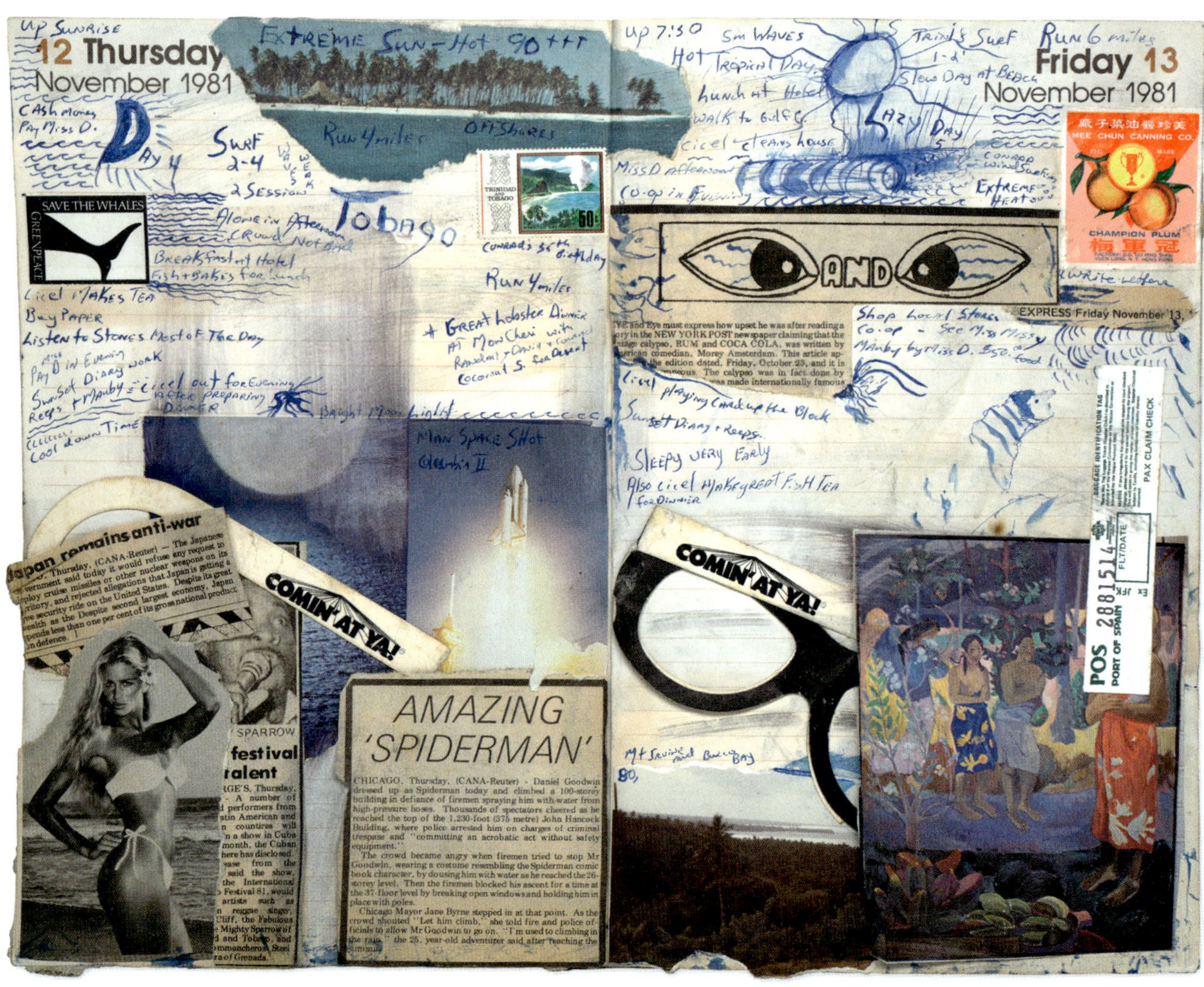
12 Thursday
November 1981
Friday 13
November 1981
SAVE THE WHALES
GREENPEACE
Tobago
TRINIDAD AND TOBAGO
50¢
MEE CHUN CANNING CO.
CHAMPION PLUM
AND
EXPRESS Friday November 13
...Eye and Eye must express how upset he was after reading a story in the NEW YORK POST newspaper claiming that the vintage calypso, RUM and COCA COLA, was written by American comedian, Morey Amsterdam. This article appeared in the edition dated, Friday, October 23, and it is ... The calypso was in fact done by ... was made internationally famous
Sleepy very Early
Also cicel make great Fish Tea for Dinner
Japan remains anti-war
COMIN' AT YA!
COMIN' AT YA!
festival talent
PAX CLAIM CHECK
POS 288151
PORT OF SPAIN
AMAZING 'SPIDERMAN'
CHICAGO, Thursday, (CANA-Reuter) - Daniel Goodwin dressed up as Spiderman today and climbed a 100-storey building in defiance of firemen spraying him with water from high-pressure hoses. Thousands of spectators cheered as he reached the top of the 1,230-foot (375 metre) John Hancock Building, where police arrested him on charges of criminal trespass and "committing an acrobatic act without safety equipment."
The crowd became angry when firemen tried to stop Mr Goodwin, wearing a costume resembling the Spiderman comic book character, by dousing him with water as he reached the 26-storey level. Then the firemen blocked his ascent for a time at the 37-floor level by breaking open windows and holding him in place with poles.
Chicago Mayor Jane Byrne stepped in at that point. As the crowd shouted "Let him climb," she told fire and police officials to allow Mr Goodwin to go on. "I'm used to climbing in the rain," the 25-year-old adventurer said after reaching the summit.

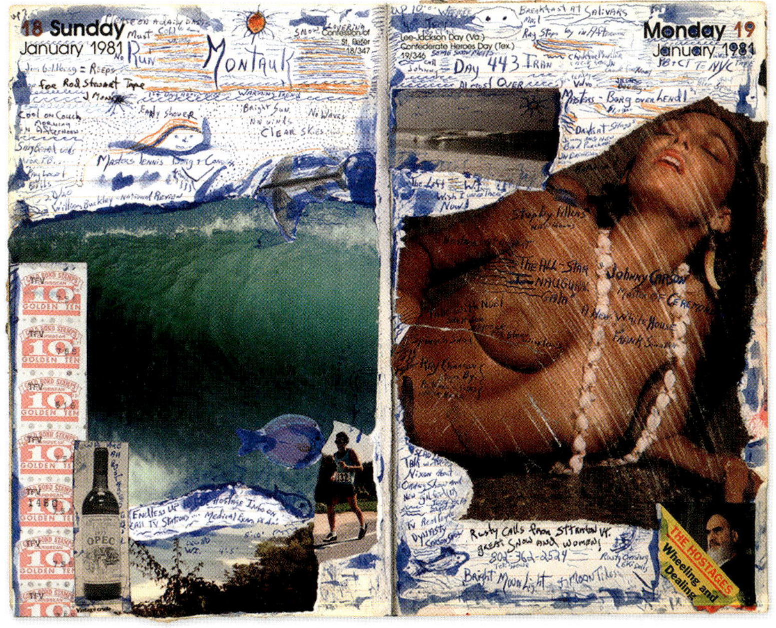
18 Sunday
January 1981
Montauk
Monday 19
January 1981
THE HOSTAGES: Wheeling and Dealing

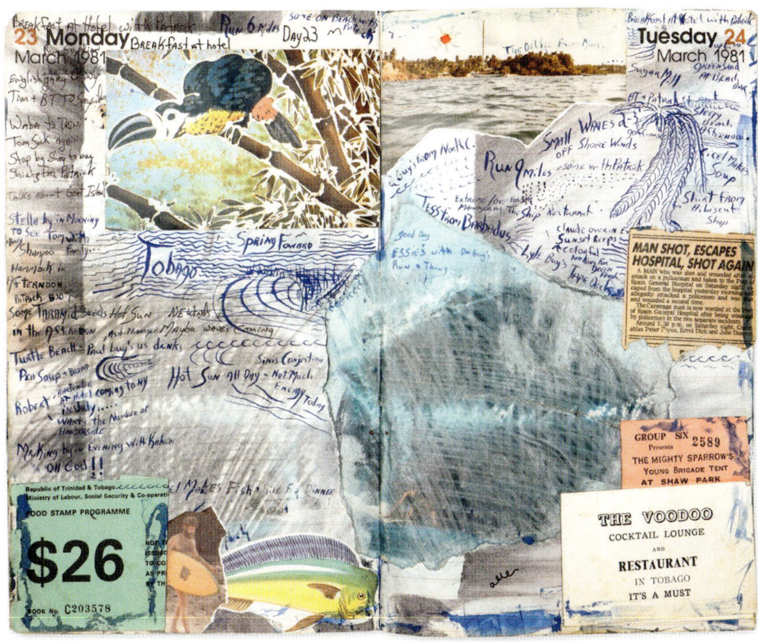
23 Monday
March 1981
Tuesday 24
March 1981
Tobago
MAN SHOT, ESCAPES HOSPITAL, SHOT AGAIN
Republic of Trinidad & Tobago
FOOD STAMP PROGRAMME
$26
GROUP SX 2589
Presents
THE MIGHTY SPARROW'S
YOUNG BRIGADE TENT
AT SHAW PARK
THE VOODOO
COCKTAIL LOUNGE
AND
RESTAURANT
IN TOBAGO
IT'S A MUST

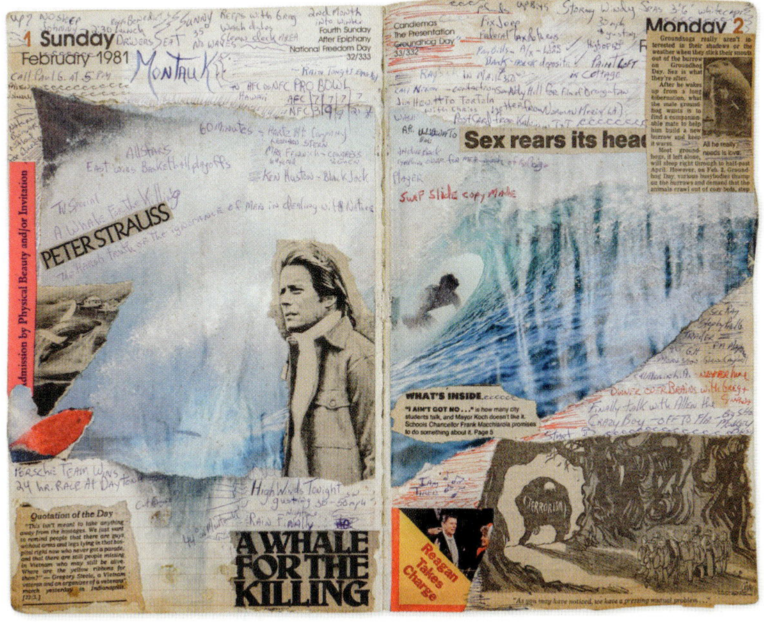
1 Sunday
February 1981
Montauk
Monday 2
Sex rears its head
PETER STRAUSS
Quotation of the Day
WHAT'S INSIDE
A WHALE FOR THE KILLING
Reagan Takes Charge

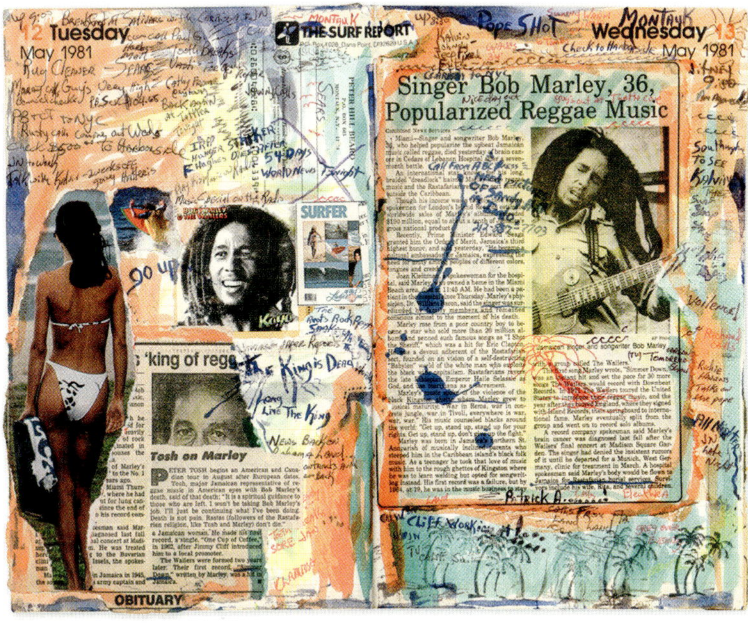
12 Tuesday
May 1981
THE SURF REPORT
Pope Shot
Wednesday 13
May 1981
Singer Bob Marley, 36,
Popularized Reggae Music
SURFER
Tosh on Marley
OBITUARY

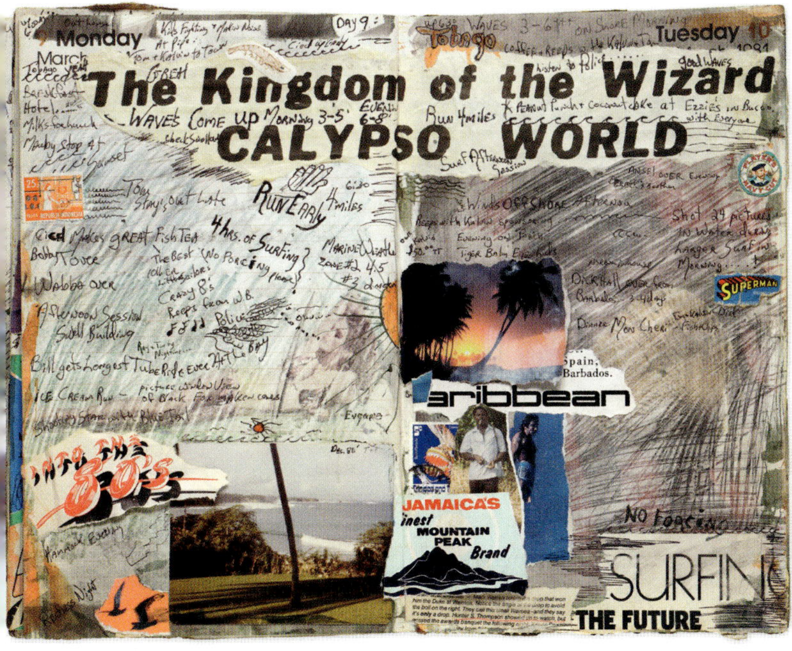
Monday
March
Tuesday 10
Tobago
The Kingdom of the Wizard
CALYPSO WORLD
SUPERMAN
aribbean
JAMAICA'S
finest
MOUNTAIN
PEAK
Brand
SURFIN
THE FUTURE

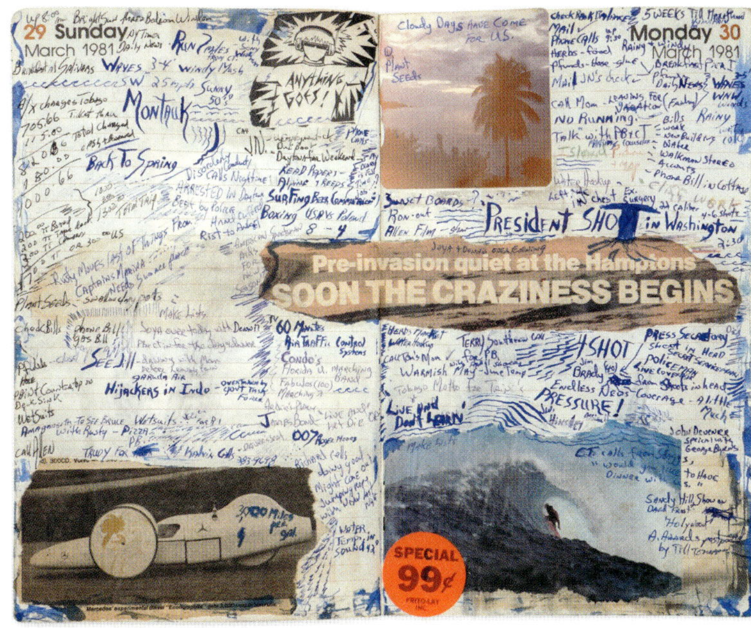
29 Sunday
March 1981
Monday 30
March 1981
Montauk
President Shot in Washington
Pre-invasion quiet at the Hamptons
SOON THE CRAZINESS BEGINS
SPECIAL
99¢

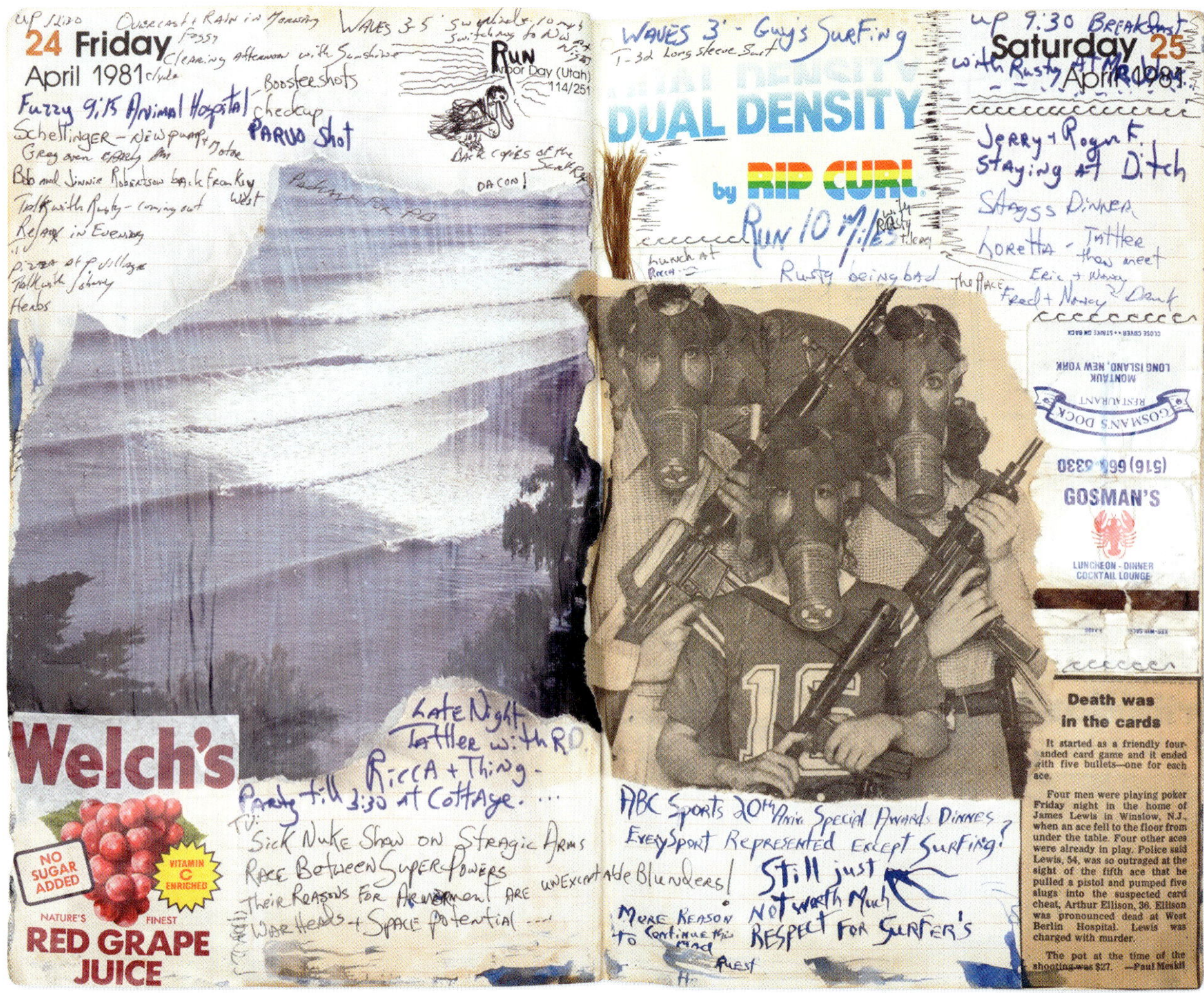

Death was in the cards

It started as a friendly four-handed card game and it ended with five bullets—one for each ace.

Four men were playing poker Friday night in the home of James Lewis in Winslow, N.J., when an ace fell to the floor from under the table. Four other aces were already in play. Police said Lewis, 54, was so outraged at the sight of the fifth ace that he pulled a pistol and pumped five slugs into the suspected card cheat, Arthur Ellison, 36. Ellison was pronounced dead at West Berlin Hospital. Lewis was charged with murder.

The pot at the time of the shooting was $27. —Paul Meskil

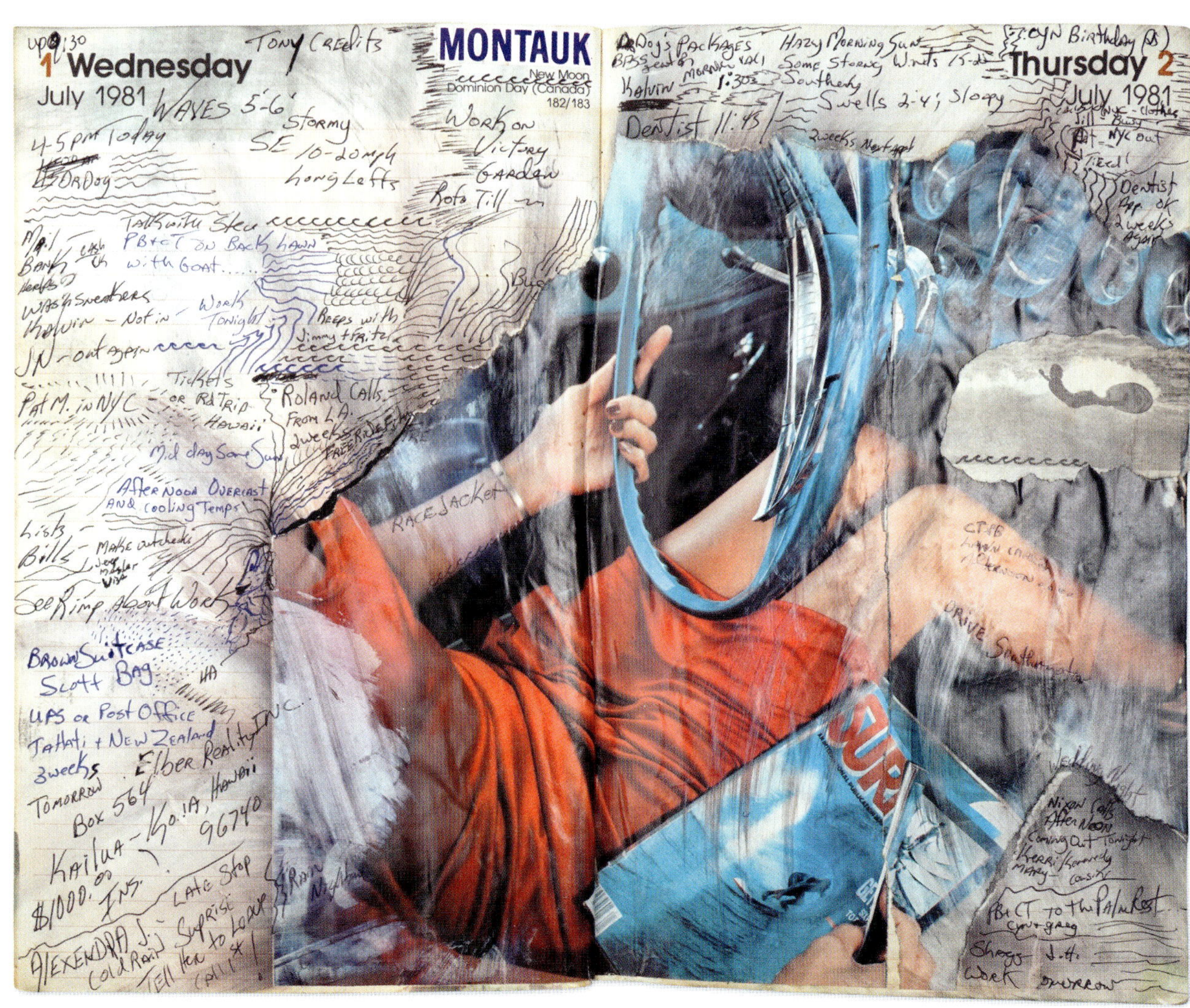

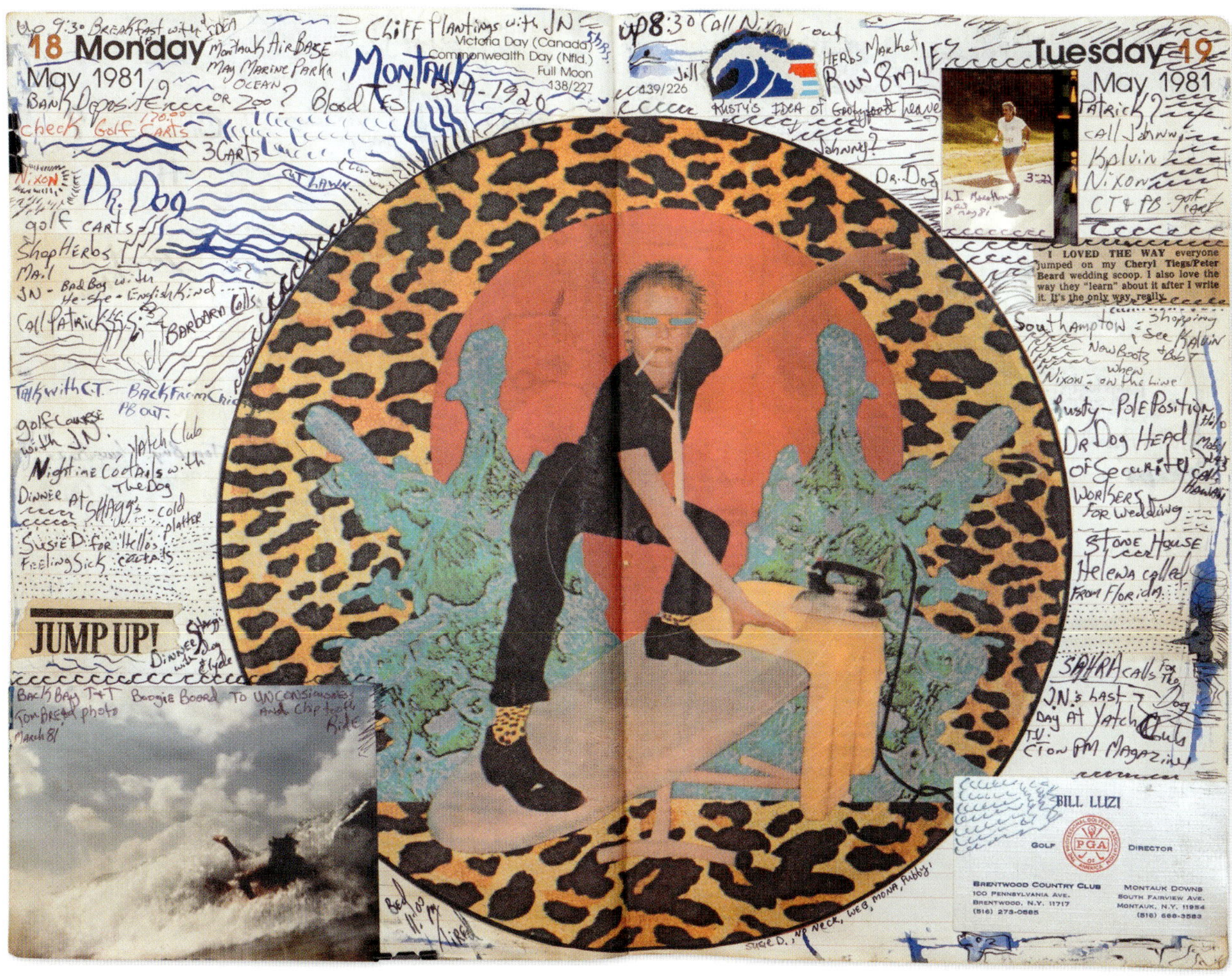
18 Monday
May 1981
Victoria Day (Canada)
Commonwealth Day (Nfld.)
Full Moon
138/227
139/226
Tuesday 19
May 1981
JUMP UP!
I LOVED THE WAY everyone jumped on my Cheryl Tiegs/Peter Beard wedding scoop. I also love the way they "learn" about it after I write it. It's the only way really.
BILL LUZI
GOLF DIRECTOR
BRENTWOOD COUNTRY CLUB
100 PENNSYLVANIA AVE.
BRENTWOOD, N.Y. 11717
(516) 273-0585
MONTAUK DOWNS
SOUTH FAIRVIEW AVE.
MONTAUK, N.Y. 11954
(516) 668-3583

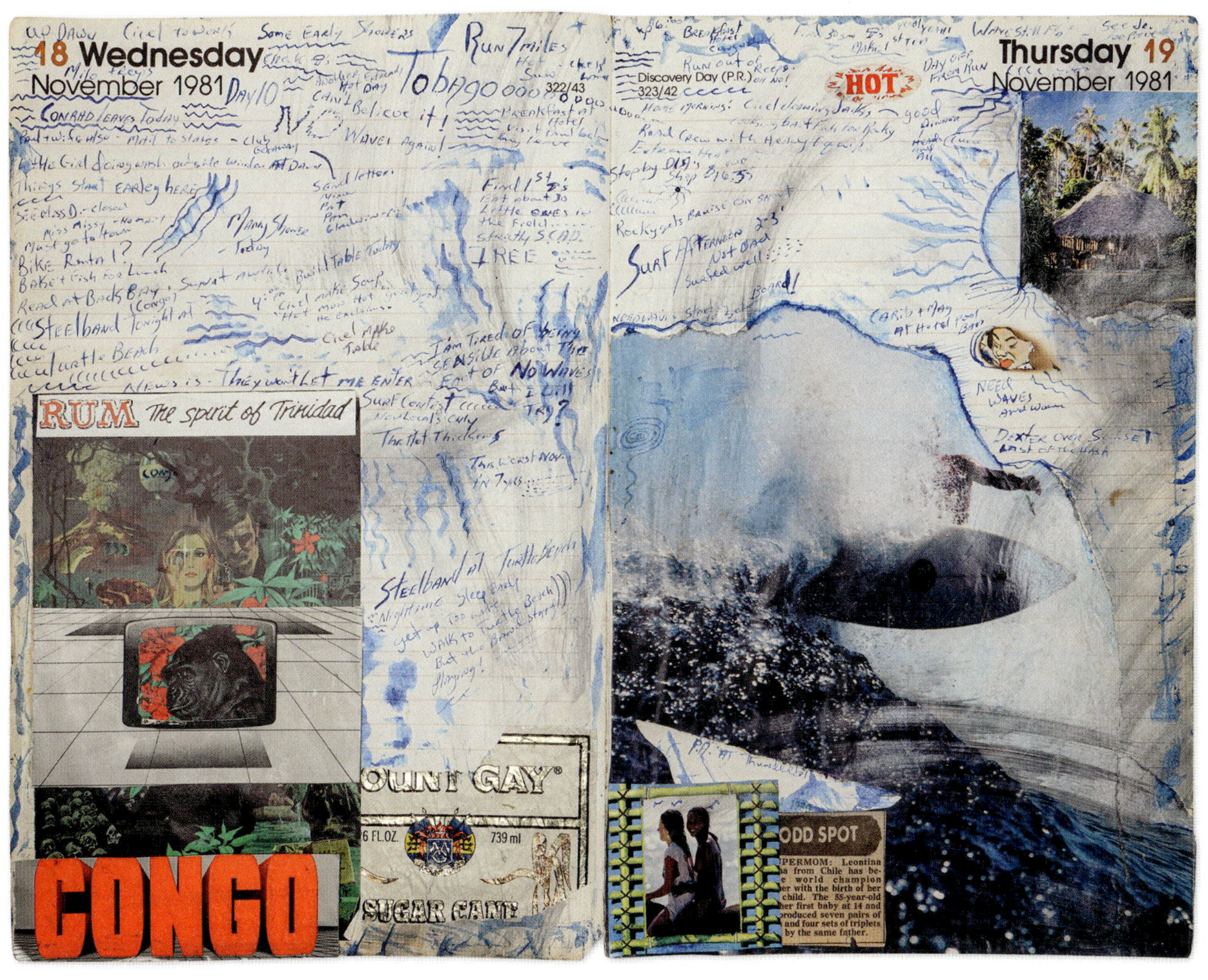
18 Wednesday
November 1981
322/43
Discovery Day (P.R.)
323/42
HOT
Thursday 19
November 1981
RUM The spirit of Trinidad
CONGO
OUNT GAY
6 FL.OZ.
739 ml
SUGAR CANE
ODD SPOT
PERMOM: Leontina
a from Chile has be-
er world champion
er with the birth of her
child. The 55-year-old
her first baby at 14 and
produced seven pairs of
and four sets of triplets
by the same father.

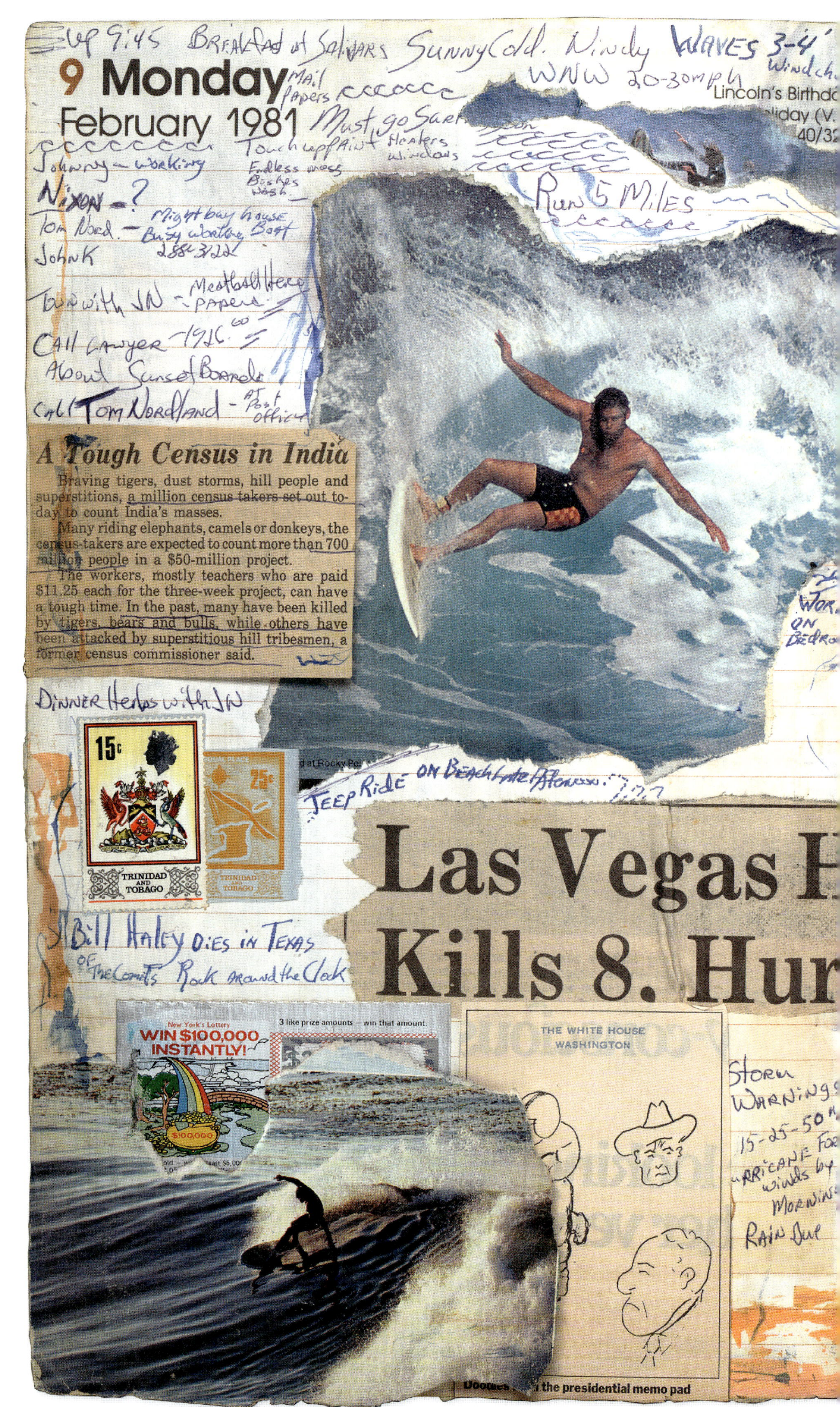

A Tough Census in India

Braving tigers, dust storms, hill people and superstitions, a million census takers set out today to count India's masses.

Many riding elephants, camels or donkeys, the census-takers are expected to count more than 700 million people in a $50-million project.

The workers, mostly teachers who are paid $11.25 each for the three-week project, can have a tough time. In the past, many have been killed by tigers, bears and bulls, while others have been attacked by superstitious hill tribesmen, a former census commissioner said.

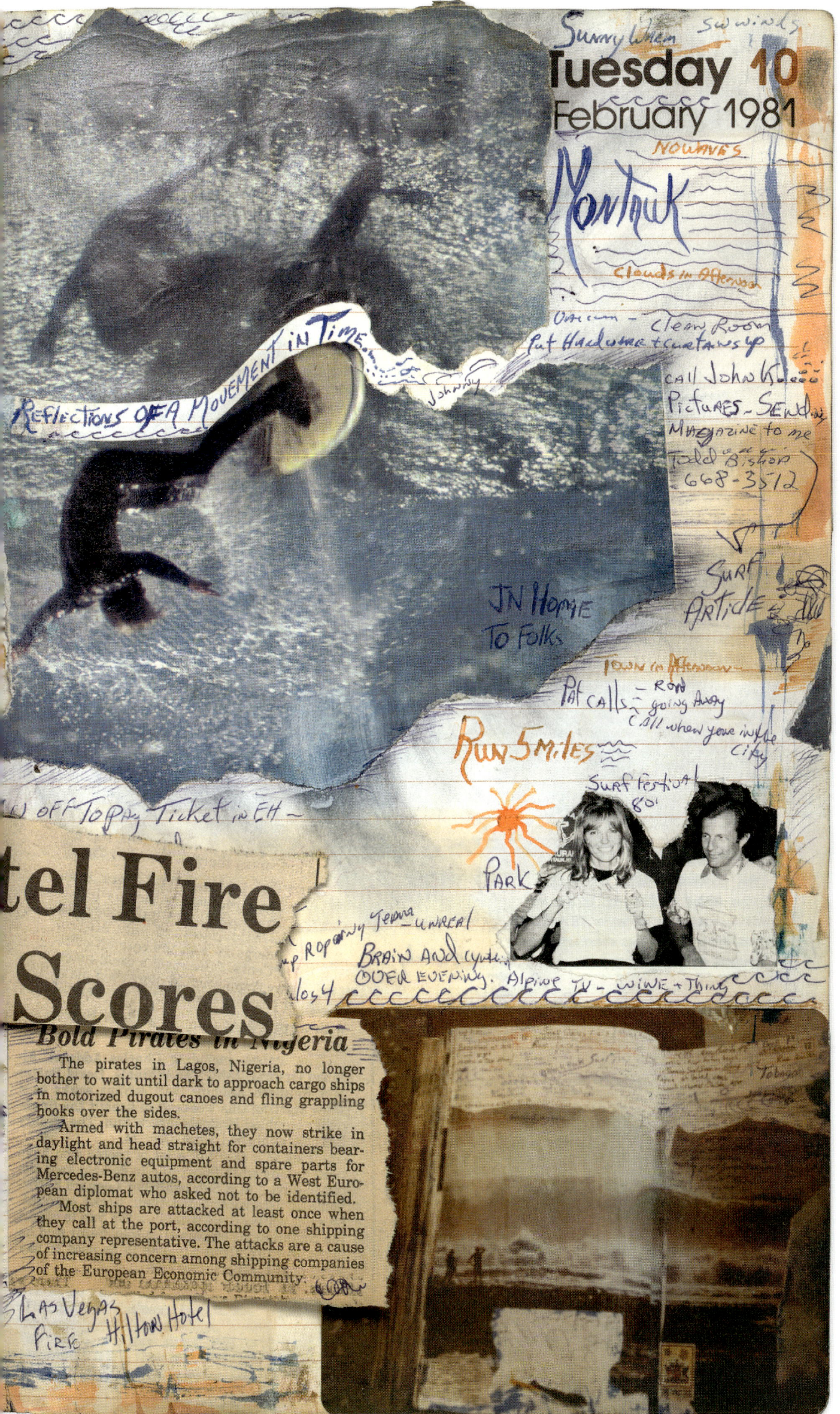

tel Fire
Scores

Bold Pirates in Nigeria

The pirates in Lagos, Nigeria, no longer bother to wait until dark to approach cargo ships in motorized dugout canoes and fling grappling hooks over the sides.

Armed with machetes, they now strike in daylight and head straight for containers bearing electronic equipment and spare parts for Mercedes-Benz autos, according to a West European diplomat who asked not to be identified.

Most ships are attacked at least once when they call at the port, according to one shipping company representative. The attacks are a cause of increasing concern among shipping companies of the European Economic Community.

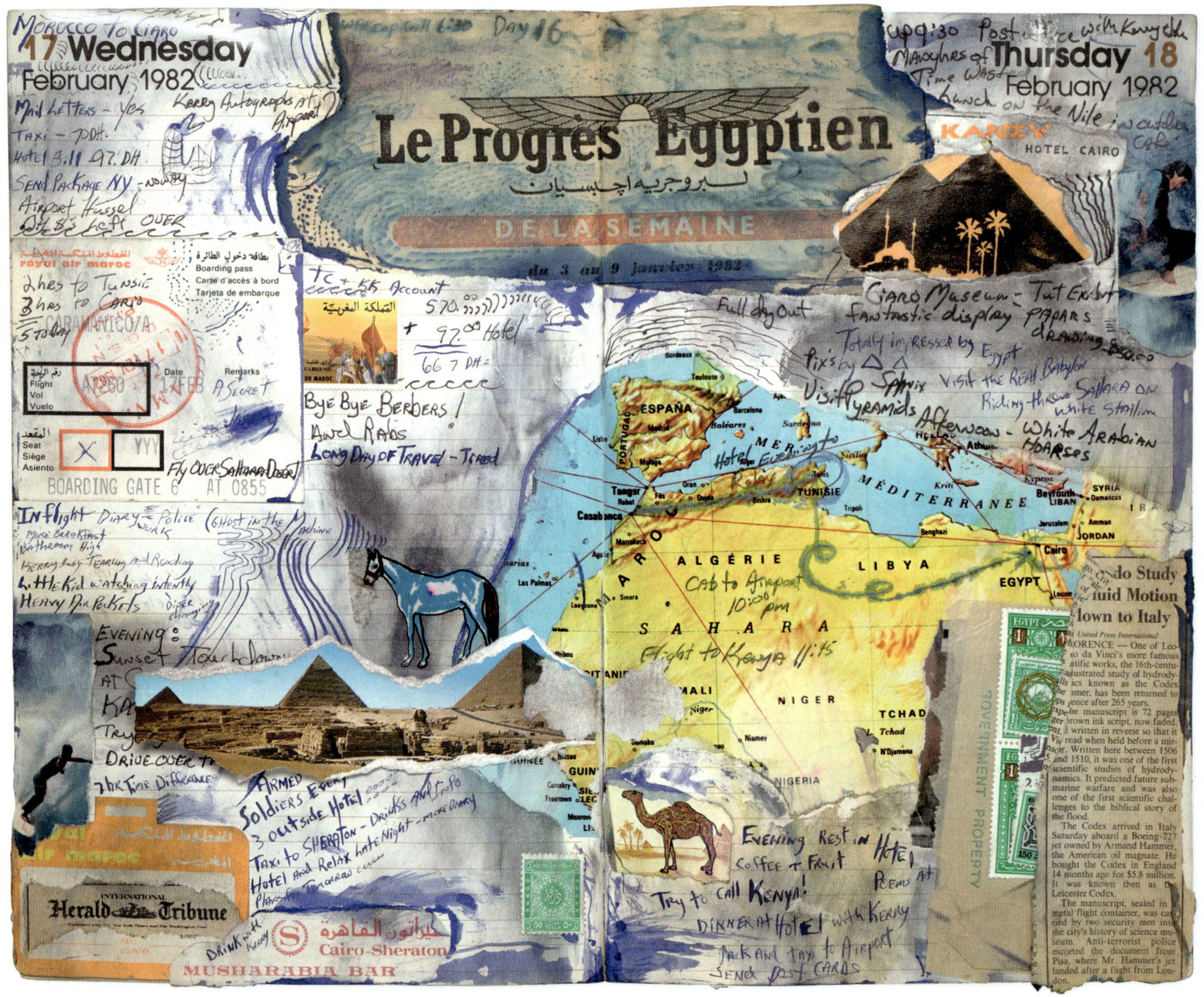

...do Study
...uid Motion
...lown to Italy

United Press International

...ORENCE — One of Leo... da Vinci's more famous ...atific works, the 16th-centu... illustrated study of hydrody... ...ics known as the Codex ...mer, has been returned to ...ence after 265 years.

...he manuscript is 72 pages ...brown ink script, now faded, ...written in reverse so that it ...read when held before a mir... Written here between 1506 and 1510, it was one of the first scientific studies of hydrodynamics. It predicted future submarine warfare and was also one of the first scientific challenges to the biblical story of the flood.

The Codex arrived in Italy Saturday aboard a Boeing 727 jet owned by Armand Hammer, the American oil magnate. He bought the Codex in England 14 months ago for $5.8 million. It was known then as the Leicester Codex.

The manuscript, sealed in a metal flight container, was carried by two security men into the city's history of science museum. Anti-terrorist police escorted the document from Pisa, where Mr. Hammer's jet landed after a flight from London.

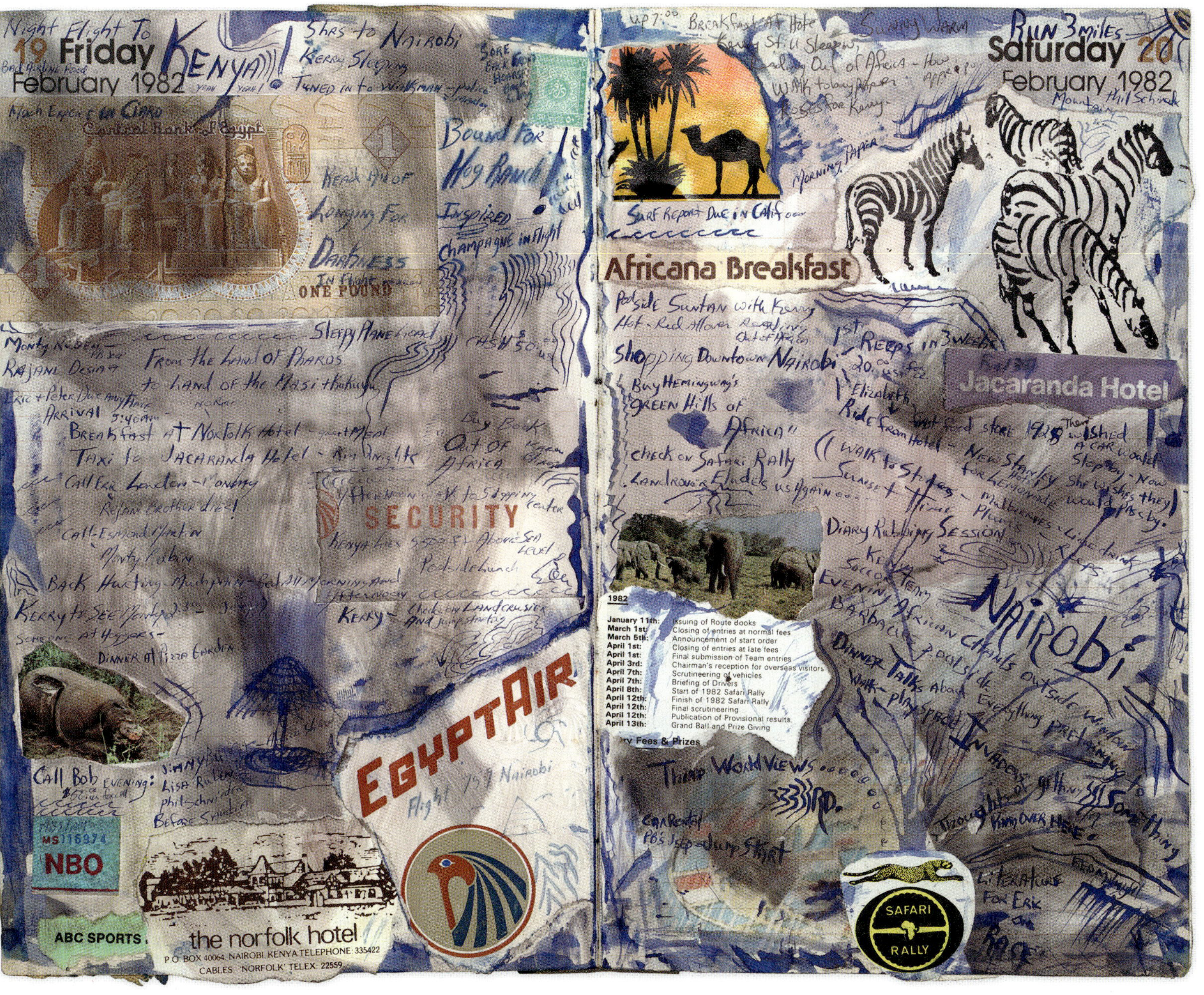
19 Friday
February 1982
Night Flight To KENYA!
Central Bank of Egypt
ONE POUND
Bound For Hog Ranch
SECURITY
EGYPTAIR
NBO
ABC SPORTS
the norfolk hotel
P.O. BOX 40064, NAIROBI, KENYA TELEPHONE 335422
CABLES 'NORFOLK' TELEX: 22559
Saturday 20
February 1982
Run 3 miles
Africana Breakfast
Jacaranda Hotel
1982
January 11th: Issuing of Route books
March 1st: Closing of entries at normal fees
March 5th: Announcement of start order
April 1st: Closing of entries at late fees
April 1st: Final submission of Team entries
April 3rd: Chairman's reception for overseas visitors
April 7th: Scrutineering of vehicles
April 7th: Briefing of Drivers
April 8th: Start of 1982 Safari Rally
April 12th: Finish of 1982 Safari Rally
April 12th: Final scrutineering
April 12th: Publication of Provisional results
April 13th: Grand Ball and Prize Giving
Entry Fees & Prizes
Nairobi
SAFARI
RALLY

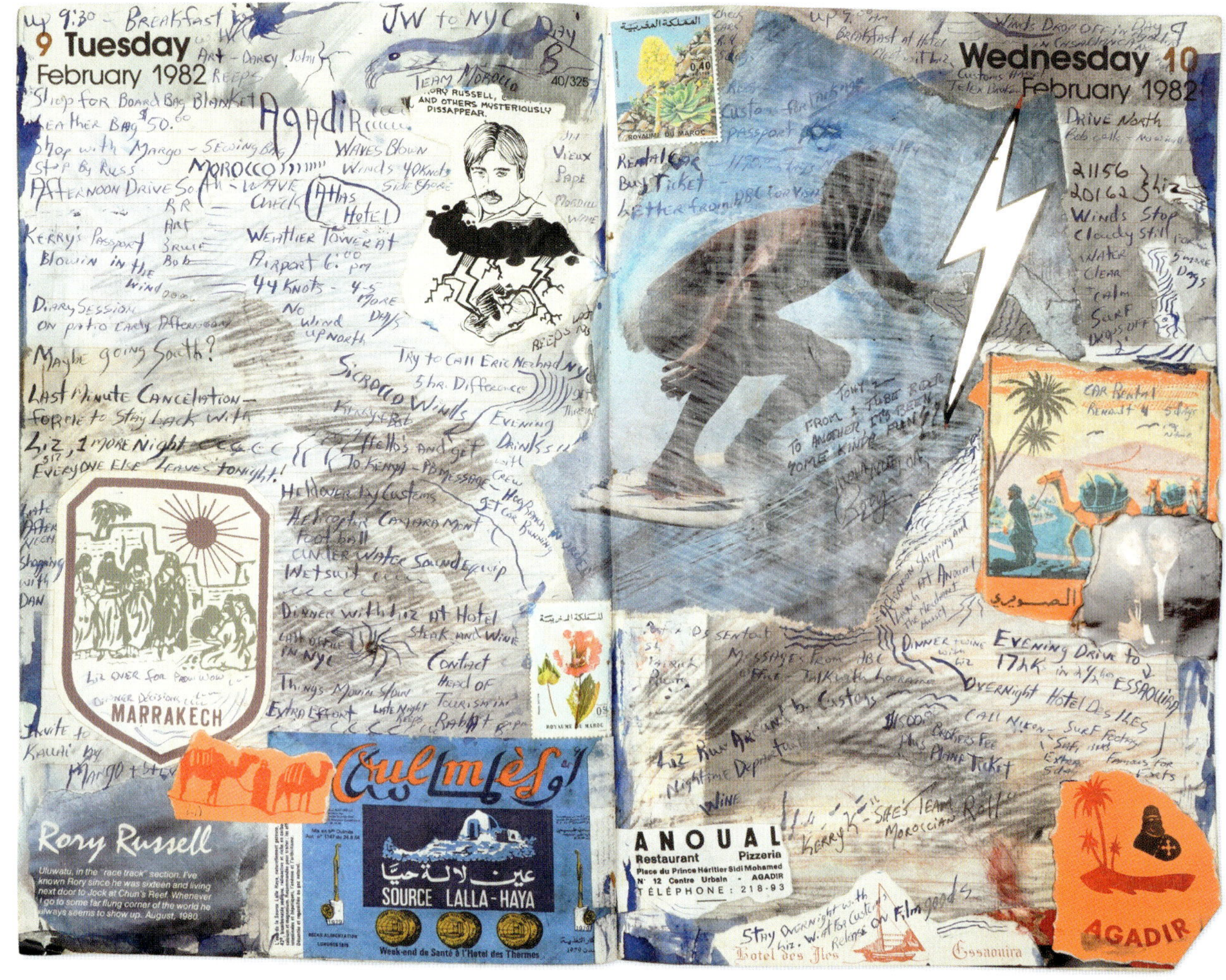

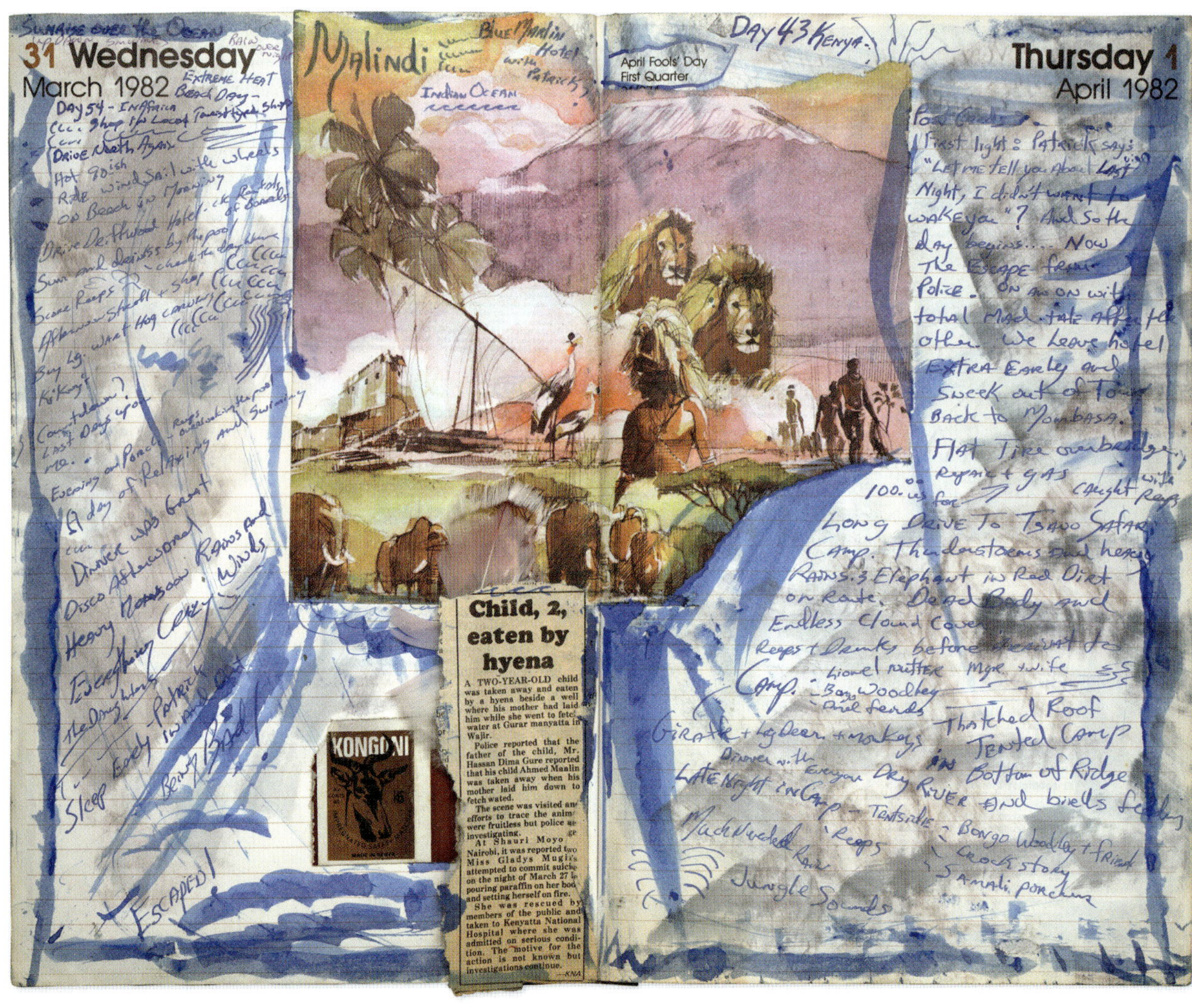

Child, 2, eaten by hyena

A TWO-YEAR-OLD child was taken away and eaten by a hyena beside a well where his mother had laid him while she went to fetch water at Gurar manyatta in Wajir.

Police reported that the father of the child, Mr. Hassan Dima Gure reported that his child Ahmed Maalin was taken away when his mother laid him down to fetch wated.

The scene was visited and efforts to trace the animal were fruitless but police are investigating.

At Shauri Moyo Nairobi, it was reported two Miss Gladys Mugi[illegible] attempted to commit suicide on the night of March 27 by pouring paraffin on her body and setting herself on fire.

She was rescued by members of the public and taken to Kenyatta National Hospital where she was admitted on serious condition. The motive for the action is not known but investigations continue.

—KNA

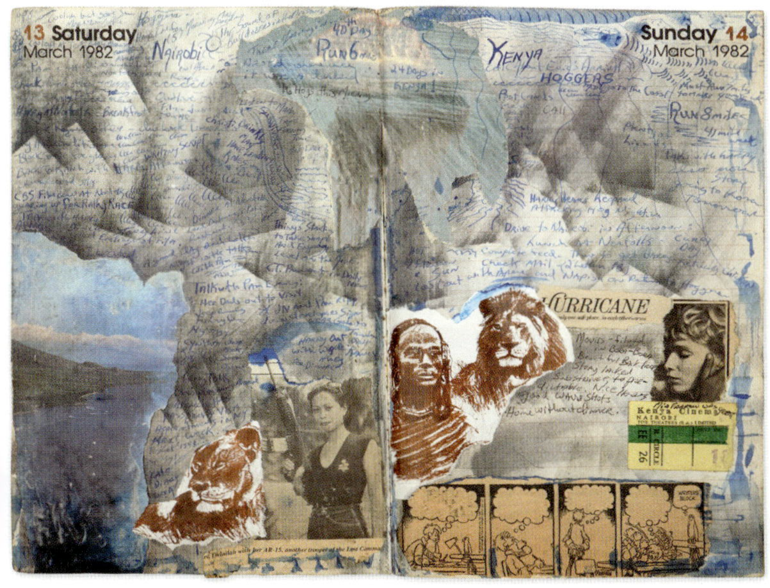
13 Saturday
March 1982
Sunday 14
March 1982
HURRICANE

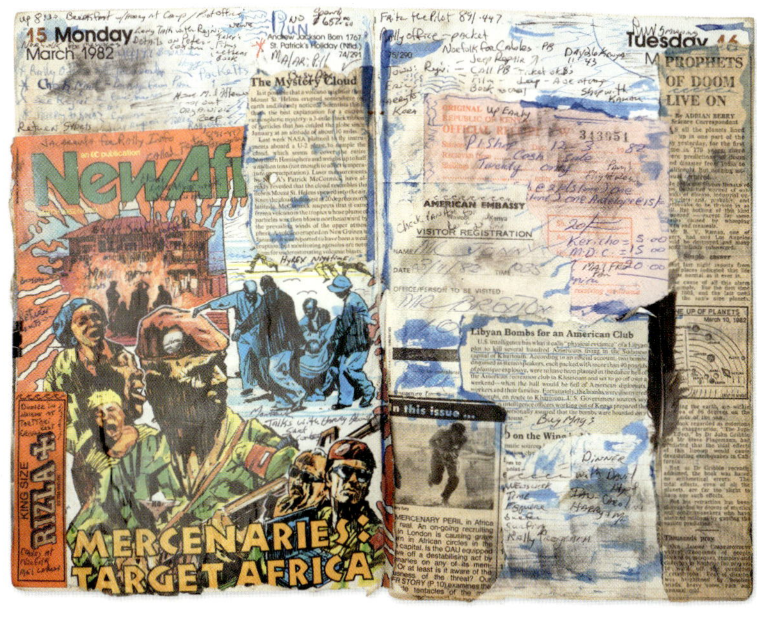
15 Monday
March 1982
Tuesday 16
The Mystery Cloud
NewAfrican
MERCENARIES: TARGET AFRICA
RIZLA+
AMERICAN EMBASSY
VISITOR REGISTRATION
Libyan Bombs for an American Club
In this issue...
PROPHETS OF DOOM LIVE ON

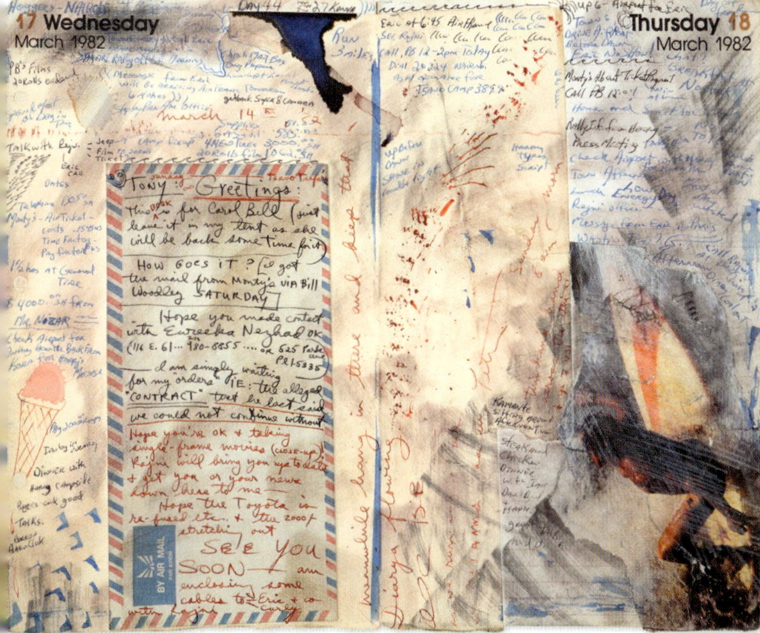
17 Wednesday
March 1982
Thursday 18
March 1982

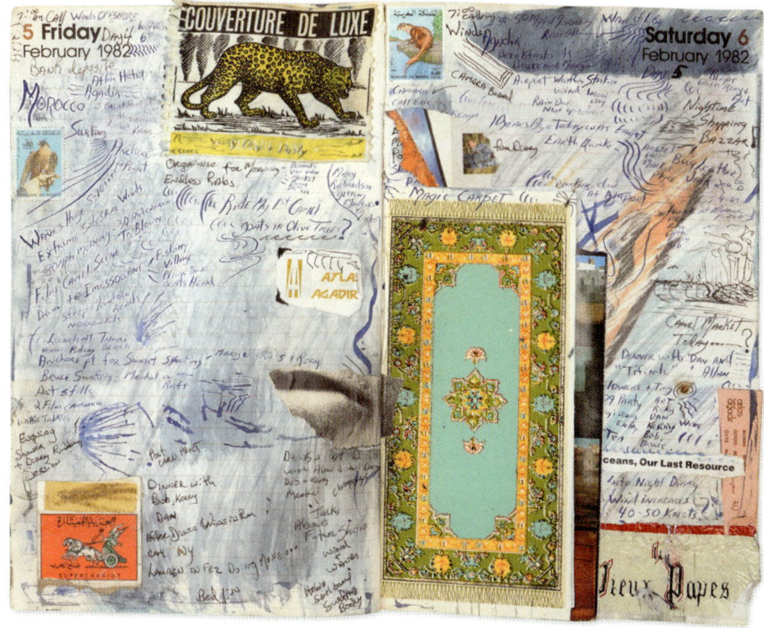
5 Friday
February 1982
Saturday 6
February 1982
COUVERTURE DE LUXE
Oceans, Our Last Resource
Vieux Papes

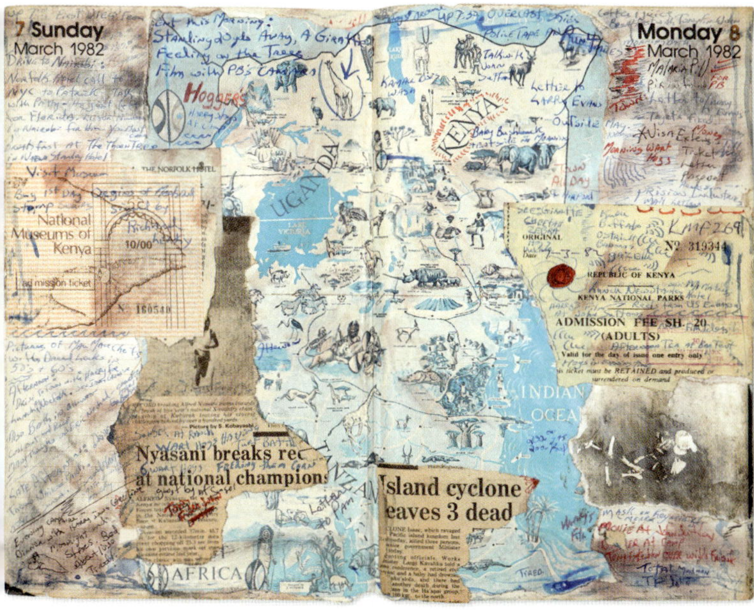
7 Sunday
March 1982
Monday 8
March 1982
National Museums of Kenya
REPUBLIC OF KENYA
KENYA NATIONAL PARKS
ADMISSION FEE SH. 20
(ADULTS)
Nyasani breaks rec
at national champion
Island cyclone
leaves 3 dead
UGANDA
KENYA
INDIAN OCEAN
AFRICA

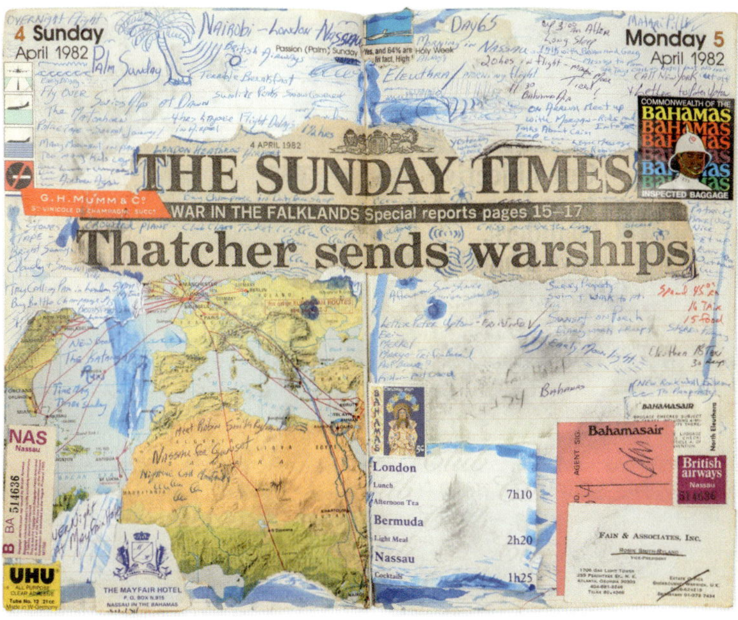
4 Sunday
April 1982
Monday 5
April 1982
THE SUNDAY TIMES
WAR IN THE FALKLANDS Special reports pages 15-17
Thatcher sends warships
COMMONWEALTH OF THE BAHAMAS
Bahamasair
British airways
London
Bermuda
Nassau
7h10
2h20
1h25
UHU
THE MAYFAIR HOTEL

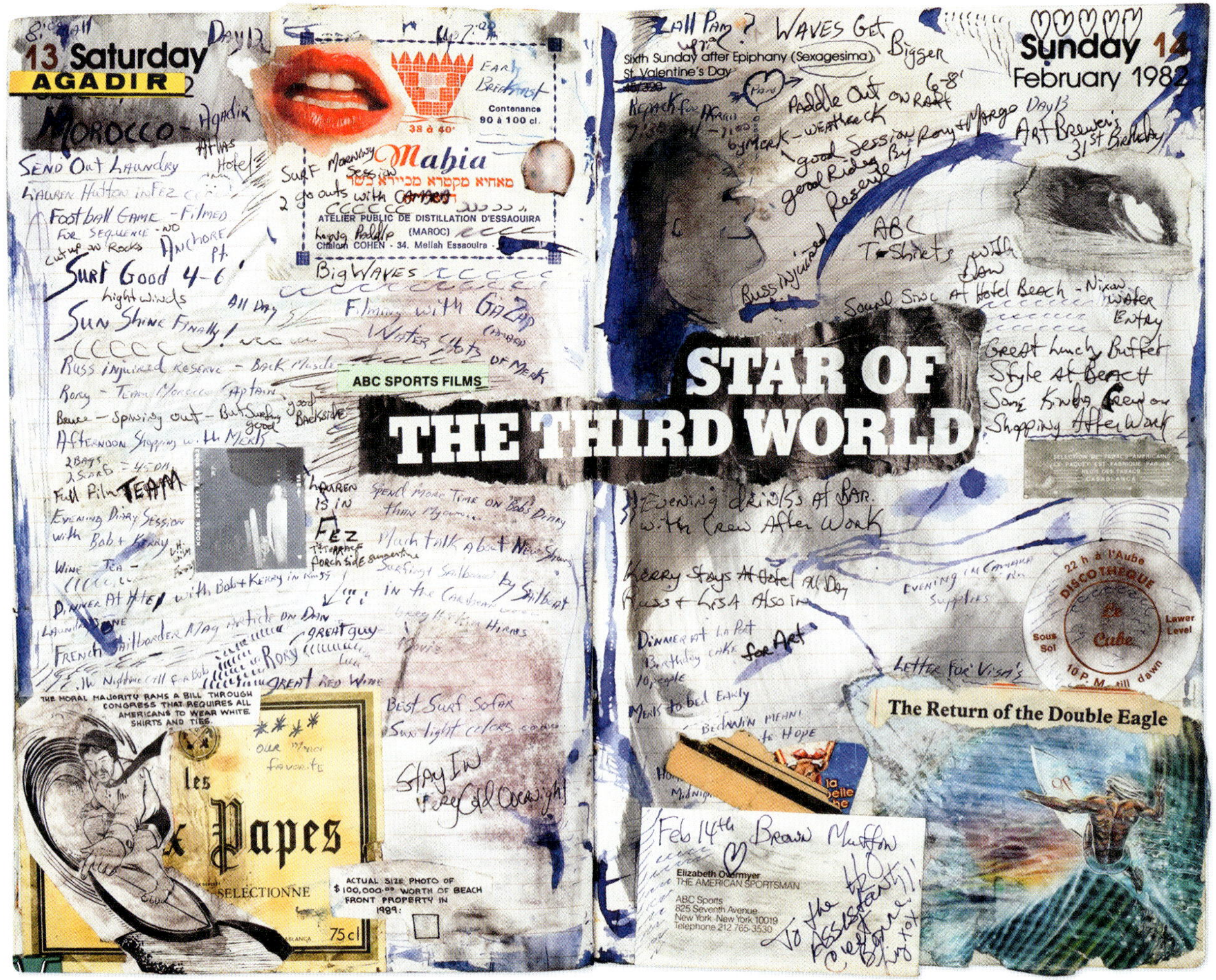
13 Saturday
AGADIR
Mahia
ATELIER PUBLIC DE DISTILLATION D'ESSAOUIRA
ABC SPORTS FILMS
THE MORAL MAJORITY BANS A BILL THROUGH CONGRESS THAT REQUIRES ALL AMERICANS TO WEAR WHITE SHIRTS AND TIES
les Papes
SELECTIONNE
75 cl
ACTUAL SIZE PHOTO OF $100,000.00 WORTH OF BEACH FRONT PROPERTY IN 1989
Sunday 14
February 1982
Sixth Sunday after Epiphany (Sexagesima)
St Valentine's Day
STAR OF THE THIRD WORLD
DISCOTHEQUE
Cube
The Return of the Double Eagle
Elizabeth Ostermyer
THE AMERICAN SPORTSMAN
ABC Sports
825 Seventh Avenue
New York, New York 10019
Telephone 212 765-3530

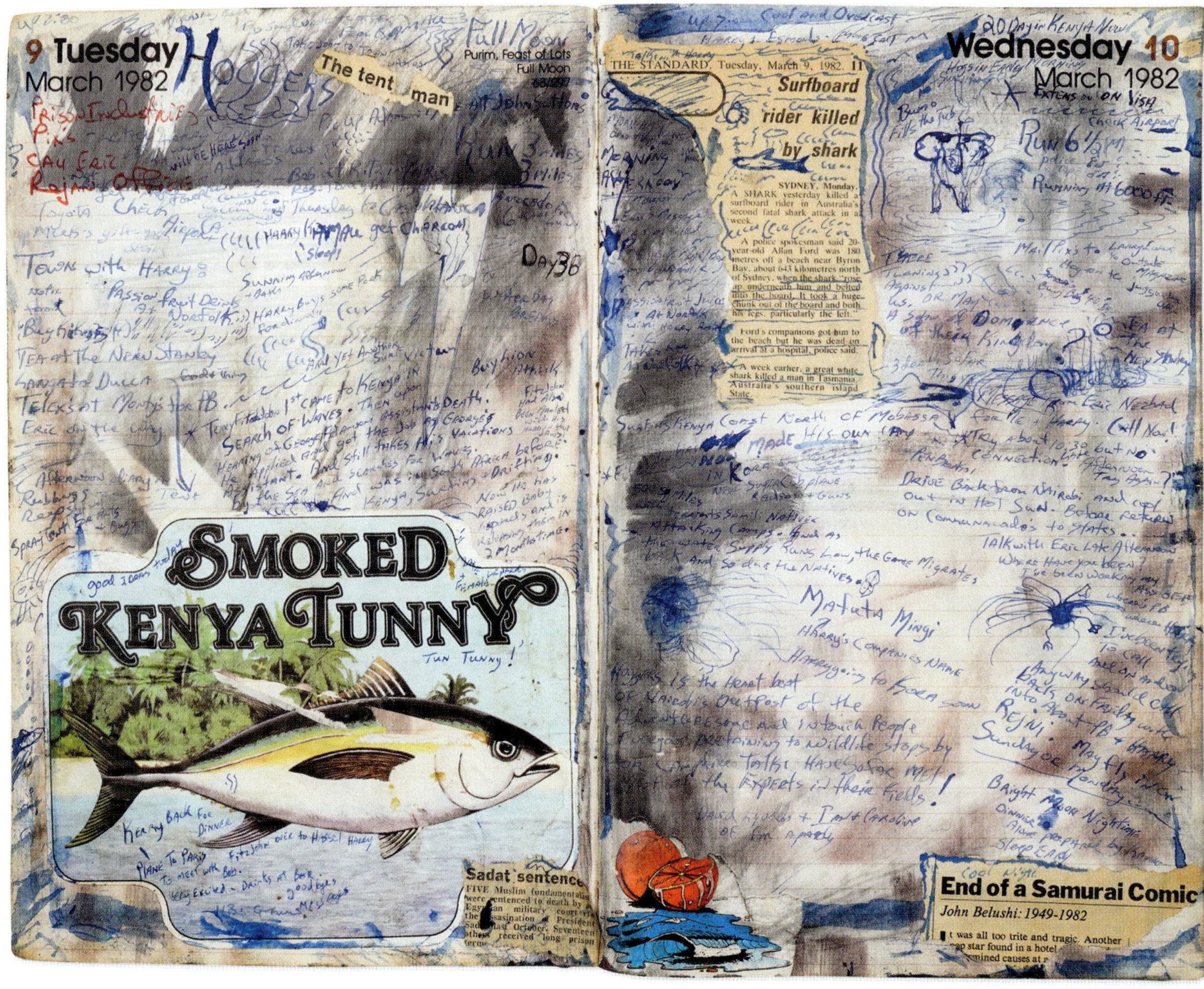
9 Tuesday
March 1982
Purim, Feast of Lots
Full Moon
The tent man
SMOKED KENYA TUNNY
Sadat sentence
Wednesday 10
March 1982
THE STANDARD, Tuesday, March 9, 1982
Surfboard rider killed by shark
SYDNEY, Monday. A SHARK yesterday killed a surfboard rider in Australia's second fatal shark attack in a week.
A police spokesman said 20-year-old Allan Ford was 180 metres off a beach near Byron Bay, about 643 kilometres north of Sydney, when the shark "rose up underneath him and belted him into the board. It took a huge chunk out of the board and both his legs, particularly the left."
Ford's companions got him to the beach but he was dead on arrival at a hospital, police said.
A week earlier, a great white shark killed a man in Tasmania, Australia's southern island State.
End of a Samurai Comic
John Belushi: 1949-1982

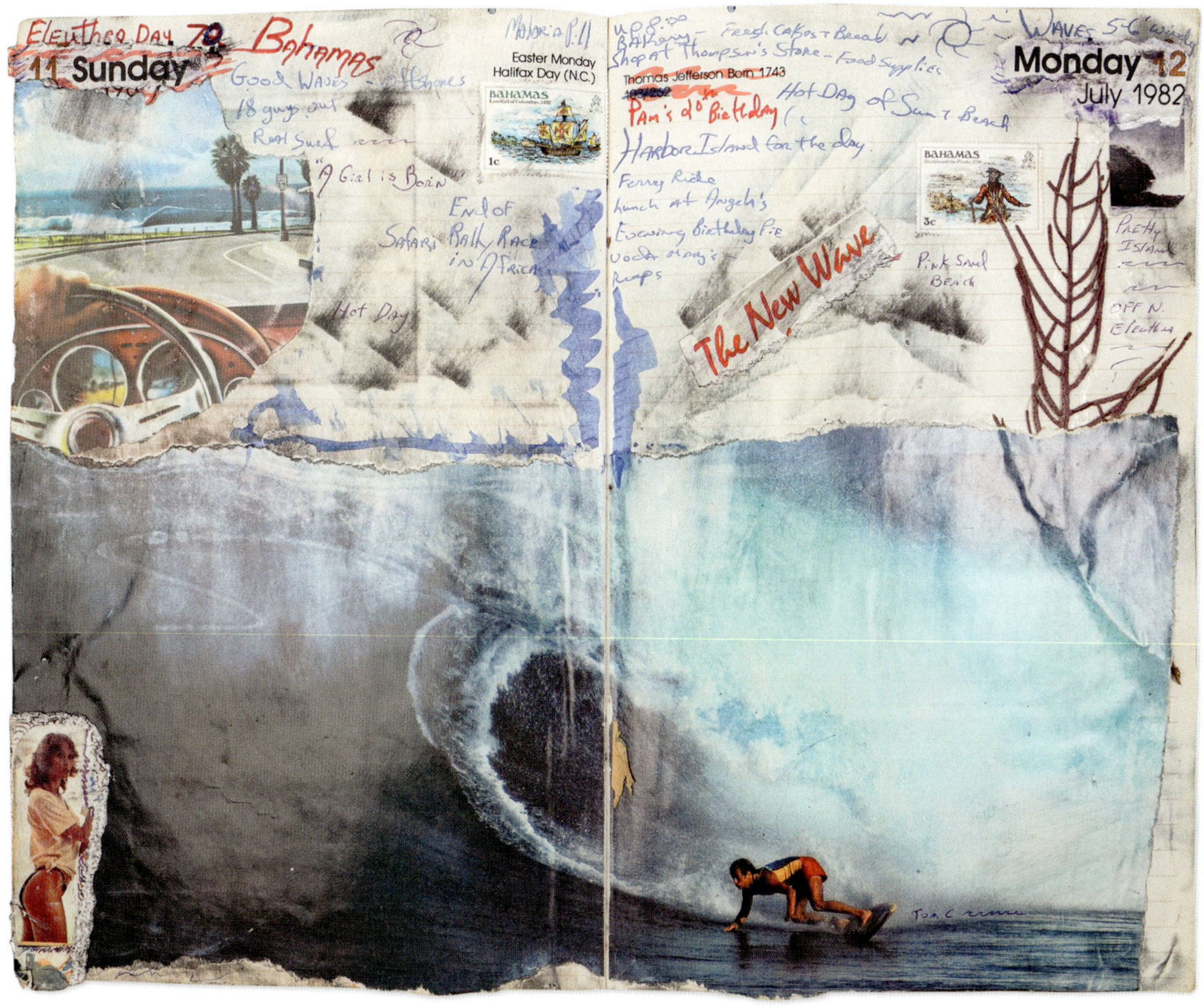
11 Sunday
Bahamas
Easter Monday
Halifax Day (N.C.)
BAHAMAS
1c
Thomas Jefferson Born 1743
Monday 12
July 1982
BAHAMAS
3c
The New Wave

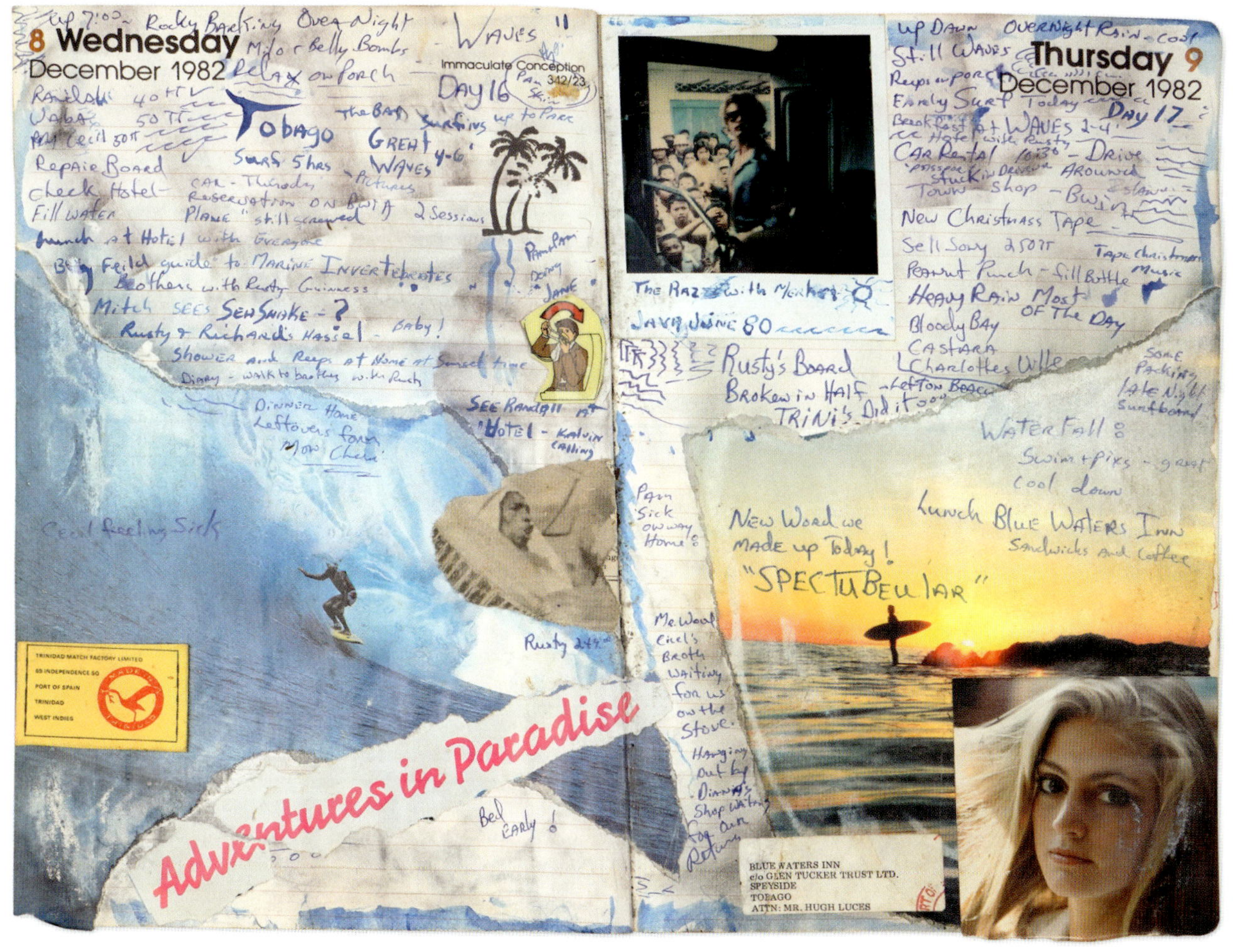
8 Wednesday
December 1982
Immaculate Conception
Tobago
Thursday 9
December 1982
TRINIDAD MATCH FACTORY LIMITED
PORT OF SPAIN
TRINIDAD
WEST INDIES
"SPECTUBEULAR"
Adventures in Paradise
BLUE WATERS INN
c/o GLEN TUCKER TRUST LTD.
SPEYSIDE
TOBAGO
ATTN: MR. HUGH LUCES

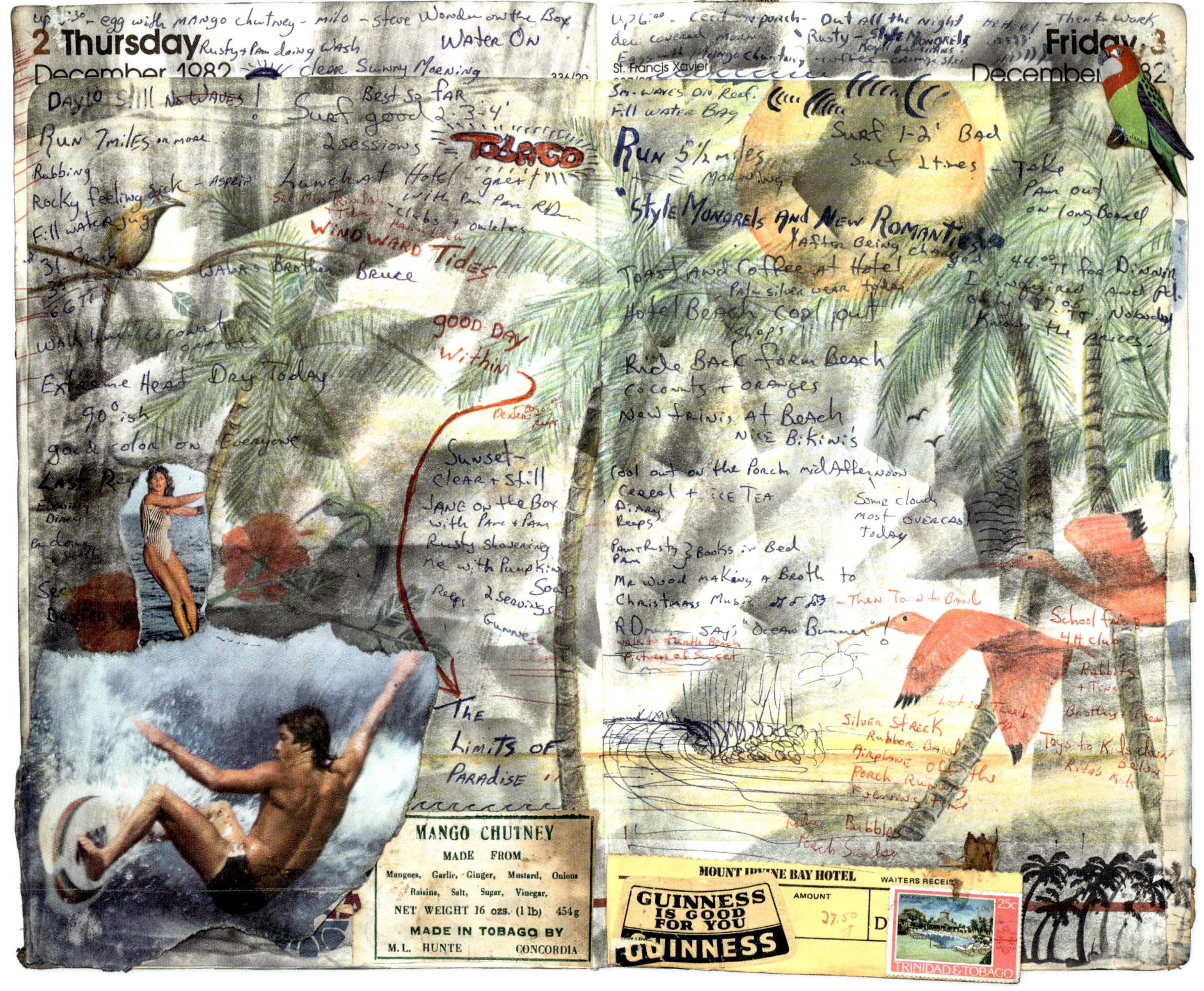
2 Thursday
December 1982
Friday 3
December 1982
St. Francis Xavier
TOBAGO
MANGO CHUTNEY
MADE FROM
Mangoes, Garlic, Ginger, Mustard, Onions
Raisins, Salt, Sugar, Vinegar.
NET WEIGHT 16 ozs. (1 lb) 454g
MADE IN TOBAGO BY
M.L. HUNTE CONCORDIA
GUINNESS IS GOOD FOR YOU
GUINNESS
AMOUNT
WAITERS RECEIPT
25c
TRINIDAD & TOBAGO

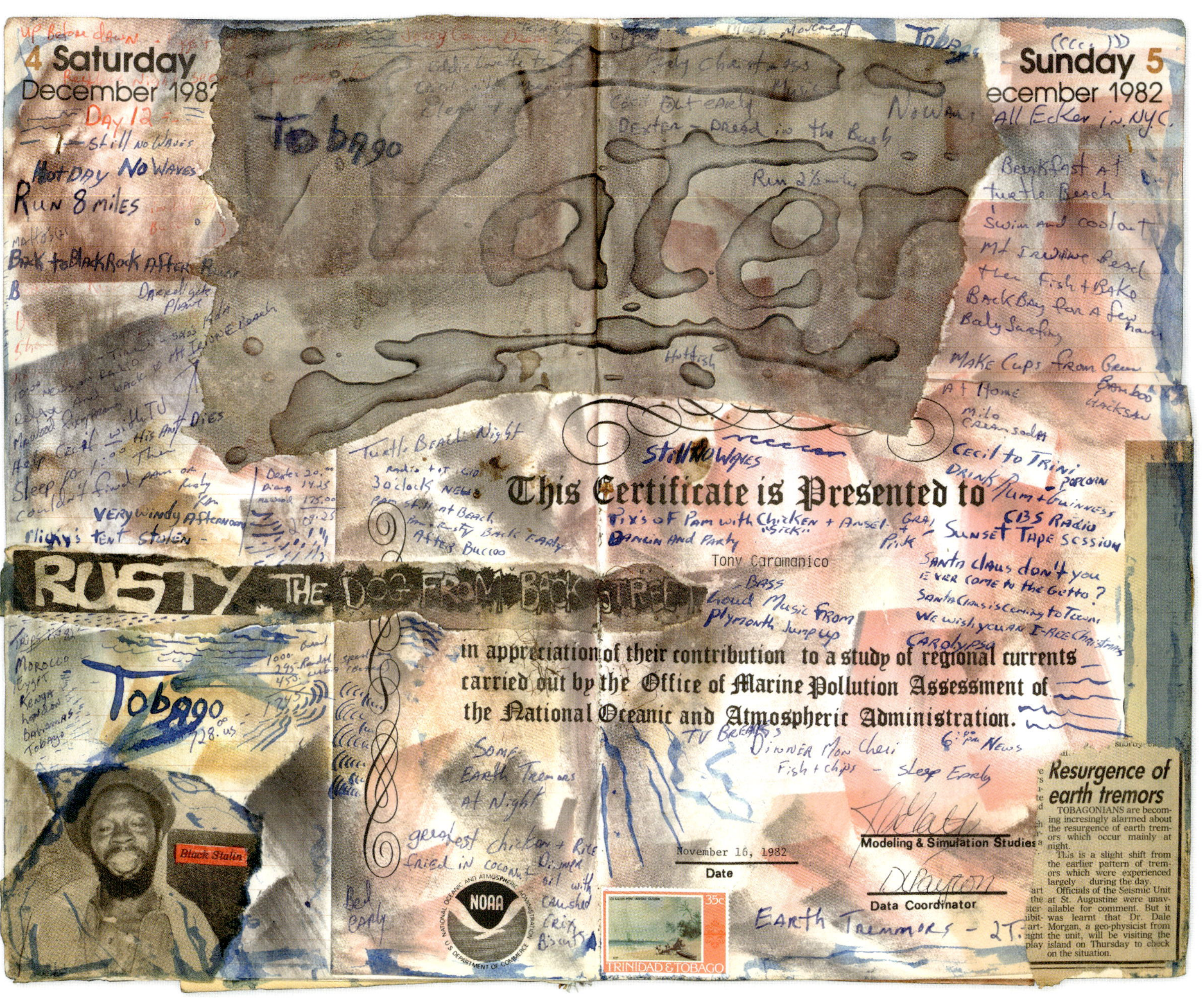

Resurgence of earth tremors

TOBAGONIANS are becoming incresingly alarmed about the resurgence of earth tremors which occur mainly at night.

This is a slight shift from the earlier pattern of tremors which were experienced largely during the day.

Officials of the Seismic Unit at St. Augustine were unavailable for comment. But it was learnt that Dr. Dale Morgan, a geo-physicist from the unit, will be visiting the island on Thursday to check on the situation.

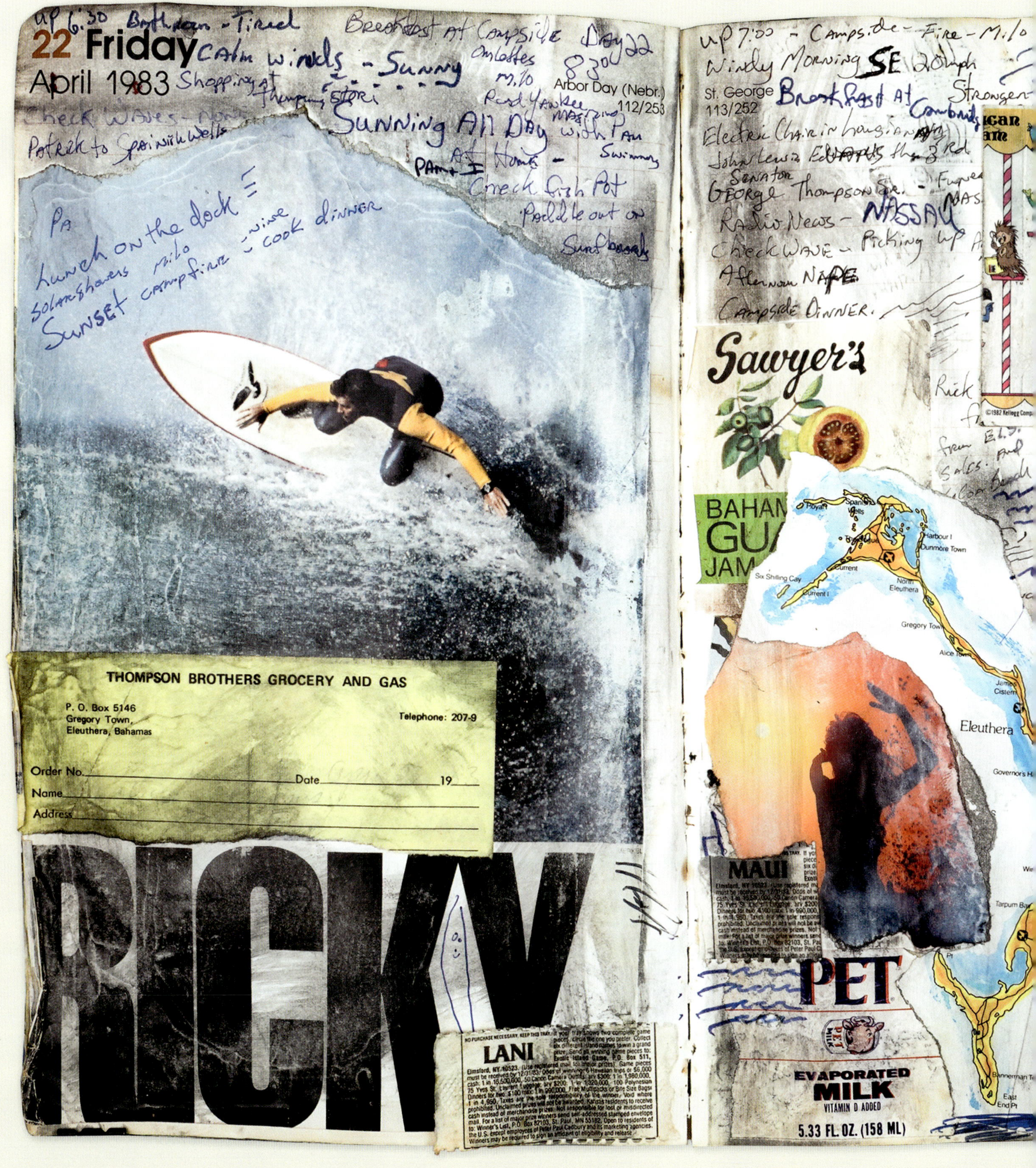

22 Friday
April 1983
Arbor Day (Nebr.)
112/253
St. George
113/252
Breakfast at Campsite
Sunning All Day
Lunch on the dock
Sunset campfire
Campside Dinner.
THOMPSON BROTHERS GROCERY AND GAS
P. O. Box 5146
Gregory Town,
Eleuthera, Bahamas
Telephone: 207-9
Order No.
Date
19
Name
Address
RICKY
LANI
Sawyer's
BAHAM
GU
JAM
Harbour I
Dunmore Town
Six Shilling Cay
Current
North Eleuthera
Gregory Town
Alice Town
Eleuthera
Governors H
Tarpum Bay
MAUI
PET
EVAPORATED
MILK
VITAMIN D ADDED
5.33 FL. OZ. (158 ML)

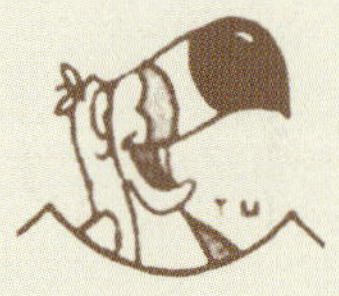

"RICK HAD BEEN IN PRISON IN BALI BEFORE OUR TRIP. THE ONLY REASON HE GOT OUT WAS BECAUSE HIS DAD WAS A TEST PILOT FOR GRUMMAN. HE WENT TO HIS BOSS, GRABBED A SOPHISTICATED FIGHTER JET, BORROWED $50K, FLEW TO BALI AND SAID I'M GETTING MY SON OUT. HE WAS EITHER GONNA PAY THEM OFF OR SHOOT THEM UP. THEN HERE I AM GOING BACK TO BALI WITH RICKY WITH THAT CONTEXT... WE'RE GETTING OFF THE PLANE WITH CARTS AND CARTS OF LUGGAGE, 16-18 SURFBOARDS, AN ENTOURAGE OF SOUND MEN, PHOTOGRAPHERS AND PRODUCERS. THERE'S ABOUT 10 OF US AND RICKY'S GOT A BIG BOOMBOX AND HE'S PLAYING PINK FLOYD, WAILING "WAAAAH, MONEY!!!!!" CRUISING THROUGH THE AIRPORT. IT WAS NUTS."

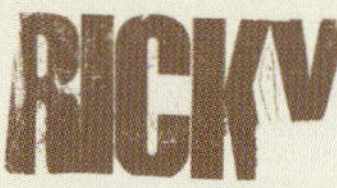

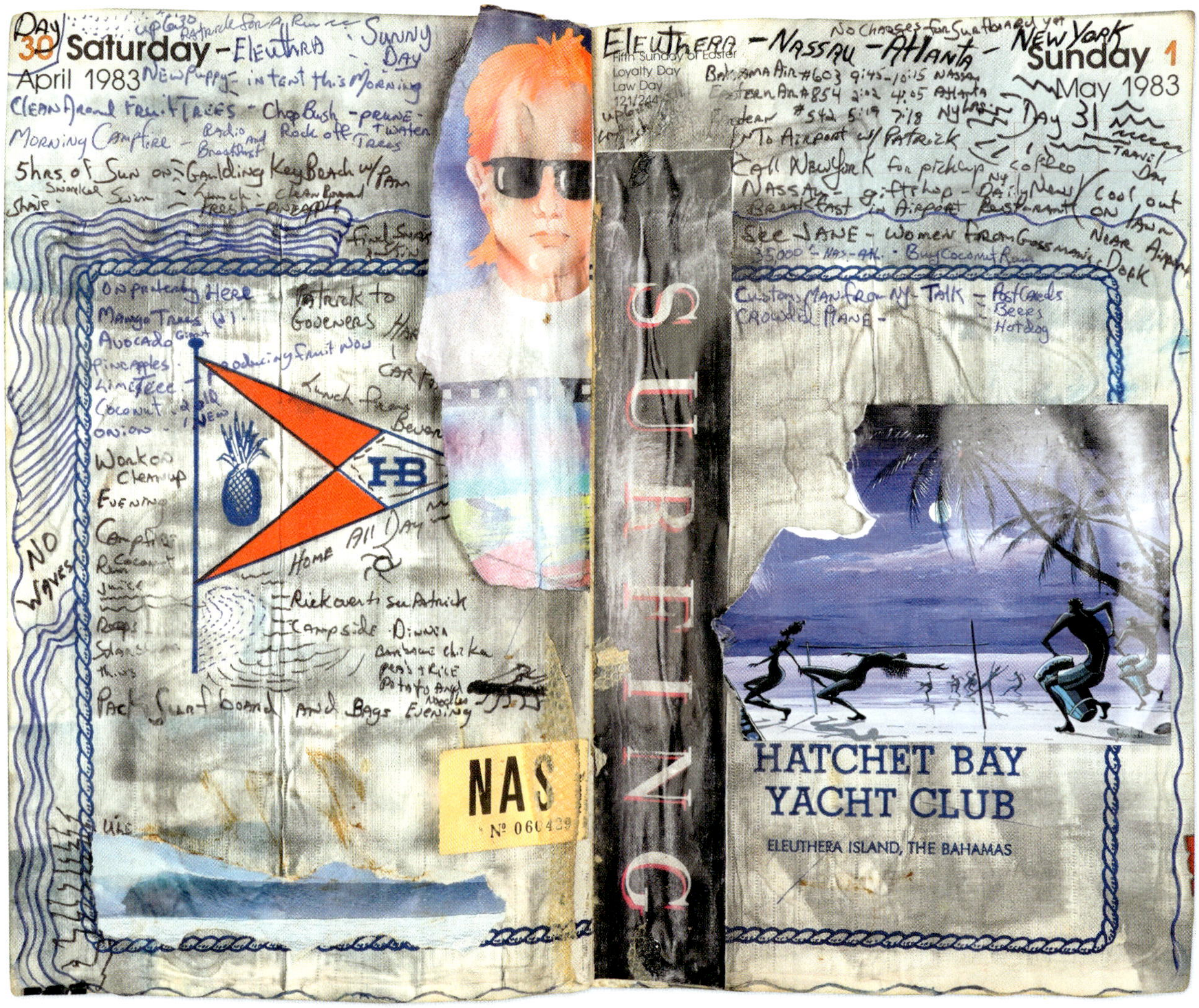

Day 30 **Saturday** – Eleuthra

April 1983

Eleuthera – Nassau – Atlanta – New York **Sunday** 1

Fifth Sunday of Easter
Loyalty Day
Law Day

May 1983

SURFING

NAS
Nº 060439

HATCHET BAY
YACHT CLUB

ELEUTHERA ISLAND, THE BAHAMAS

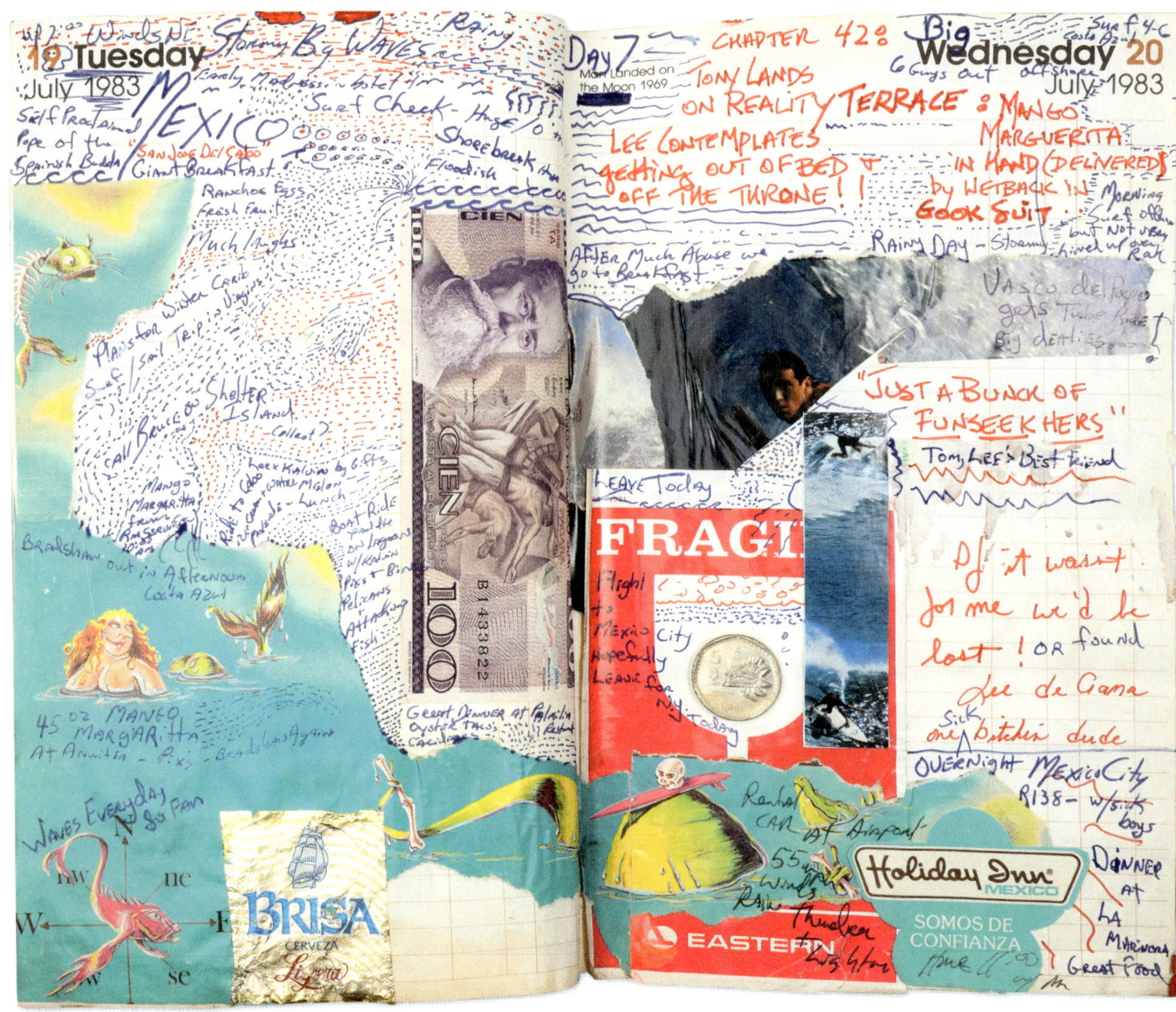

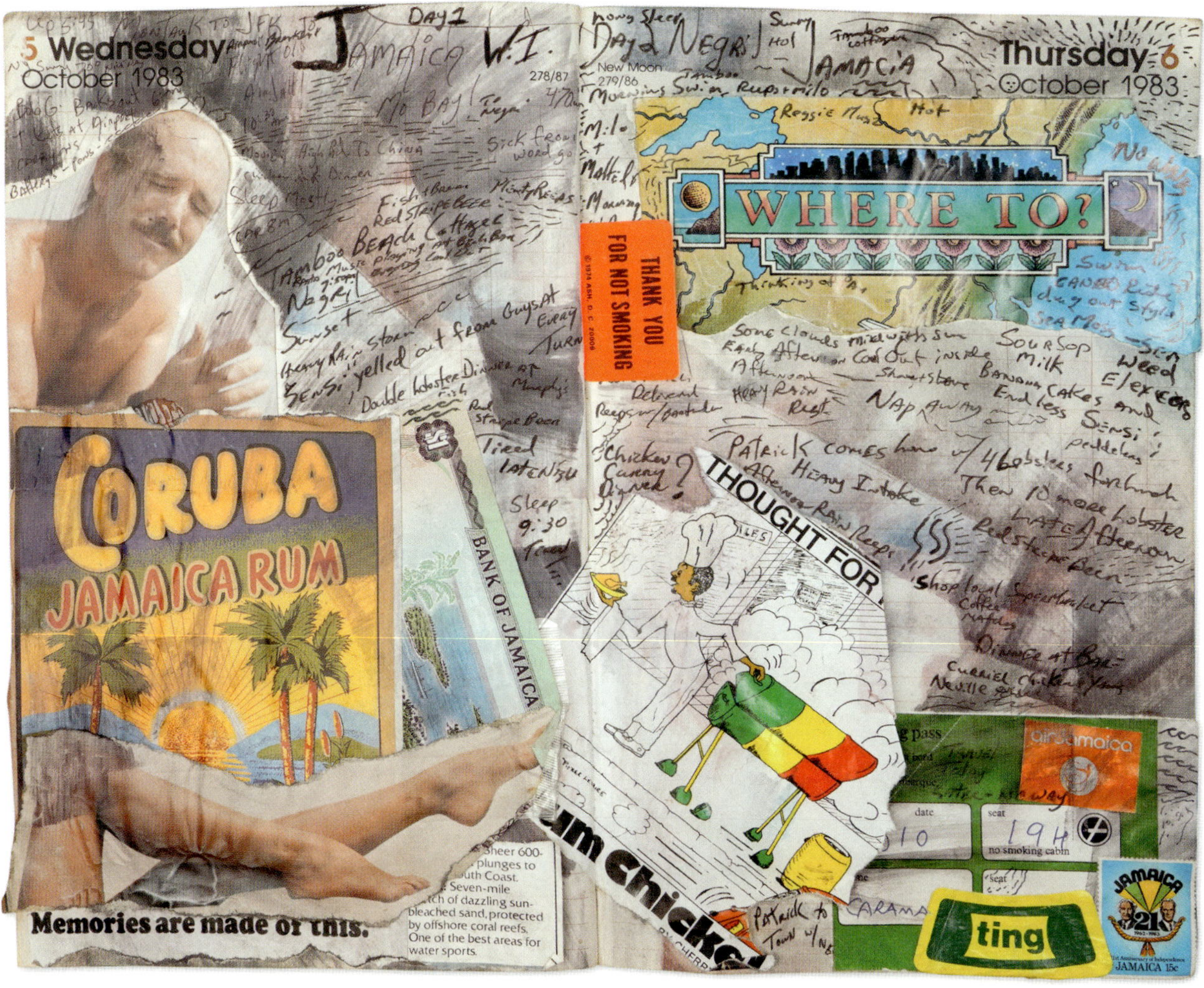

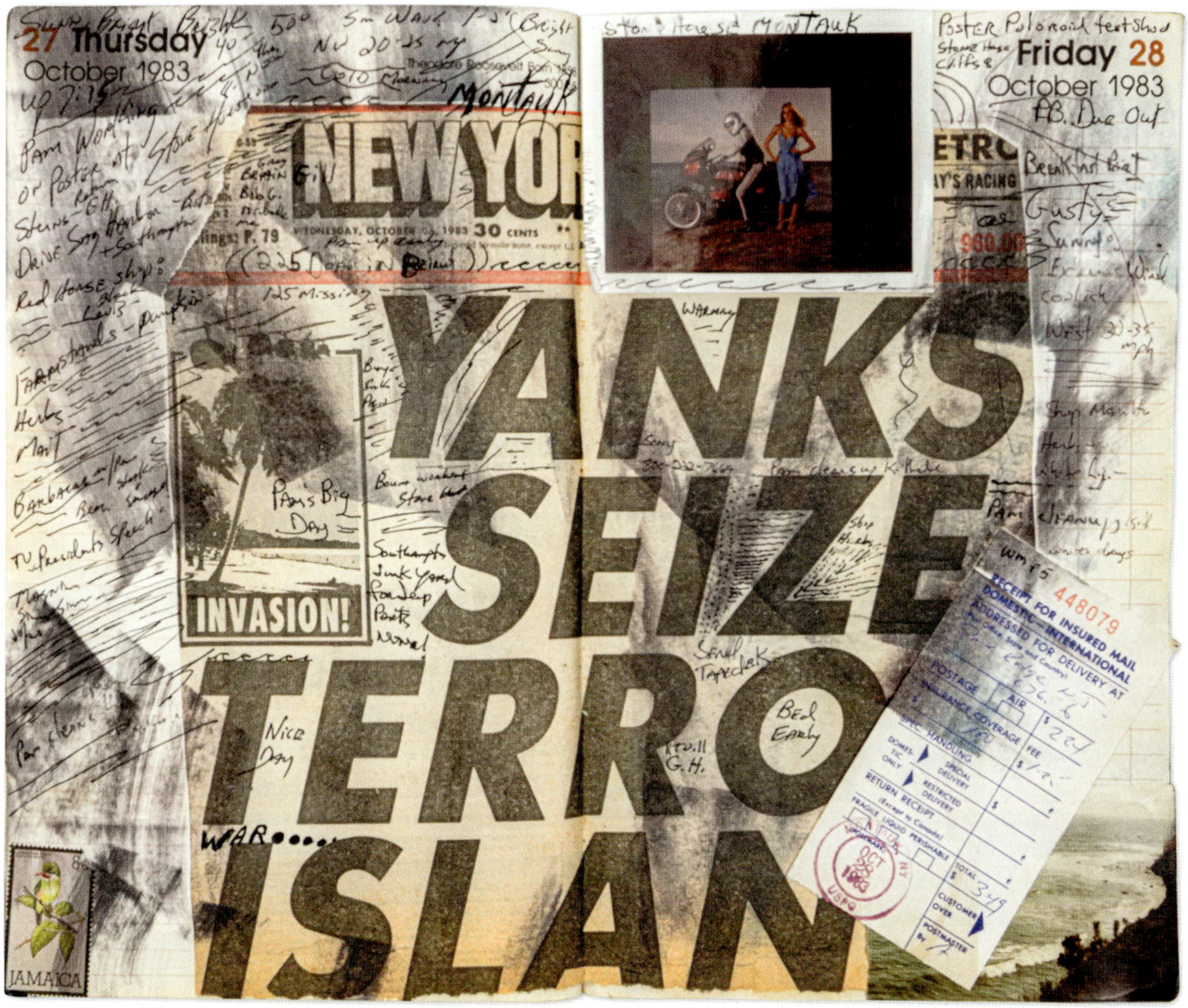

27 Thursday
October 1983

Friday 28
October 1983

NEW YOR

30 CENTS

YANKS
SEIZE
TERRO
ISLAN

INVASION!

RECEIPT FOR INSURED MAIL
DOMESTIC - INTERNATIONAL
448079

JAMAICA

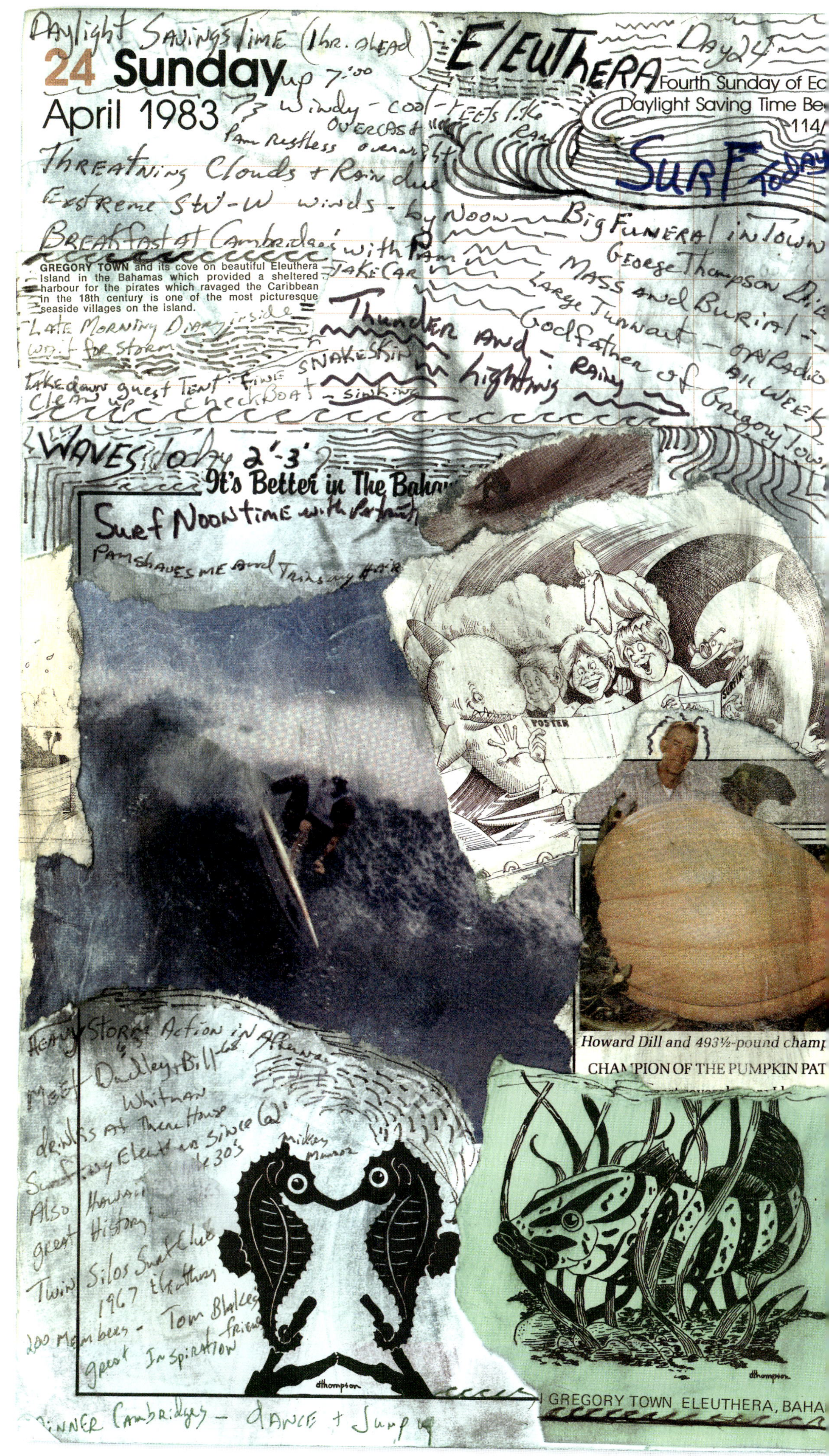
24 Sunday
April 1983
Fourth Sunday of Ea
Daylight Saving Time Be
114/
Daylight Savings Time (1hr. ahead)
Eleuthera
Day 24
up 7:00
Windy - cool - feels like rain
Overcast
Surf Today
Threatning Clouds + Rain due
Extreme SW-W winds - by Noon
Big Funeral in Town
Breakfast at Cambridge's with Pam
Take Car
George Thompson
Mass and Burial
Large Turnout
Godfather of Gregory Town
GREGORY TOWN and its cove on beautiful Eleuthera Island in the Bahamas which provided a sheltered harbour for the pirates which ravaged the Caribbean in the 18th century is one of the most picturesque seaside villages on the island.
Late Morning Drawing inside
wait for storm
Thunder and lightning
Snakeskin
Waves Today 2'-3'
It's Better in The Baha
Surf Noon time
POSTER
Howard Dill and 493½-pound champ
CHAMPION OF THE PUMPKIN PAT
Heavy Storm Action in Afternoon
Meet Dudley + Bill Whitman
drinks at Their House
Also Hawaii
great History
Twin Silos Surf Club
1967
200 Members - Tom Blake
great Inspiration
dthompson
GREGORY TOWN ELEUTHERA, BAHA
Dinner Cambridges - dance + Jump up

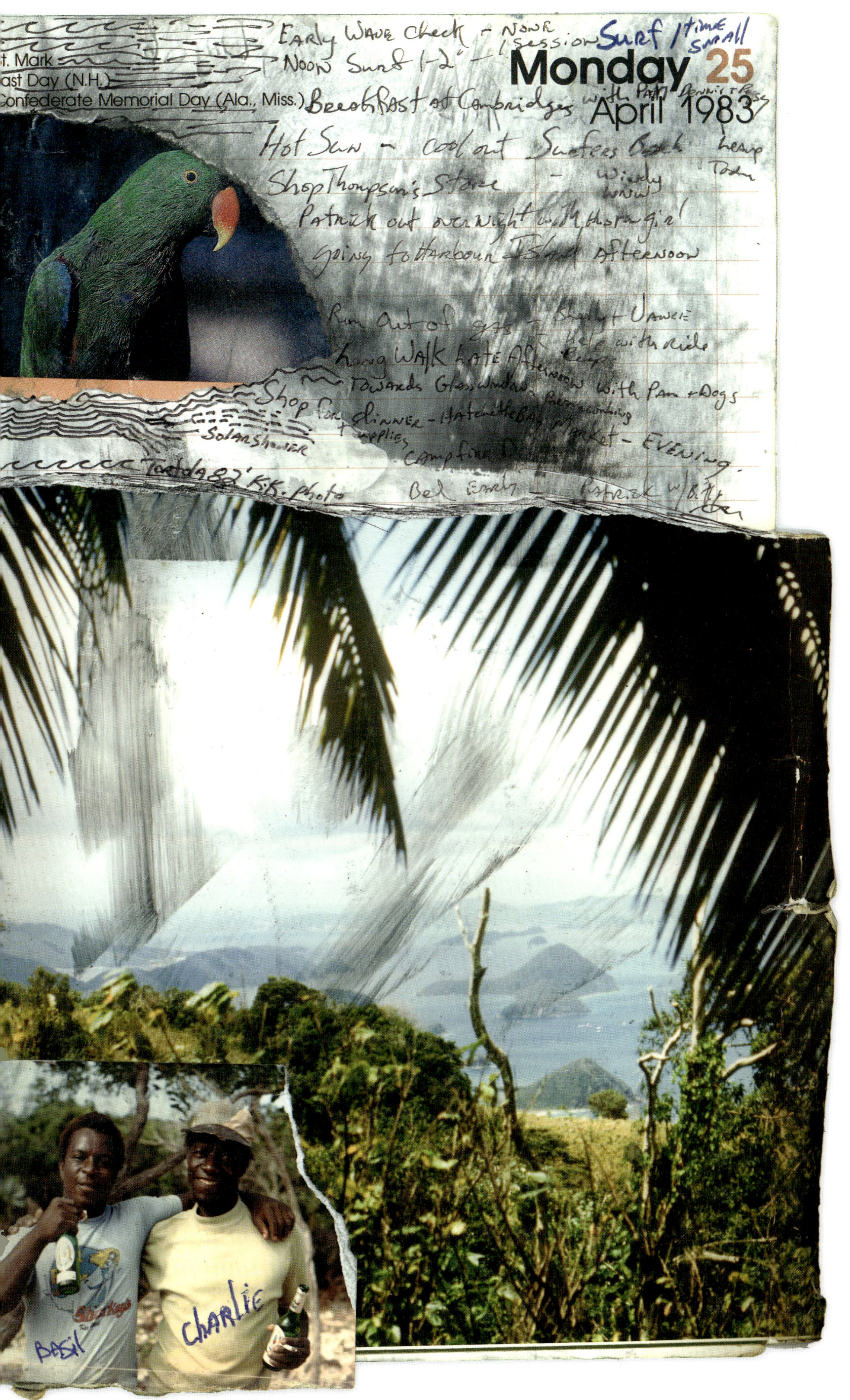
Monday 25
April 1983
t. Mark
ast Day (N.H.)
Confederate Memorial Day (Ala., Miss.)
Surf 1 time small
Early Wave check
Noon Surf 1-2'
Breakfast at Cambridges
Hot Sun - cool out Surfers Beach
Shop Thompson's Store
Patrick out overnight
going to Harbour Island Afternoon
Run out of gas
Long Walk Late Afternoon
Towards Glass Window
Shop for dinner - Hatchet Bay Market - Evening
campfire
Bed Early
Solar shower
K.K. photo
Basil
Charlie

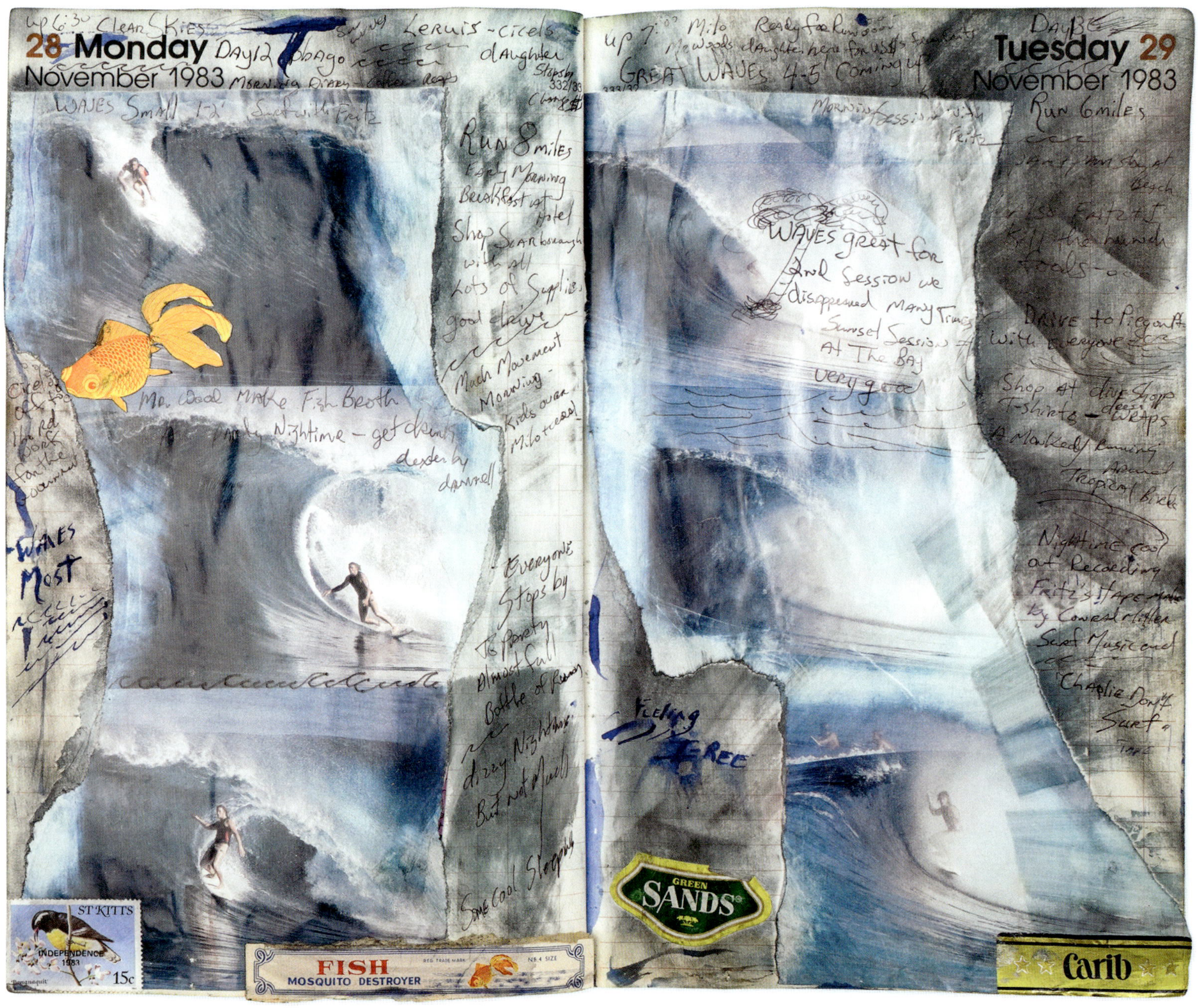
28 Monday
November 1983
Tuesday 29
November 1983
ST KITTS
INDEPENDENCE
1983
15c
FISH
MOSQUITO DESTROYER
No.4 SIZE
GREEN
SANDS
Carib

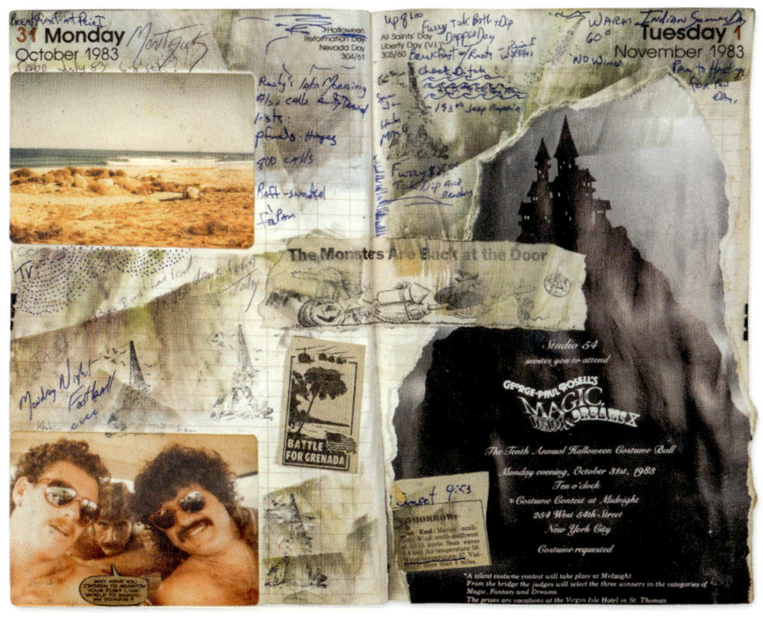

31 Monday
October 1983
Tuesday 1
November 1983
The Monsters Are Back at the Door
BATTLE FOR GRENADA
Costume requested

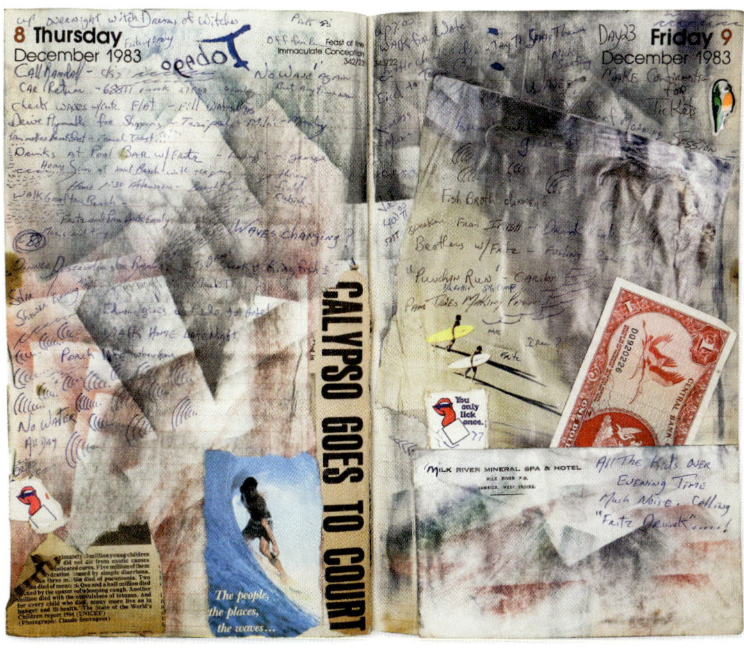

8 Thursday
December 1983
Friday 9
December 1983
CALYPSO GOES TO COURT
MILK RIVER MINERAL SPA & HOTEL
The people, the places, the waves...

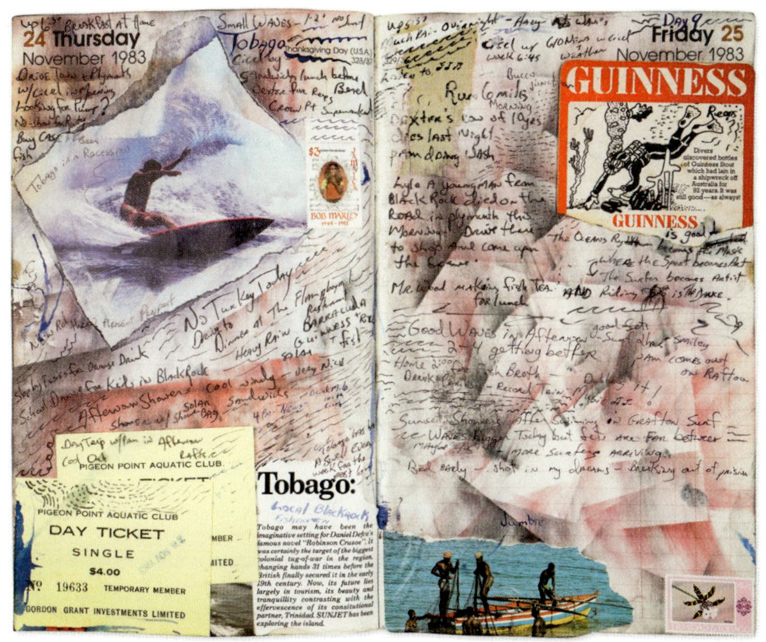

24 Thursday
November 1983
Friday 25
November 1983
GUINNESS
Tobago:
PIGEON POINT AQUATIC CLUB
DAY TICKET
SINGLE
$4.00
TEMPORARY MEMBER
GORDON GRANT INVESTMENTS LIMITED

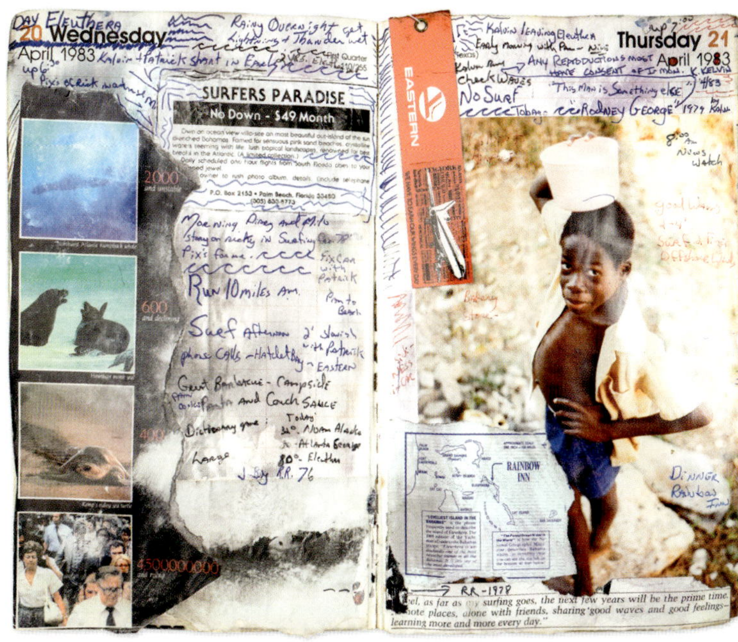

20 Wednesday
April 1983
Thursday 21
April 1983
SURFERS PARADISE
No Down - $49 Month
EASTERN
RAINBOW INN

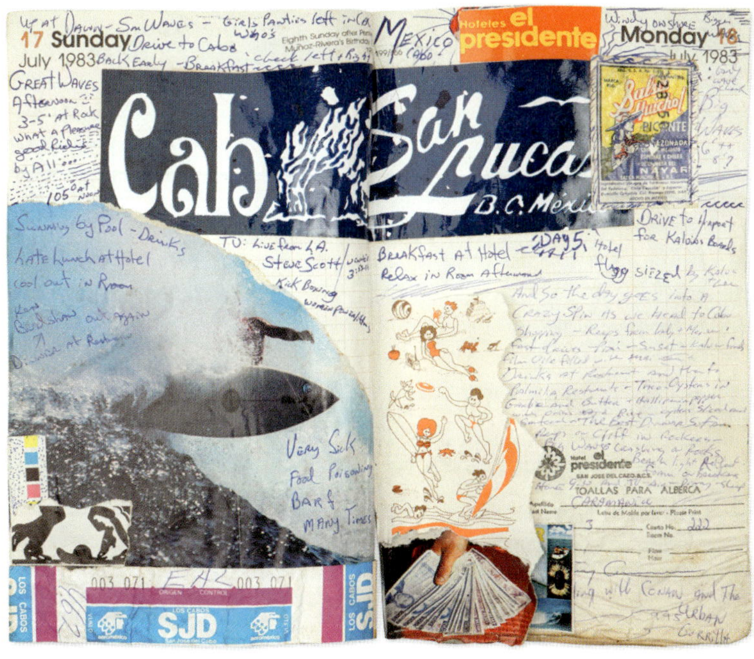

17 Sunday
July 1983
Monday 18
July 1983
Hoteles el presidente
Cabo San Lucas
B.C. México
TOALLAS PARA ALBERCA
SJD
LOS CABOS

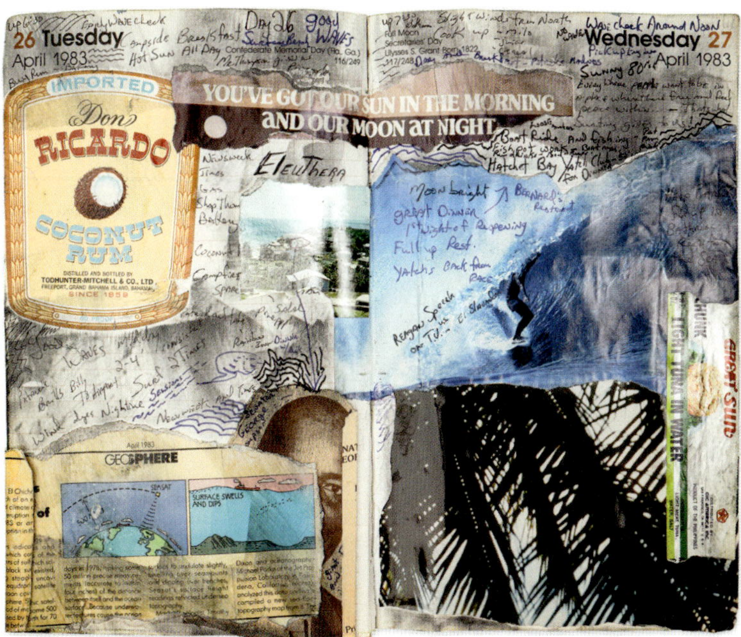

26 Tuesday
April 1983
Wednesday 27
April 1983
IMPORTED
Don RICARDO
COCONUT RUM
YOU'VE GOT OUR SUN IN THE MORNING AND OUR MOON AT NIGHT
GEOSPHERE

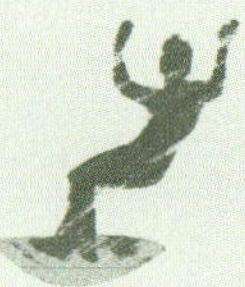

"WHEN WE GOT THE JOURNALS AT THE BEGINNING OF EACH YEAR PETER AND I WOULD PREP THE BACKGROUNDS WITH 'RUBBINGS'. WE WOULD TAKE PICTURES AND TRANSFER THE IMAGES FROM A MAGAZINE OR NEWSPAPER TO THE PAGE WITH A CHEMICAL CALLED AFTA CLEANING FLUID, A SUPER TOXIC DEGREASER. WE'D BE LOCKED UP IN A ROOM, ESPECIALLY IN THE WINTER, DOING ALL-NIGHTERS STARTING AT 7 OR 8 O'CLOCK. WE'D HAVE EVERYTHING SPREAD OUT AND WOULD SPEND HOURS AND HOURS SMOKING AND DRINKING AND DOING THESE RUBBINGS UNTIL THE NEXT DAY, PREPPING 40 OR 50 PAGES AT A TIME FOR US TO COLLAGE OVER."

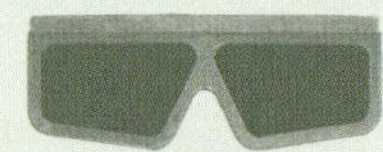

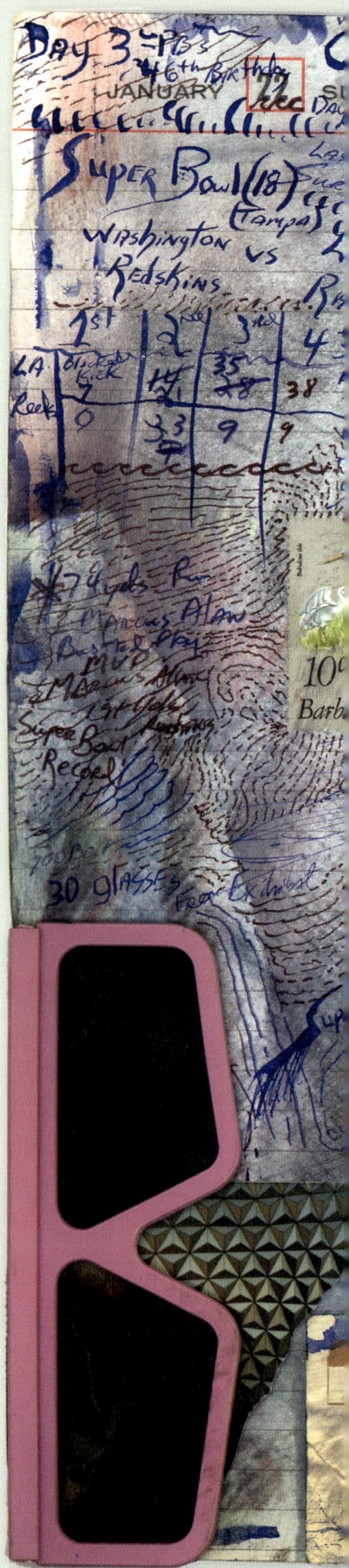

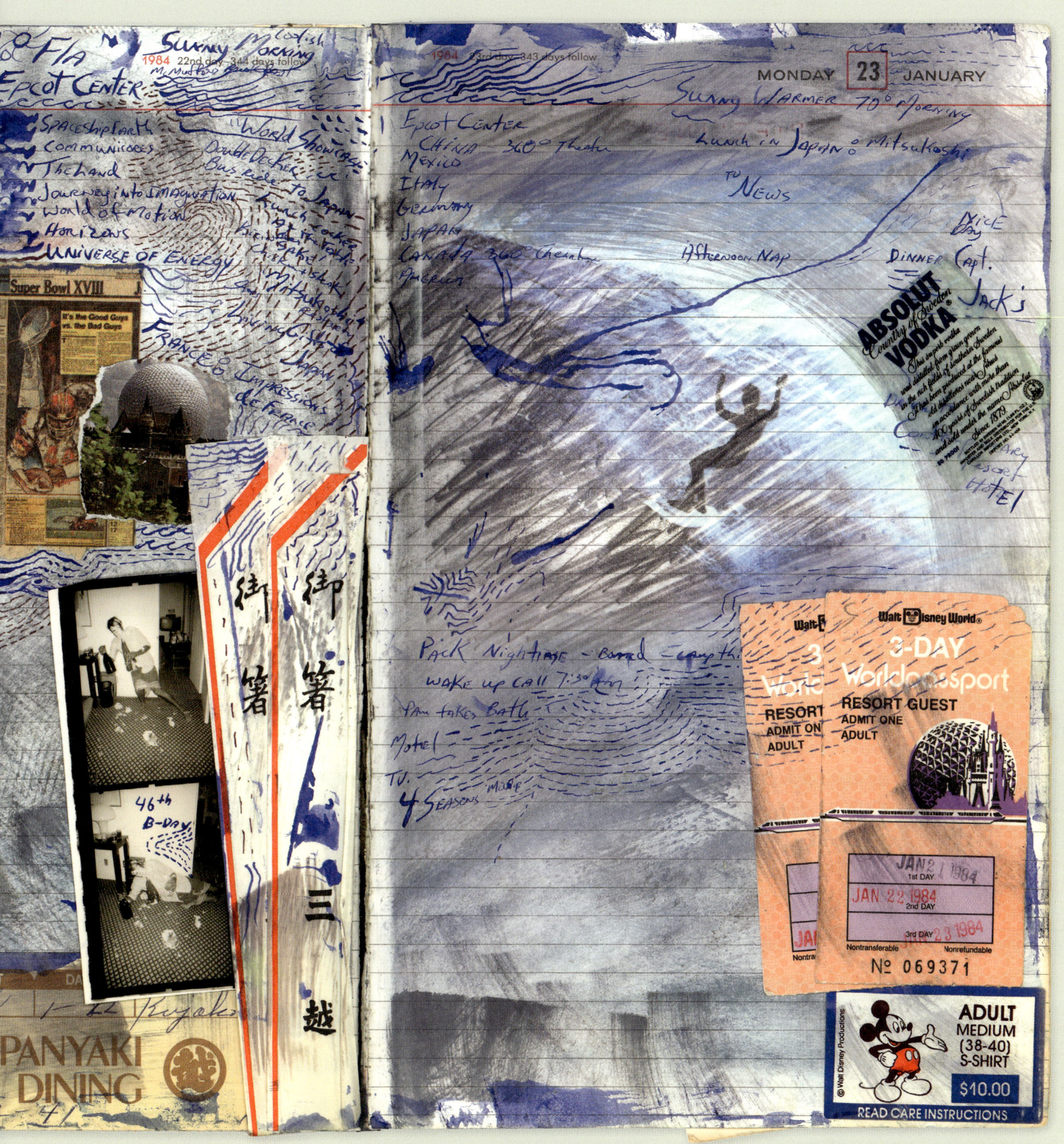

1984 22nd day 344 days follow
FLA
Epcot Center
Spaceship Earth
The Land
Journey into Imagination
World of Motion
Horizons
Universe of Energy
World Showcase
Super Bowl XVIII
It's the Good Guys vs. the Bad Guys
France Impressions de France
46th B-Day
Panyaki
PANYAKI DINING
1984 23rd day 343 days follow
MONDAY 23 JANUARY
Sunny Warmer 70° Morning
Epcot Center
China 360° Theater
Mexico
Italy
Germany
Japan
Canada 360° Theater
America
Lunch in Japan Mitsukoshi
TV News
Afternoon Nap
Nice Day
Dinner Capt. Jack's
Pack Nightime
Wake up call 7:30 AM
Motel
TV.
4 Seasons
ABSOLUT
Country of Sweden
VODKA
御箸
御箸
三越
Walt Disney World
3-DAY
World Passport
RESORT GUEST
ADMIT ONE
ADULT
JAN 21 1984
1st DAY
JAN 22 1984
2nd DAY
3rd DAY
JAN 23 1984
Nontransferable
Nonrefundable
№ 069371
ADULT
MEDIUM
(38-40)
S-SHIRT
$10.00
READ CARE INSTRUCTIONS

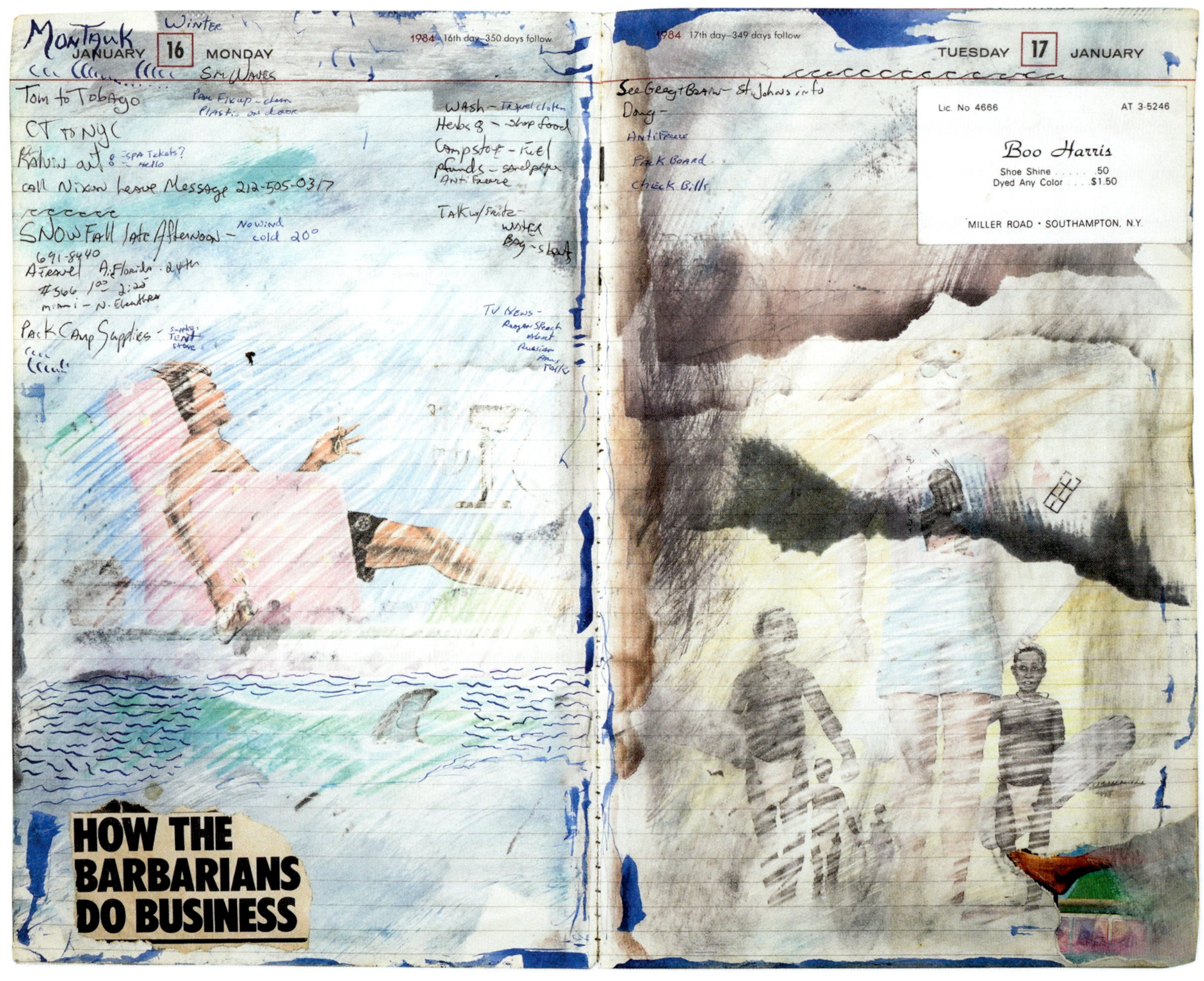
Montauk
Winter
JANUARY 16 MONDAY
1984 16th day–350 days follow
Tom to Tobago
CT to NYC
call Nixon Leave Message 212-505-0317
SNOW Fall late Afternoon – No wind cold 20°
691-8440
Pack Camp Supplies
WASH
Compstop – fuel
TV News –
1984 17th day–349 days follow
TUESDAY 17 JANUARY
Doug –
Antifreeze
Pack Board
Check Bills
Lic. No 4666
AT 3-5246
Boo Harris
Shoe Shine 50
Dyed Any Color $1.50
MILLER ROAD • SOUTHAMPTON, N.Y.
HOW THE
BARBARIANS
DO BUSINESS

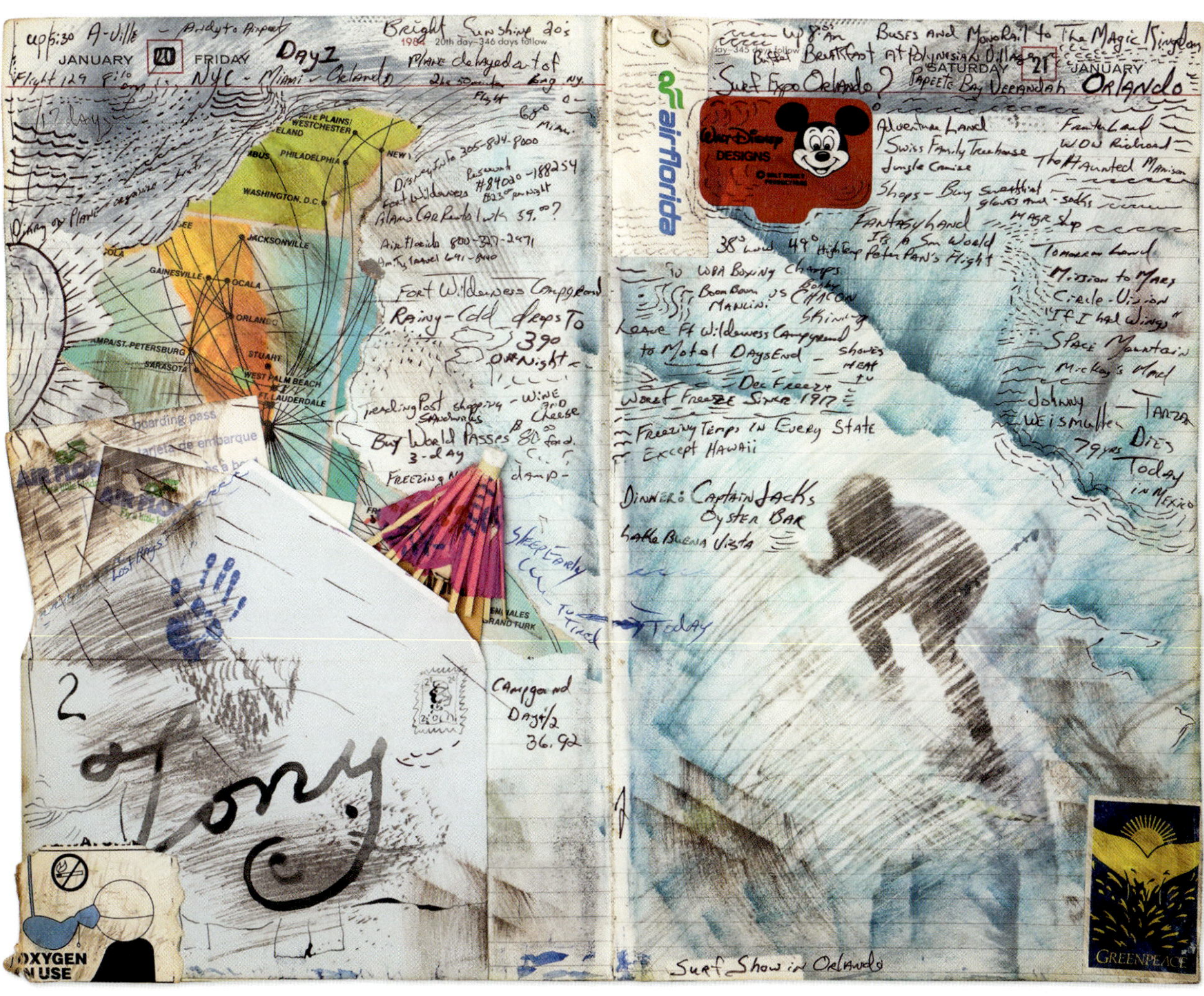

JANUARY
20
FRIDAY
Day 2
1984 20th day—346 days follow
Bright Sunshine 20's
Plane delayed
SATURDAY
21
JANUARY
Orlando
airflorida
WALT DISNEY DESIGNS
Adventure Land
Swiss Family Treehouse
Jungle Cruise
Fantasyland
Peter Pan's Flight
Tomorrow Land
Mission to Mars
Space Mountain
Haunted Mansion
Fort Wilderness Campground
Rainy-Cold drops to 39° at Night
Buy World Passes 3-day
Freezing Temps in Every State Except Hawaii
Dinner: Captain Jacks Oyster Bar
Lake Buena Vista
Johnny Weismuller – Tarzan Dies Today in Mexico
boarding pass
tarjeta de embarque
Tony
OXYGEN IN USE
Surf Show in Orlando
GREENPEACE

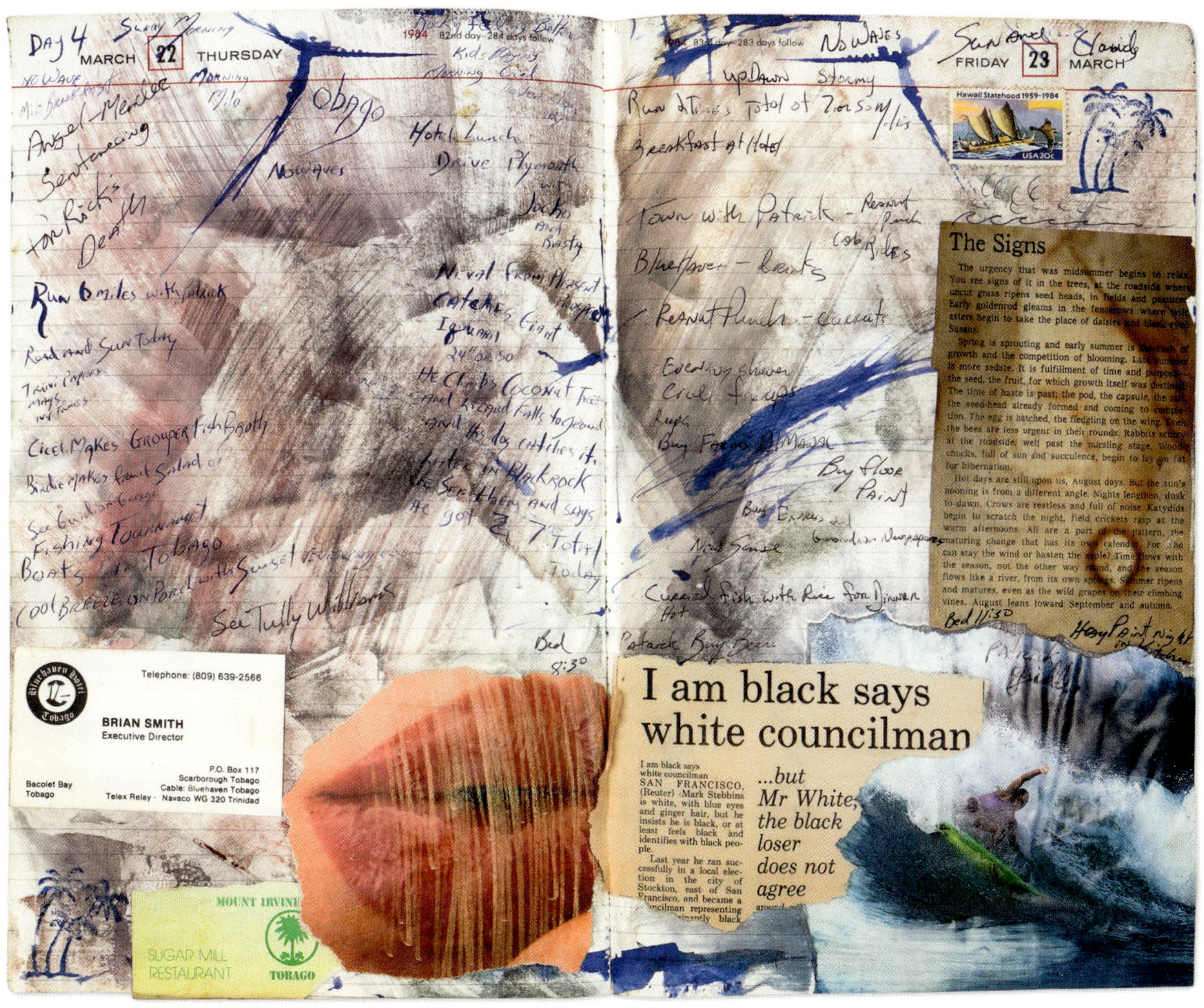

Day 4
MARCH
22
THURSDAY
1984 82nd day—284 days follow
Tobago
No Waves
Run 6 miles
FRIDAY
23
MARCH
Breakfast at Hotel
Hawaii Statehood 1959-1984
USA 20c
The Signs
Telephone: (809) 639-2566
BRIAN SMITH
Executive Director
Bacolet Bay
Tobago
P.O. Box 117
Scarborough Tobago
Cable: Bluehaven Tobago
Telex Relay · Navaco WG 320 Trinidad
I am black says white councilman
...but Mr White, the black loser does not agree
MOUNT IRVINE
SUGAR MILL RESTAURANT
TOBAGO
Bed 9:30

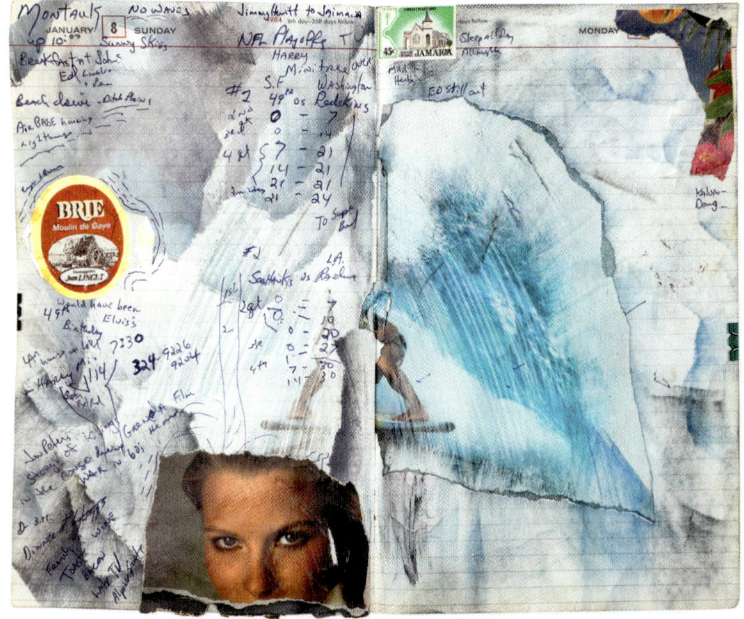
JANUARY
SUNDAY
MONDAY
BRIE
Moulin de Gaye

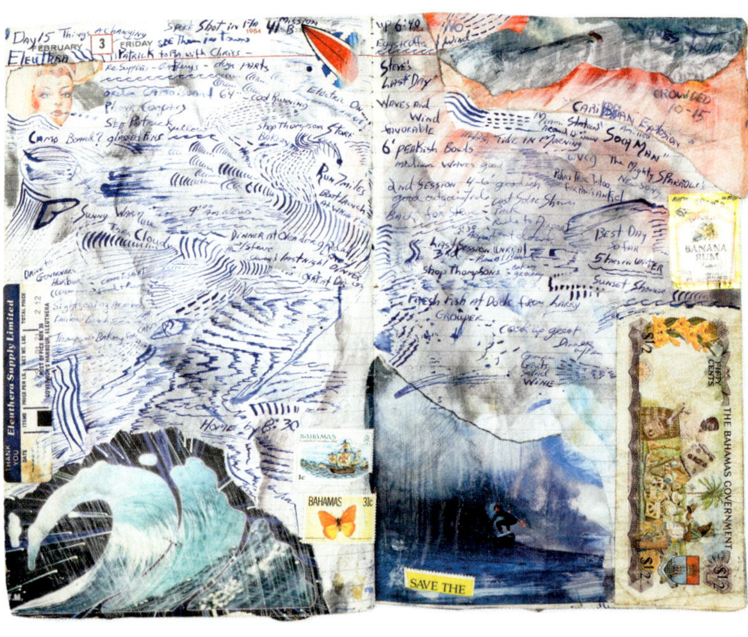
FEBRUARY
FRIDAY
Eleuthera Supply Limited
BAHAMAS
SAVE THE
THE BAHAMAS GOVERNMENT

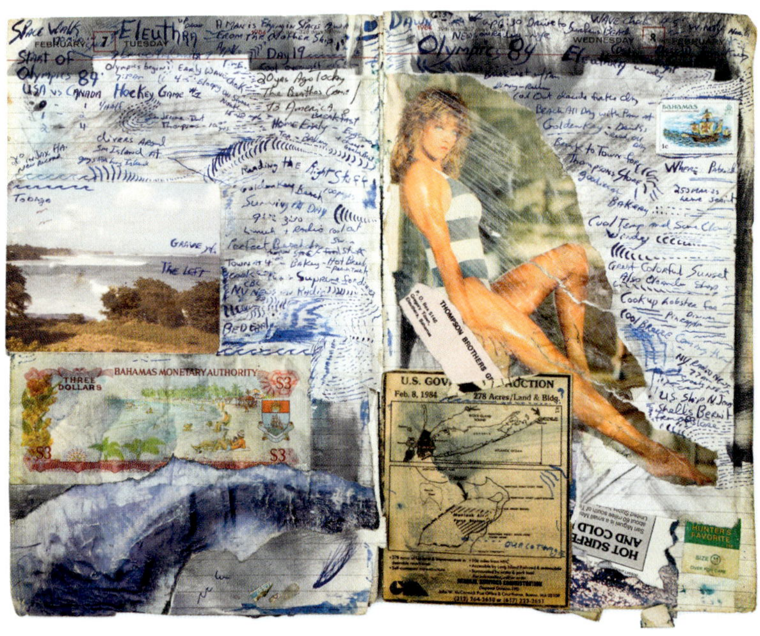
BAHAMAS MONETARY AUTHORITY
THREE DOLLARS
BAHAMAS
WEDNESDAY
HOT SURF AND COLD

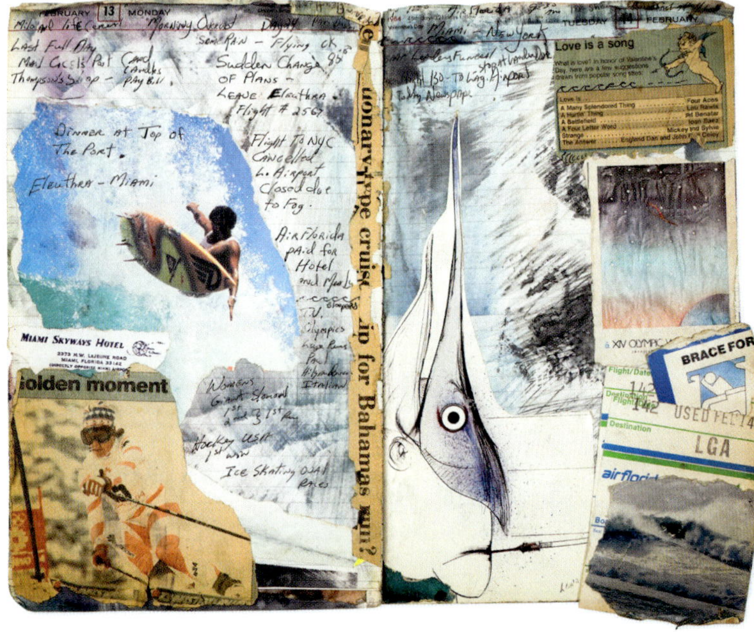
FEBRUARY
MONDAY
TUESDAY
MIAMI SKYWAYS HOTEL
olden moment
ip for Bahamas sun?
Love is a song
BRACE FOR
LGA

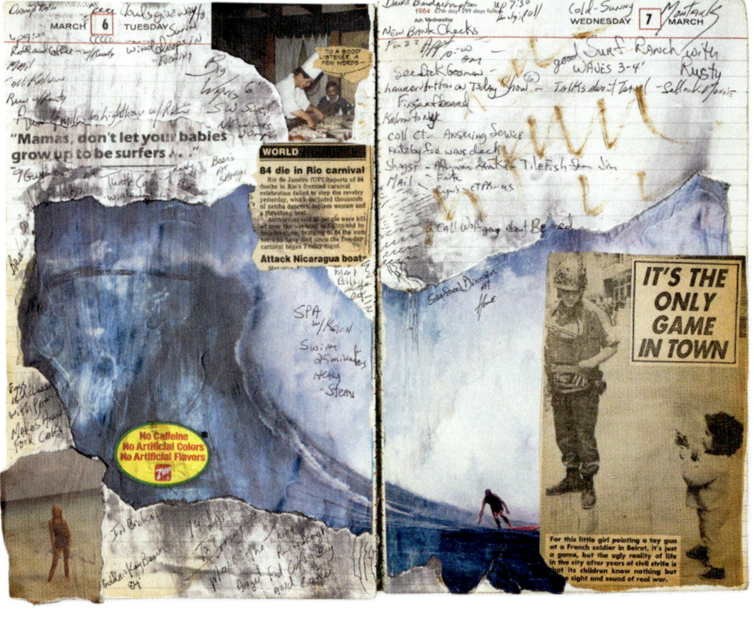
MARCH
TUESDAY
WEDNESDAY
"Mamas, don't let your babies grow up to be surfers"
WORLD
84 die in Rio carnival
Attack Nicaragua boat
No Caffeine
No Artificial Colors
No Artificial Flavors
IT'S THE ONLY GAME IN TOWN

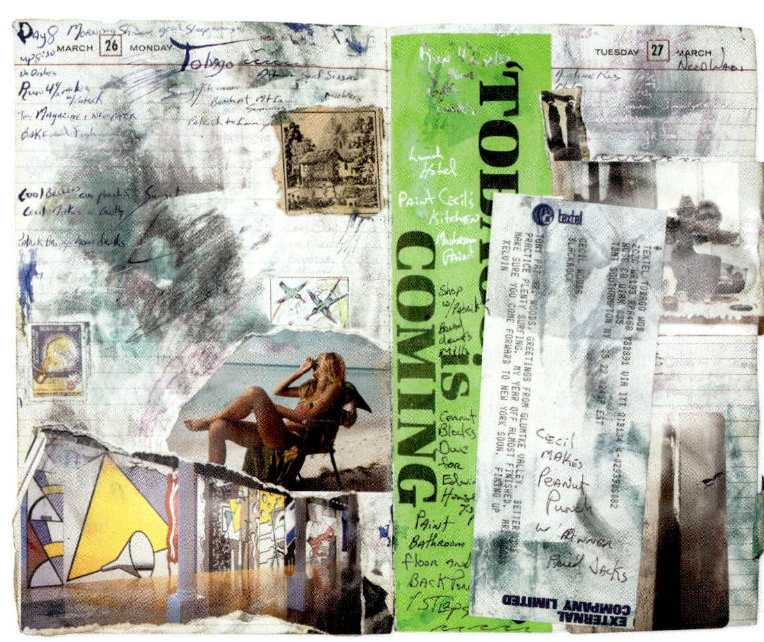
MARCH
MONDAY
TUESDAY
COMING
EXTERNAL COMPANY LIMITED

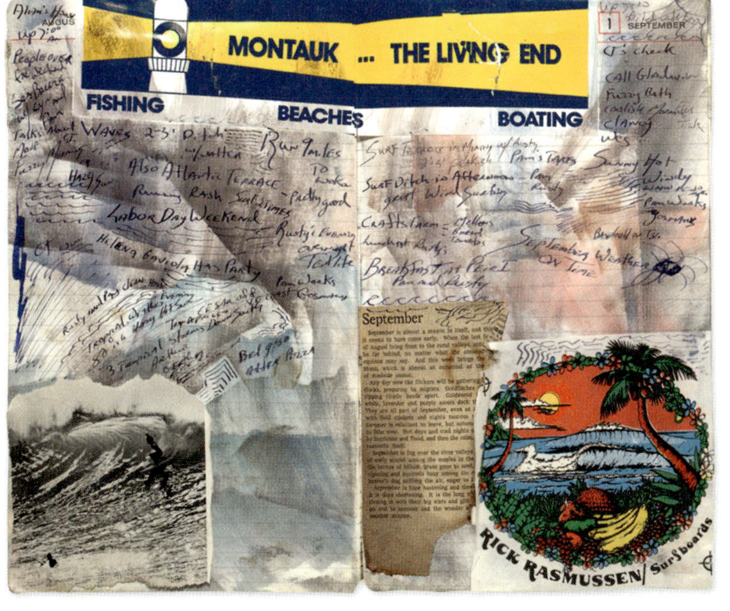
MONTAUK ... THE LIVING END
FISHING
BEACHES
BOATING
September
RICK RASMUSSEN Surfboards

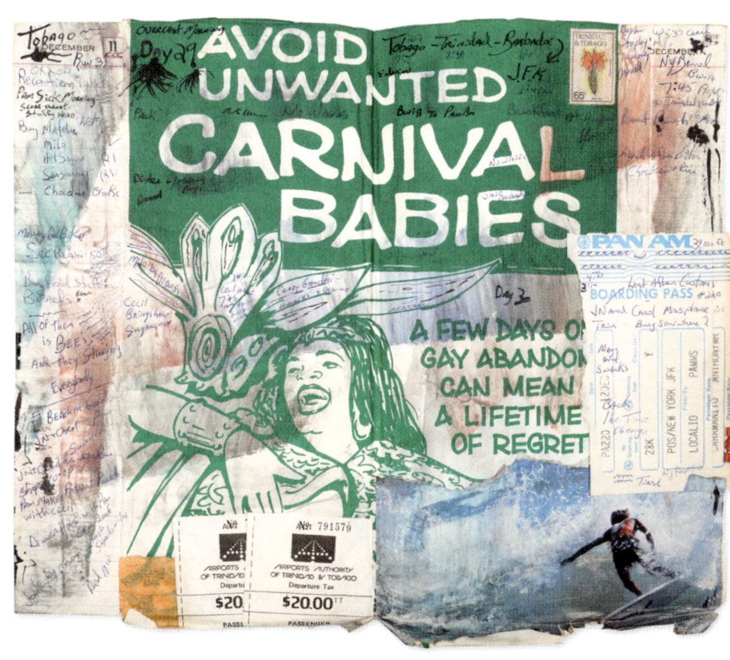
AVOID
UNWANTED
CARNIVAL
BABIES
A FEW DAYS OF
GAY ABANDON
CAN MEAN
A LIFETIME
OF REGRET
PAN AM
BOARDING PASS
$20
$20.00

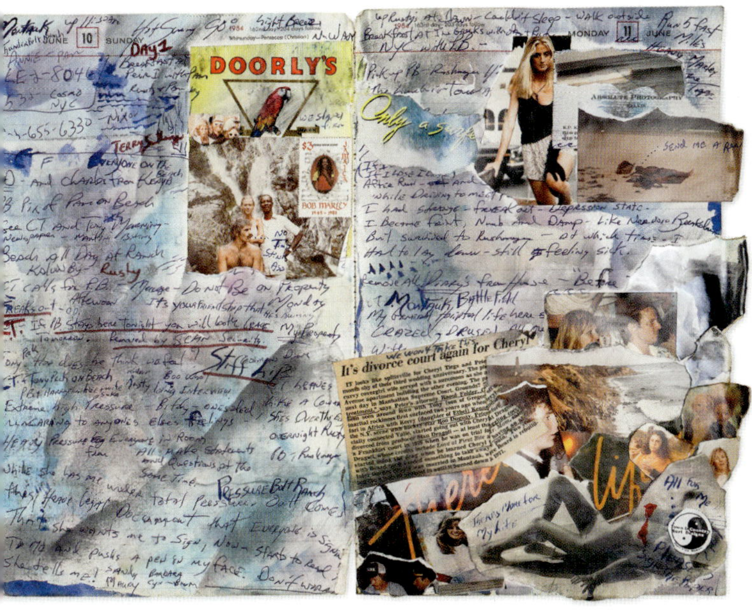
DOORLY'S
It's divorce court again for Cheryl

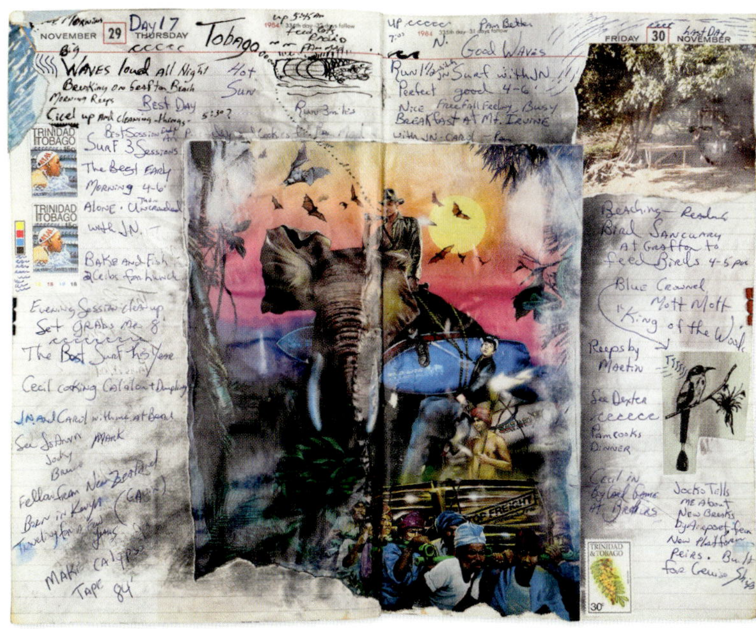
NOVEMBER 29 THURSDAY
FRIDAY 30 NOVEMBER
TRINIDAD & TOBAGO

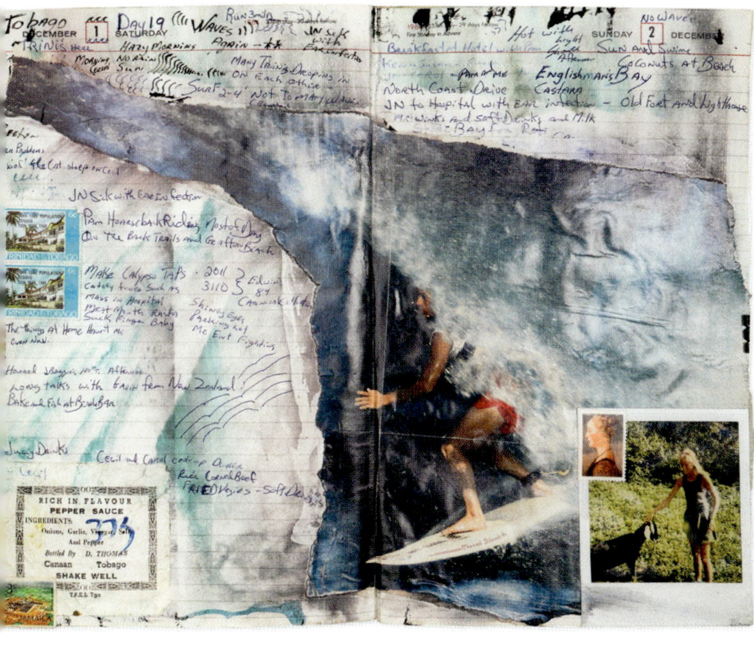
DECEMBER 1 SATURDAY
SUNDAY 2 DECEMBER
RICH IN FLAVOUR
PEPPER SAUCE
SHAKE WELL

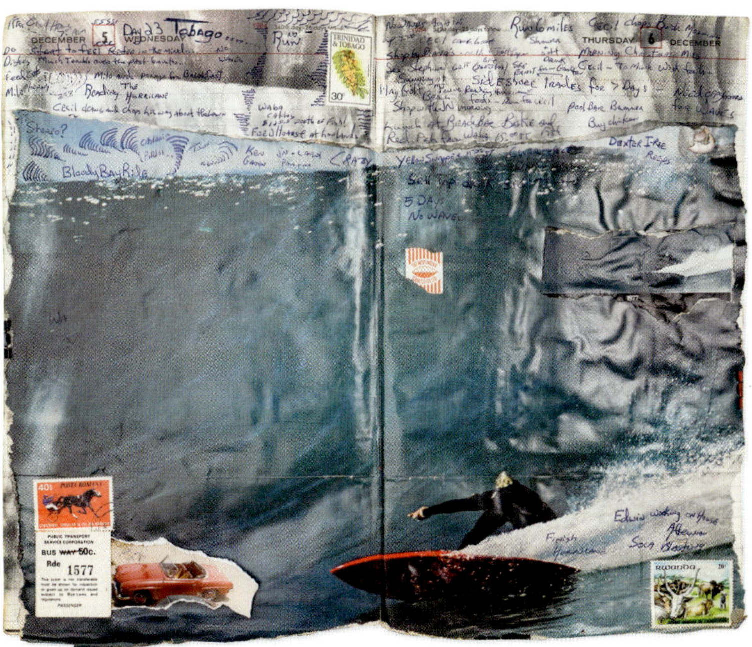
DECEMBER 5 WEDNESDAY
THURSDAY 6 DECEMBER
BUS 50c.
1577

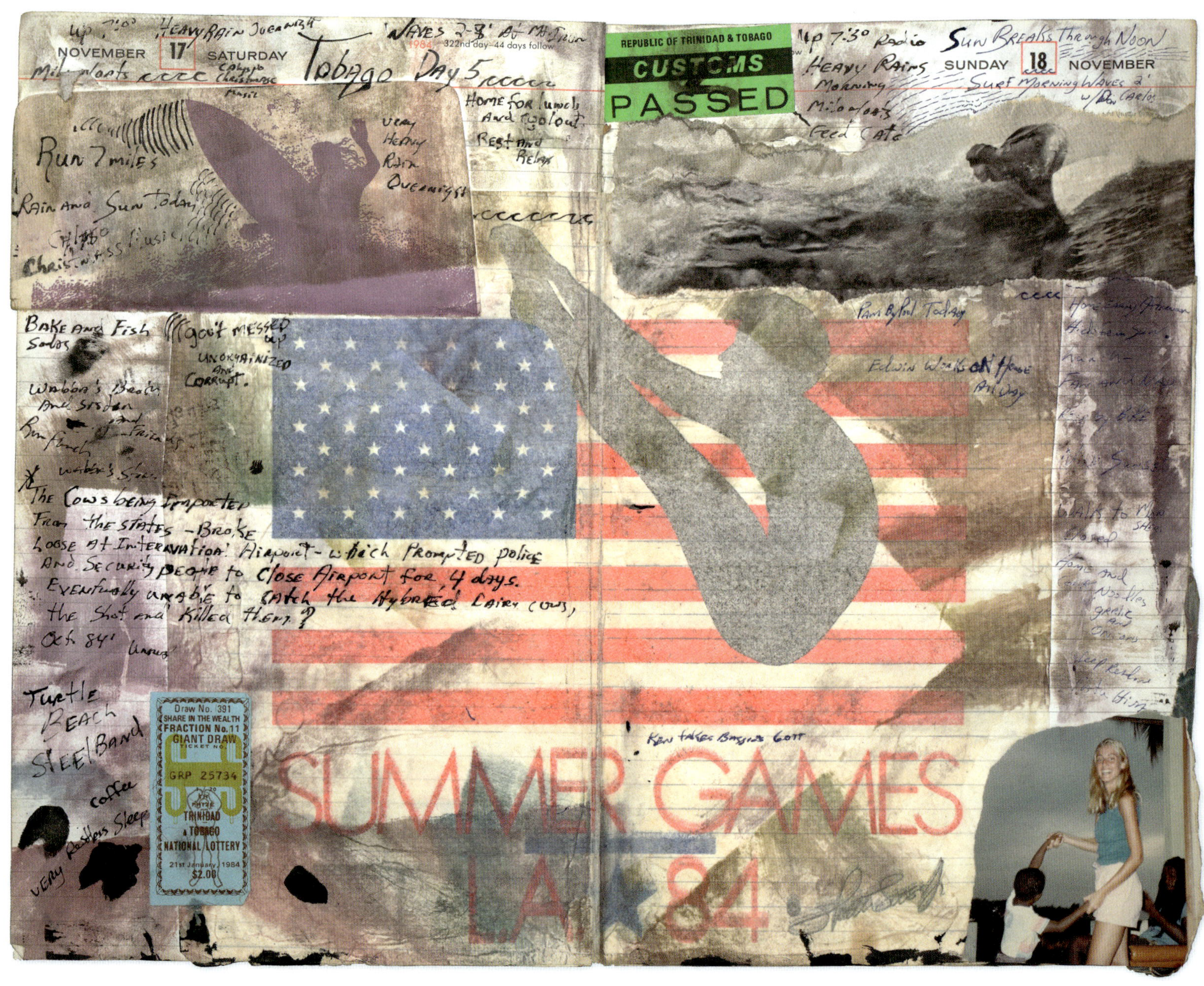
NOVEMBER 17 SATURDAY
Tobago Day 5
REPUBLIC OF TRINIDAD & TOBAGO
CUSTOMS
PASSED
SUNDAY 18 NOVEMBER
Run 7 miles
Rain and Sun Today
Bake and Fish
The Cows being Imported From the States - Broke Loose at International Airport - which prompted police and Security people to Close Airport for 4 days.
Turtle Beach Steel Band
Draw No. 391
SHARE IN THE WEALTH
FRACTION No. 11
GIANT DRAW
GRP 25734
TRINIDAD & TOBAGO NATIONAL LOTTERY
21st January 1984
$2.00
SUMMER GAMES
L.A. 84

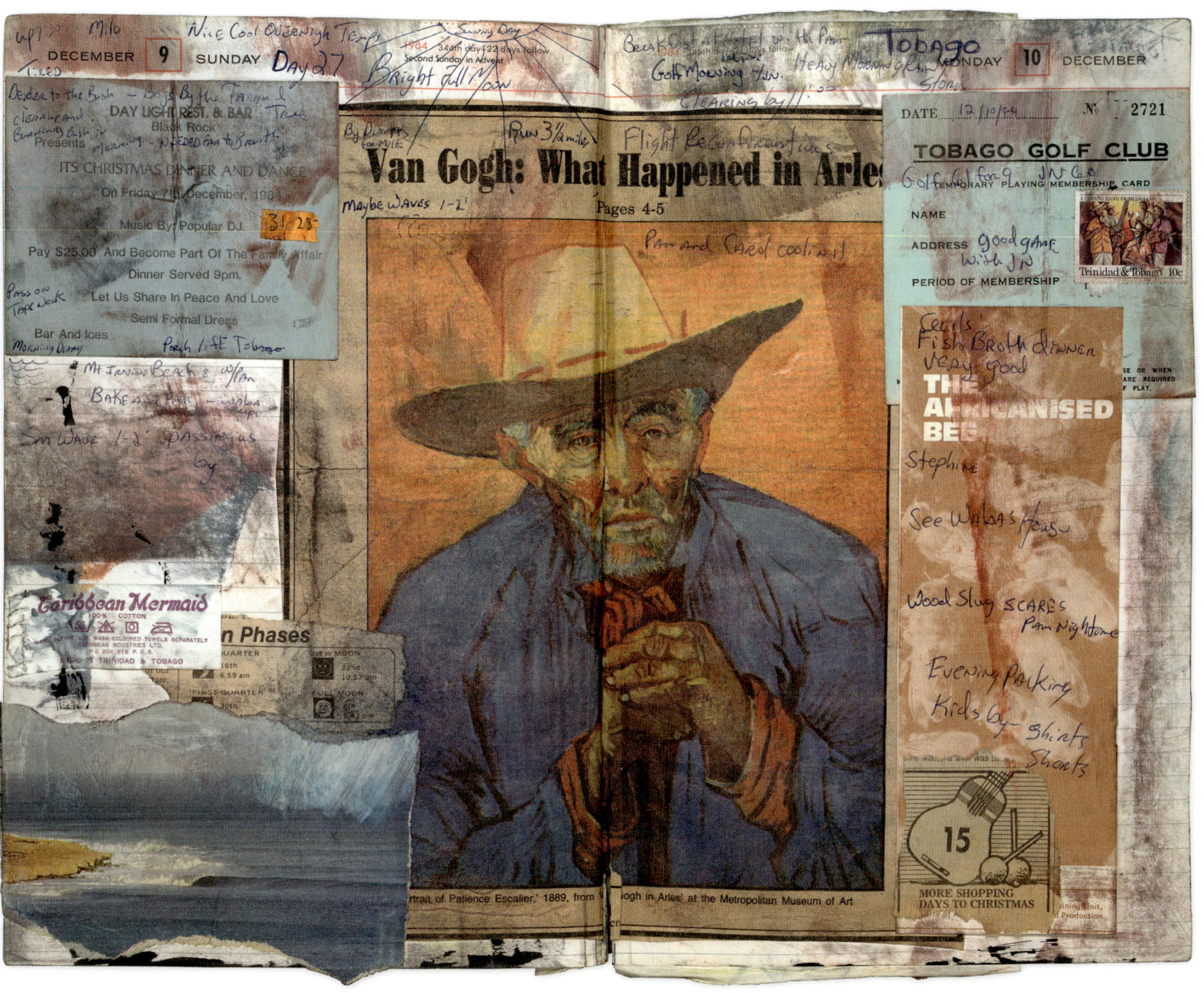
DECEMBER 9 SUNDAY
Day 27
Bright Full Moon
Second Sunday in Advent
MONDAY 10 DECEMBER
Tobago
Van Gogh: What Happened in Arles
Pages 4-5
Run 3½ miles
Flight Reconfirmations
Maybe waves 1-2'
Pam and Carol cooling
DAY LIGHT REST. & BAR
Black Rock
Presents
ITS CHRISTMAS DINNER AND DANCE
On Friday 7th December, 1984
Music By Popular DJ.
Pay $25.00 And Become Part Of The Family Affair
Dinner Served 9pm.
Let Us Share In Peace And Love
Semi Formal Dress
Bar And Ices
DATE
No 2721
TOBAGO GOLF CLUB
TEMPORARY PLAYING MEMBERSHIP CARD
NAME
ADDRESS
good game with JN
PERIOD OF MEMBERSHIP
Trinidad & Tobago 10c
Cecils
Fish Broth dinner
very good
Stephine
Wood Slug scares
Pam Nightime
Evening Parking
Kids by Shirts
Shorts
Caribbean Mermaid
100% COTTON
TRINIDAD & TOBAGO
n Phases
NEW MOON
FULL MOON
15
MORE SHOPPING DAYS TO CHRISTMAS
rtrait of Patience Escalier,' 1889, from ogh in Arles' at the Metropolitan Museum of Art

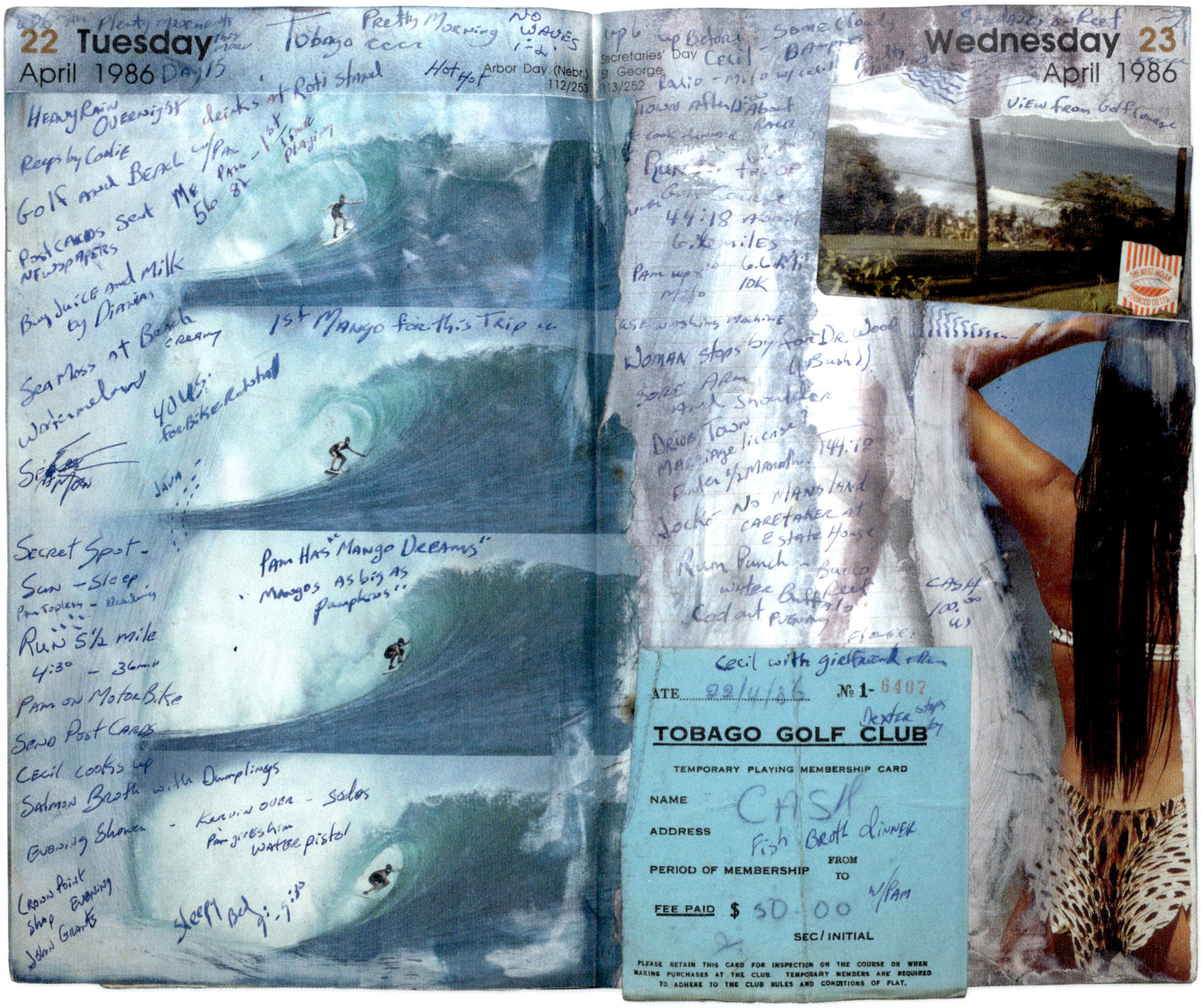

22 Tuesday
April 1986

Arbor Day (Nebr.)
112/253

Secretaries' Day
St George
113/252

Wednesday 23
April 1986

ATE 22/4/86 № 1- 6407

TOBAGO GOLF CLUB

TEMPORARY PLAYING MEMBERSHIP CARD

NAME CASH

ADDRESS

PERIOD OF MEMBERSHIP FROM TO

FEE PAID $ 50.00

SEC/INITIAL

PLEASE RETAIN THIS CARD FOR INSPECTION ON THE COURSE OR WHEN MAKING PURCHASES AT THE CLUB. TEMPORARY MEMBERS ARE REQUIRED TO ADHERE TO THE CLUB RULES AND CONDITIONS OF PLAY.

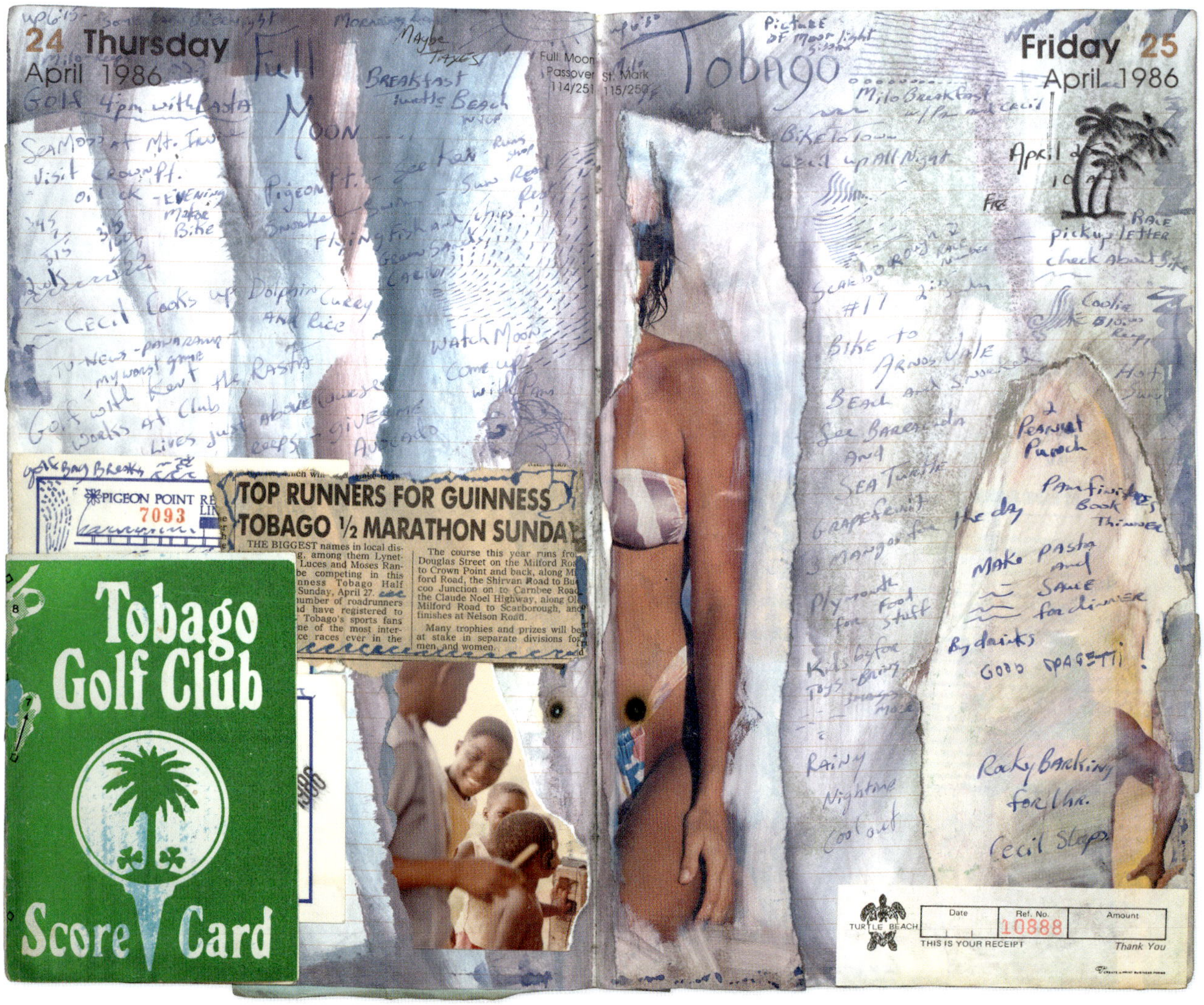

24 Thursday
April 1986

Full Moon
Passover
114/251

St Mark
115/250

Friday 25
April 1986

PIGEON POINT RE LIN
7093

TOP RUNNERS FOR GUINNESS TOBAGO ½ MARATHON SUNDAY

THE BIGGEST names in local dis- ...g, among them Lynet- ... Luces and Moses Ran- ... be competing in this ...nness Tobago Half ... Sunday, April 27. ...umber of roadrunners ...d have registered to ... Tobago's sports fans ...ne of the most inter- ...ce races ever in the

The course this year runs fro[m] Douglas Street on the Milford Roa[d] to Crown Point and back, along Mi[l]ford Road, the Shirvan Road to Bu[c]coo Junction on to Carnbee Road, the Claude Noel Highway, along Ol[d] Milford Road to Scarborough, and finishes at Nelson Road.

Many trophies and prizes will be at stake in separate divisions for men and women.

Tobago Golf Club

Score Card

TURTLE BEACH

Date	Ref. No.	Amount
	10888	

THIS IS YOUR RECEIPT

Thank You

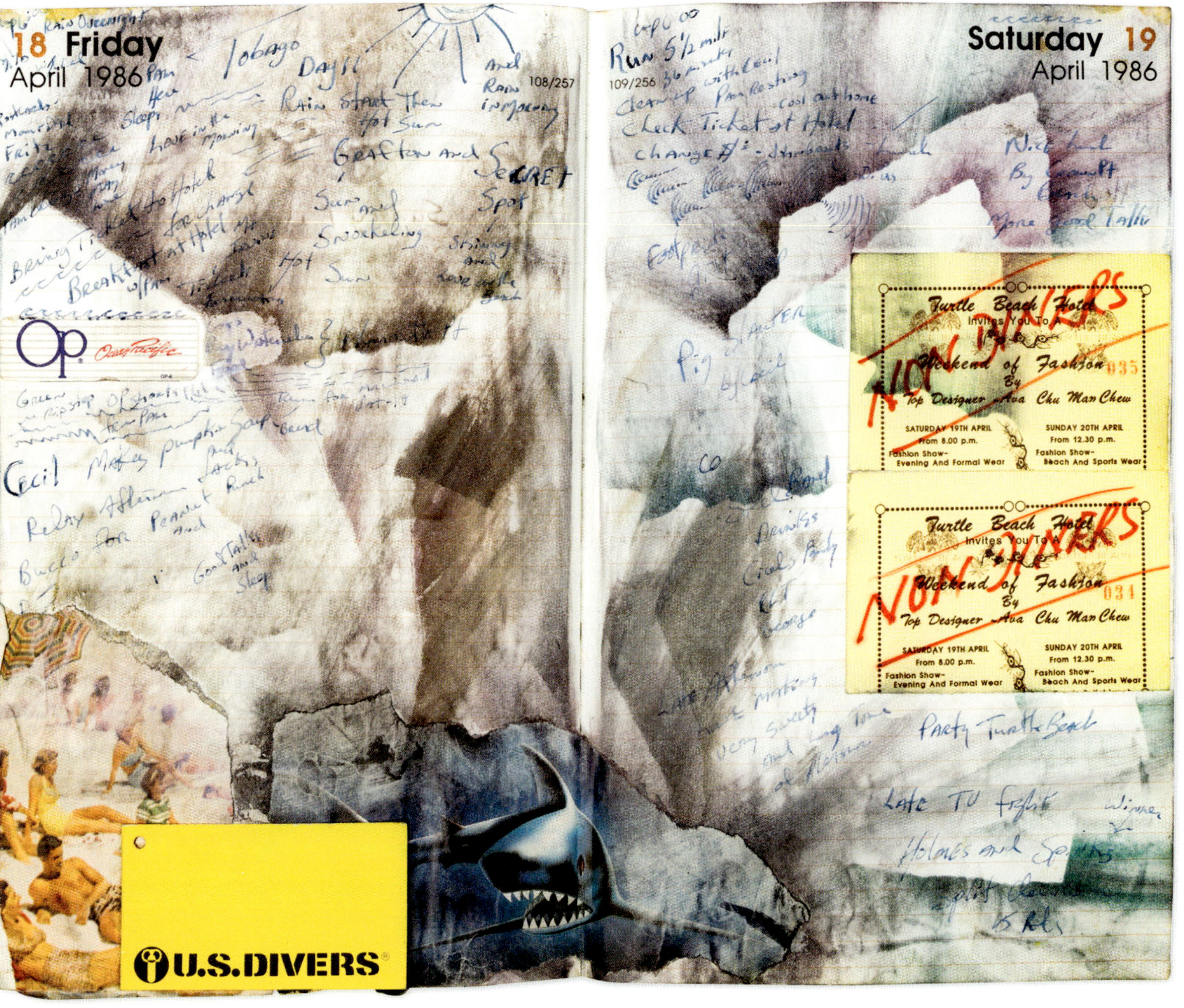
18 Friday
April 1986
108/257
109/256
Saturday 19
April 1986
Op
Turtle Beach Hotel
Invites You To A
Weekend of Fashion
By
Top Designer Ava Chu Man Chew
SATURDAY 19TH APRIL
From 8.00 p.m.
Fashion Show-
Evening And Formal Wear
SUNDAY 20TH APRIL
From 12.30 p.m.
Fashion Show-
Beach And Sports Wear
035
034
NON DIVERS
U.S.DIVERS

1987

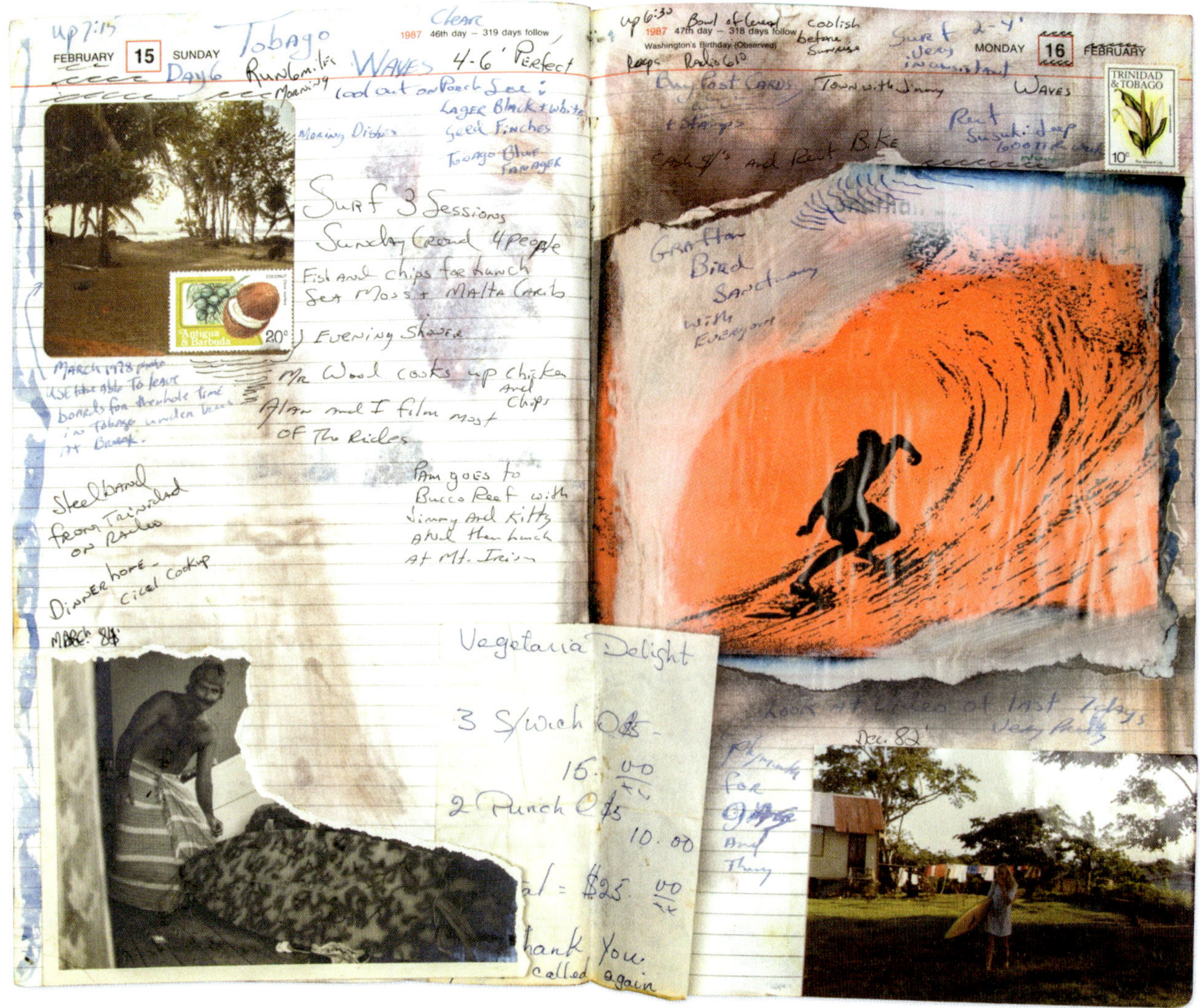

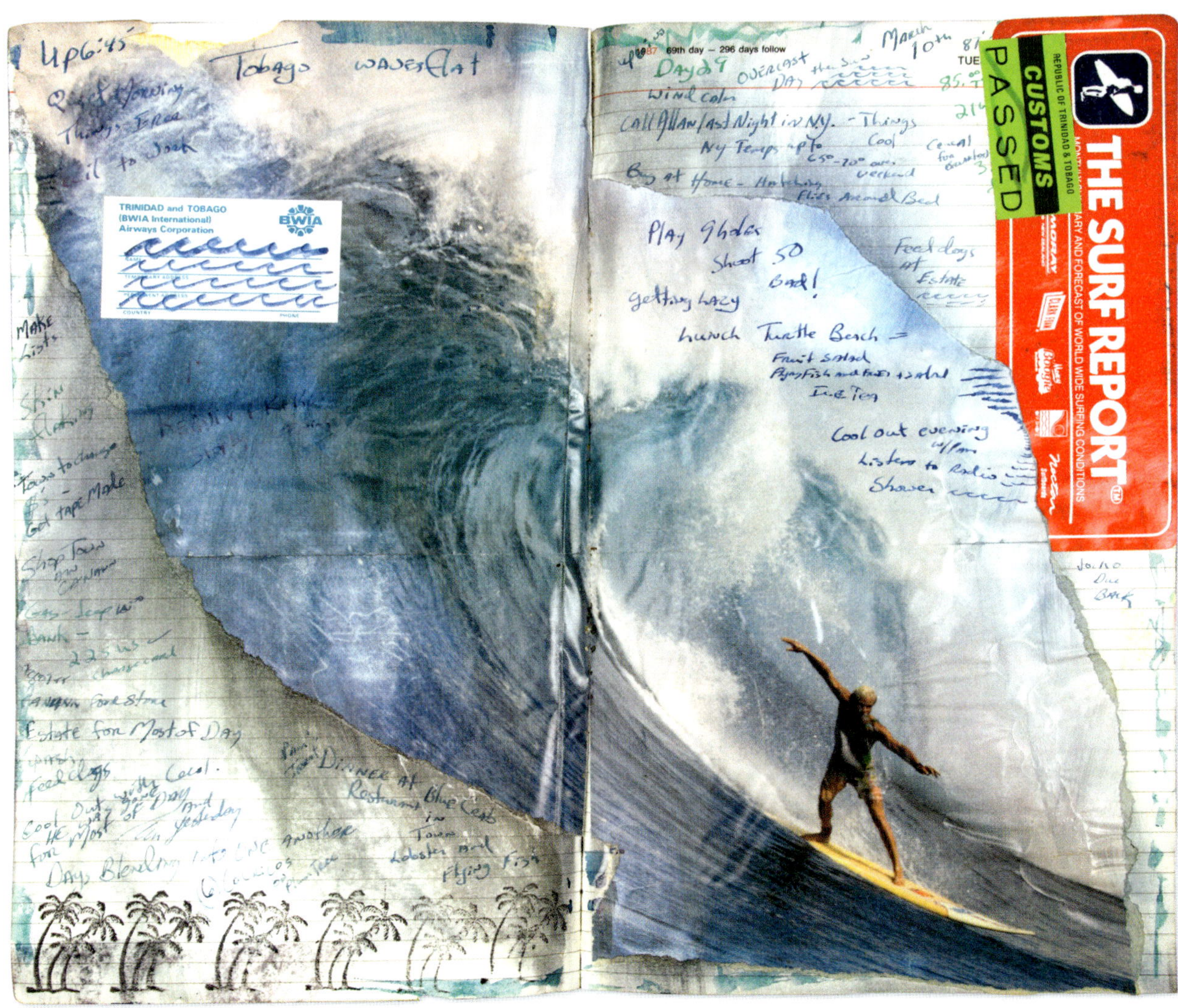

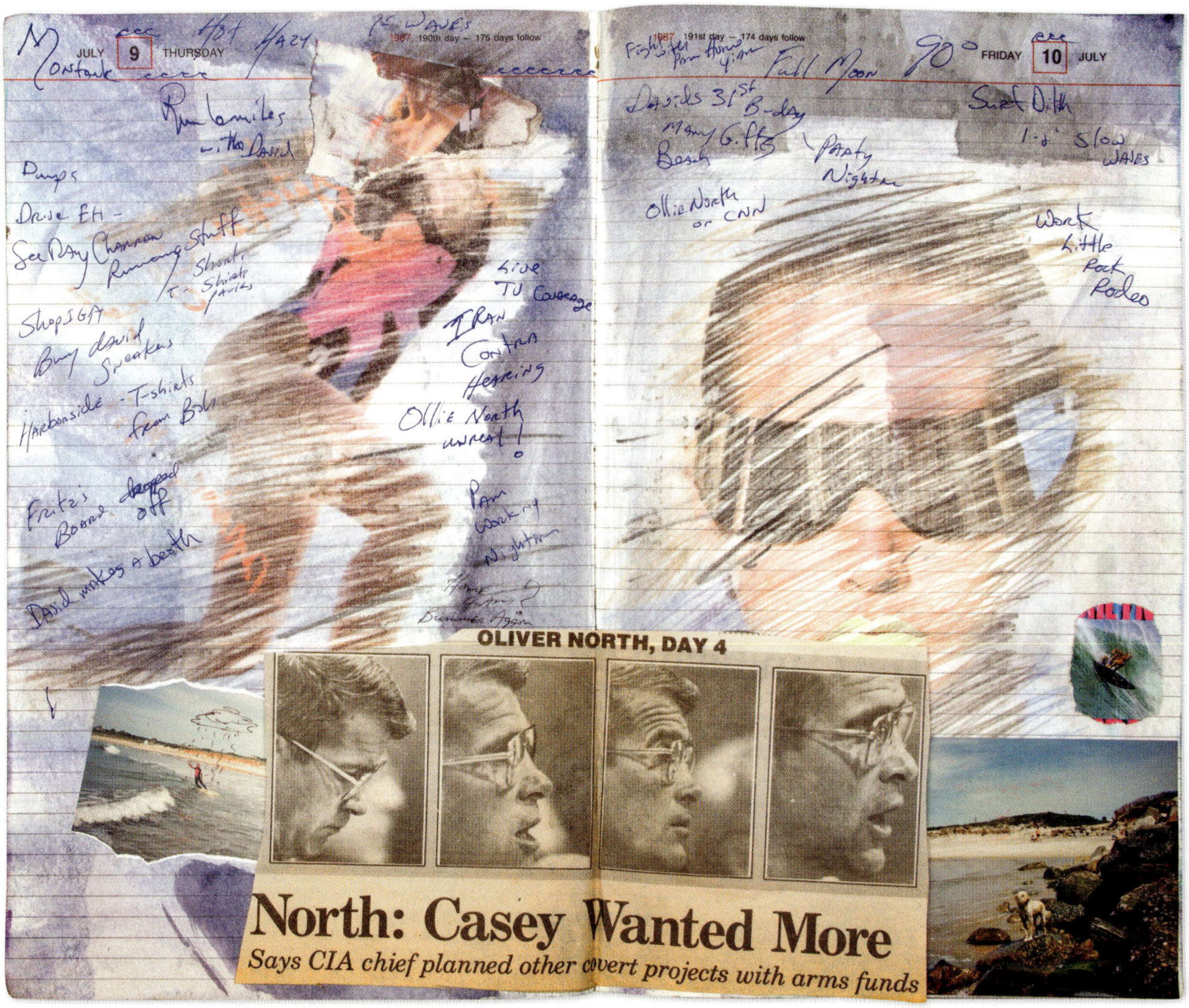

FEBRUARY 15 SUNDAY
1987 46th day – 319 days follow
1987 47th day – 318 days follow
Washington's Birthday (Observed)
MONDAY 16 FEBRUARY
TRINIDAD & TOBAGO
Antigua & Barbuda 20c

1987 69th day – 296 days follow
TRINIDAD and TOBAGO
(BWIA International)
Airways Corporation
BWIA
REPUBLIC OF TRINIDAD & TOBAGO
CUSTOMS
PASSED
THE SURF REPORT

JULY 9 THURSDAY

1987 190th day – 175 days follow

1987 191st day – 174 days follow

FRIDAY 10 JULY

OLIVER NORTH, DAY 4

North: Casey Wanted More

Says CIA chief planned other covert projects with arms funds

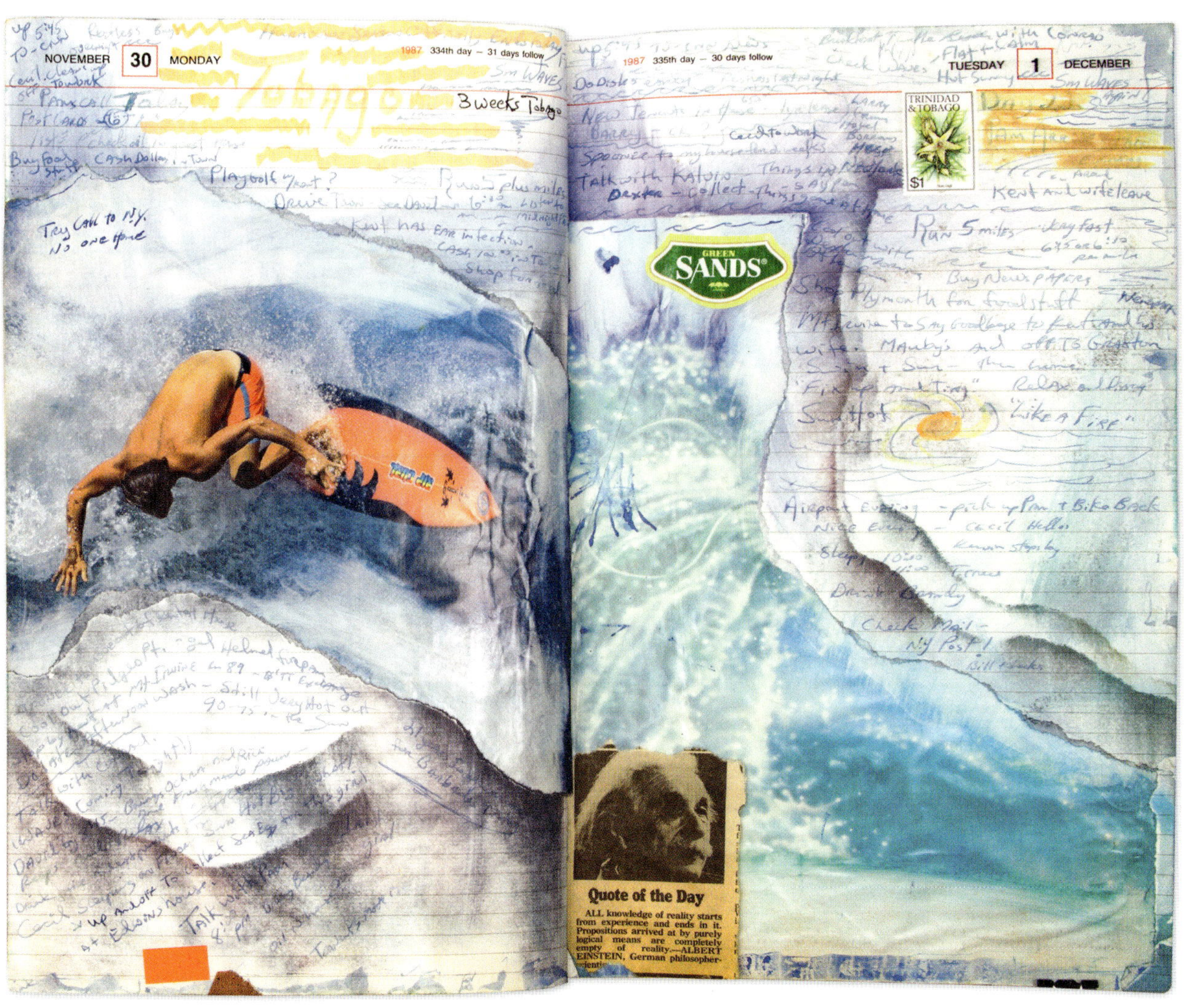

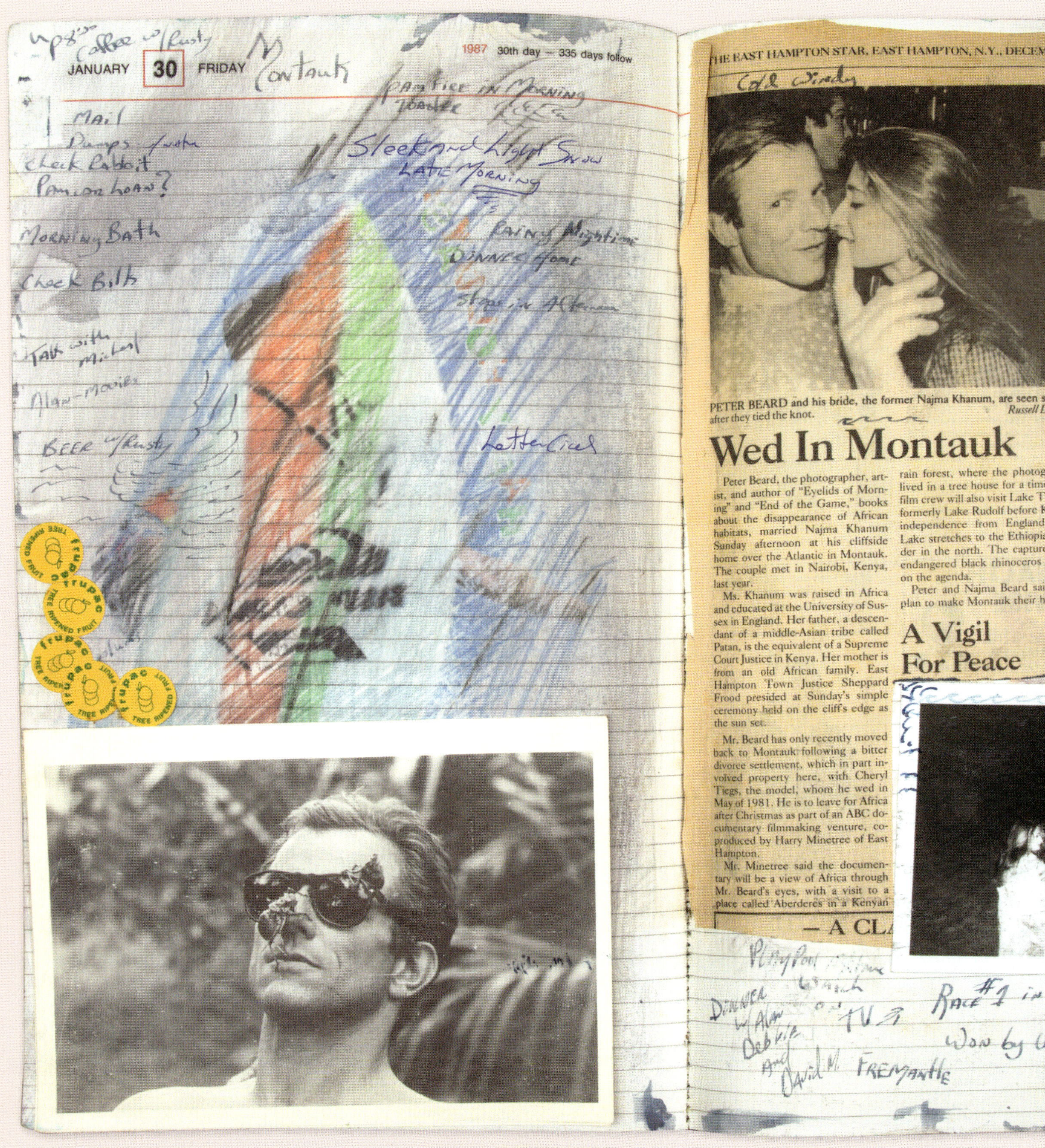

THE EAST HAMPTON STAR, EAST HAMPTON, N.Y., DECEM

PETER BEARD and his bride, the former Najma Khanum, are seen sh
after they tied the knot. *Russell Dr*

Wed In Montauk

Peter Beard, the photographer, artist, and author of "Eyelids of Morning" and "End of the Game," books about the disappearance of African habitats, married Najma Khanum Sunday afternoon at his cliffside home over the Atlantic in Montauk. The couple met in Nairobi, Kenya, last year.

Ms. Khanum was raised in Africa and educated at the University of Sussex in England. Her father, a descendant of a middle-Asian tribe called Patan, is the equivalent of a Supreme Court Justice in Kenya. Her mother is from an old African family. East Hampton Town Justice Sheppard Frood presided at Sunday's simple ceremony held on the cliff's edge as the sun set.

Mr. Beard has only recently moved back to Montauk following a bitter divorce settlement, which in part involved property here, with Cheryl Tiegs, the model, whom he wed in May of 1981. He is to leave for Africa after Christmas as part of an ABC documentary filmmaking venture, co-produced by Harry Minetree of East Hampton.

Mr. Minetree said the documentary will be a view of Africa through Mr. Beard's eyes, with a visit to a place called Aberderes in a Kenyan rain forest, where the photogr
lived in a tree house for a time.
film crew will also visit Lake Tu
formerly Lake Rudolf before K
independence from England.
Lake stretches to the Ethiopia
der in the north. The capture
endangered black rhinoceros i
on the agenda.

Peter and Najma Beard said
plan to make Montauk their ho

A Vigil For Peace

— A CL

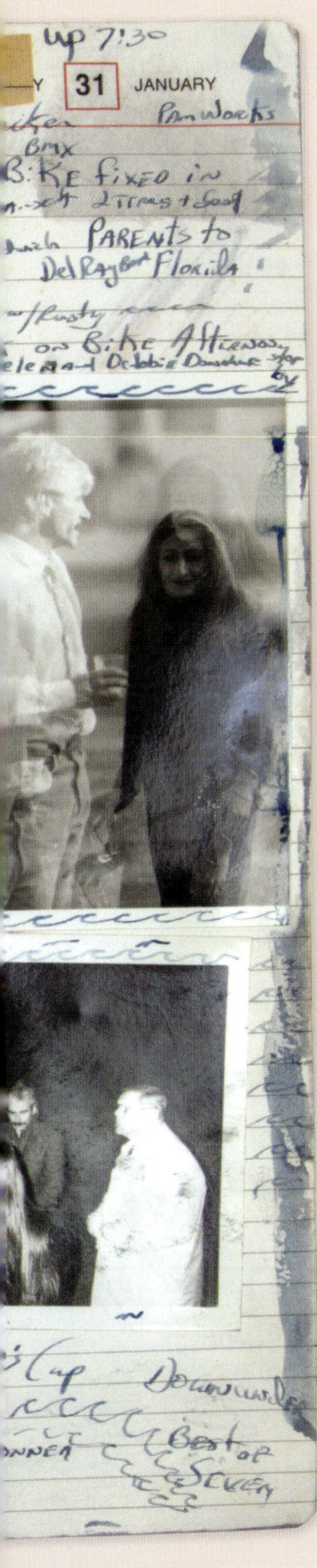

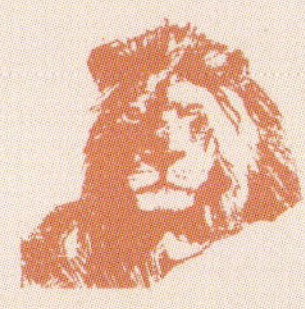

"BEARD WAS THE MAN ABOUT TOWN IN MONTAUK. HE WOULD HAVE WHAT HE CALLED 'THE BULKHEAD PARTY.' HE HAD THE GOVERNOR, JACKIE O, WARHOL, ENDLESS CELEBS, LOCALS IN TOWN, PEOPLE FROM THE BAR. THE GOVERNOR'S HELICOPTER IS LANDING AT THE PROPERTY NEXT DOOR. WE'RE SMOKING JOINTS, THERE'S COPS EVERYWHERE. DURING THAT PERIOD HE COULD DO NO WRONG. THE MAIN HOOK OF THE WHOLE PROPERTY WAS THE WAVE IN THE BACKYARD – THE RANCH. THE RANCH IS TO YOUR RIGHT AND TO THE LEFT IS THE AIRBASE ON THE SAME COVE. OUR CREW SCORED SO MANY DAYS OF AMAZING WAVES WITH NO ONE ELSE AROUND."

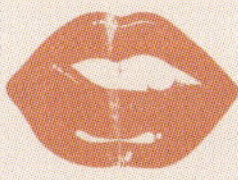

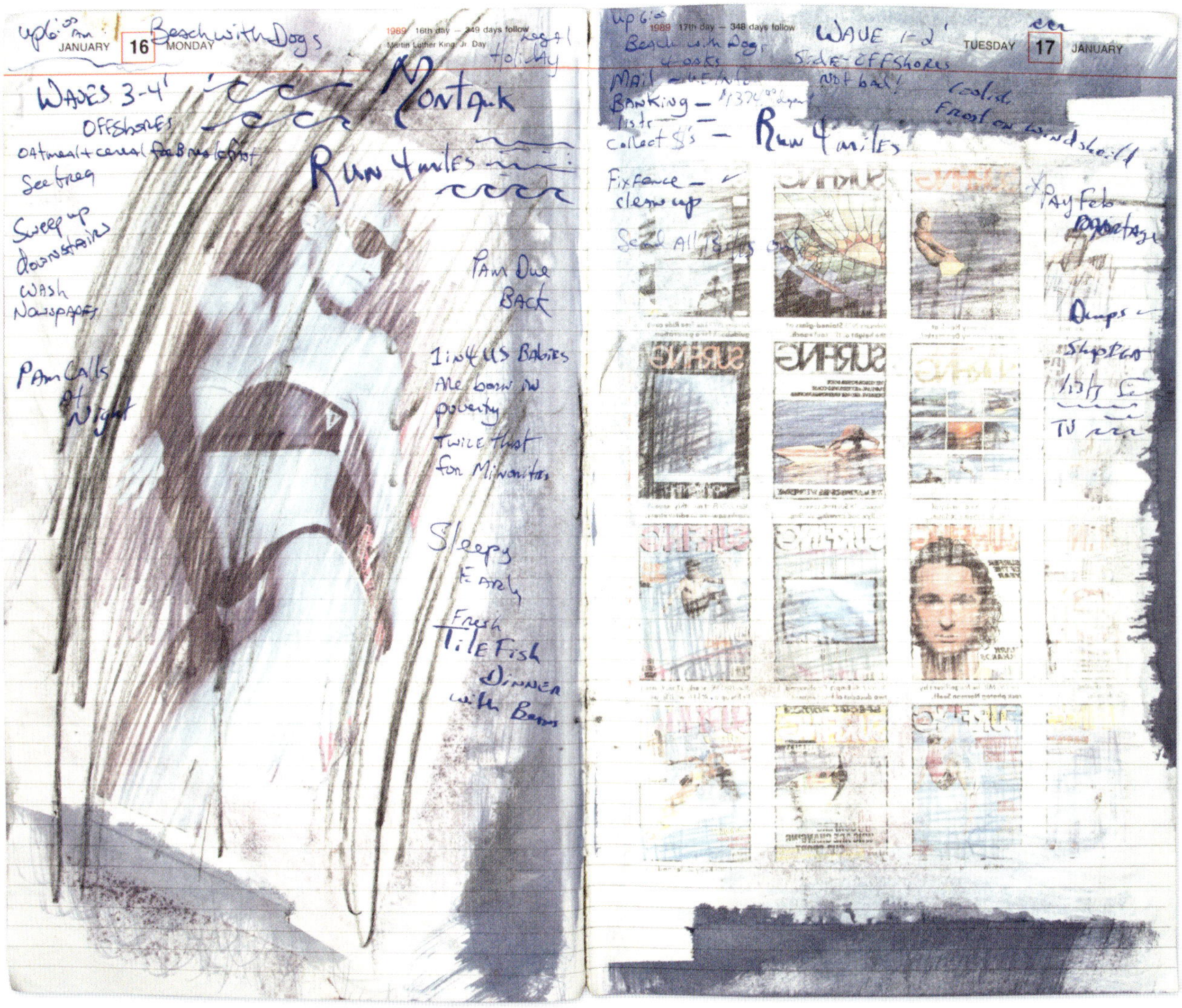

Up 6:00 am JANUARY 16 MONDAY Beach with Dogs 1989 16th day – 349 days follow Martin Luther King, Jr. Day Legal Holiday

WAVES 3-4'
OFFSHORES
Oatmeal + cereal for Bree (Dogs?)
See Greg
Sweep up downstairs
Wash Newspapers
Pam Calls at Night

Montauk
Run 4 miles

Pam Due Back
1 in 4 US Babies are born in poverty
Twice that for Minorities

Sleeps Early
Fresh Tile Fish Dinner with Barry

Up 6:00 1989 17th day – 348 days follow Beach with Dogs
WAVE 1-2'
Side-Offshores
not bad!
TUESDAY 17 JANUARY
Mail
Banking
Collect $'s
Run 4 miles
Cool, Frost on windshield
Fix Fence
Clean up
Pay Feb Mortgage
Dumps 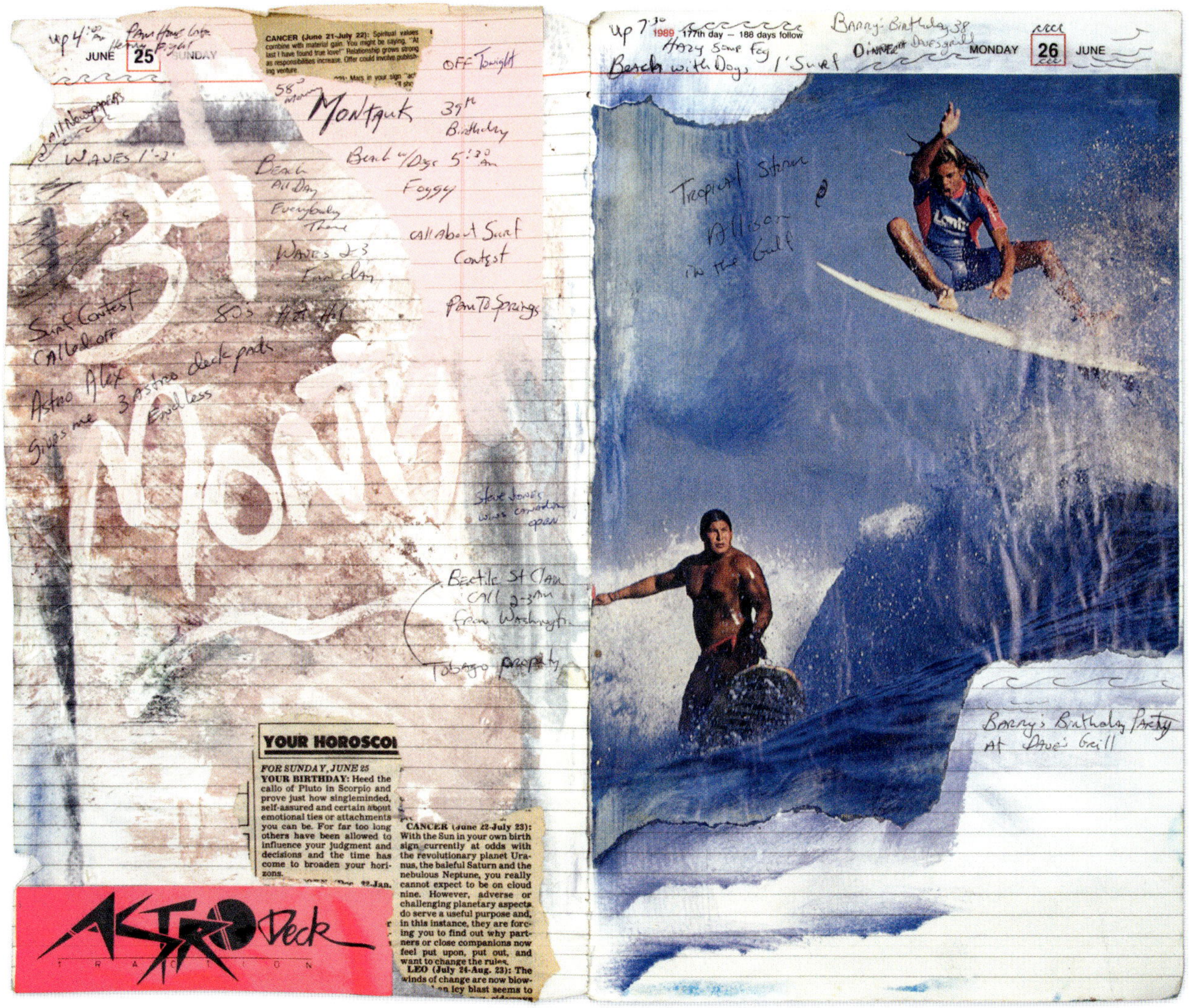
Shopping list
TV

Up 4:30 am JUNE 25 SUNDAY
OFF Tonight
58° mean
Montauk 37th Birthday
Beach w/Dogs 5:30 am
Foggy
WAVES 1-2'
Beach All Day
Everybody There
Waves 2-3
Call about Surf Contest
Pam To Springs
Surf Contest Called off
Astro Alex gives me 3 Astro deck pads
Steve Jones wins Canadian Open
Beetle St Clair Call 2-3am from Washington
Tobago property

CANCER (June 21-July 22): Spiritual values combine with material gain. You might be saying, "At last I have found true love!" Relationship grows strong as responsibilities increase. Offer could involve publishing venture.

YOUR HOROSCO[PE]

FOR SUNDAY, JUNE 25
YOUR BIRTHDAY: Heed the callo of Pluto in Scorpio and prove just how singleminded, self-assured and certain about emotional ties or attachments you can be. For far too long others have been allowed to influence your judgment and decisions and the time has come to broaden your horizons.

CANCER (June 22-July 23): With the Sun in your own birth sign currently at odds with the revolutionary planet Uranus, the baleful Saturn and the nebulous Neptune, you really cannot expect to be on cloud nine. However, adverse or challenging planetary aspects do serve a useful purpose and, in this instance, they are forcing you to find out why partners or close companions now feel put upon, put out, and want to change the rules.

LEO (July 24-Aug. 23): The winds of change are now blow- ... an icy blast seems to

ASTRO Deck TRACTION

Up 7:30 1989 177th day – 188 days follow
Hazy Some Fog
Barry Birthday 38
MONDAY 26 JUNE
Beach with Dogs 1' Surf
Tropical Storm Allison in the Gulf
Barry's Birthday Party At Dave's Grill

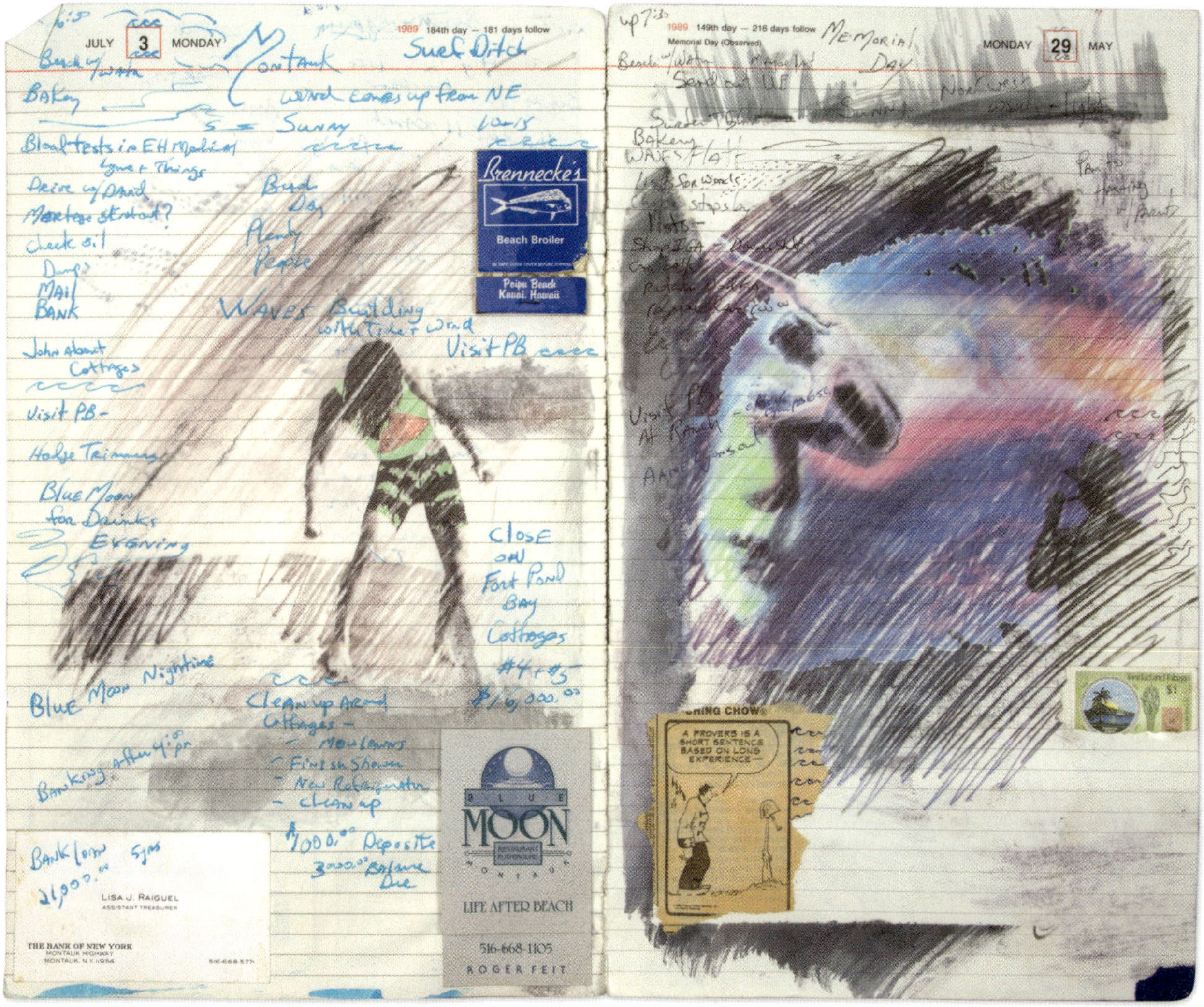

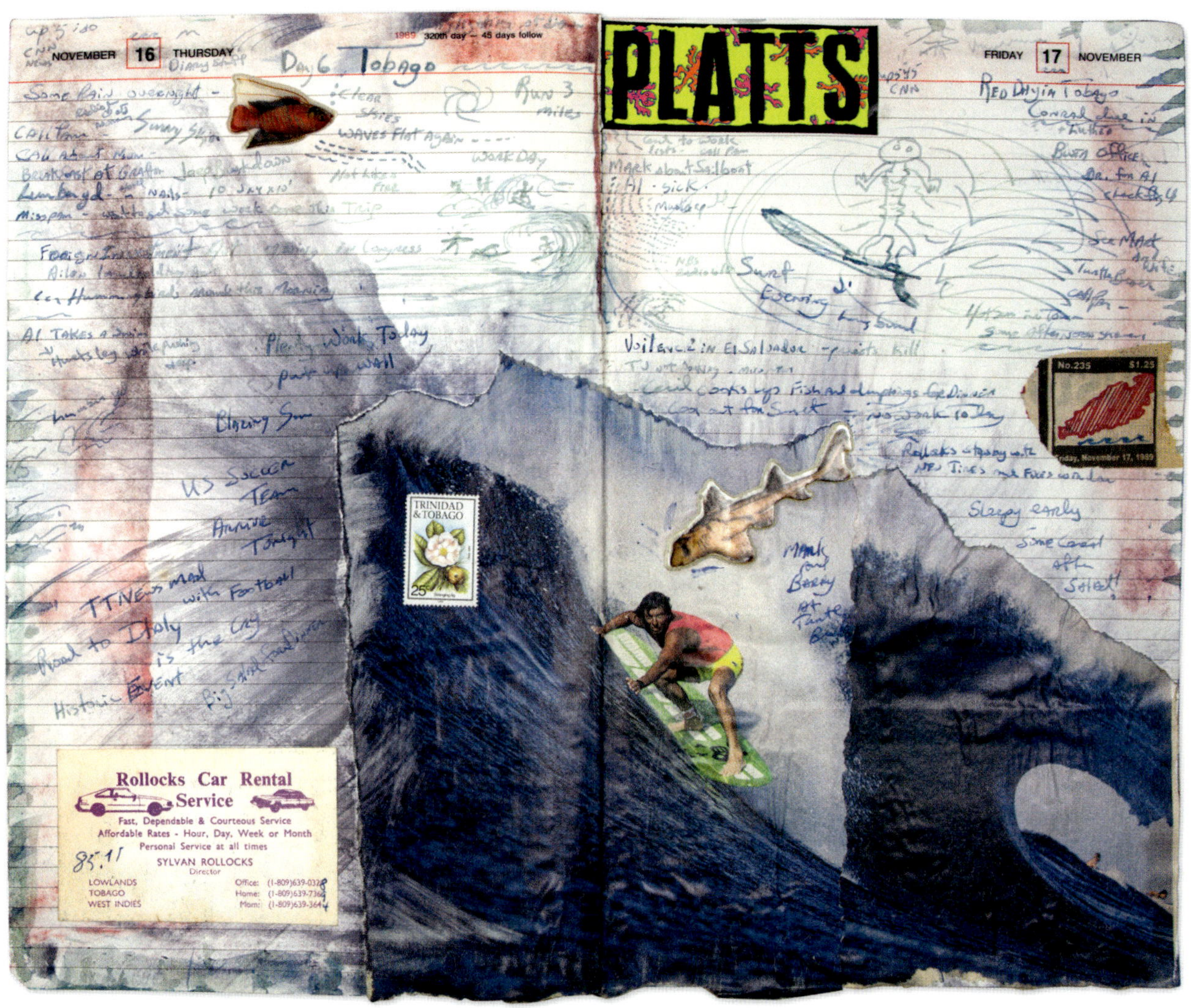
NOVEMBER 16 THURSDAY
PLATTS
FRIDAY 17 NOVEMBER
TRINIDAD & TOBAGO
Rollocks Car Rental Service
Fast, Dependable & Courteous Service
Affordable Rates - Hour, Day, Week or Month
Personal Service at all times
SYLVAN ROLLOCKS
Director
LOWLANDS
TOBAGO
WEST INDIES

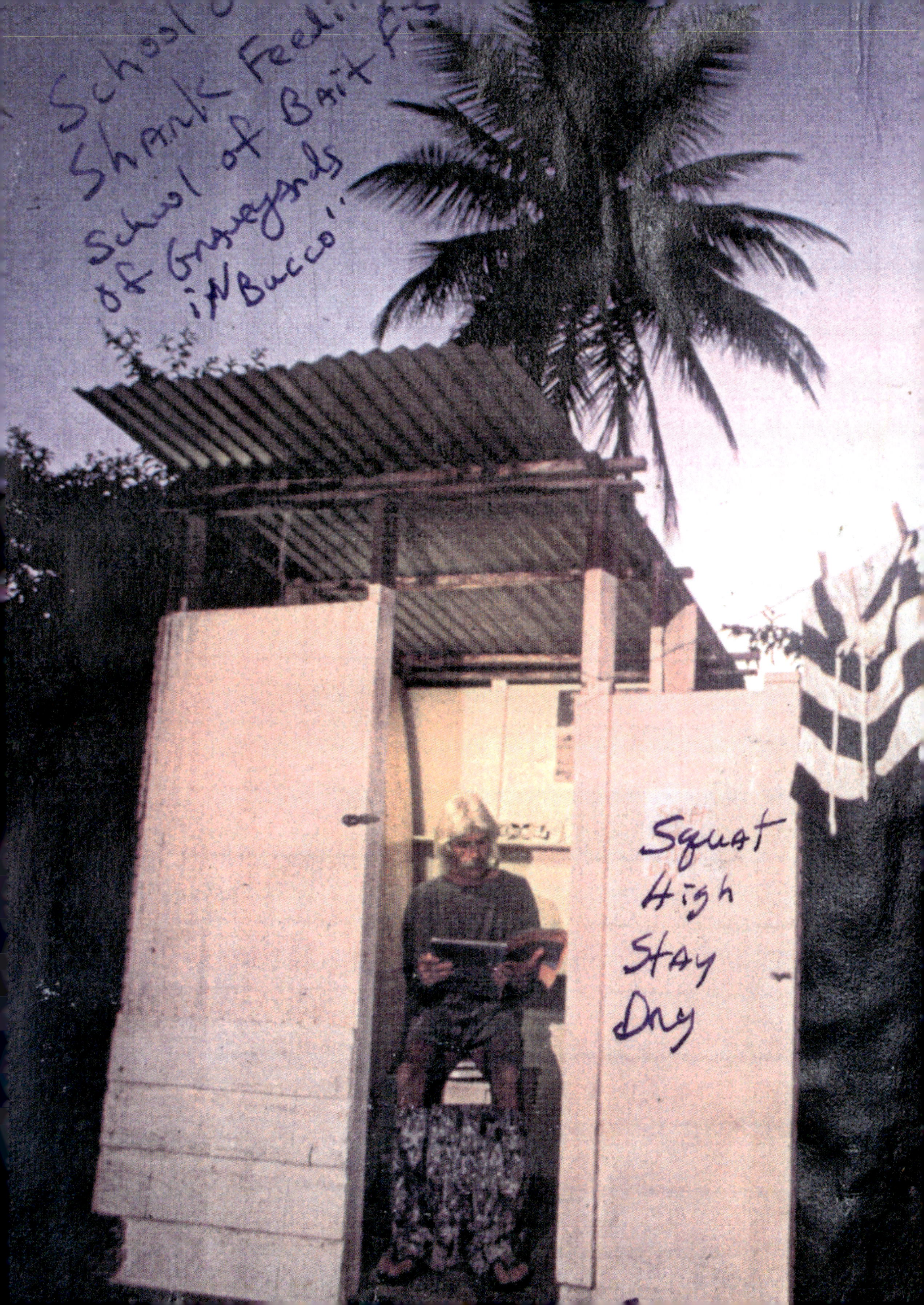
Shark Feedi
School of Bait fi
of Graveyards
in Bucco!
Squat
High
Stay
Dry

JOURNALS

1990s

Tony's relentlessly unconventional approach to life sets the stage for his '90s journals.

Moving out of Beard's house in 1984, Tony set sail into adulthood and laid roots in Montauk in the form of property ownership. Nowhere near the exorbitant price point the zip code is now famous for, he got a job working construction so he could qualify for a mortgage. He worked for 6 months on the renovation of Montauk Manor and the day that he was approved by the bank, he quit, again freeing him to chase waves around the world. As Tony would say, "Whenever I was doing something else, I always felt like I was turning my back on the ocean."

You'll notice an ever-present theme throughout the '90s and '00s comes in the form of a bright red 'Tobago News' typeface. While on a surf trip to Barbados in 1974, a man named Chris Schwank planted the seed of a dreamy right-hand point break on the island of Tobago. Exactly what Tony was looking for, he set off the following winter to explore the island and discovered exactly that: a picture-perfect, tropical right-hander that had a familiar glow about it he just couldn't shake. "It's the place I was looking for ever since I was a kid and I watched Swiss Family Robinson. I fell in love with the tropics, the reefs, and the treehouses. Lo and behold after I visited I found out that the movie was filmed in Tobago! It was full circle, and the waves were great."

Tony continued to travel to Tobago as much as he could between '75 to '89 when he finally zeroed in on a lot for $17,000. He re-financed his Montauk property, got the down payment, and achieved what every surfer hopes to obtain at one point in their life: his own slice of tropical surf heaven. Tony even used the construction skills he learned while working on Montauk Manor to frame the house himself, although he did call in contractors to build his infamous outhouse pictured to the left.

Now, with a roof over his head and warm waves at his disposal, Tony doubled down on surfing. Most competitive sports sagas are done and dusted by age 40, but at 41 Tony felt drawn to return to competition and the culture that brought him so much joy as a kid. He dove back in full force, entering and winning a contest in New Jersey. He carried that momentum into Da Bull's Surf Legends Classic in Jaco, Costa Rica, a contest organized by one of his childhood heroes, Greg Noll. In what would be yet another career-defining moment, Tony won the comp, which led to Noll asking him to create a pro model under his Da Bull surfboard label.

Now a team rider for one of surfing's most historic companies, Tony was on the road again. With surf culture emerging in East Asia and longboard surfing experiencing a resurgence in popularity, business was ripe for the taking. Tony would accompany Noll on annual trips to Japan while promoting Da Bull Surfboards, where he would continue to compete on his signature model. With friends who worked as flight attendants on United Airlines that had no problem sharing their flight coupons, Tony continued to explore new waves in Honolulu, Singapore, Thailand, and Bali, where he befriended Tony "Doris" Eltherington. Legendary pioneer of the Indonesian archipelago and one of Bali's maddest dogs, Tony joined Doris for his first Indo-boat trip to Lombok and Desert Point, one of the world's best, most remote waves.

With his own surfboard model came the opportunity to sell and distribute Da Bull surfboards. In 1993, Tony opened Real Surfers, his Montauk-based surf shop. Still needing to scratch the itch whenever the waves got good meant hiring someone to help manage the business. After striking up a conversation with a Carolina-born fisherman whose girlfriend, Charlotte, was stuck down south, Tony offered her the job so long as she could make it to New York. Charlotte's relationship didn't last, but she and Tony's friendship did, and they began dating in 1998. A year later, they decided to get married while sitting on the beach in Bali and, in 2000, said 'I Do' on Tony's property in Tobago… where he still only had an outhouse. The consummate gentleman, Tony, went down a week before the wedding and built an addition to the house, including a bathroom... and it's been happily ever after ever since!

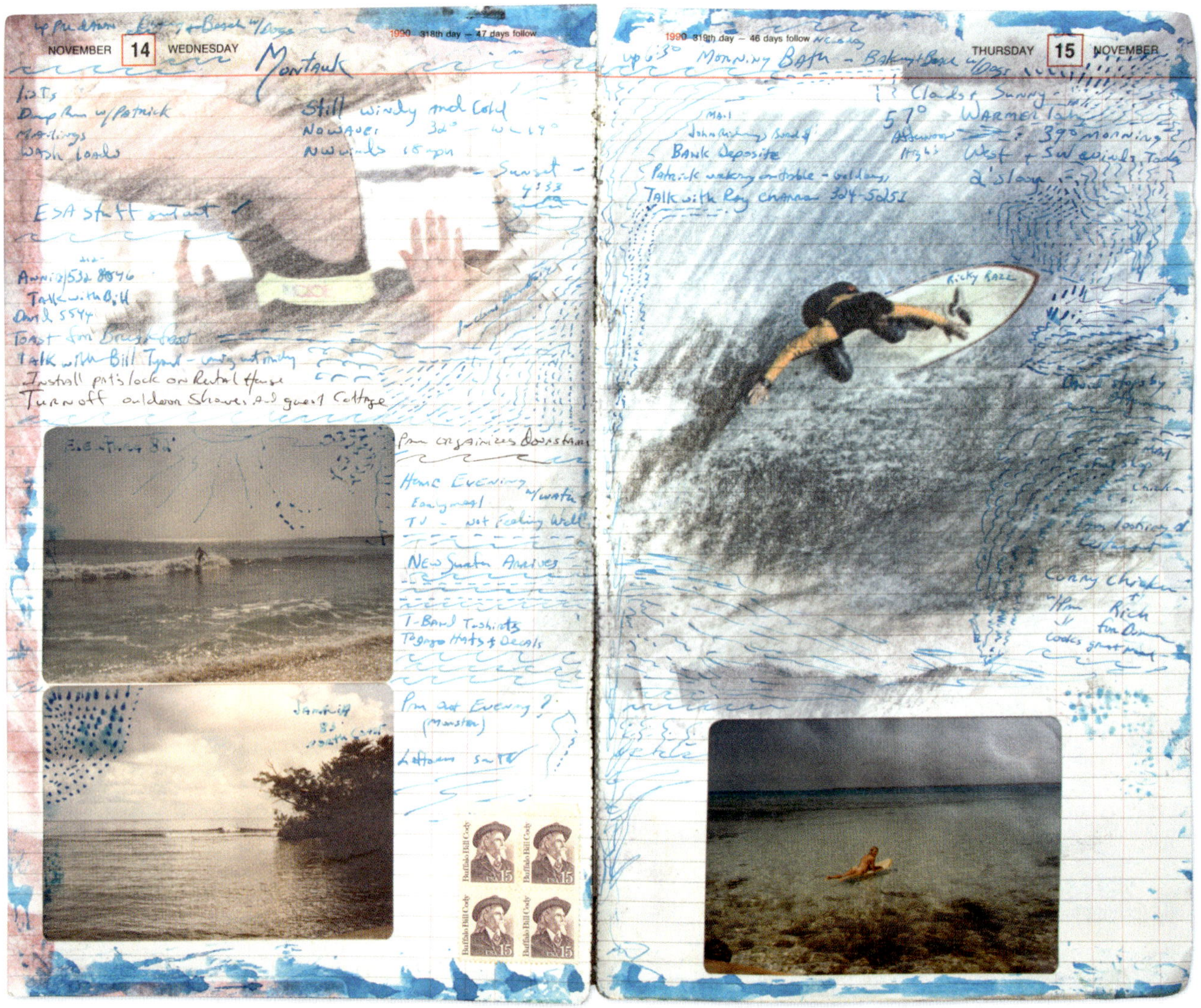

NOVEMBER 14 WEDNESDAY

1990 318th day – 47 days follow

1990 319th day – 46 days follow

THURSDAY 15 NOVEMBER

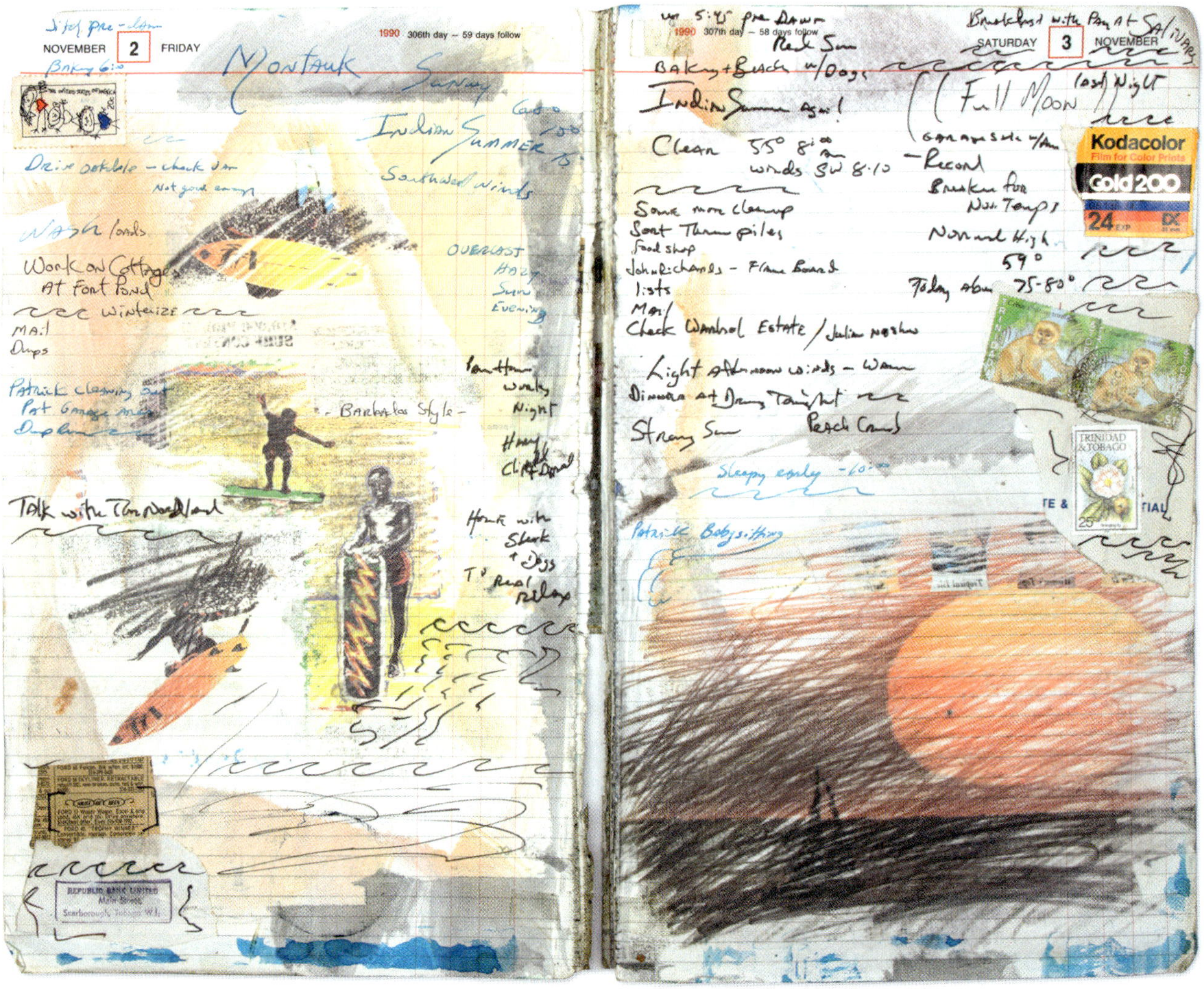

NOVEMBER 2 FRIDAY

1990 306th day – 59 days follow

1990 307th day – 58 days follow

SATURDAY 3 NOVEMBER

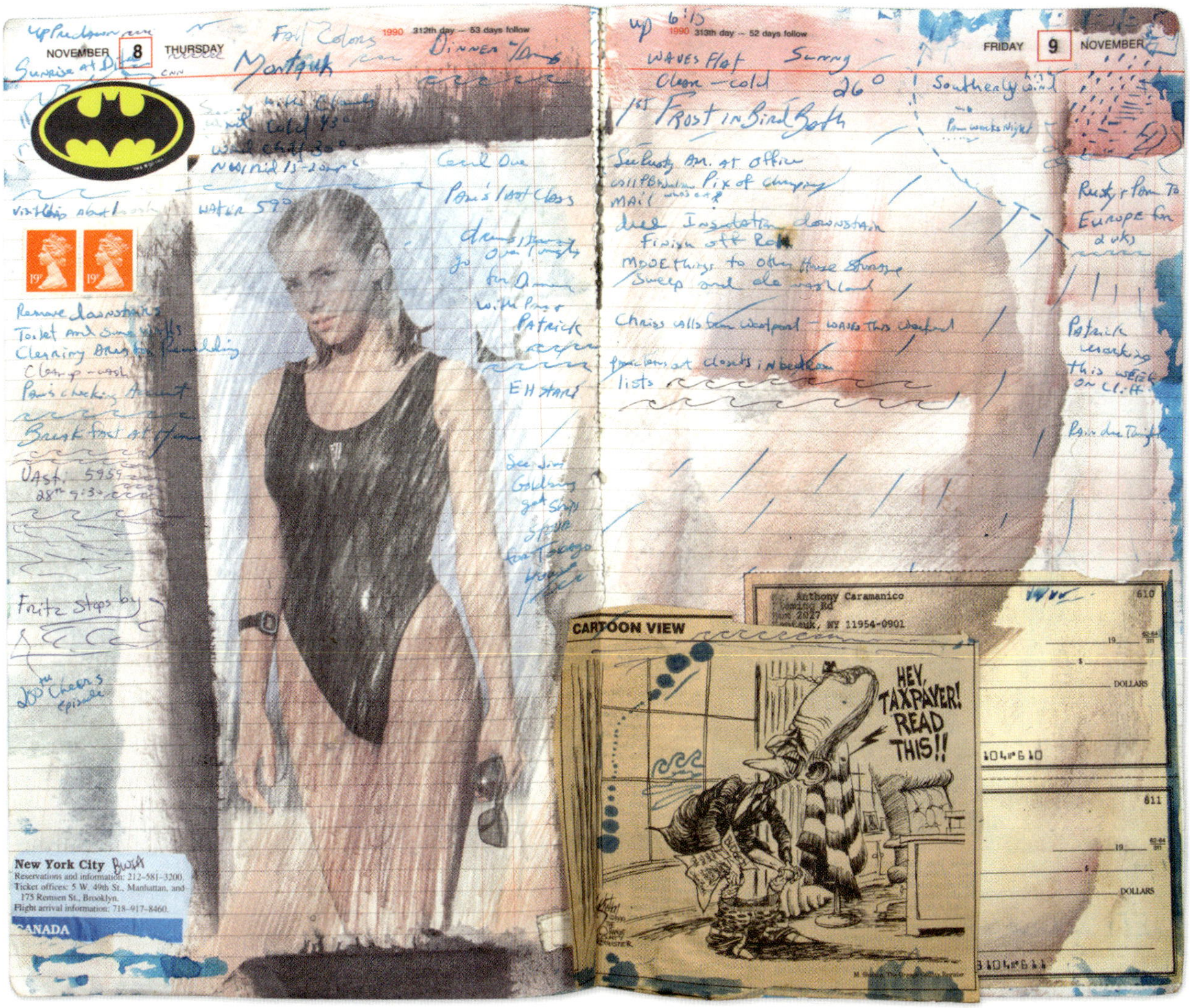

NOVEMBER 8 THURSDAY 1990 312th day – 53 days follow

New York City
Reservations and information: 212-581-3200.
Ticket offices: 5 W. 49th St., Manhattan, and 175 Remsen St., Brooklyn.
Flight arrival information: 718-917-8460.

CANADA

1990 313th day – 52 days follow FRIDAY 9 NOVEMBER

CARTOON VIEW

HEY, TAXPAYER! READ THIS!!

Anthony Caramanico
Montauk, NY 11954-0901

610
19
DOLLARS

611
19
DOLLARS

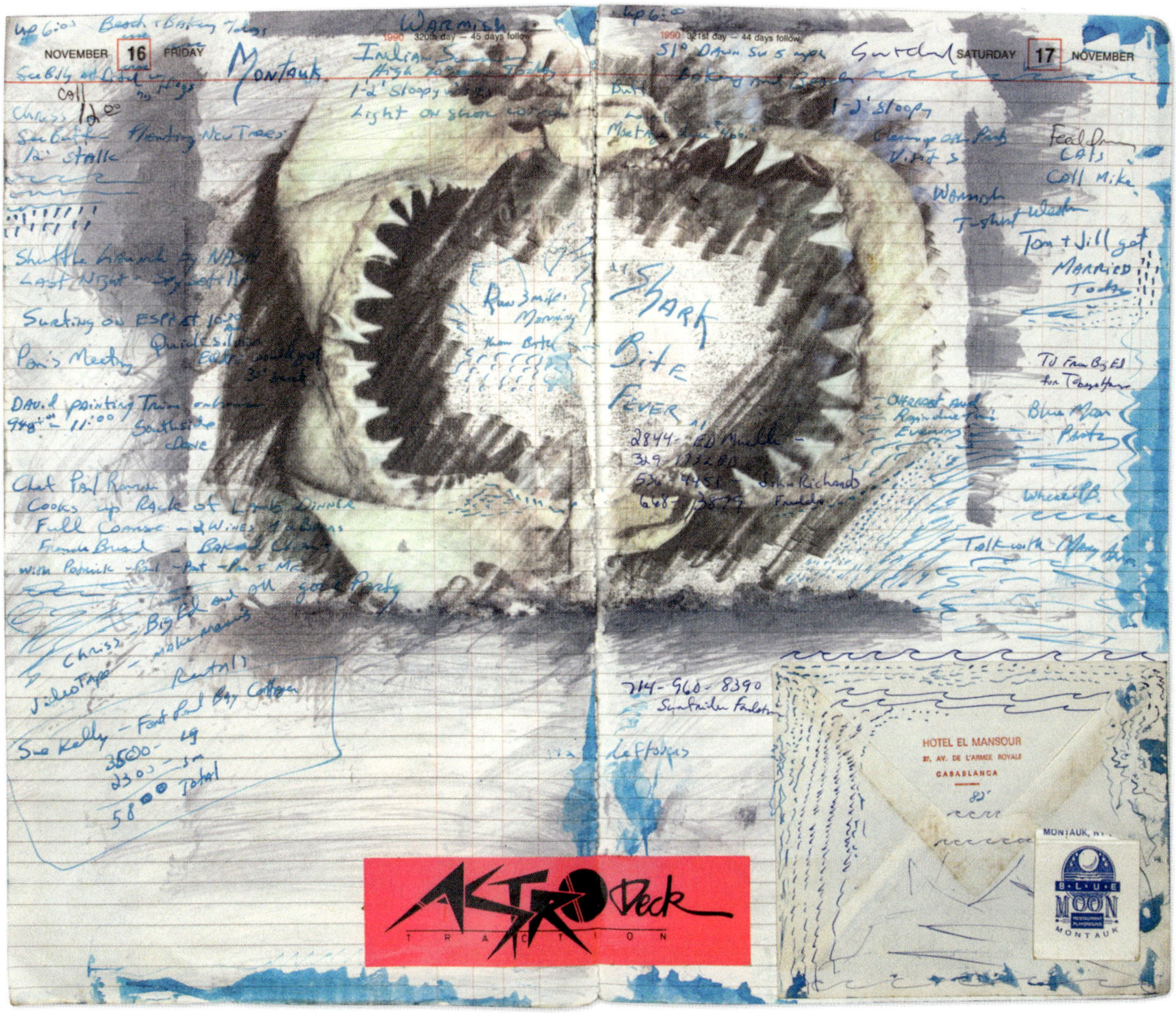

NOVEMBER 16 FRIDAY 1990 320th day – 45 days follow

1990 321st day – 44 days follow SATURDAY 17 NOVEMBER

HOTEL EL MANSOUR
27, AV. DE L'ARMEE ROYALE
CASABLANCA

ASTRO Deck
TRACTION

MONTAUK, N.Y.
BLUE MOON
MONTAUK

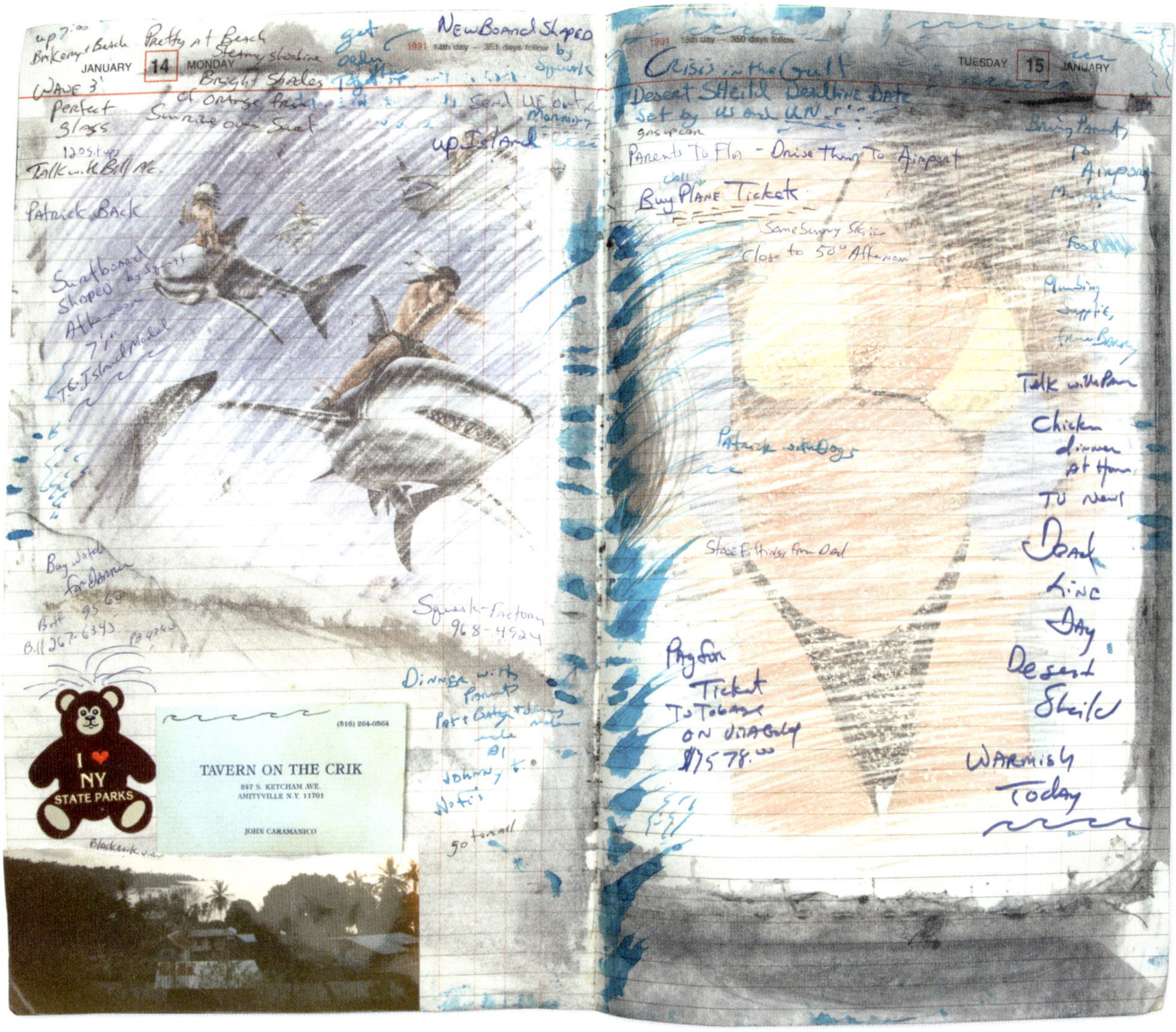

JANUARY 14 MONDAY
1991 14th day – 351 days follow

1991 15th day – 350 days follow
TUESDAY 15 JANUARY

I ♥ NY STATE PARKS

(516) 264-0504
TAVERN ON THE CRIK
847 S. KETCHAM AVE.
AMITYVILLE N.Y. 11701
JOHN CARAMANICO

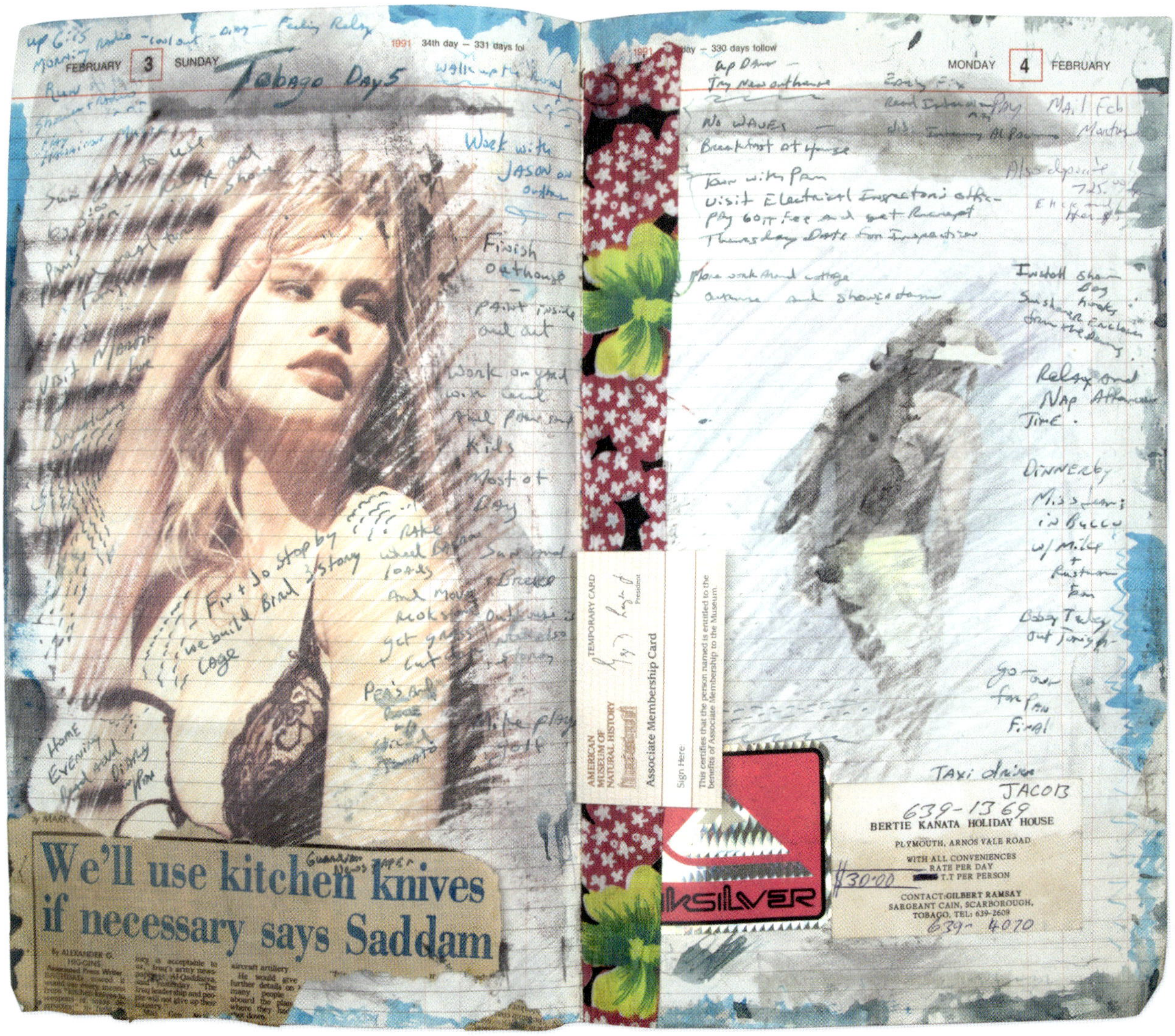

FEBRUARY 3 SUNDAY
1991 34th day – 331 days fol

day – 330 days follow
MONDAY 4 FEBRUARY

We'll use kitchen knives if necessary says Saddam

TEMPORARY CARD
AMERICAN MUSEUM OF NATURAL HISTORY
Associate Membership Card
Sign Here
This certifies that the person named is entitled to the benefits of Associate Membership to the Museum.

QUIKSILVER

BERTIE KANATA HOLIDAY HOUSE
PLYMOUTH, ARNOS VALE ROAD
WITH ALL CONVENIENCES
RATE PER DAY
T.T PER PERSON
CONTACT: GILBERT RAMSAY
SARGEANT CAIN, SCARBOROUGH,
TOBAGO, TEL: 639-2609

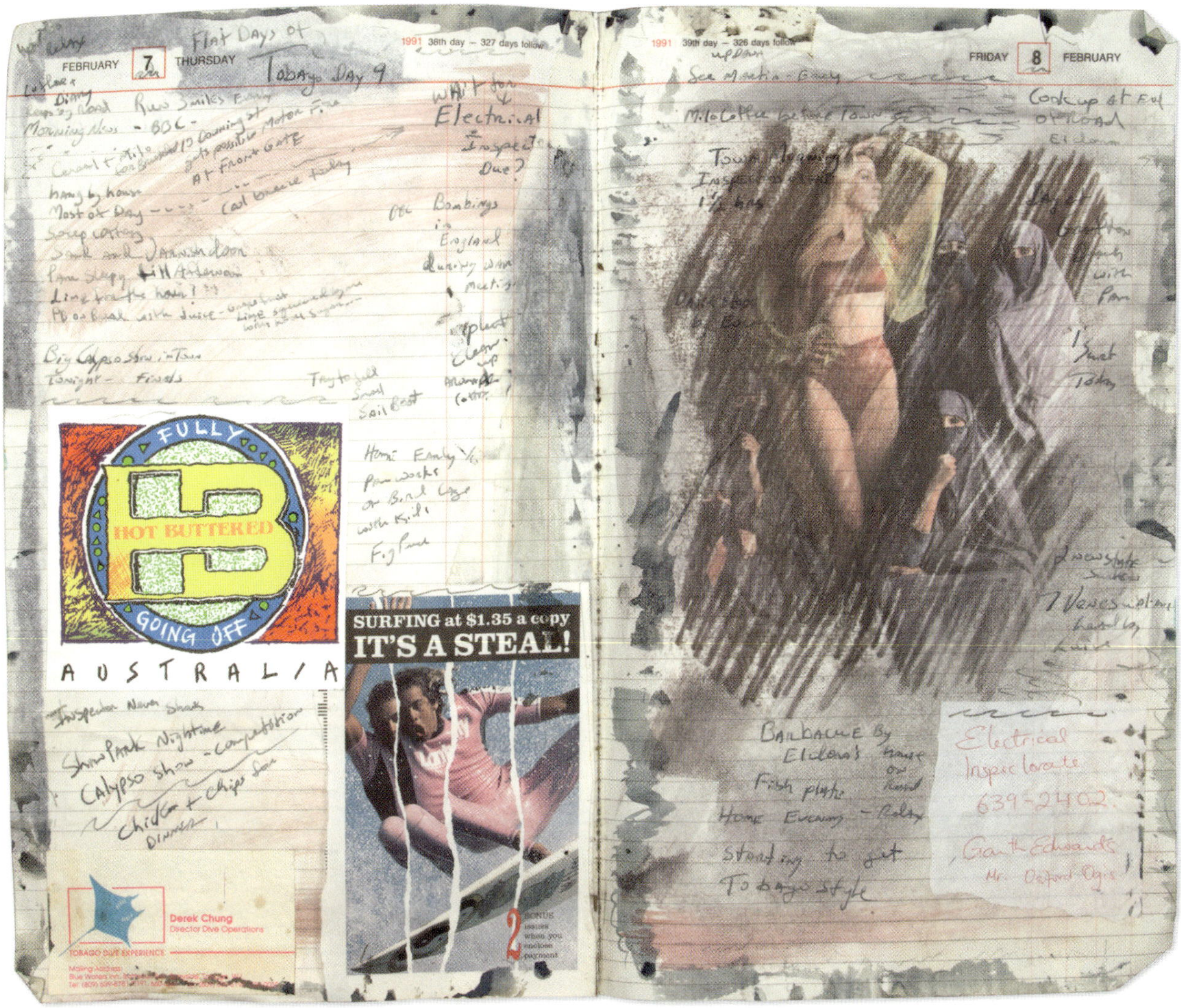

FEBRUARY 7 THURSDAY

1991 38th day – 327 days follow

FULLY
HOT BUTTERED
GOING OFF
AUSTRALIA

SURFING at $1.35 a copy
IT'S A STEAL!

Derek Chung
Director Dive Operations
TOBAGO DIVE EXPERIENCE

1991 39th day – 326 days follow

FRIDAY 8 FEBRUARY

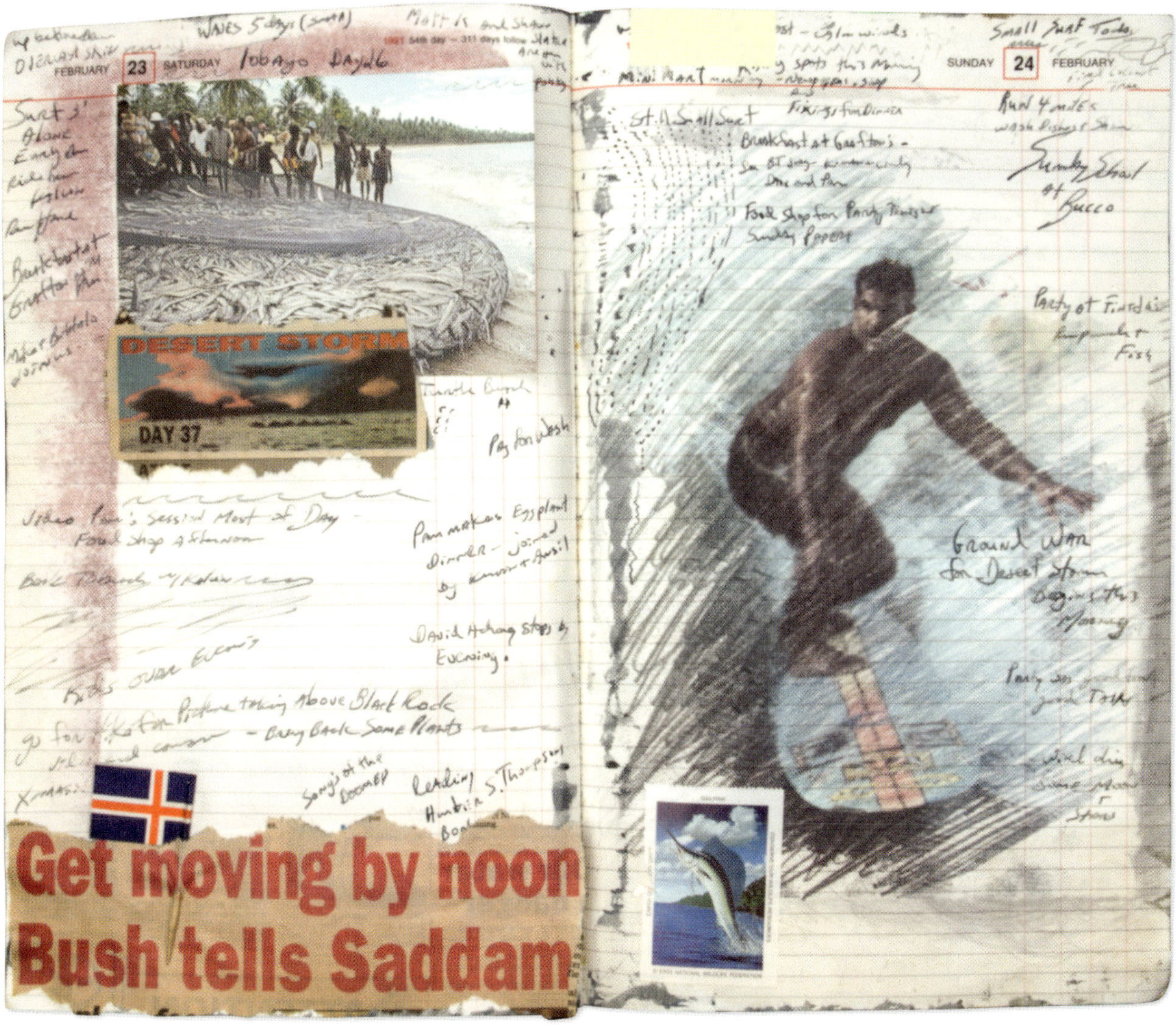

FEBRUARY 23 SATURDAY

1991 54th day – 311 days follow

DESERT STORM
DAY 37

Get moving by noon
Bush tells Saddam

SUNDAY 24 FEBRUARY

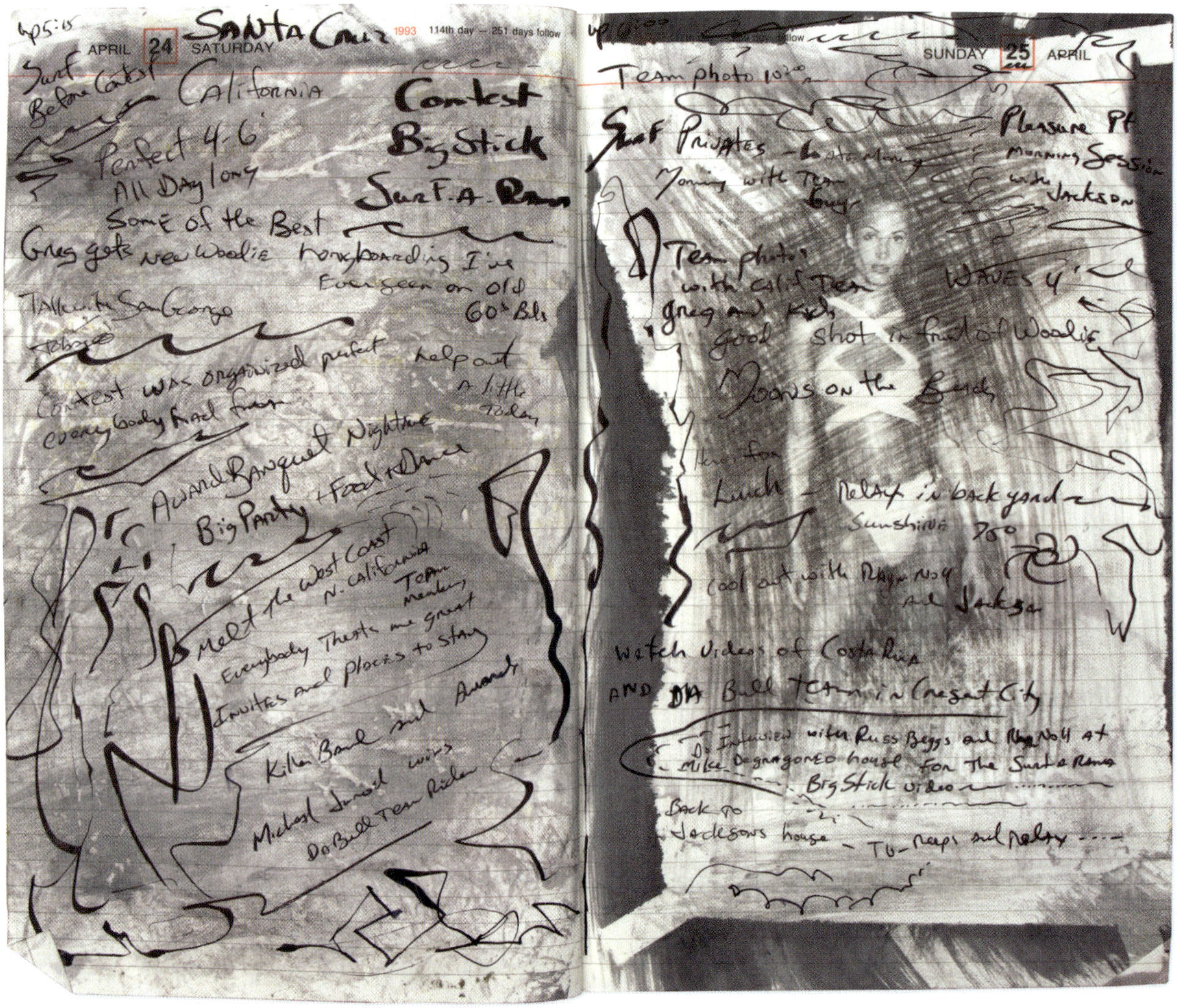

APRIL 24 SATURDAY 1993 114th day – 251 days follow

Santa Cruz California

Contest Big Stick Surf-A-Rama

Surf Before Contest

Perfect 4-6' All Day long

Some of the Best longboarding I've Ever seen on old 60's Bds

Greg gets new Woodie

Contest was organized perfect

everybody had fun

Award Banquet Nighttime

Big Party + Food + Dance

Meet the West Coast N. California Team members

Everybody There are great

Invites and Places to stay

Killer Band and Awards

Michael Junod wins DaBull Team Rider

SUNDAY 25 APRIL

Team photo 10:00

Surf Privates

Pleasure Pt Morning Session with Jackson

Morning with Team Guys

Team photos with Calif Team Greg and Kids

WAVES 4'

Good shot in front of Woodie

Moons on the Beach

Lunch – Relax in back yard

Sunshine 75°

Cool out with Ragu Noll and Jackson

Watch Videos of Costa Rica AND DA Bull Team in Crescent City

Do Interview with Russ Beggs and Ragu Noll at Mike Dogangoreo house for the Surf a Rama Big Stick video

Back to Jacksons house – TV naps and relax

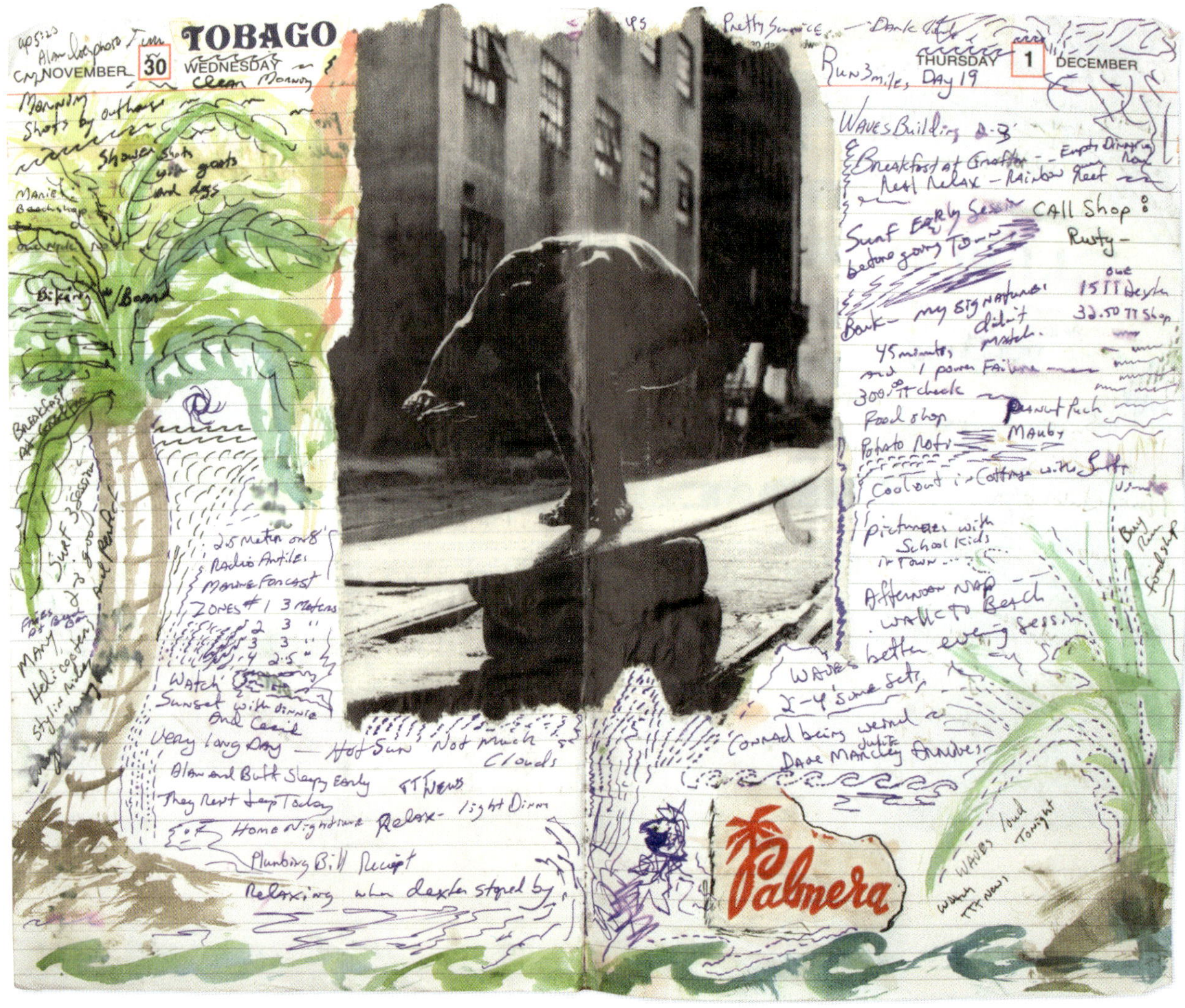

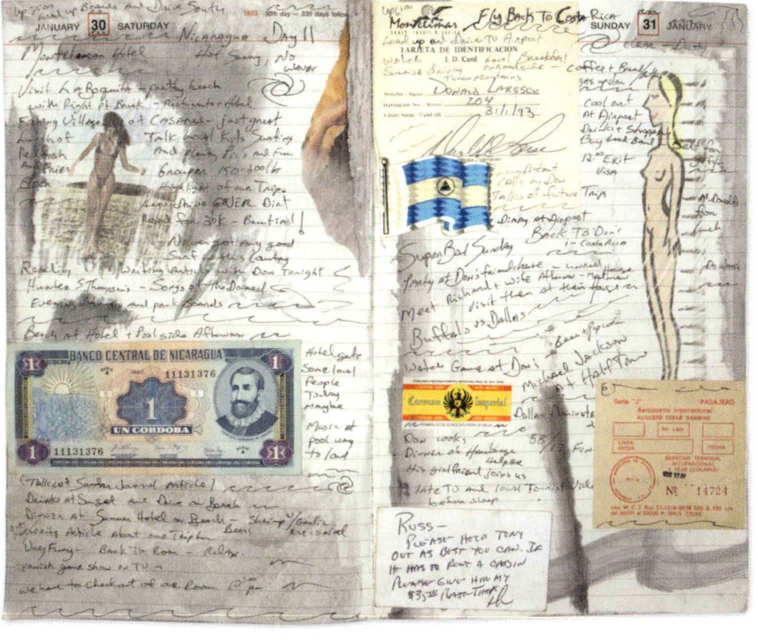
BANCO CENTRAL DE NICARAGUA
UN CORDOBA
JANUARY 30 SATURDAY
SUNDAY 31 JANUARY

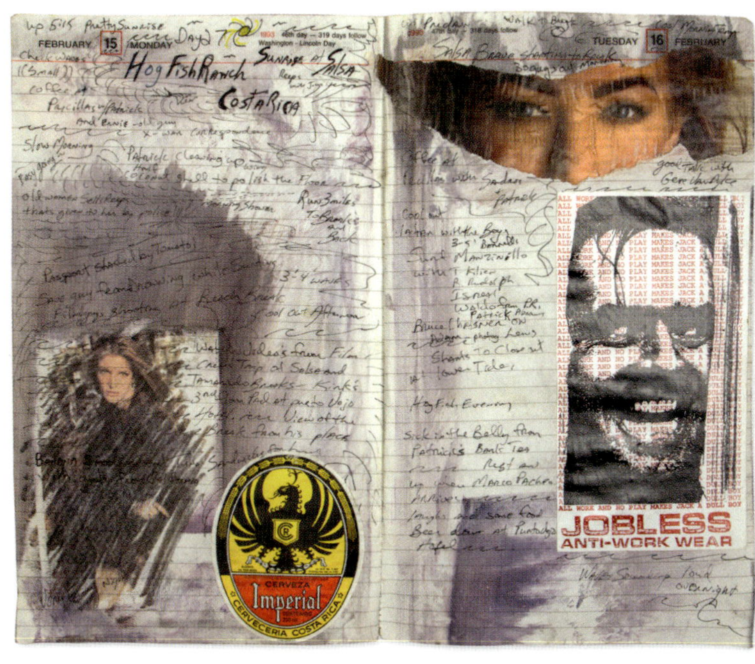
FEBRUARY 15 MONDAY
TUESDAY 16 FEBRUARY
JOBLESS
ANTI-WORK WEAR
CERVEZA
Imperial
CERVECERIA COSTA RICA

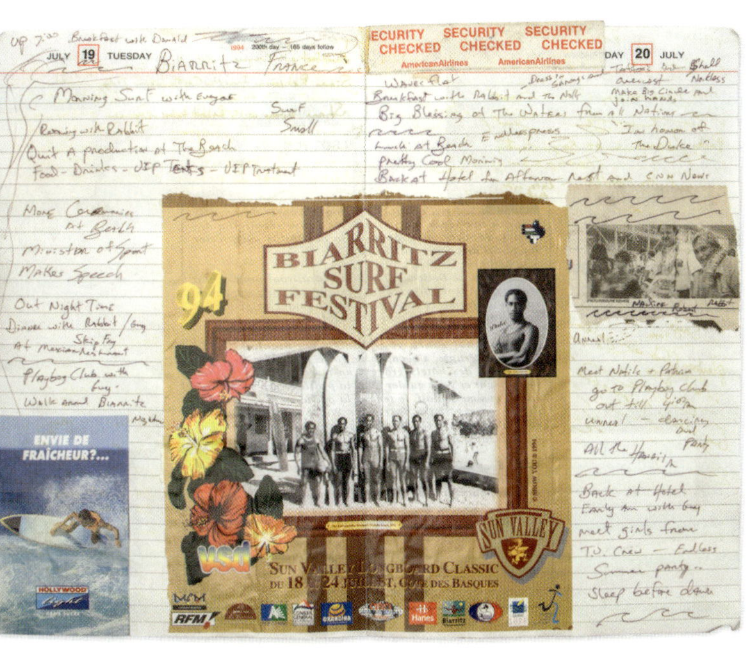
JULY 19 TUESDAY
20 JULY
SECURITY CHECKED
BIARRITZ SURF FESTIVAL
94
ENVIE DE FRAÎCHEUR?...
SUN VALLEY

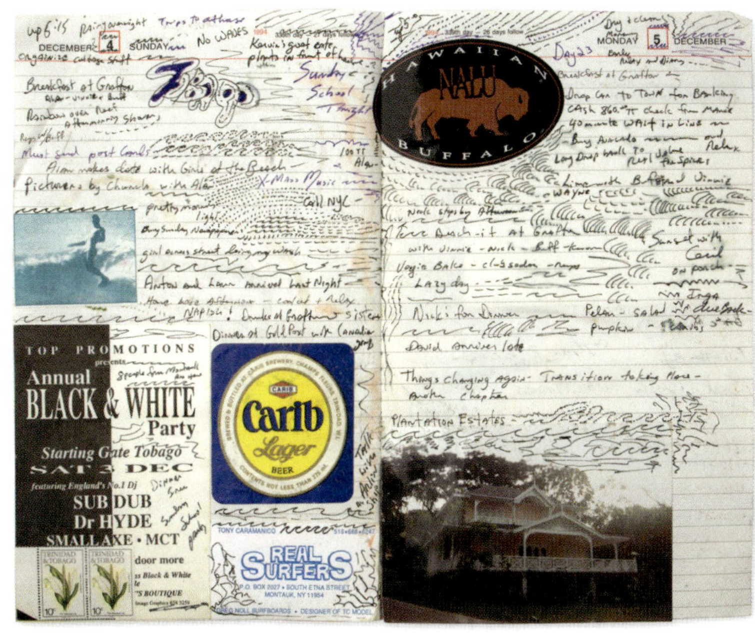
DECEMBER 4 SUNDAY
MONDAY 5 DECEMBER
HAWAIIAN
NALU
BUFFALO
TOP PROMOTIONS
Annual
BLACK & WHITE
Party
Starting Gate Tobago
SAT 3 DEC
SUB DUB
Dr HYDE
SMALL AXE • MCT
Carib
Lager
REAL SURFERS

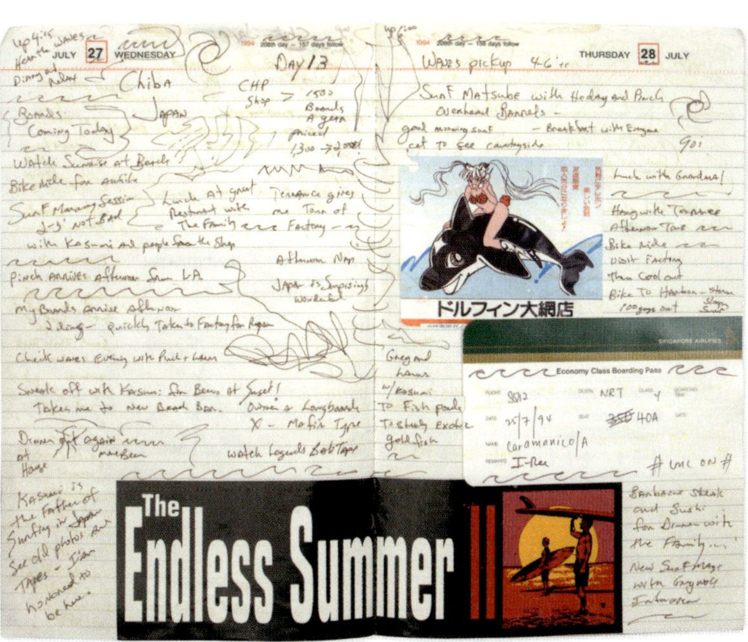
JULY 27 WEDNESDAY
THURSDAY 28 JULY
ドルフィン大網店
Economy Class Boarding Pass
The Endless Summer II

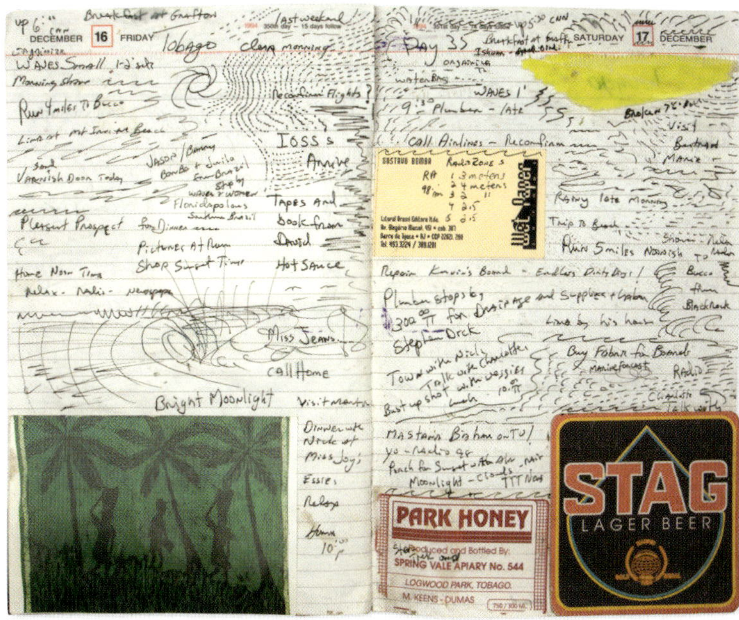
DECEMBER 16 FRIDAY
SATURDAY 17 DECEMBER
PARK HONEY
SPRING VALE APIARY No. 544
STAG
LAGER BEER

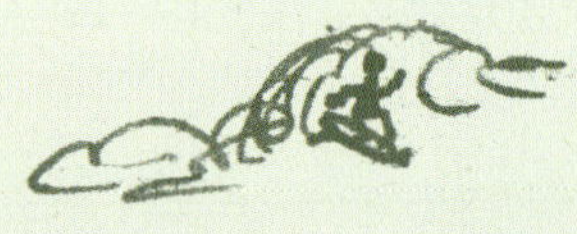

THE BEST RUN OF WAVES I'VE EVER HAD WAS IN TOBAGO. I SPENT SO MUCH TIME THERE, BUT I'LL NEVER FORGET DECEMBER OF '95. I WAS THERE WITH MY FRIEND DAVE FROM SANTA CRUZ WHO WAS A REALLY GOOD SURFER. WE HAD 28 OUT OF 30 DAYS OF SURFING WITH JUST A COUPLE GUYS OUT. WE HAD SO MUCH SURF. IT NEVER DROPPED BELOW 4 FOOT AND SOME DAYS WAS 10+ FEET AND PERFECT. IT WAS DREAMY.

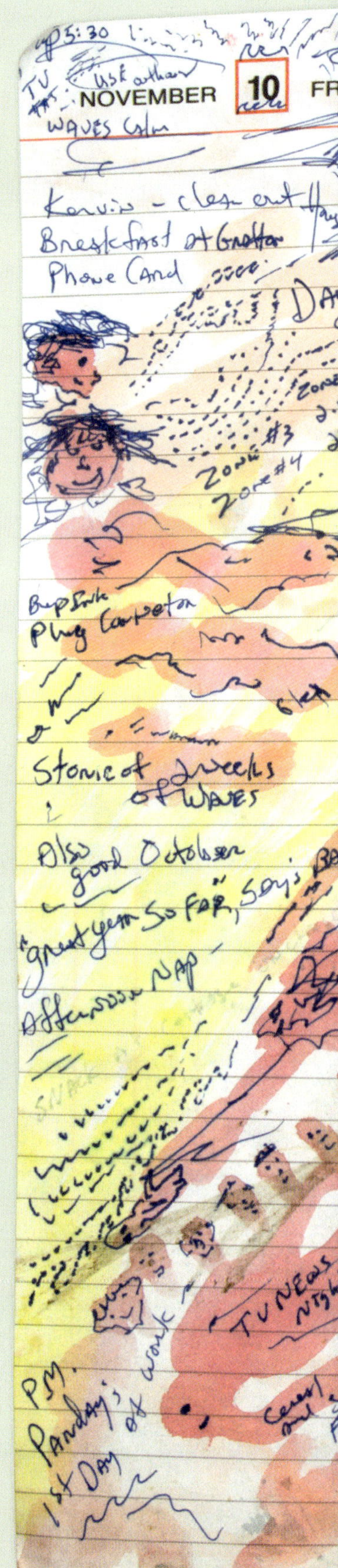

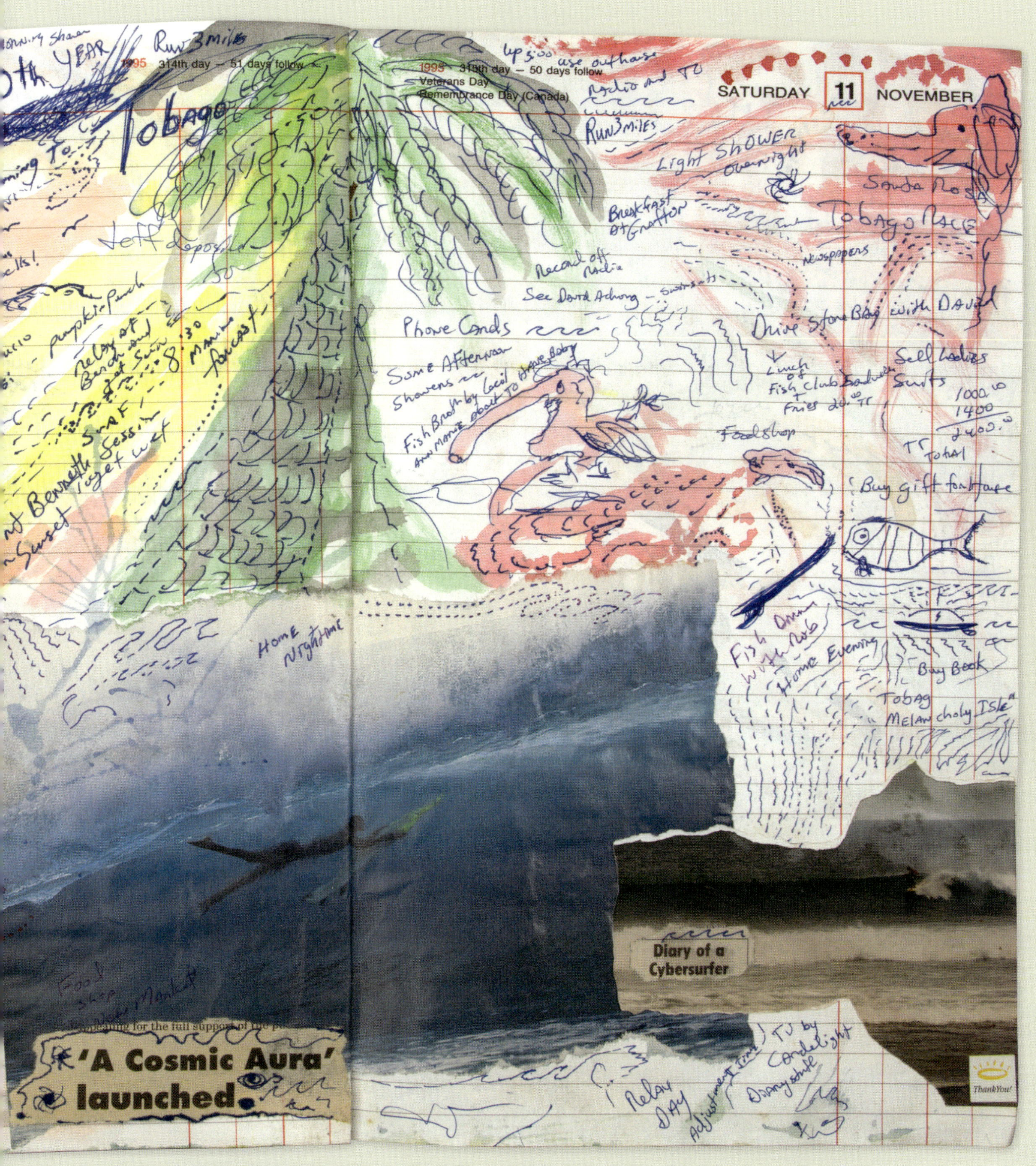
1995 314th day — 51 days follow
1995 315th day — 50 days follow
Veterans Day
Remembrance Day (Canada)
SATURDAY 11 NOVEMBER
Tobago
Run 3 miles
Light SHOWER overnight
Phone Cards
Drive Store Bay with David
Buy gift for Haze
Home Evening
Buy Book
Diary of a Cybersurfer
'A Cosmic Aura' launched
ThankYou!

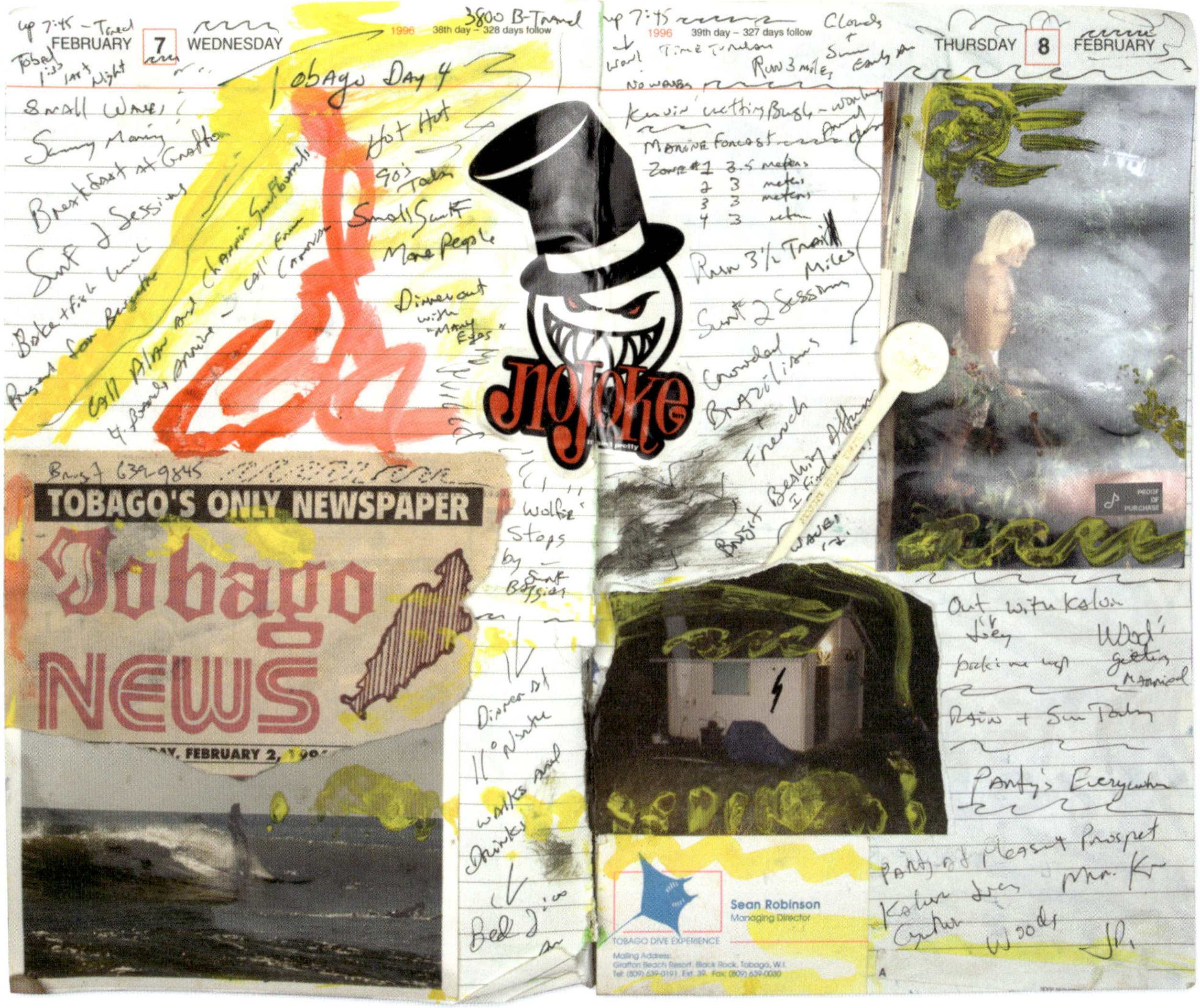

FEBRUARY 7 WEDNESDAY

1996 38th day – 328 days follow

Tobago Day 4

TOBAGO'S ONLY NEWSPAPER

Tobago NEWS

1996 39th day – 327 days follow

THURSDAY 8 FEBRUARY

Sean Robinson
Managing Director
TOBAGO DIVE EXPERIENCE

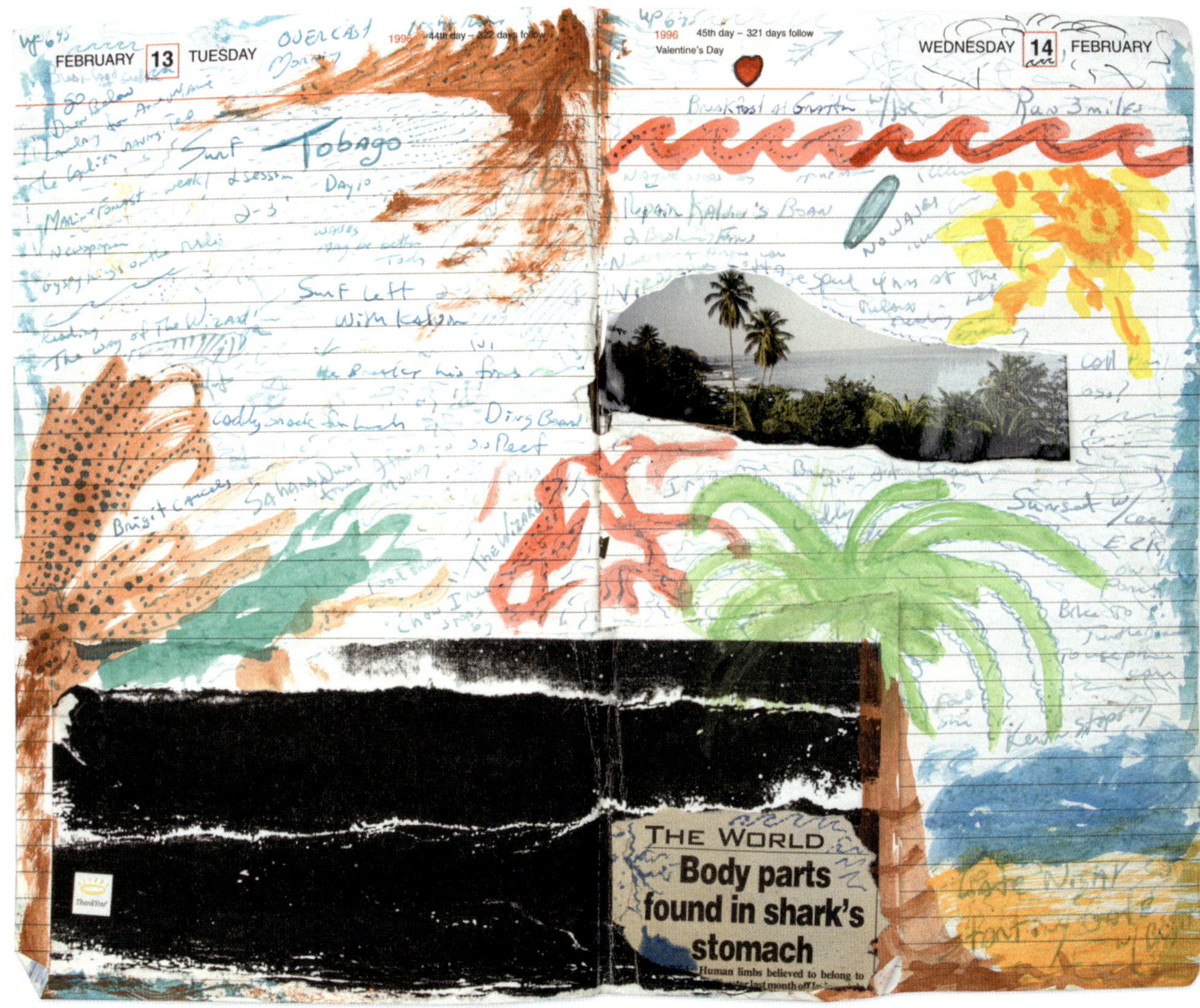

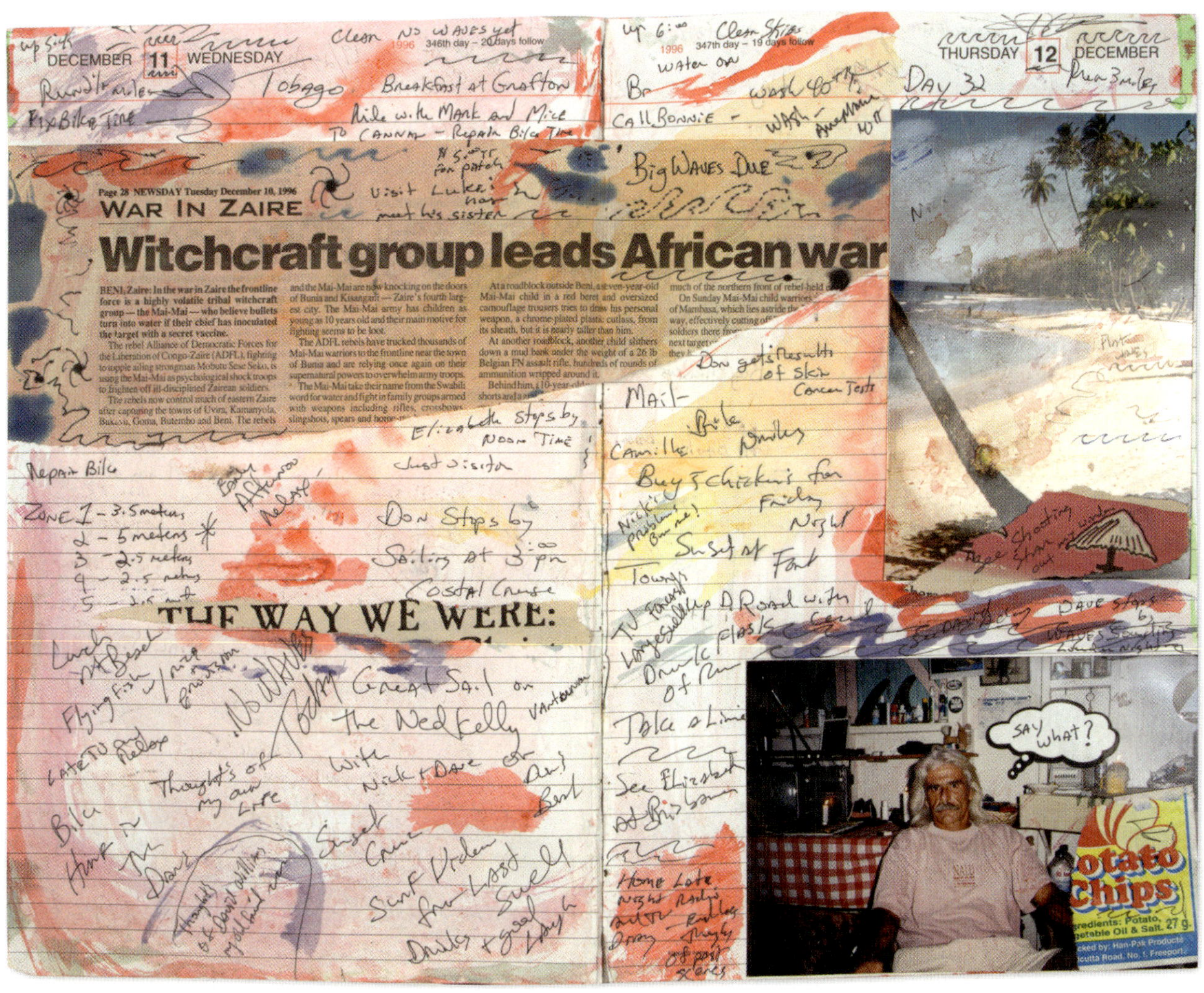
DECEMBER 11 WEDNESDAY
1996 346th day – 20 days follow
Tobago
Breakfast at Grafton
1996 347th day – 19 days follow
THURSDAY 12 DECEMBER
Day 32
Big Waves Due
Page 28 NEWSDAY Tuesday December 10, 1996
WAR IN ZAIRE
Witchcraft group leads African war
Repair Bike
Don Stops by
Sailing at 3 pm
THE WAY WE WERE:
Great Sail on The Ned Kelly
Mail
Buy Chicken for Friday Night
Sunset at Fort
SAY WHAT?
Potato Chips

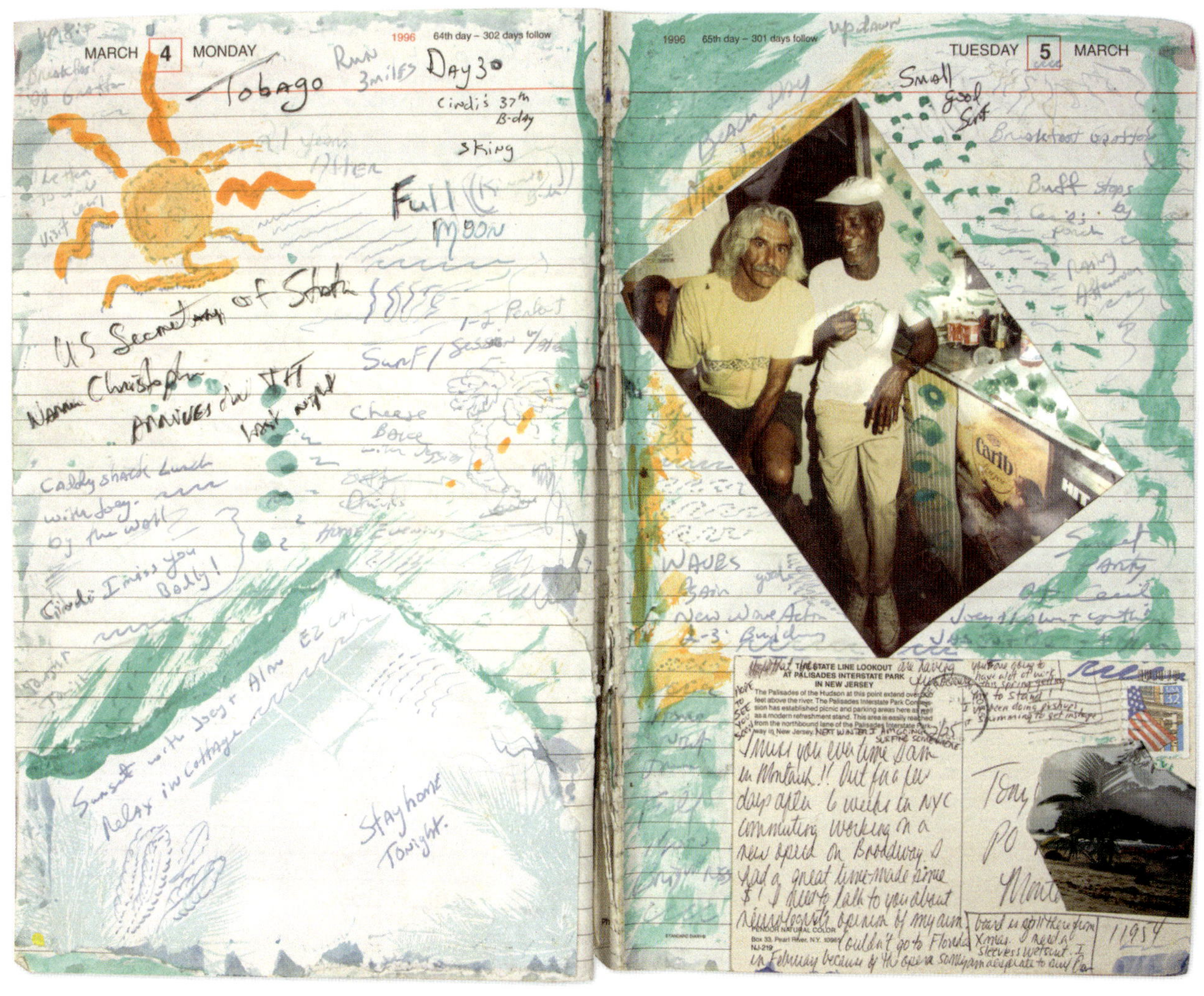
MARCH 4 MONDAY
1996 64th day – 302 days follow
Tobago
Run 3 miles
Day 30
Full Moon
US Secretary of State
Caddy shack Lunch
Stay home Tonight
1996 65th day – 301 days follow
TUESDAY 5 MARCH
Small good Surf
THE STATE LINE LOOKOUT AT PALISADES INTERSTATE PARK IN NEW JERSEY
Carib

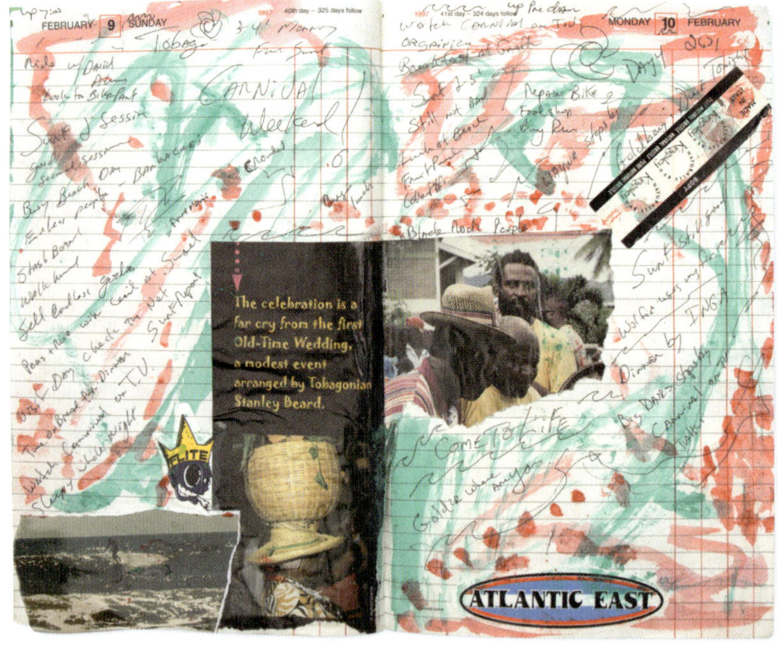
FEBRUARY 9 SUNDAY
MONDAY 10 FEBRUARY
The celebration is a far cry from the first Old-Time Wedding, a modest event arranged by Tobagonian Stanley Beard.
ATLANTIC EAST

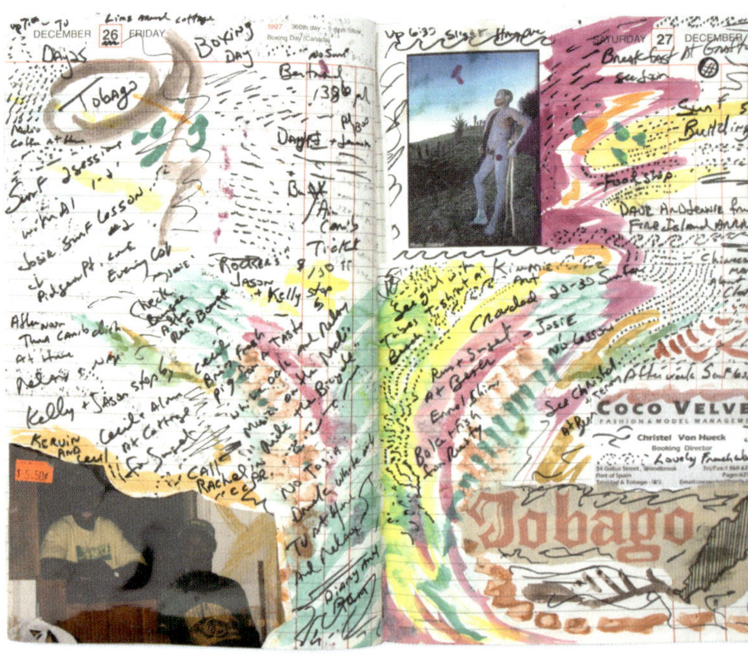
DECEMBER 26 FRIDAY
27 DECEMBER
COCO VELVE
Christel Von Hueck
Booking Director
Tobago

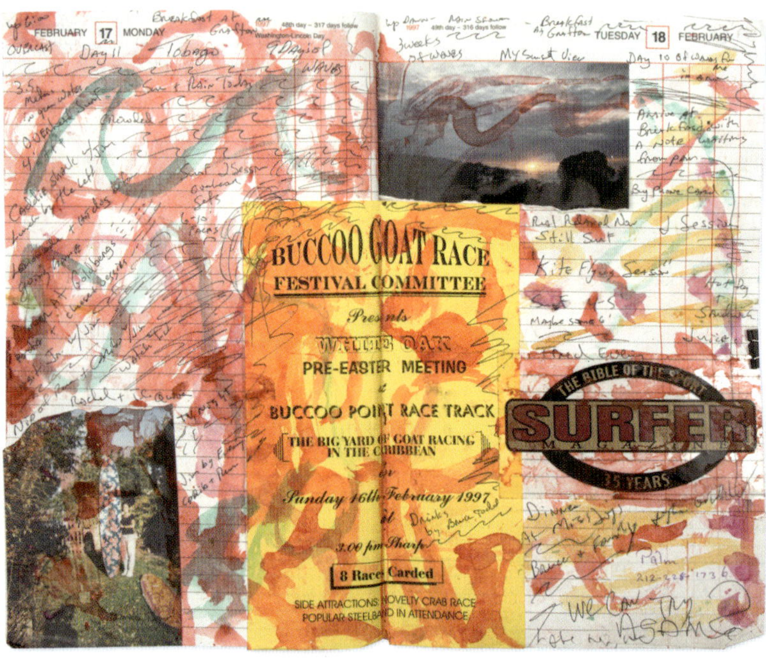
FEBRUARY 17 MONDAY
TUESDAY 18 FEBRUARY
BUCCOO GOAT RACE
FESTIVAL COMMITTEE
Presents
PRE-EASTER MEETING
BUCCOO POINT RACE TRACK
THE BIG YARD OF GOAT RACING IN THE CARIBBEAN
Sunday 16th February 1997
3.00 pm Sharp
8 Races Carded
SIDE ATTRACTIONS NOVELTY CRAB RACE
POPULAR STEELBAND IN ATTENDANCE
THE BIBLE OF THE SPORT
SURFER
35 YEARS

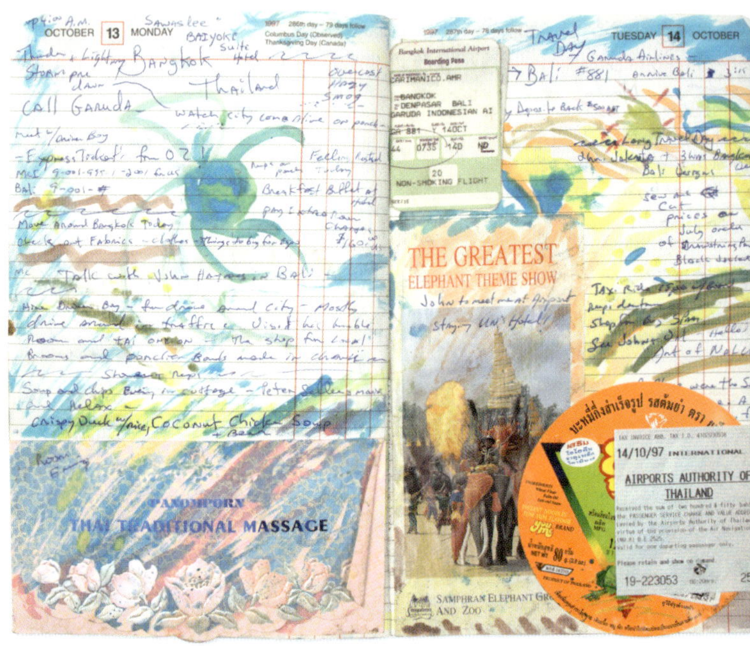
OCTOBER 13 MONDAY
TUESDAY 14 OCTOBER
Bangkok International Airport
Boarding Pass
BANGKOK
DENPASAR BALI
GARUDA INDONESIAN AI
NON-SMOKING FLIGHT
THE GREATEST
ELEPHANT THEME SHOW
THAI TRADITIONAL MASSAGE
14/10/97 INTERNATIONAL
AIRPORTS AUTHORITY OF THAILAND
19-223053
SAMPHRAN ELEPHANT GROUND AND ZOO

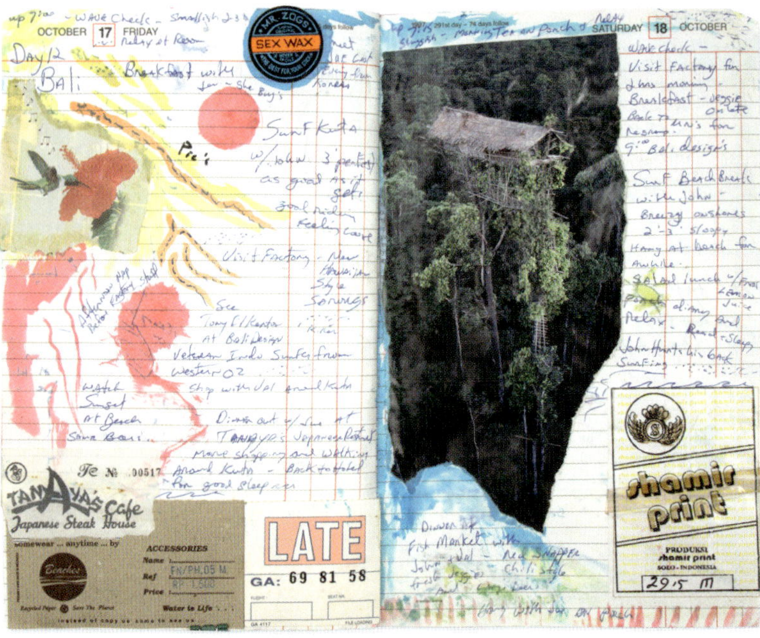
OCTOBER 17 FRIDAY
SATURDAY 18 OCTOBER
SEX WAX
TANAYA'S Cafe
Japanese Steak House
No 00517
ACCESSORIES
LATE
GA: 69 81 58
shamir print
29.5 m

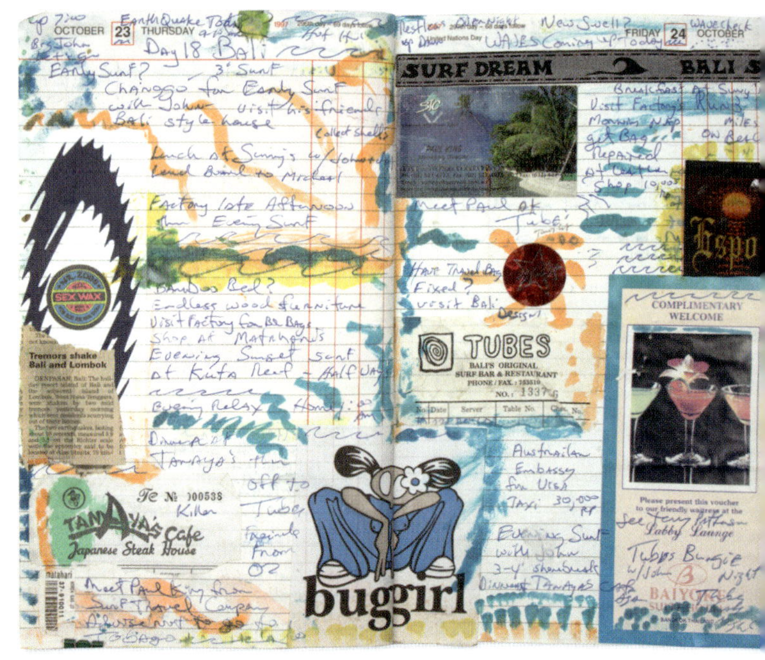
OCTOBER 23 THURSDAY
FRIDAY 24 OCTOBER
SURF DREAM
BALI
SEX WAX
Tremors shake Bali and Lombok
TUBES
BALI'S ORIGINAL SURF BAR & RESTAURANT
COMPLIMENTARY
WELCOME
TANAYA'S Cafe
Japanese Steak House
No 00538
buggirl

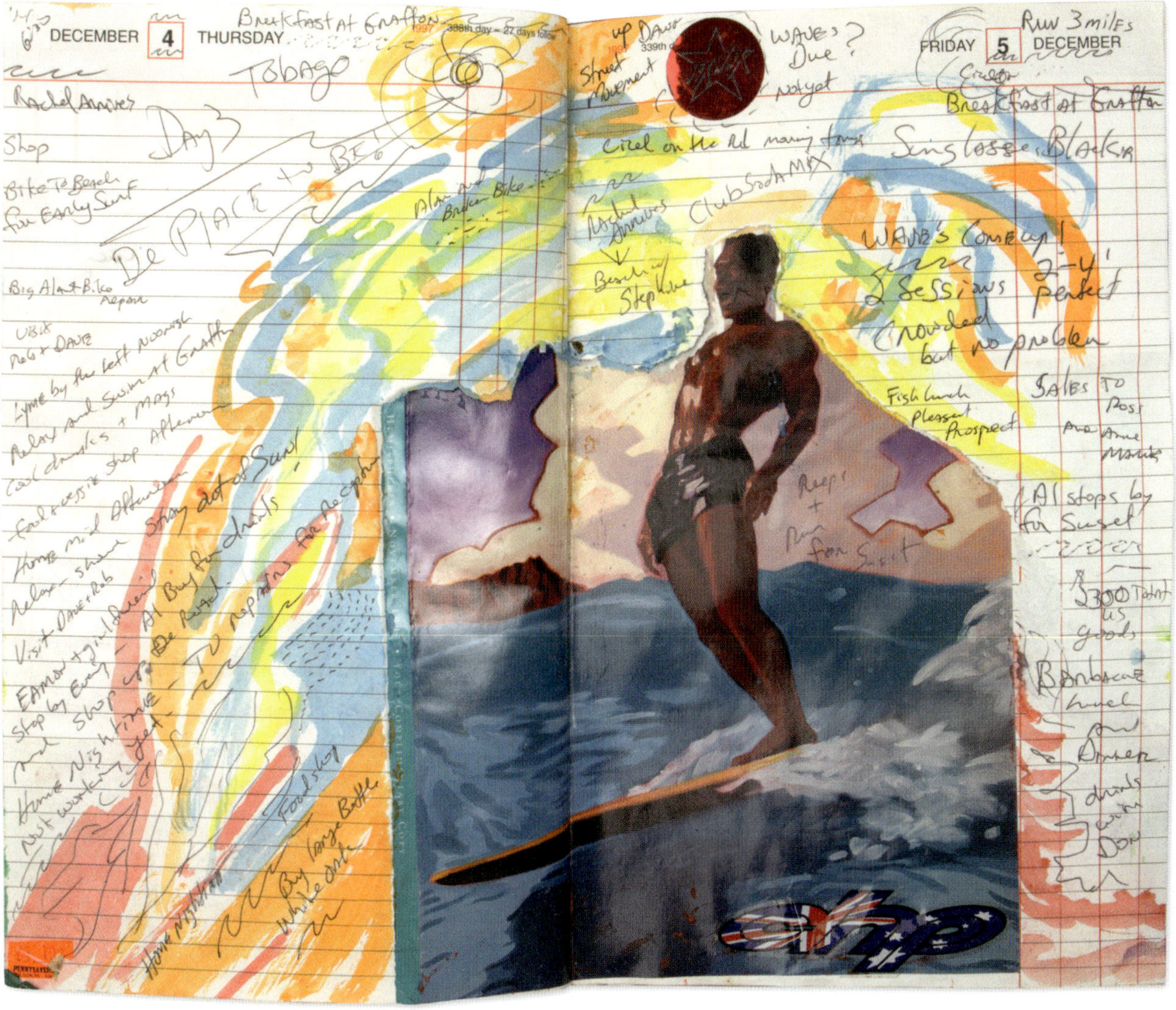

DECEMBER 4 THURSDAY

Breakfast at Grafton

Tobago

Day 3

Be place to be

FRIDAY 5 DECEMBER

Run 3 miles

Breakfast at Grafton

Waves? Due? Not yet

Waves Come up! 3-4' perfect
2 sessions
Crowded but no problem

Fish lunch

Sales to

Barbecue

Dinner

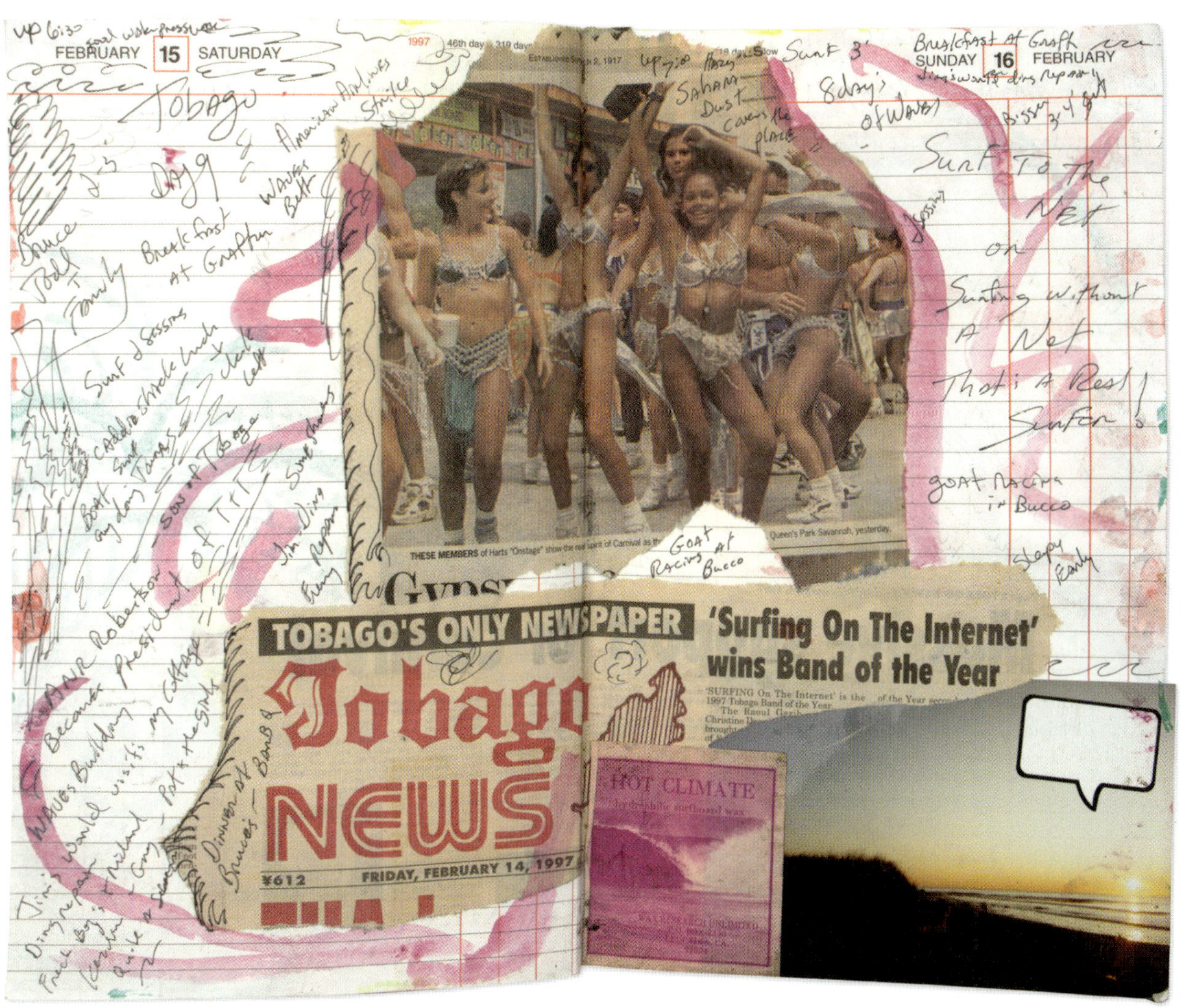

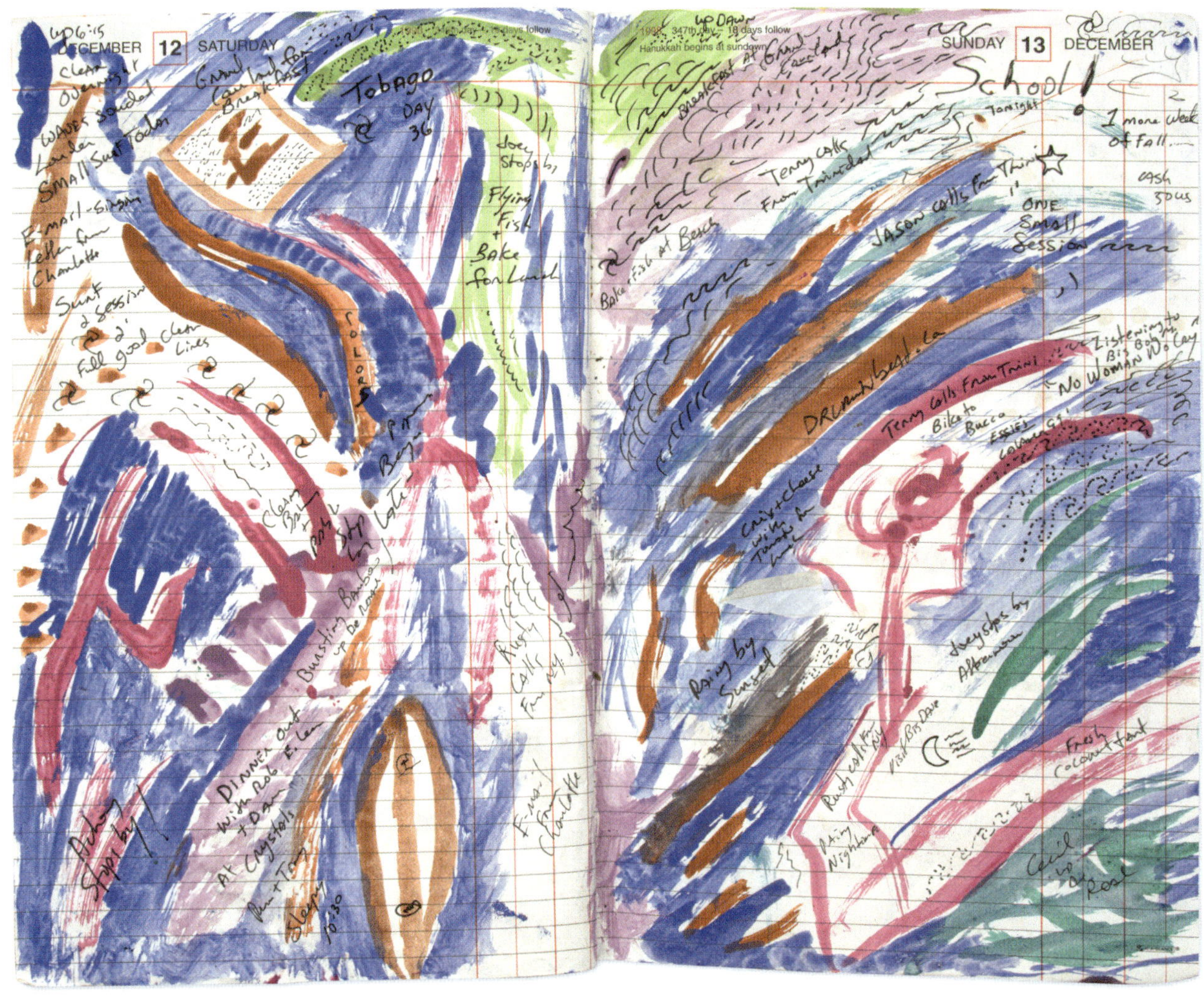
DECEMBER 12 SATURDAY
SUNDAY 13 DECEMBER
Tobago
School!

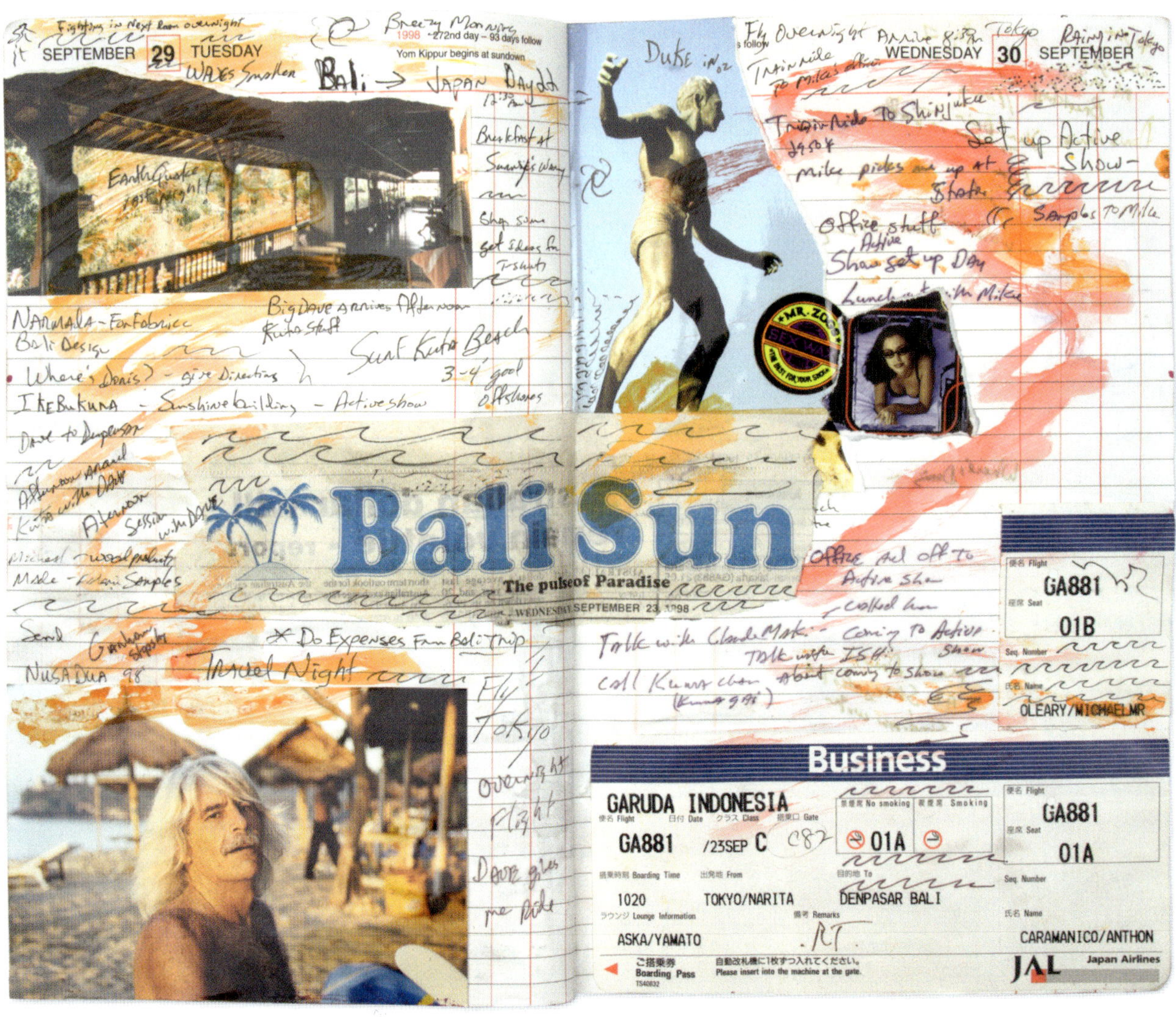
SEPTEMBER 29 TUESDAY
1998 272nd day – 93 days follow
Yom Kippur begins at sundown
WEDNESDAY 30 SEPTEMBER
Bali Sun
The pulse of Paradise
WEDNESDAY SEPTEMBER 23, 1998
GA881
01B
OLEARY/MICHAELMR
Business
GARUDA INDONESIA
GA881
/23SEP C
01A
1020
TOKYO/NARITA
DENPASAR BALI
ASKA/YAMATO
CARAMANICO/ANTHON
Boarding Pass
JAL Japan Airlines

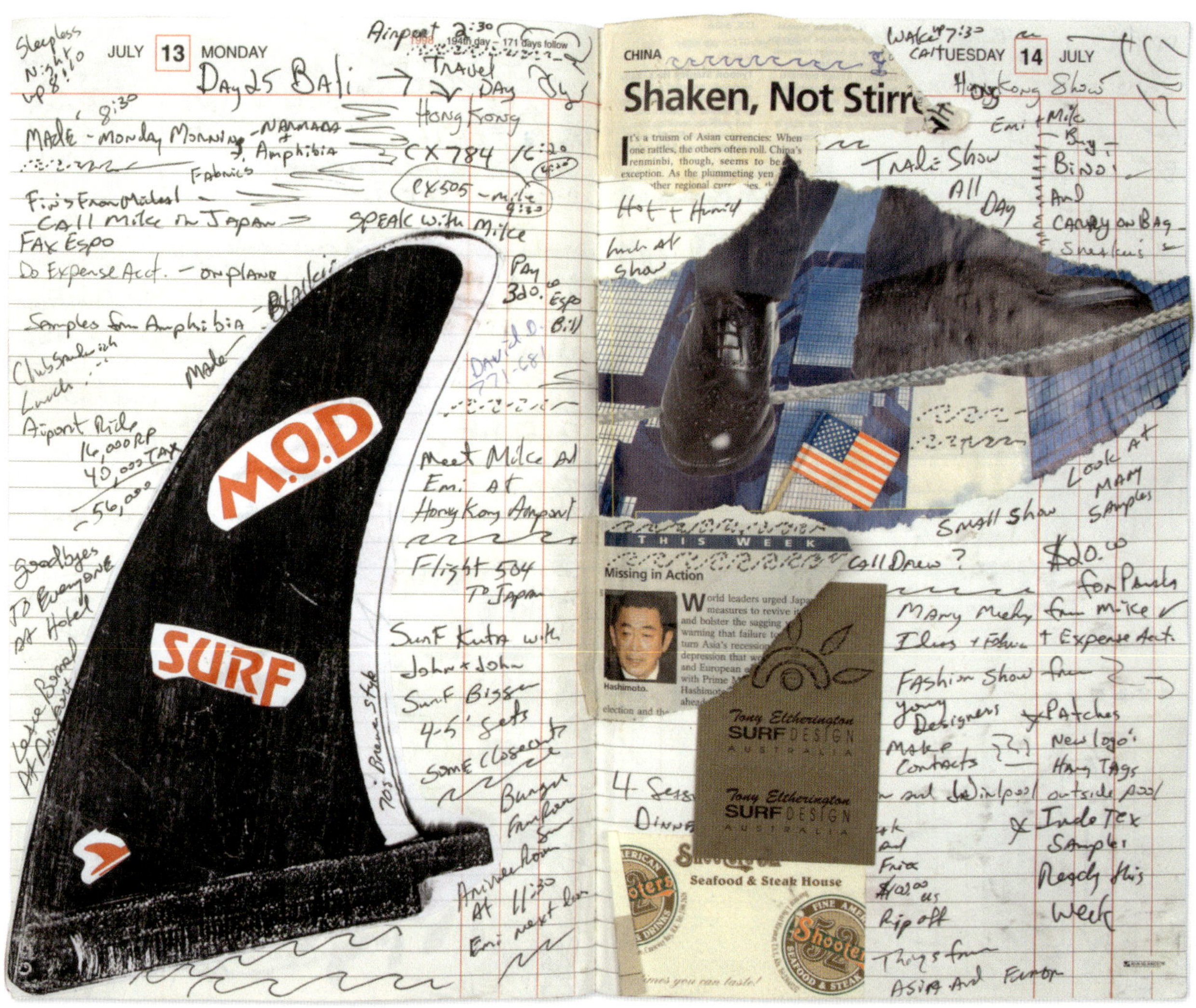
JULY 13 MONDAY
M.O.D
SURF
CHINA
Shaken, Not Stirr
TUESDAY 14 JULY
THIS WEEK
Missing in Action
Hashimoto
Tony Ettherington
SURF DESIGN
AUSTRALIA
Seafood & Steak House
Shooters

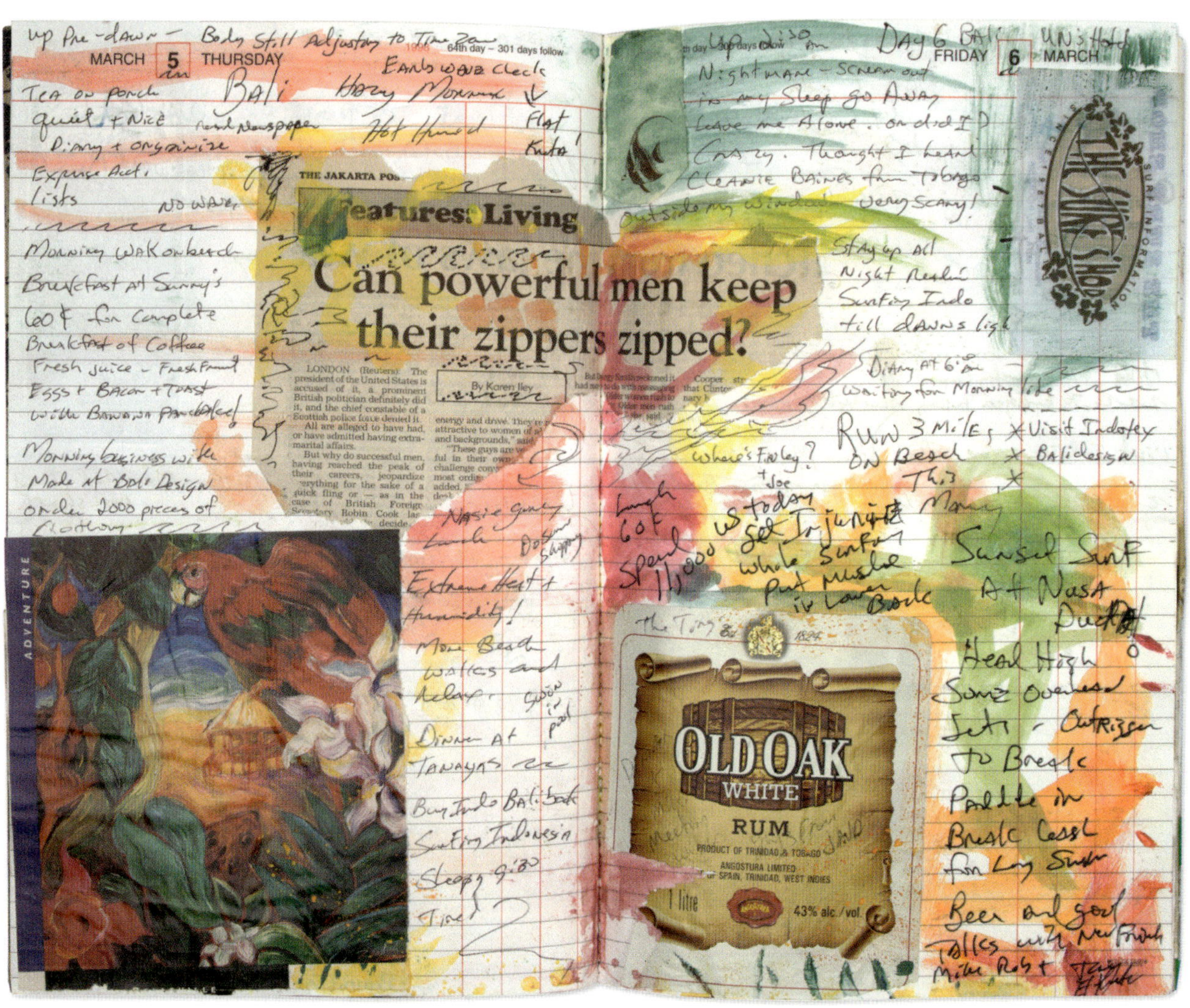
MARCH 5 THURSDAY
64th day – 301 days follow
THE JAKARTA POST
Features: Living
Can powerful men keep their zippers zipped?
By Karen Iley
ADVENTURE
FRIDAY 6 MARCH
THE SURF SHOP
SURF INFORMATION
OLD OAK
WHITE
RUM
1 litre
43% alc./vol.

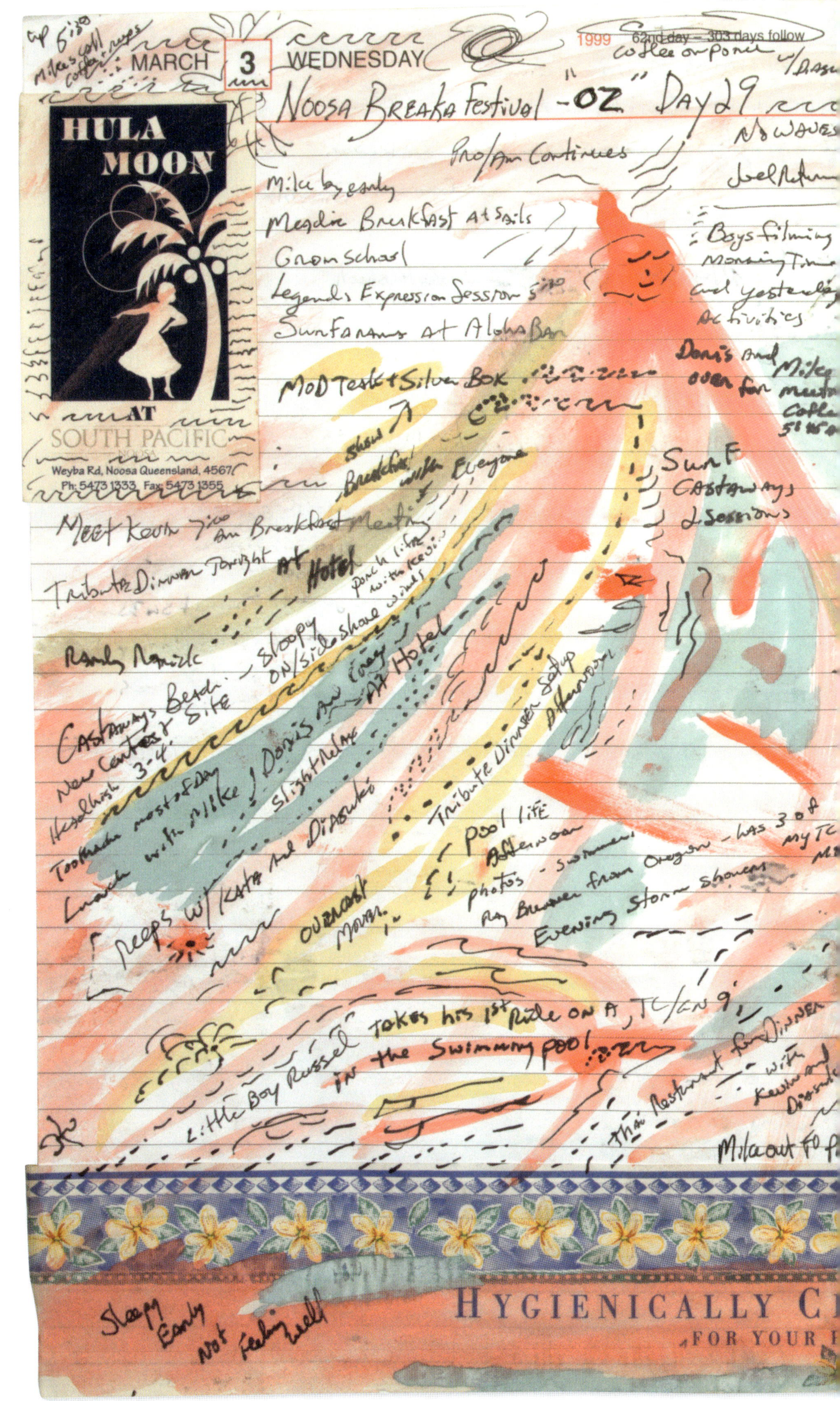
MARCH 3 WEDNESDAY
1999 62nd day – 303 days follow
HULA MOON
AT
SOUTH PACIFIC
NOOSA
Weyba Rd, Noosa Queensland, 4567
Ph: 5473 1333 Fax: 5473 1355
HYGIENICALLY C
FOR YOUR

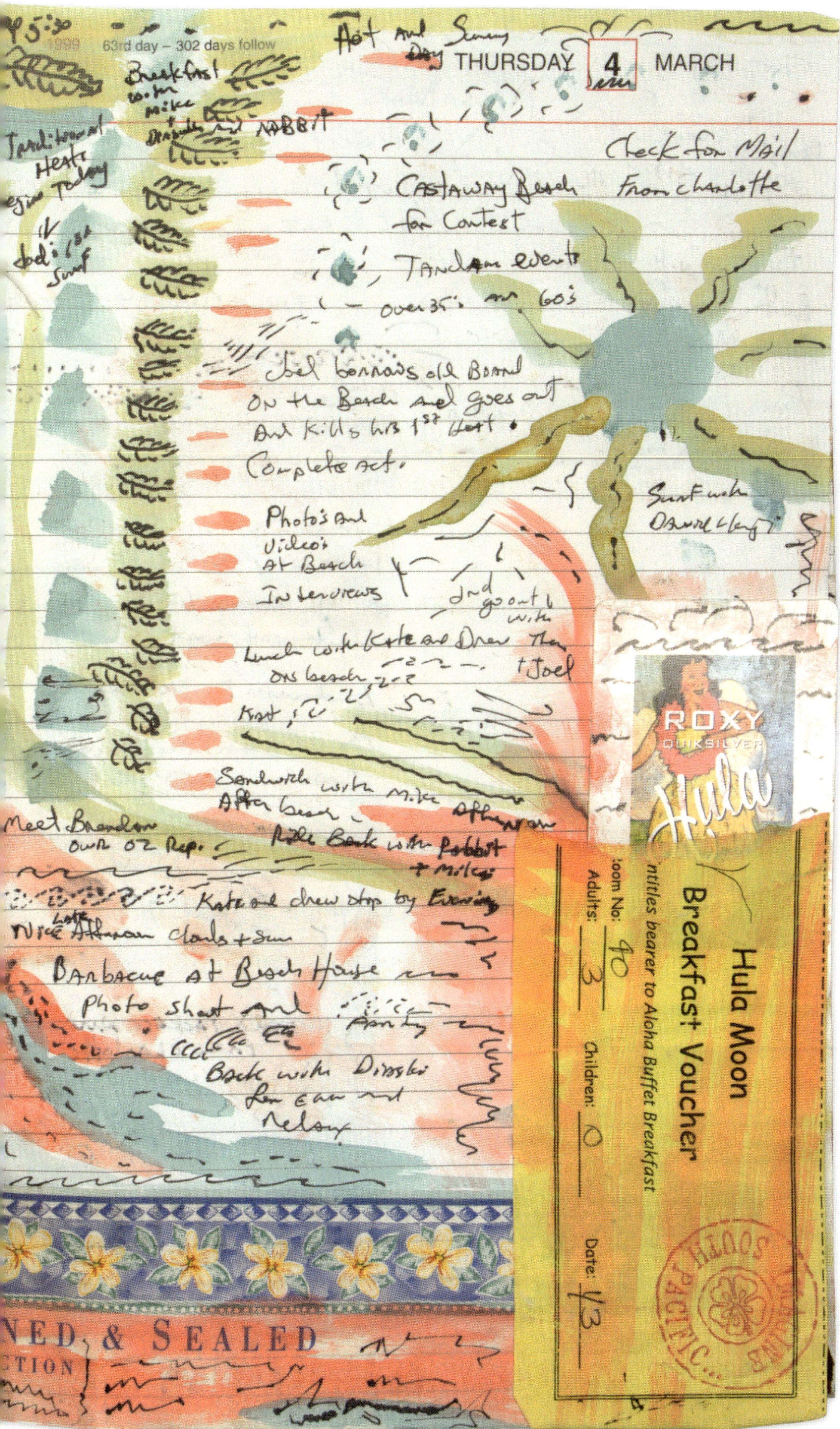
1999 63rd day – 302 days follow
THURSDAY 4 MARCH
ROXY
QUIKSILVER
Hula
Hula Moon
Breakfast Voucher
ntitles bearer to Aloha Buffet Breakfast
oom No: 40
Adults: 3
Children: 0
Date: 4/3
SOUTH PACIFIC
NED & SEALED
CTION

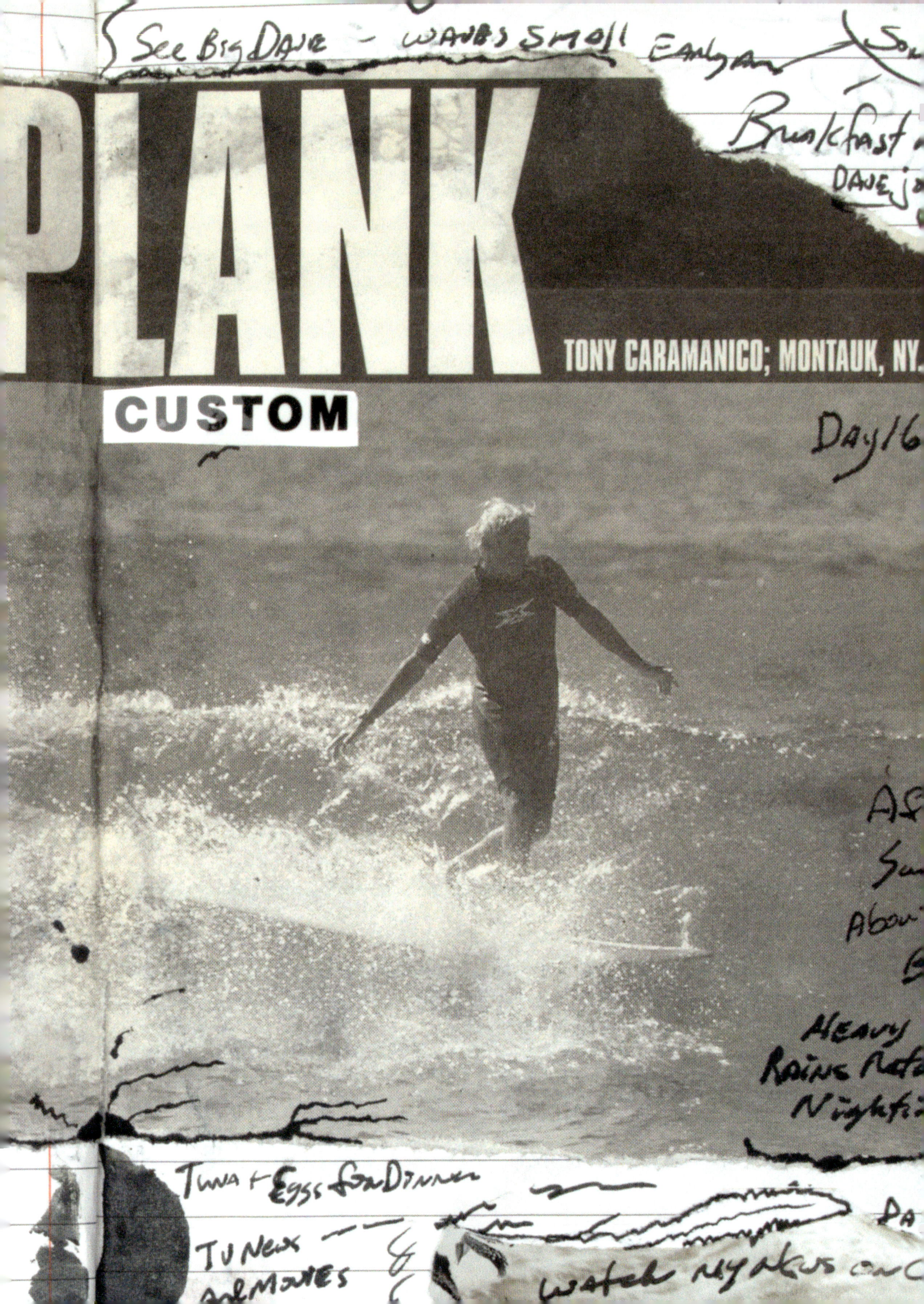

PLANK

TONY CARAMANICO; MONTAUK, NY.

CUSTOM

See Big Dave – waves small Early am

Breakfast

Day 16

Heavy Rains

Tuna + Eggs for Dinner

TV News and Movies

watch my news

JOURNALS

2000s

The 2000s marks yet another significant chapter in T.C.'s life: his emergence as an artist.

After meeting world champion surfer and modern longboarding pioneer Joel Tudor in the mid-90s in California, Tony invited Joel to visit him in New York. After falling in love with Montauk Joel would often return to visit Tony, surf uncrowded waves, and explore NYC's jazz scene. Tony wound up introducing Joel to legendary photographer Michael Halsband in the Ditch lot, who then collaborated with Joel on a portrait book, taking a deep dive into surf culture via portraits of its many characters. Upon the book's release came multiple exhibitions, including one with artist Michael Solomon at the Horowitz Gallery in East Hampton.

Halsband and Solomon knew of Tony's journals and convinced him to add some of his work into the show. With the help of East End artist Warren Padula, Tony minted the first prints of his journals and joined the party. To his surprise, it was a success.

"I sold a piece of work, and I said, 'I guess I'm an artist now.'"

An essential underpinning to Tony's story is that of the quintessential New York hustler. Yes, he's driven by his love of the ocean, but it's the constant tinkering, toying, and finagling to get there that creates his many layered story. He never set out to be an artist, but at 50, he began his most successful career arc yet.

On the back of the show came representation: Beach Ambiance in Sag Harbor, then Clic via Christian Celle with whom Tony had his first titled show in collaboration with the Warhol Estate in St. Barths. If he wasn't an artist before, there was no denying it now.

With Greg Noll's surfboard brand fizzling out, Tony began working with Channin Surfboards to continue production of his signature model. In conjunction with his selling prints, they began printing the journals onto surfboards themselves, with the boards becoming a smashing success. Being the functional works of art that they are, you couldn't paddle out at Ditch without seeing one of Tony's boards, with many of his customers doubling down and buying one to hang on their walls as well.

It was in the early 2000's that Montauk began a notable metamorphosis. Development on the East End is nothing new, but Montauk, known as a "drinking town with a fishing problem," was long absolved of the same ritzy crowd that was attracted to towns west of Amagansett. It seemed the time had come. The crowd came spilling in, and the prices rose... with hotel rooms reaching $2,000/night and some establishments charging upwards of $50 for chicken tenders.

Although Montauk's change was inevitable, the tenacity of its long-tenured, unwavering locals was never in question. Tony sits firmly within that category.

He and Charlotte still live on the same piece of property Tony bought in 1988. With two houses and a handful of quaint cottages that pre-date zoning law, Tony is now a landlord with a community of delightful summer tenants. At 73, his relationship with surfing is as strong as ever. While you can imagine he isn't logging the same 6-8 hour sessions he was when he was 25, Tony is still on it when it comes to which nook of Montauk's jagged coastline will be best on any given day.

And what comes next? "I just want to keep going. I want to keep expressing myself and getting my journals out there. I'm still stoked. I wish I could surf more; the passion is still there. I've been able to take that need for surfing every day and put it into this."

Focused on delivering his story through his journals, he is still sharing his love of surfing with the world in the same way he did when he first started at Beachcomber Surf Shop in 1964.

And isn't that a beautiful thing.

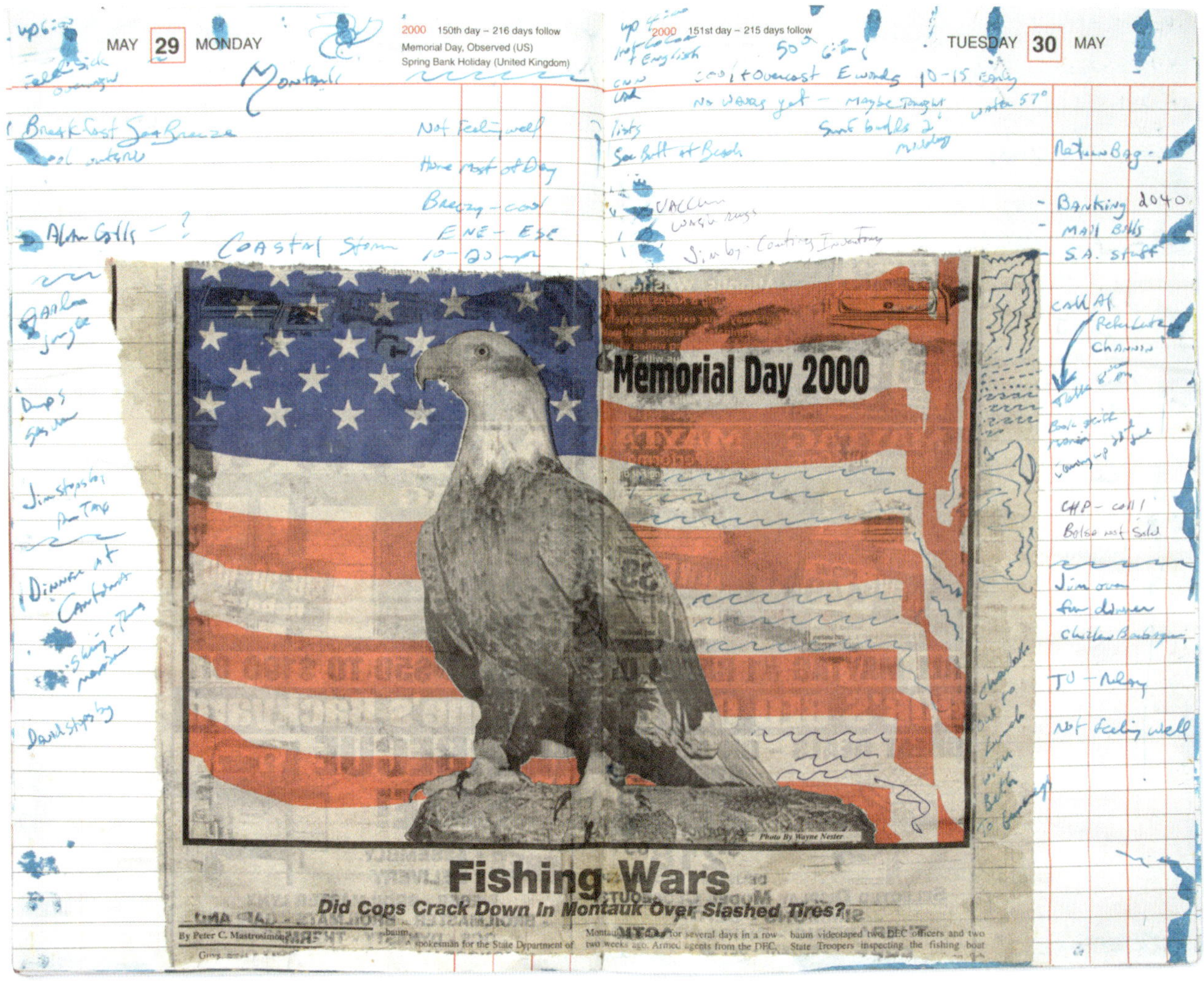
MAY 29 MONDAY
2000 150th day – 216 days follow
Memorial Day, Observed (US)
Spring Bank Holiday (United Kingdom)
2000 151st day – 215 days follow
TUESDAY 30 MAY
Montauk
Memorial Day 2000
Photo By Wayne Nester
Fishing Wars
Did Cops Crack Down In Montauk Over Slashed Tires?
By Peter C. Mastrosimone

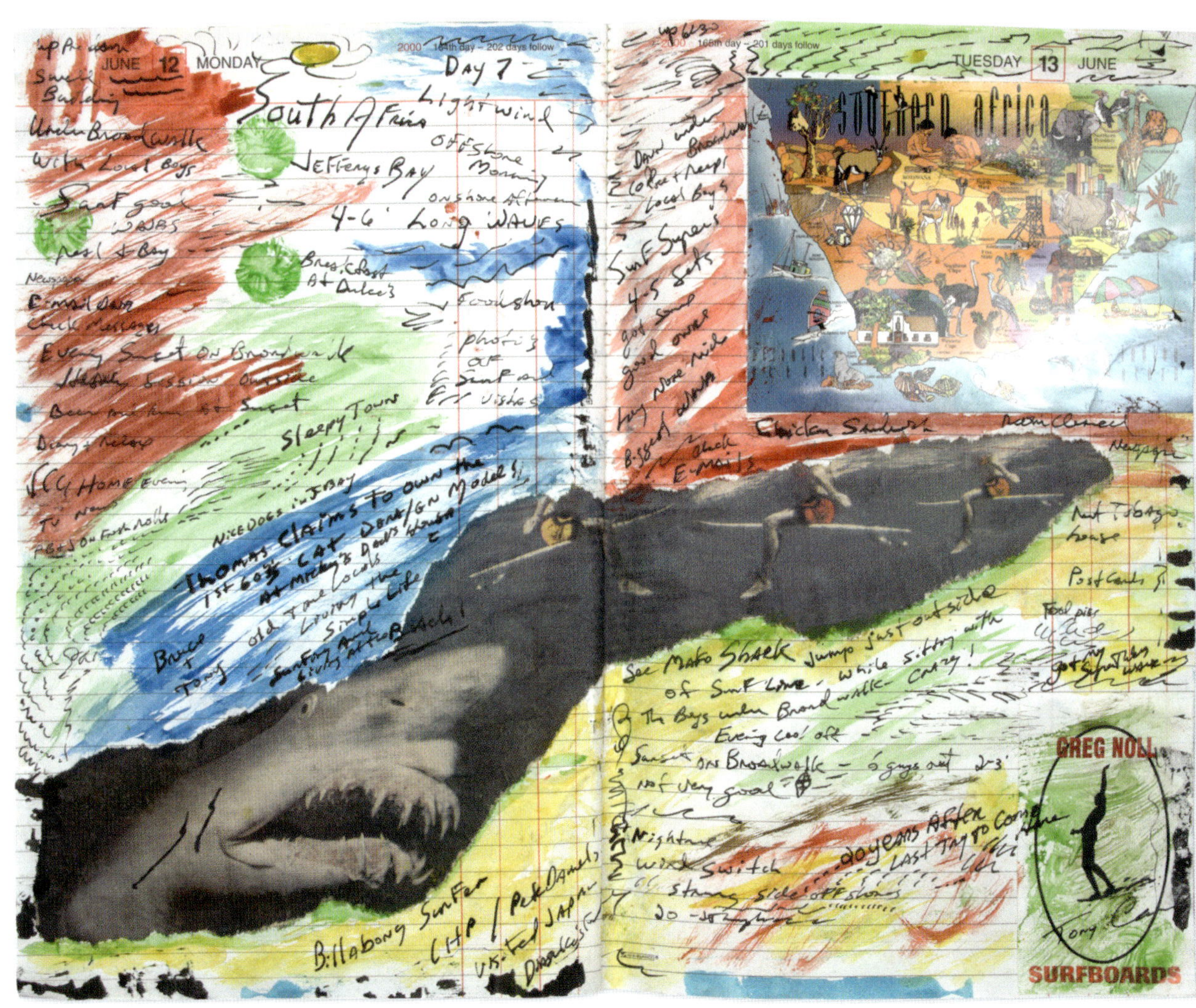
JUNE 12 MONDAY
TUESDAY 13 JUNE
Day 7
South Africa
Light wind
Jeffreys Bay
4-6' Long Waves
southern africa
GREG NOLL
SURFBOARDS

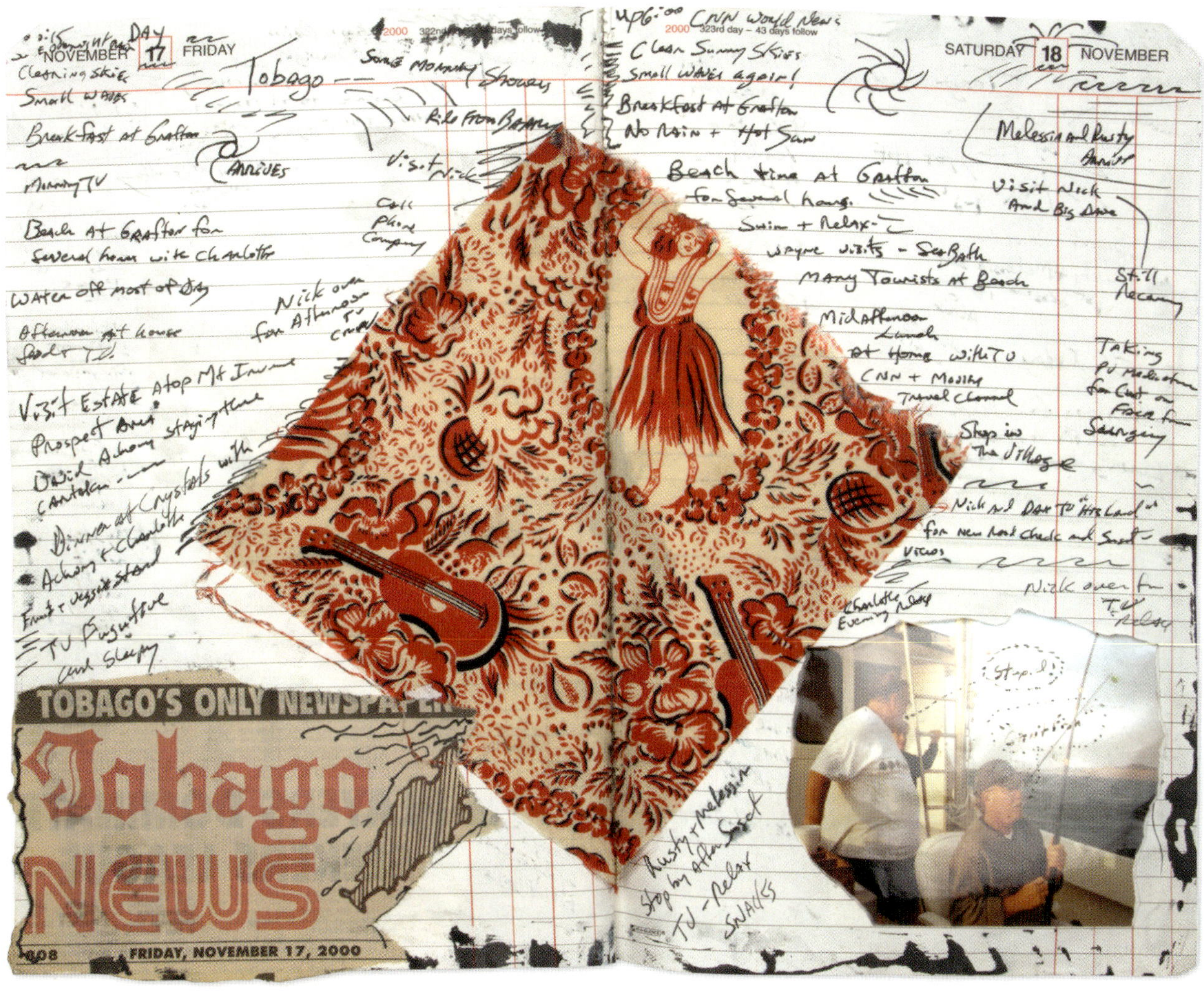
NOVEMBER 17 FRIDAY
SATURDAY 18 NOVEMBER
Tobago
TOBAGO'S ONLY NEWSPA
Tobago
NEWS
FRIDAY, NOVEMBER 17, 2000

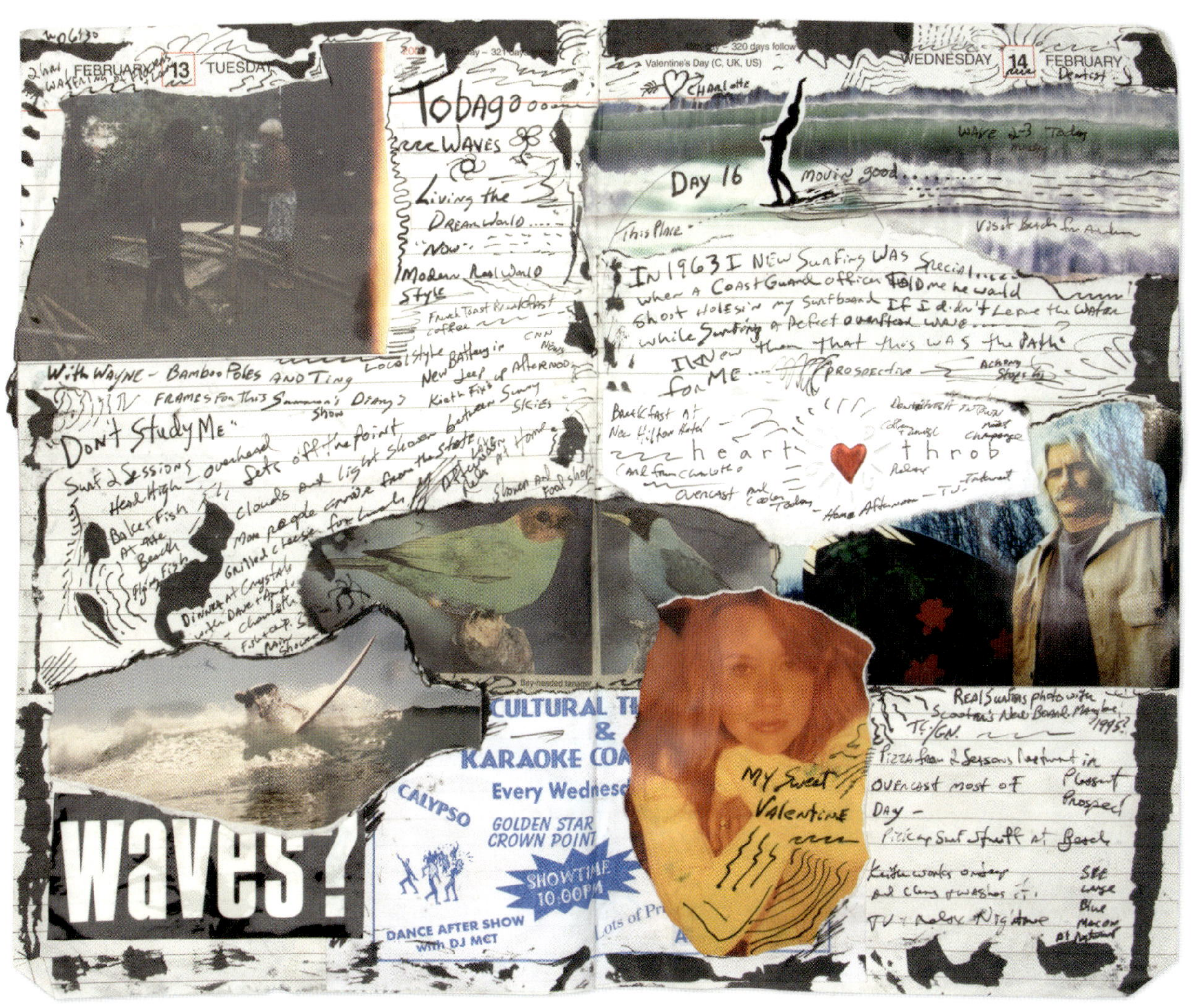
FEBRUARY 13 TUESDAY
Valentine's Day (C, UK, US)
WEDNESDAY 14 FEBRUARY
Tobago
Day 16
heart
throb
waves?
CULTURAL TH
&
KARAOKE CO
Every Wednesd
CALYPSO
GOLDEN STAR
CROWN POINT
SHOWTIME 10:00PM
DANCE AFTER SHOW
with DJ MCT
MY Sweet Valentine

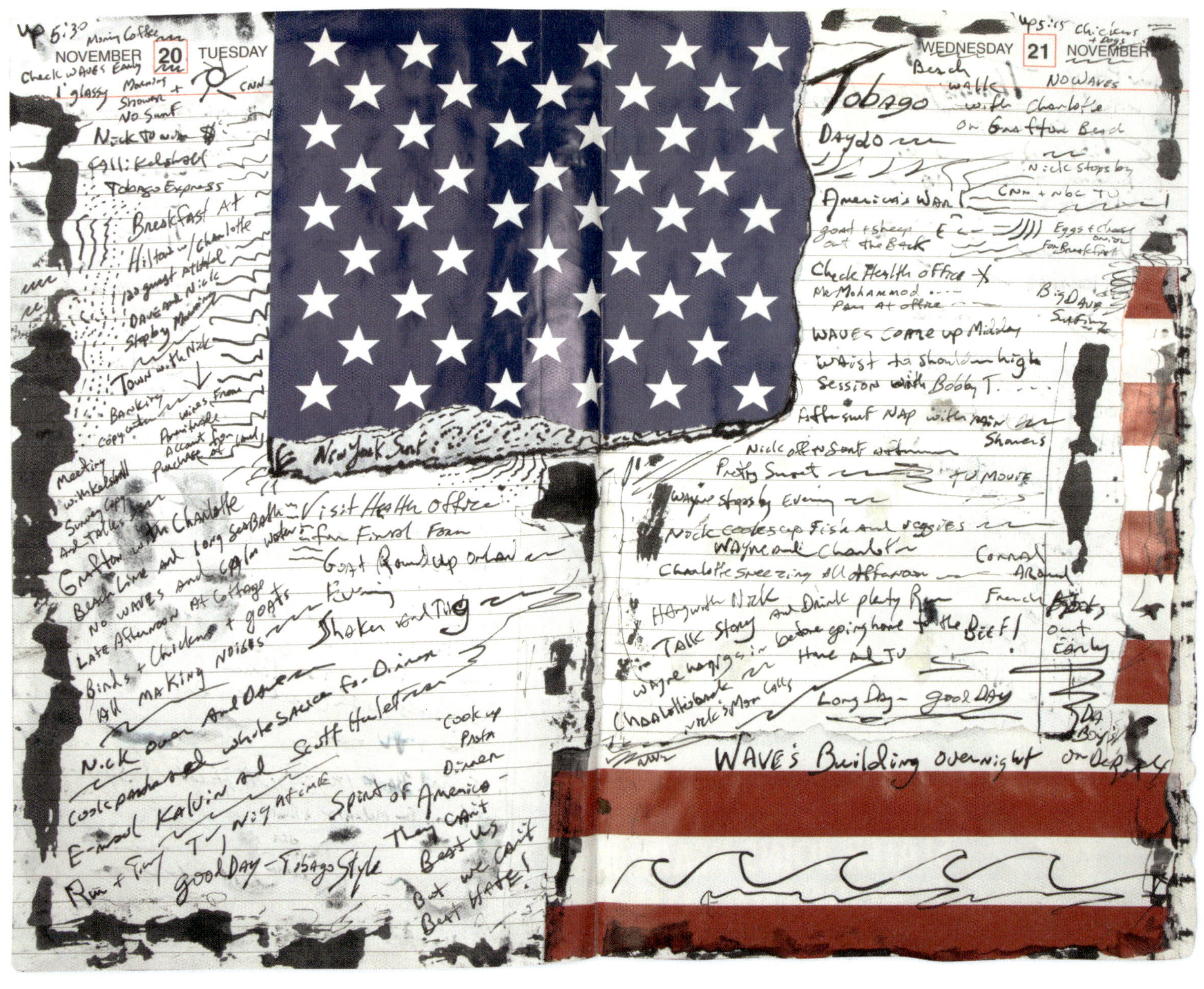
NOVEMBER 20 TUESDAY
WEDNESDAY 21 NOVEMBER
Tobago
New York Surf
Visit Health office
Goat Roundup
Spirit of America
Good Day - Tobago Style
Check Health office
Waves come up Midday
Session with Bobby T.
Long Day - Good Day
WAVES Building overnight

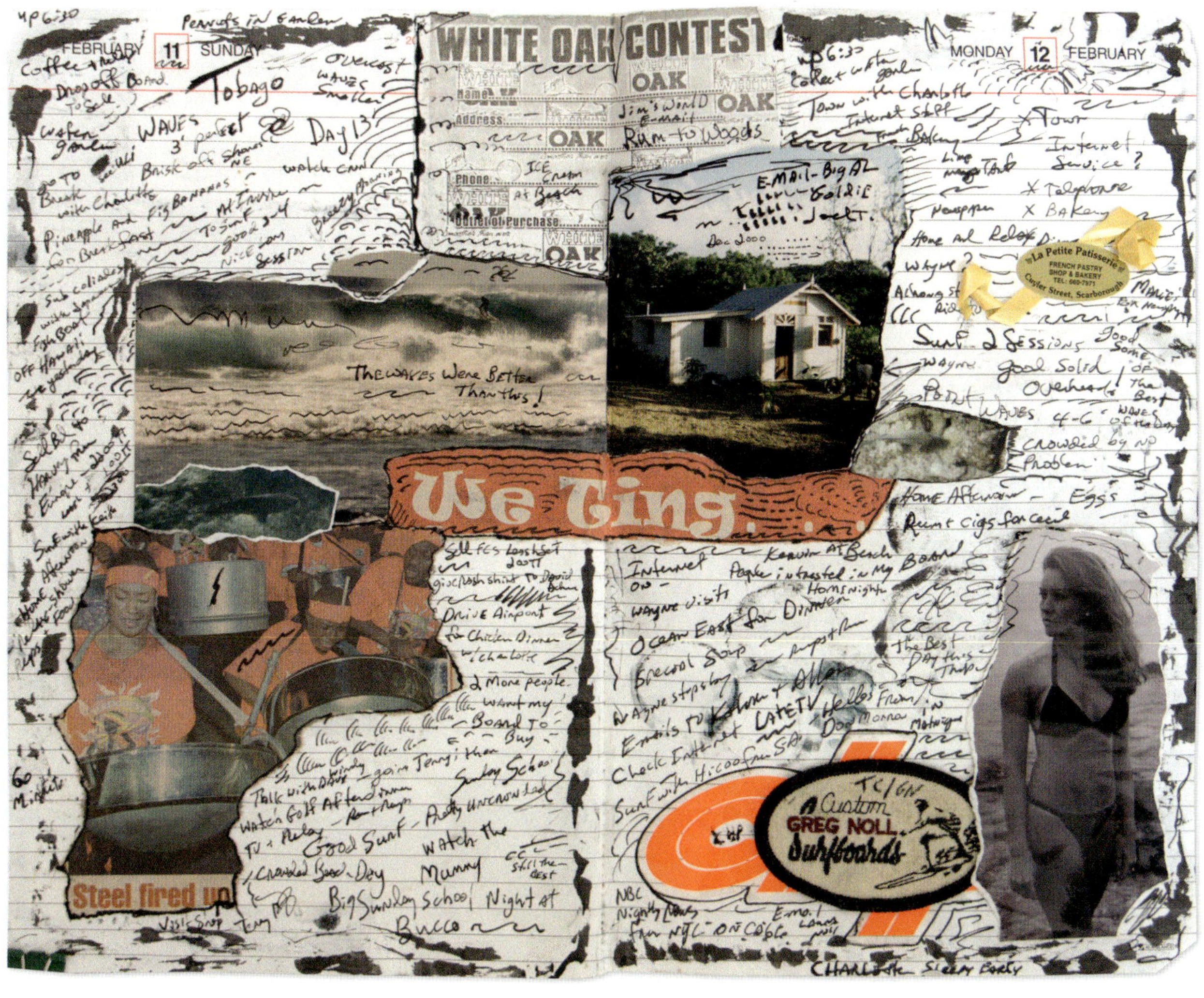
FEBRUARY 11 SUNDAY
MONDAY 12 FEBRUARY
WHITE OAK CONTEST
Tobago
Day 13
The waves were better than this!
La Petite Patisserie
FRENCH PASTRY SHOP & BAKERY
We Ting
Steel fired up
A Custom
GREG NOLL
Surfboards

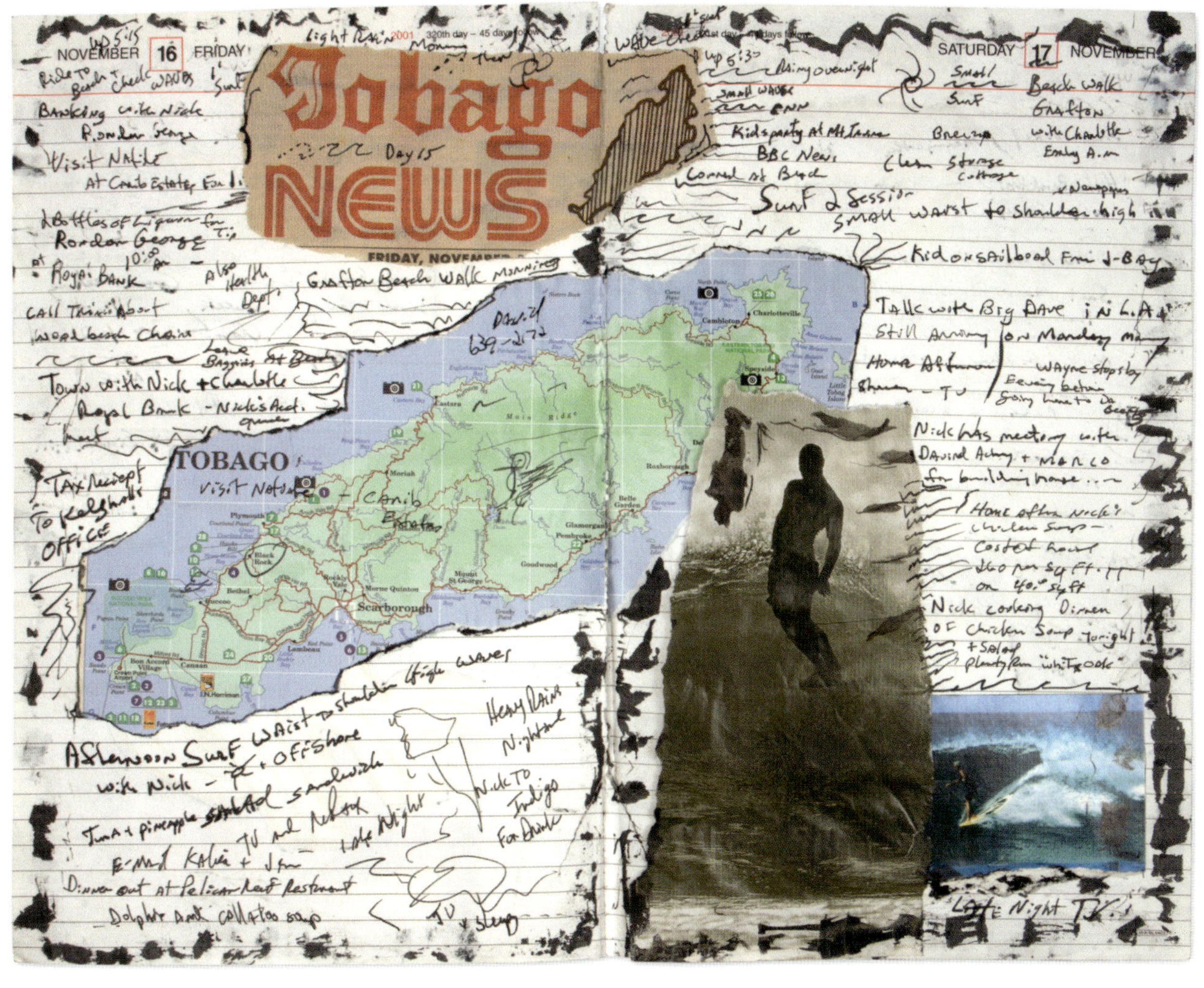
NOVEMBER 16 FRIDAY
SATURDAY 17 NOVEMBER
Tobago
NEWS
Day 15
TOBAGO
Scarborough

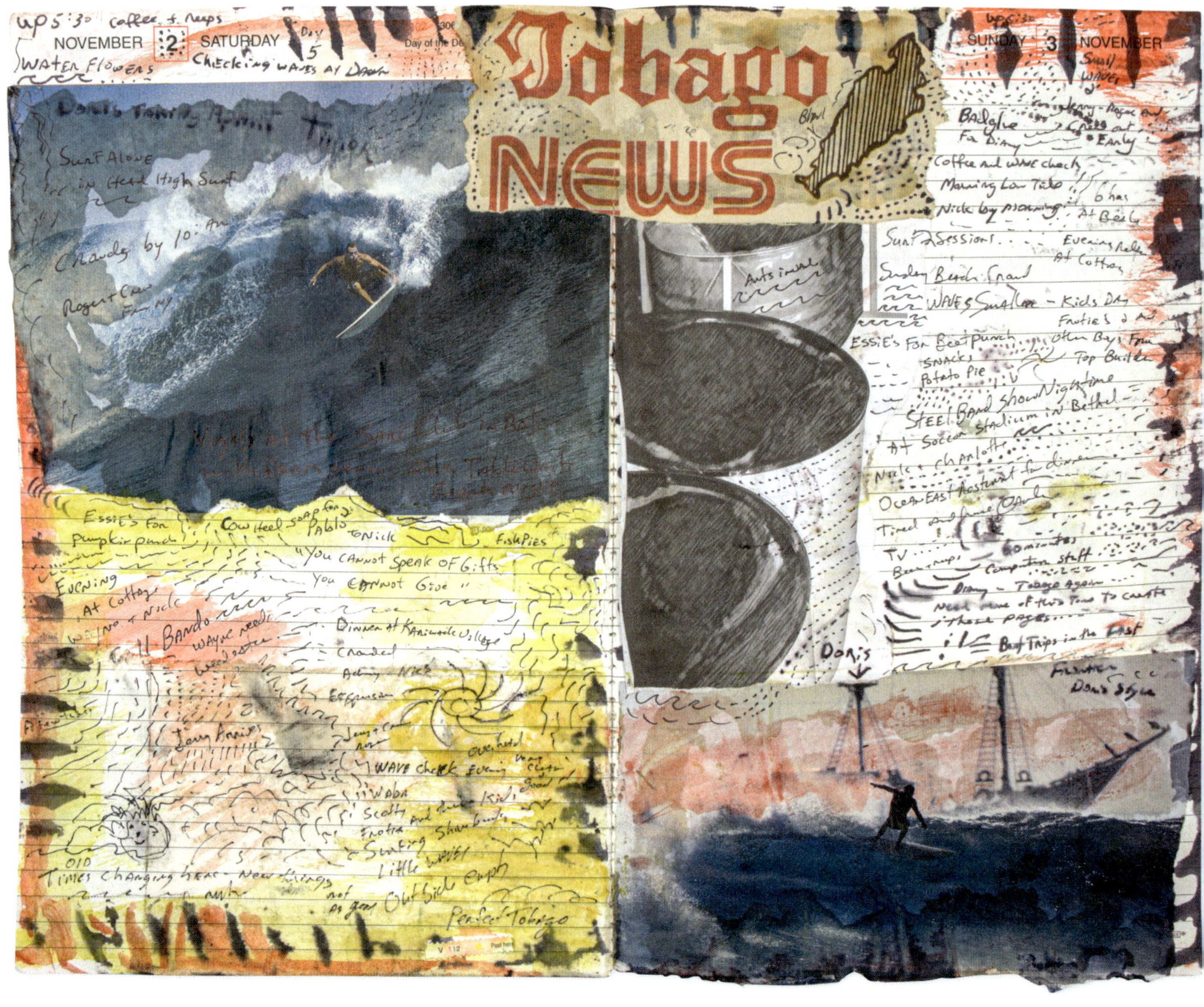
NOVEMBER 2 SATURDAY
Tobago NEWS
SUNDAY 3 NOVEMBER
Perfect Tobago

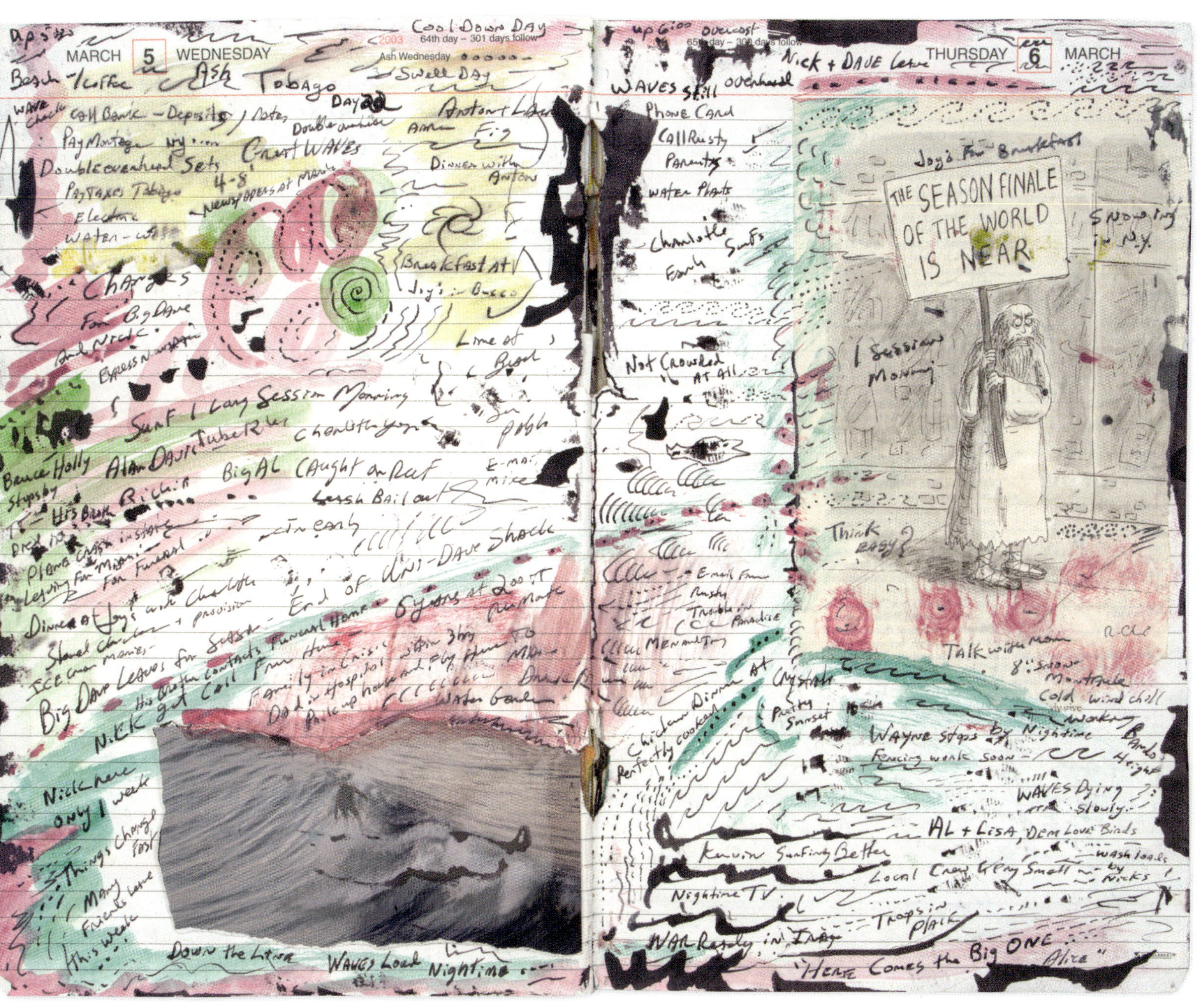
MARCH 5 WEDNESDAY
2003 64th day – 301 days follow
Ash Wednesday
Cool Down Day
Ash Tobago
Swell Day
Doubleoverhead Sets
Great WAVES
Breakfast At Joy's in Bucco
THURSDAY 6 MARCH
65th day – 300 days follow
Nick + Dave Leave
WAVES Still overhead
Phone Card
Call Rusty
Not Crowded At All
Joy's For Breakfast
THE SEASON FINALE OF THE WORLD IS NEAR
Talk with mom
Wayne stops by Nightime
WAVES Dying Slowly
AL + LISA, Dem Love Birds
Nightime TV
WAR Ready in IRAQ
"Here Comes the Big ONE"
Down the Line
Waves Load
Nightime

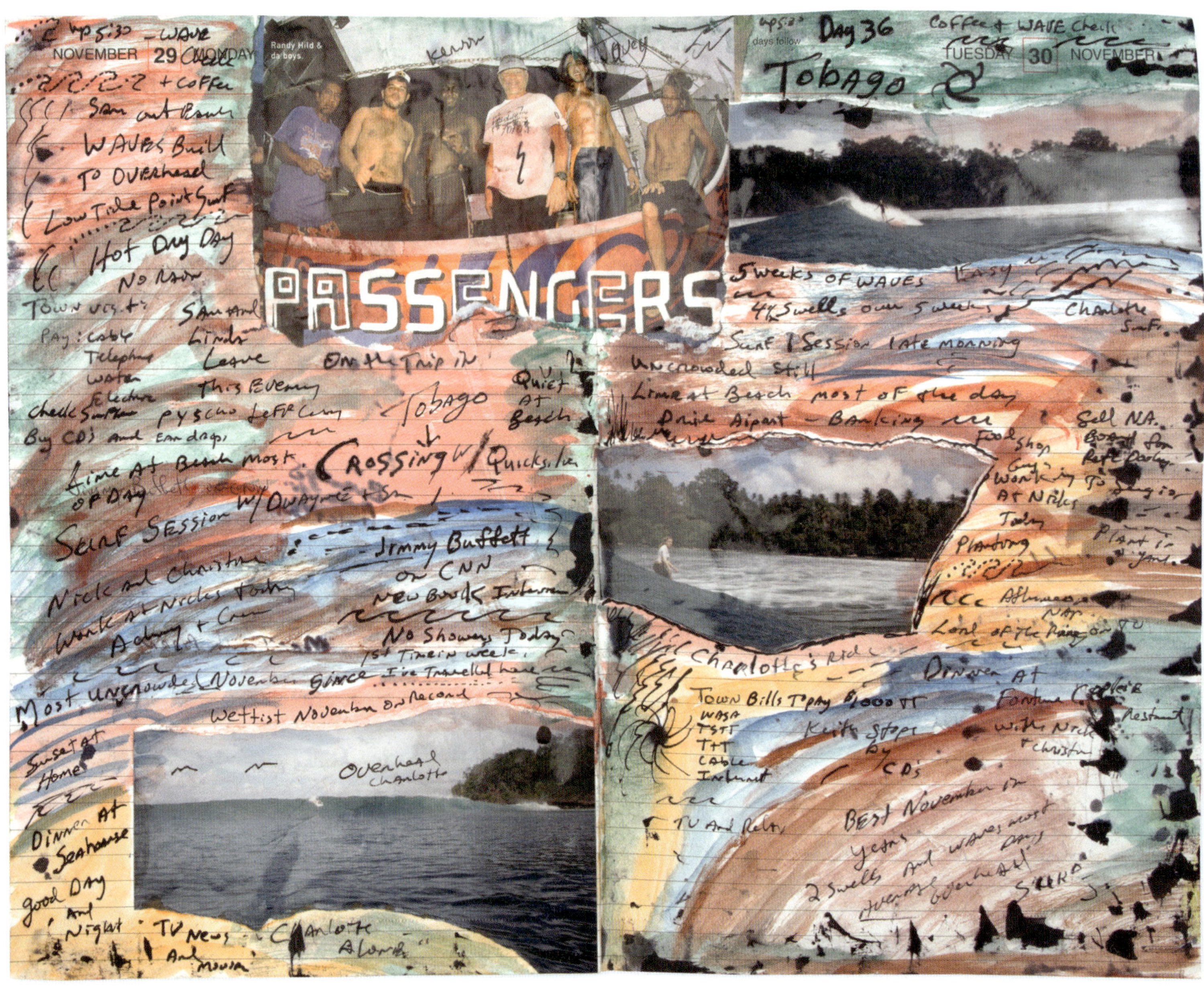
NOVEMBER 29 MONDAY
Randy Hild & da boys.
TUESDAY 30 NOVEMBER
days follow
Day 36
Coffee + WAVE Check
Tobago
WAVES Build
TO Overhead
Low Tide Point Surf
Hot Day
No Rain
PASSENGERS
On the Trip in
Tobago
Quiet At Beach
CROSSING W/ Quicksilver
Surf Session
Jimmy Buffett
on CNN
No Showers Today
1st Time in weeks
Most Uncrowded November Since I've Travelled here
Wettest November on Record
Overhead Charlotte
Sunset At Home
Dinner At Seahouse
Good Day And Night
TV News And Movie
Charlotte Alone
5 weeks of WAVES
Surf Session Late Morning
Uncrowded Still
Lime at Beach most of the day
Drive Airport - Banking
Sell NA. Board for Ref. Darby
Charlotte's Ride
Dinner At
Town Bills Today
WASA
TSTT
T&T
Cable
Internet
TV And Relax
Best November in years
2 Swells And waves most days
Overhead

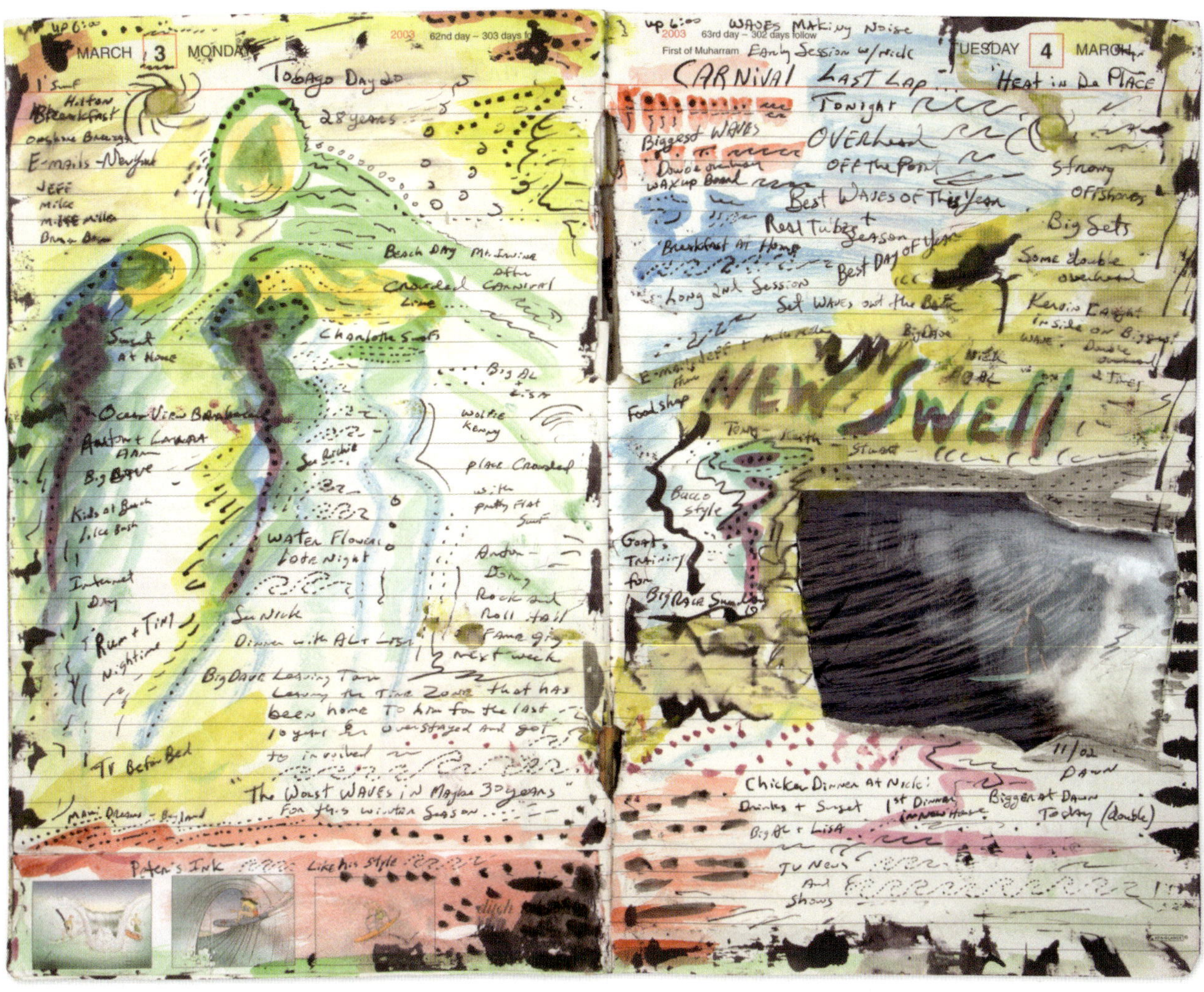
MARCH 3 MONDAY
2003 62nd day – 303 days follow
First of Muharram
2003 63rd day – 302 days follow
TUESDAY 4 MARCH
Tobago Day 20
CARNIVAL Last Lap
NEW Swell

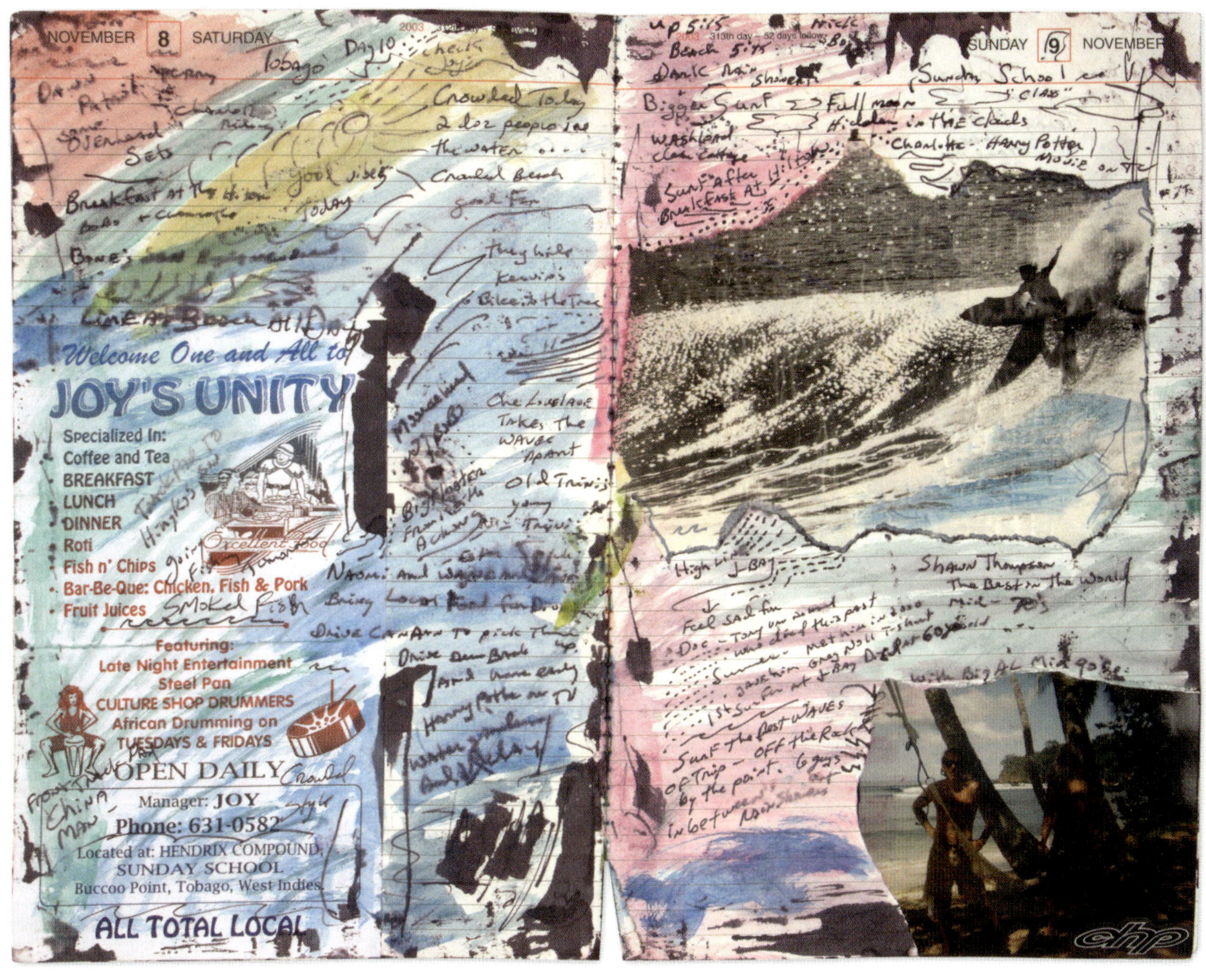
NOVEMBER 8 SATURDAY
SUNDAY 9 NOVEMBER
Welcome One and All to
JOY'S UNITY
Specialized In:
Coffee and Tea
BREAKFAST
LUNCH
DINNER
Roti
Fish n' Chips
Bar-Be-Que: Chicken, Fish & Pork
Fruit Juices
Excellent Food
Featuring:
Late Night Entertainment
Steel Pan
CULTURE SHOP DRUMMERS
African Drumming on
TUESDAYS & FRIDAYS
OPEN DAILY
Manager: JOY
Phone: 631-0582
Located at: HENDRIX COMPOUND,
SUNDAY SCHOOL
Buccoo Point, Tobago, West Indies
ALL TOTAL LOCAL

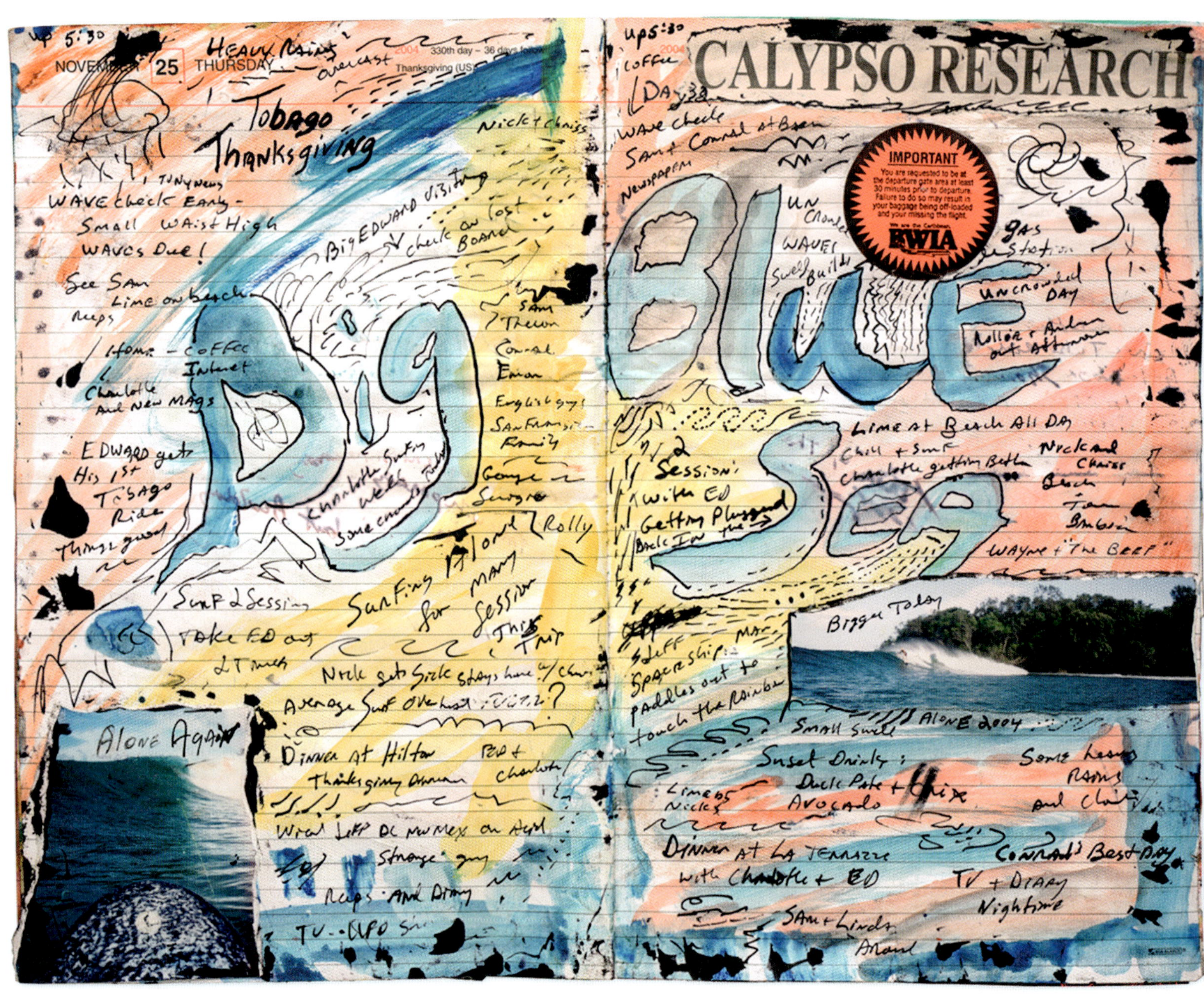

NOVEMBER 25 THURSDAY
2004 330th day
Thanksgiving (US)
Tobago
Thanksgiving
Big
Blue
Sea
CALYPSO RESEARCH
IMPORTANT
You are requested to be at the departure gate area at least 30 minutes prior to departure. Failure to do so may result in your baggage being off-loaded and your missing the flight.
BWIA
Alone Again
Bigger Today
Small Waist High
Waves Due!
Dinner at Hilton
Lime at Beach All Day
Dinner at La Terrazze
Conrad's Best Day
TV + Diary
Nightime

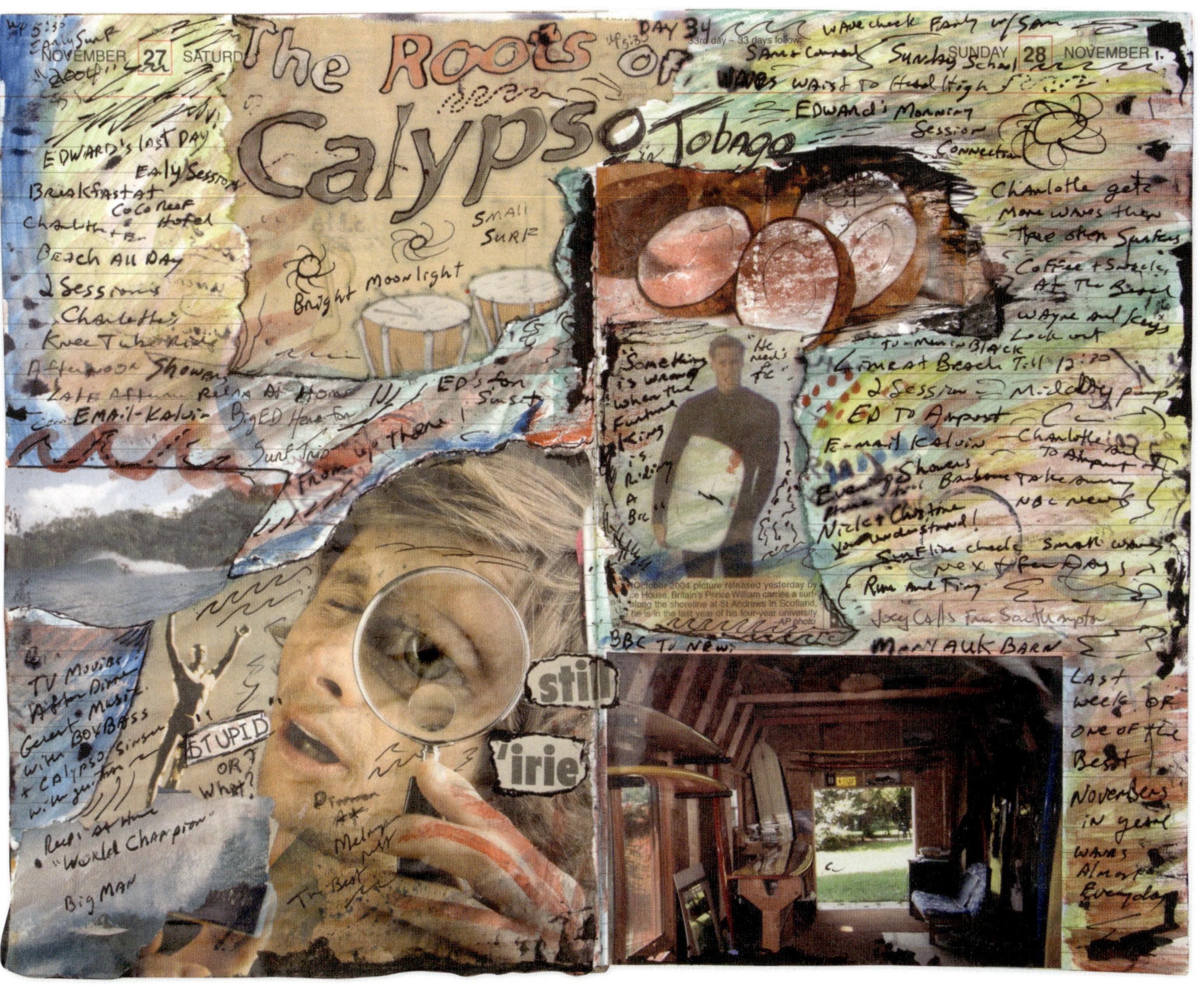
NOVEMBER 27 SATURDAY
The Roots of
Calypso
Tobago
SUNDAY 28 NOVEMBER
still
STUPID
'irie
MONTAUK BARN

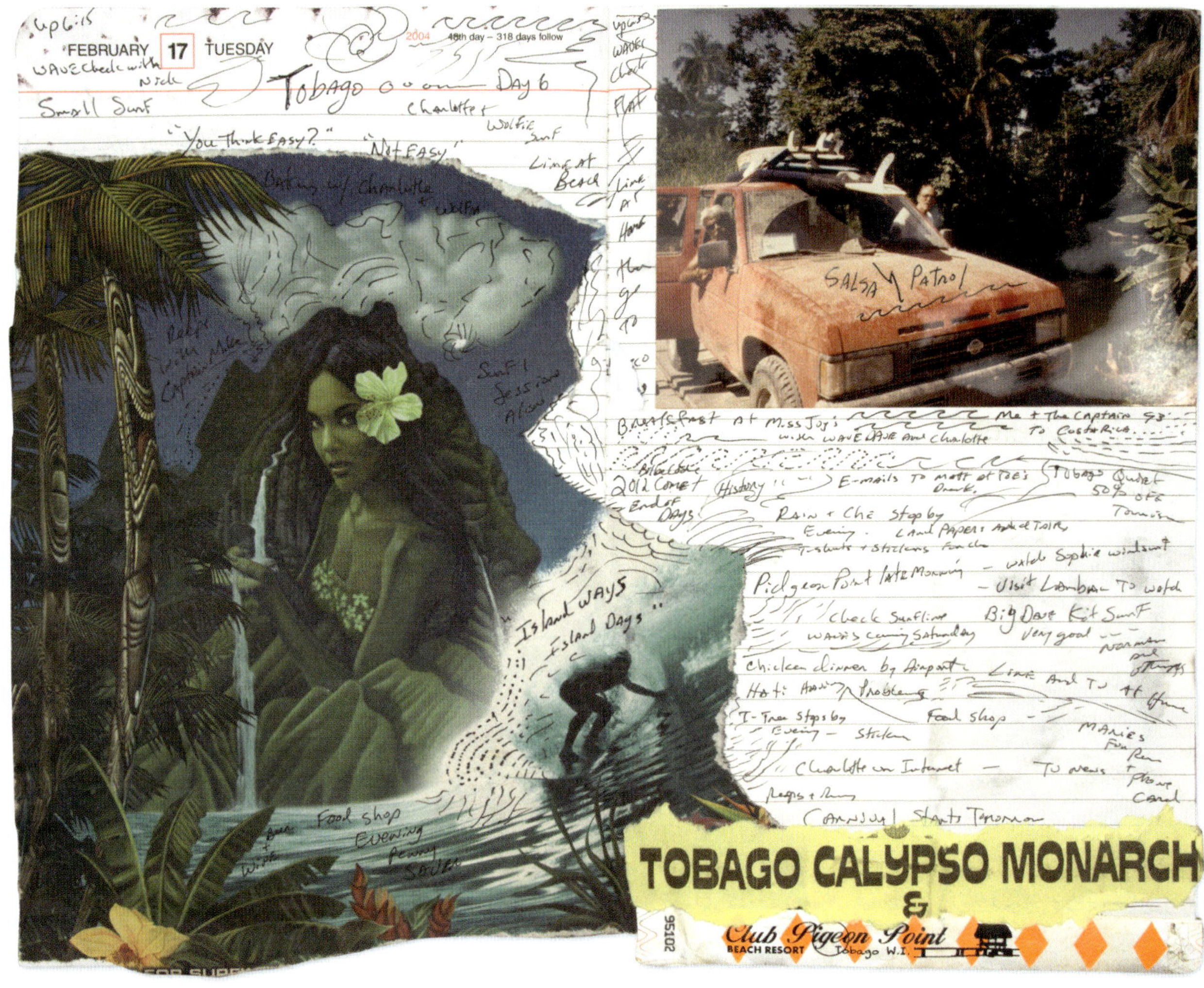

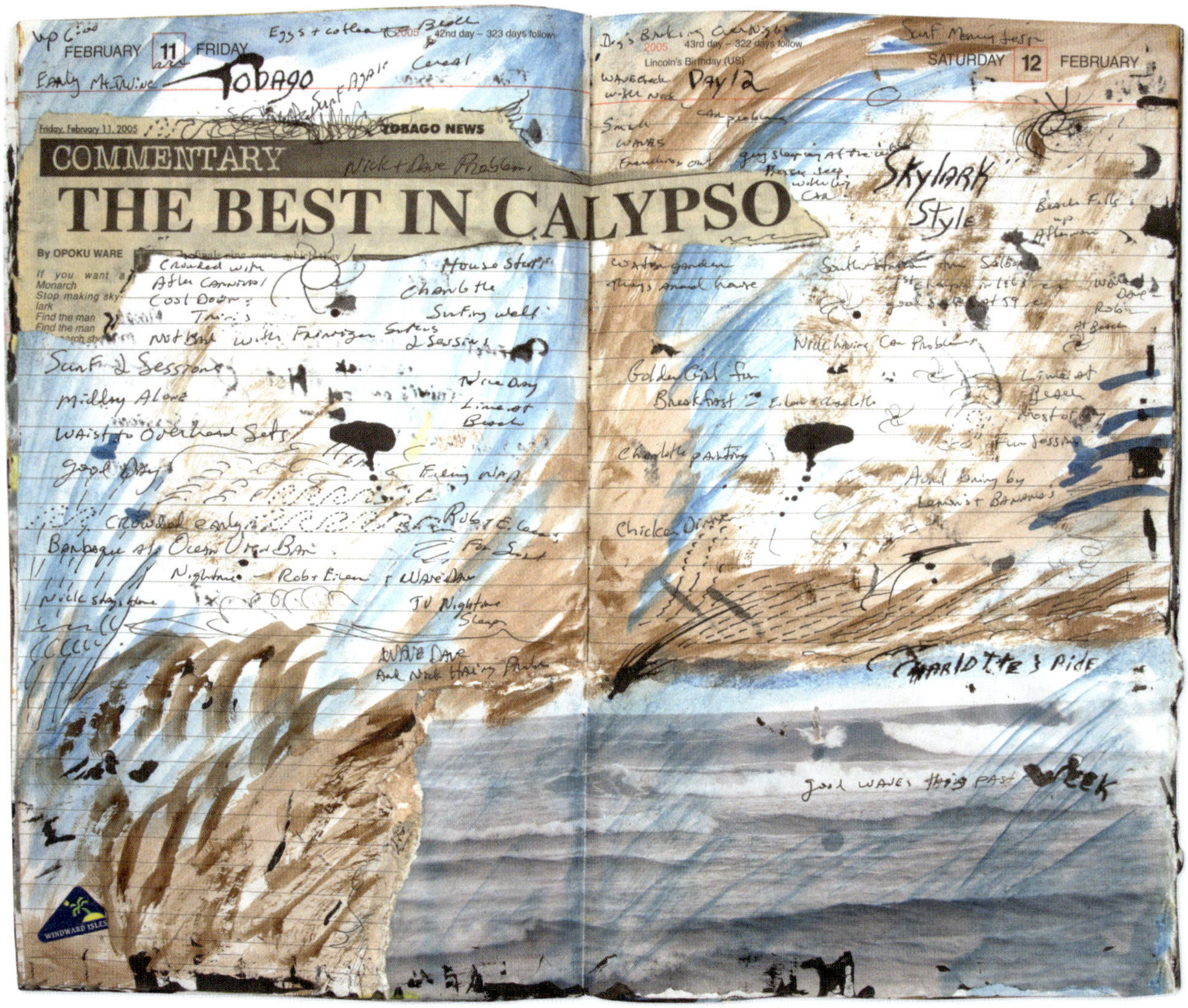

FEBRUARY 11 FRIDAY

2005 42nd day – 323 days follow

Friday, February 11, 2005

TOBAGO NEWS

COMMENTARY

THE BEST IN CALYPSO

By OPOKU WARE

If you want a Monarch
Stop making sky-
lark
Find the man
Find the man

2005 43rd day – 322 days follow

Lincoln's Birthday (US)

SATURDAY 12 FEBRUARY

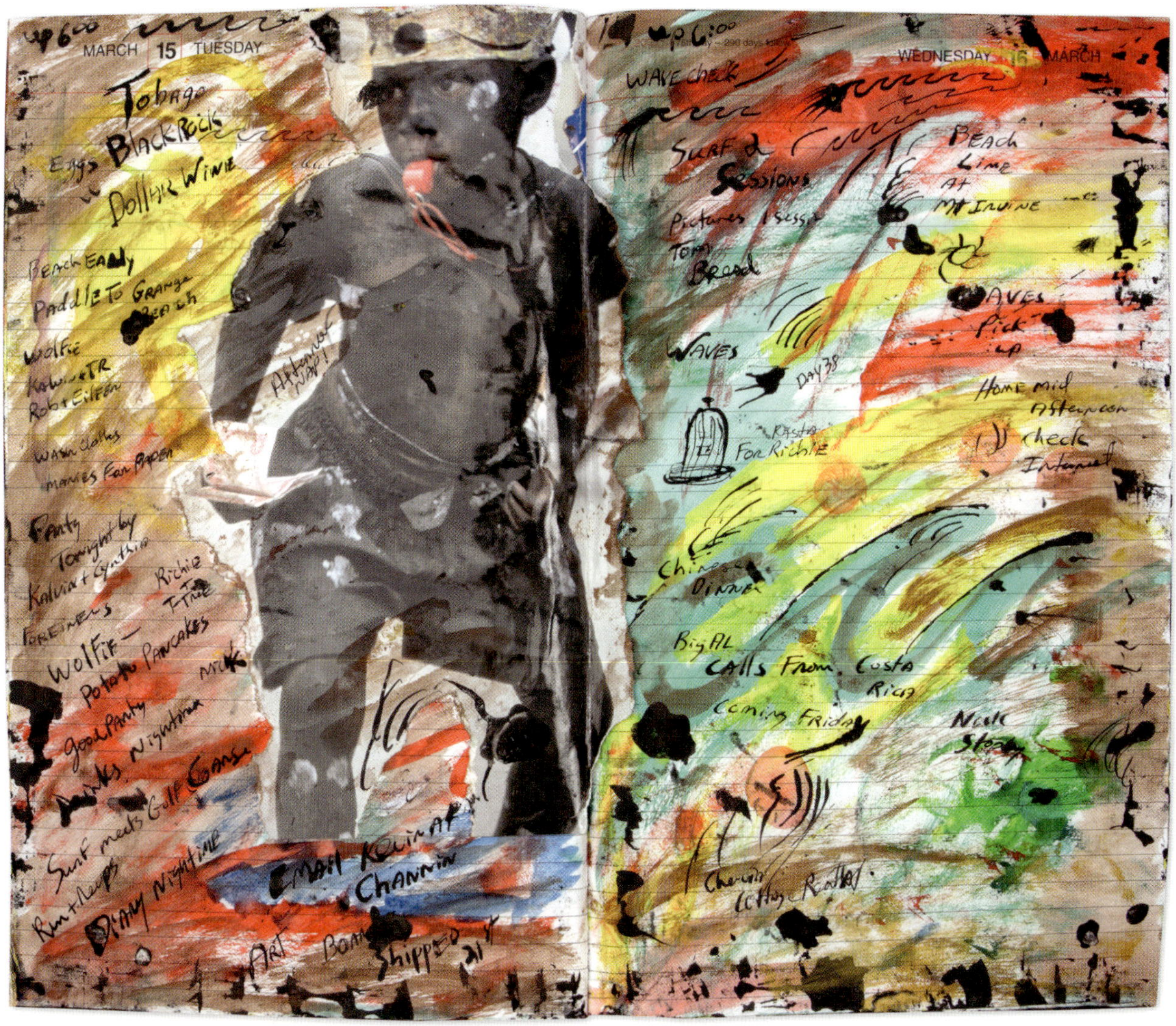

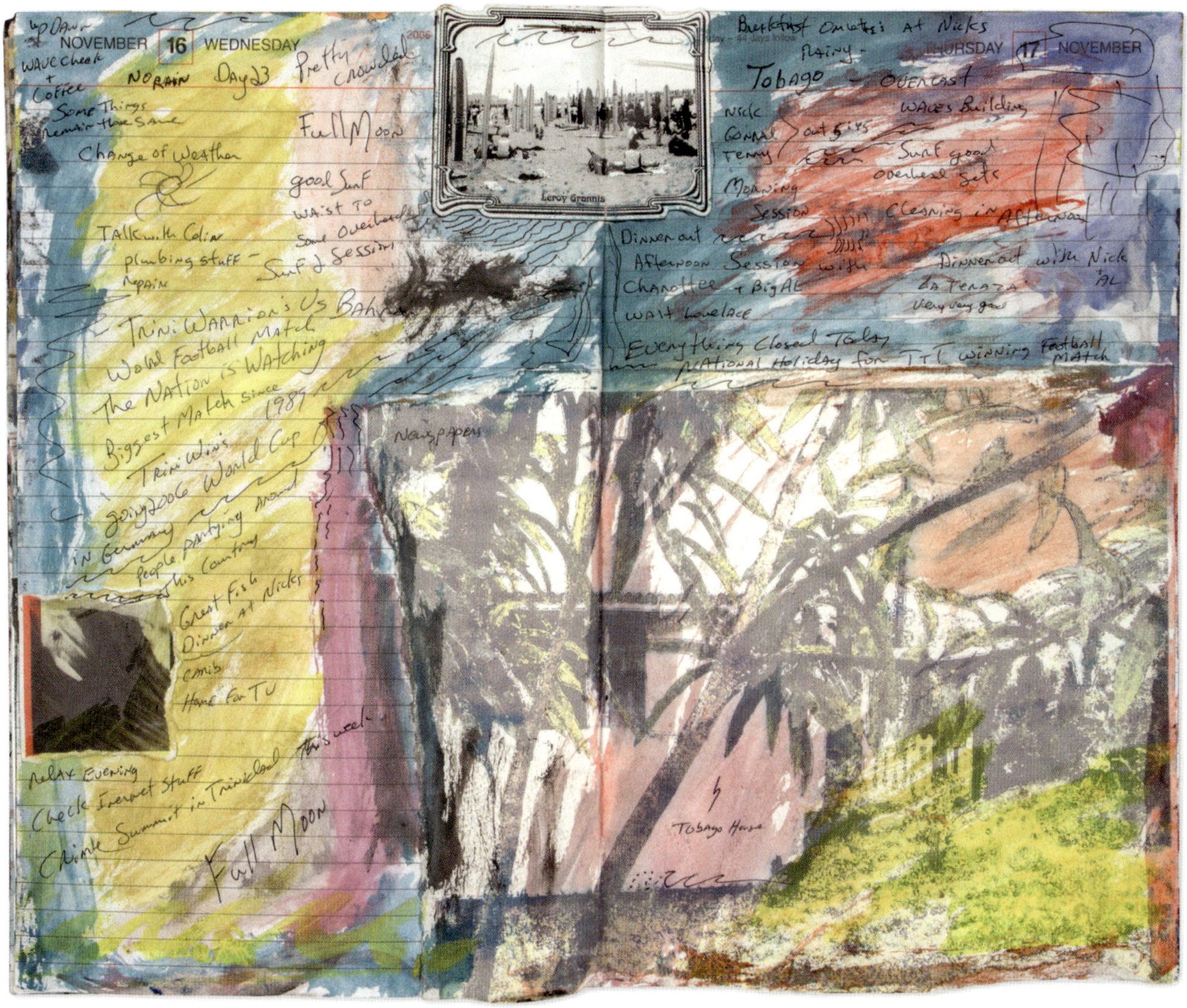

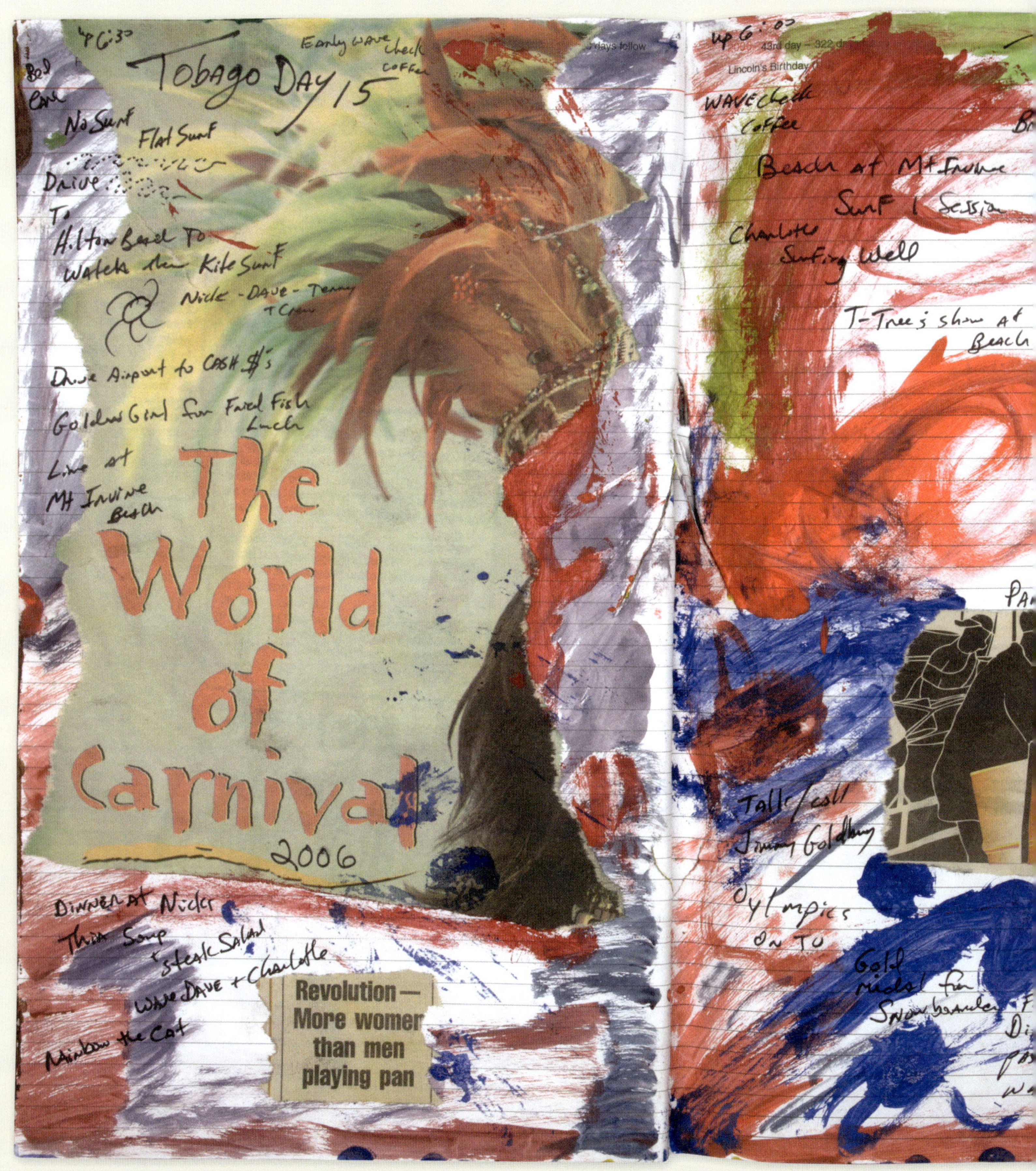
Tobago Day 15
Early wave check
coffee
No Surf
Flat Surf
Drive to
Hilton Beach to
watch the Kite Surf
Drive Airport to CASH $'s
Live at
Mt Irvine
Beach
The
World
of
Carnival
2006
Dinner at Nicks
Thai Soup
+ Steak Salad
Revolution —
More women
than men
playing pan
43rd day – 322 d
Lincoln's Birthday
Wave check
coffee
Beach at Mt Irvine
Surf 1 Session
Charlotte
Surfing Well
T-Tree's show at
Beach
Olympics
on TV
Gold
Medal for
Snowboarder

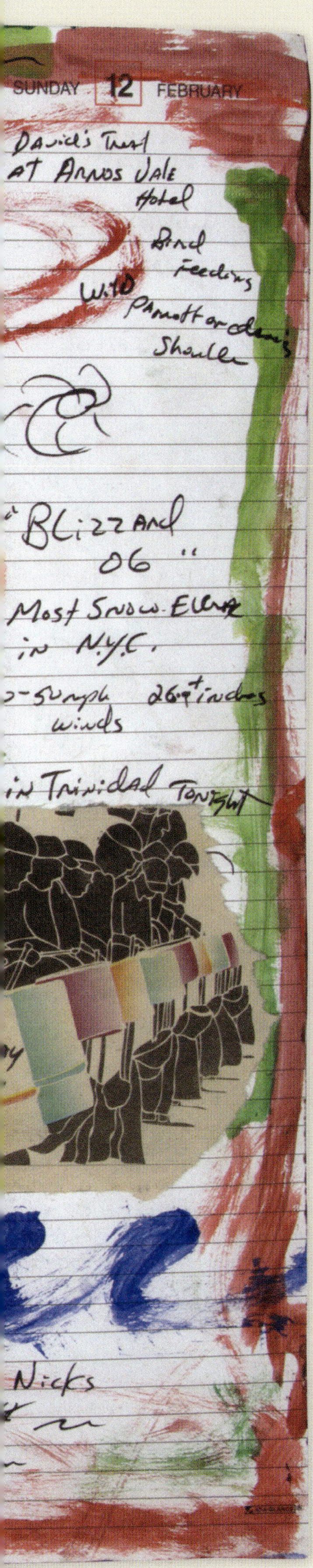

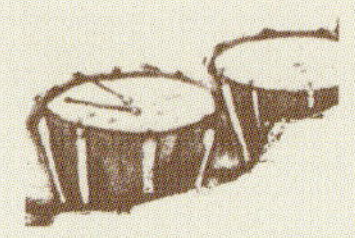

CALYPSO STARTED IN TRINIDAD AND TOBAGO. IT'S A BLEND OF WEST AFRICAN AND CARIBBEAN RHYTHMS. ONE GUY FROM TRINIDAD INVENTED THE STEEL DRUM BY POUNDING OUT LEFTOVER OIL BARRELS FROM THE US NAVAL BASE. IT JUST SO HAPPENED THAT THE HILL BEHIND MY HOUSE WAS WHERE THE TOWN'S BAND HAD THEIR TENT. AT NIGHT YOU'D HEAR THEM PRACTICING 100 STRONG PLAYING THIS INCREDIBLE, COLORFUL MUSIC. EACH YEAR THAT MARKED THE BUILD UP TO CARNIVAL.

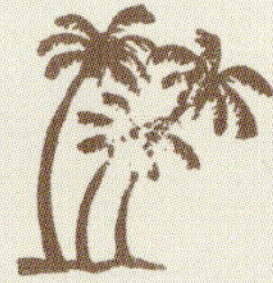

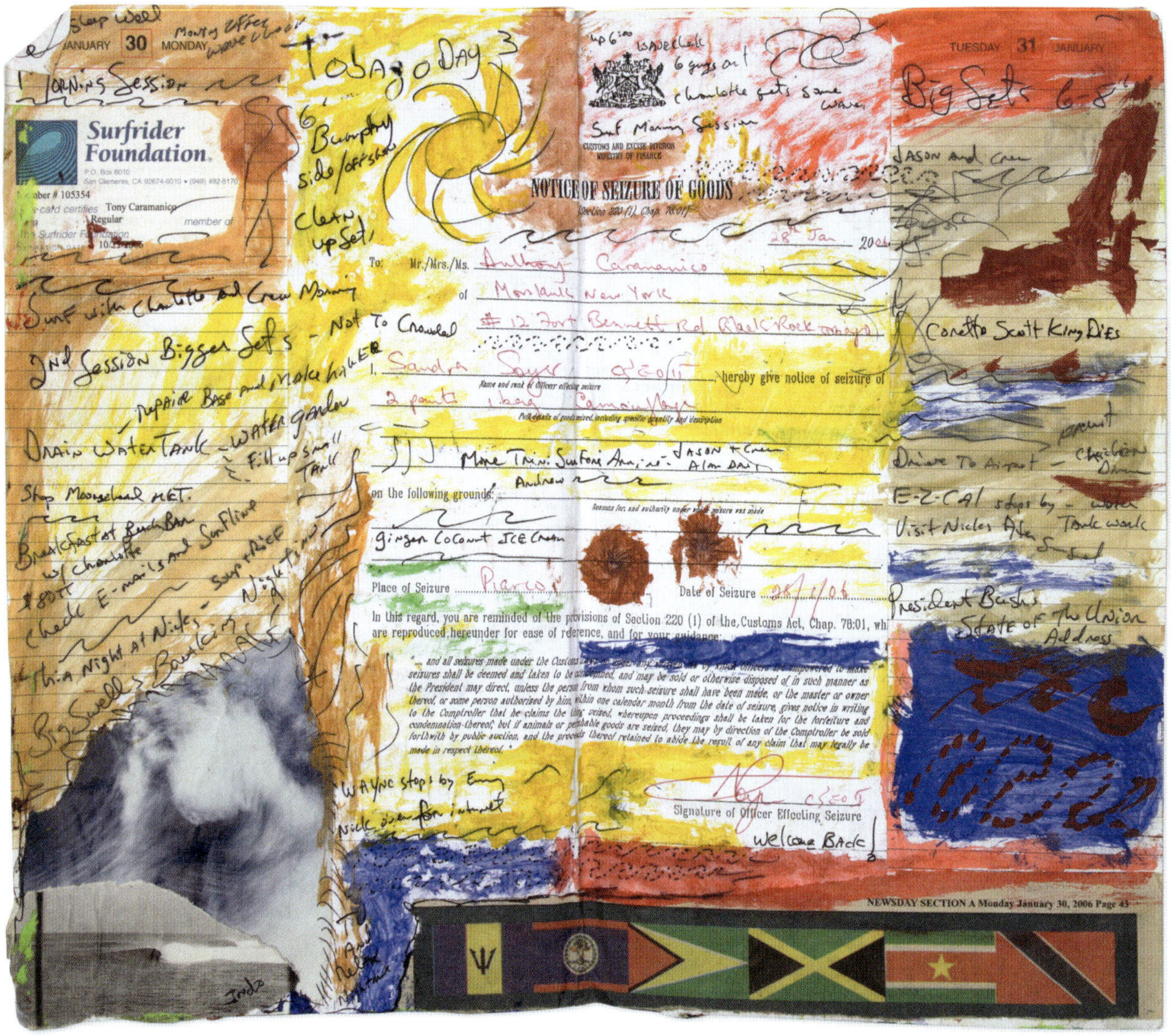

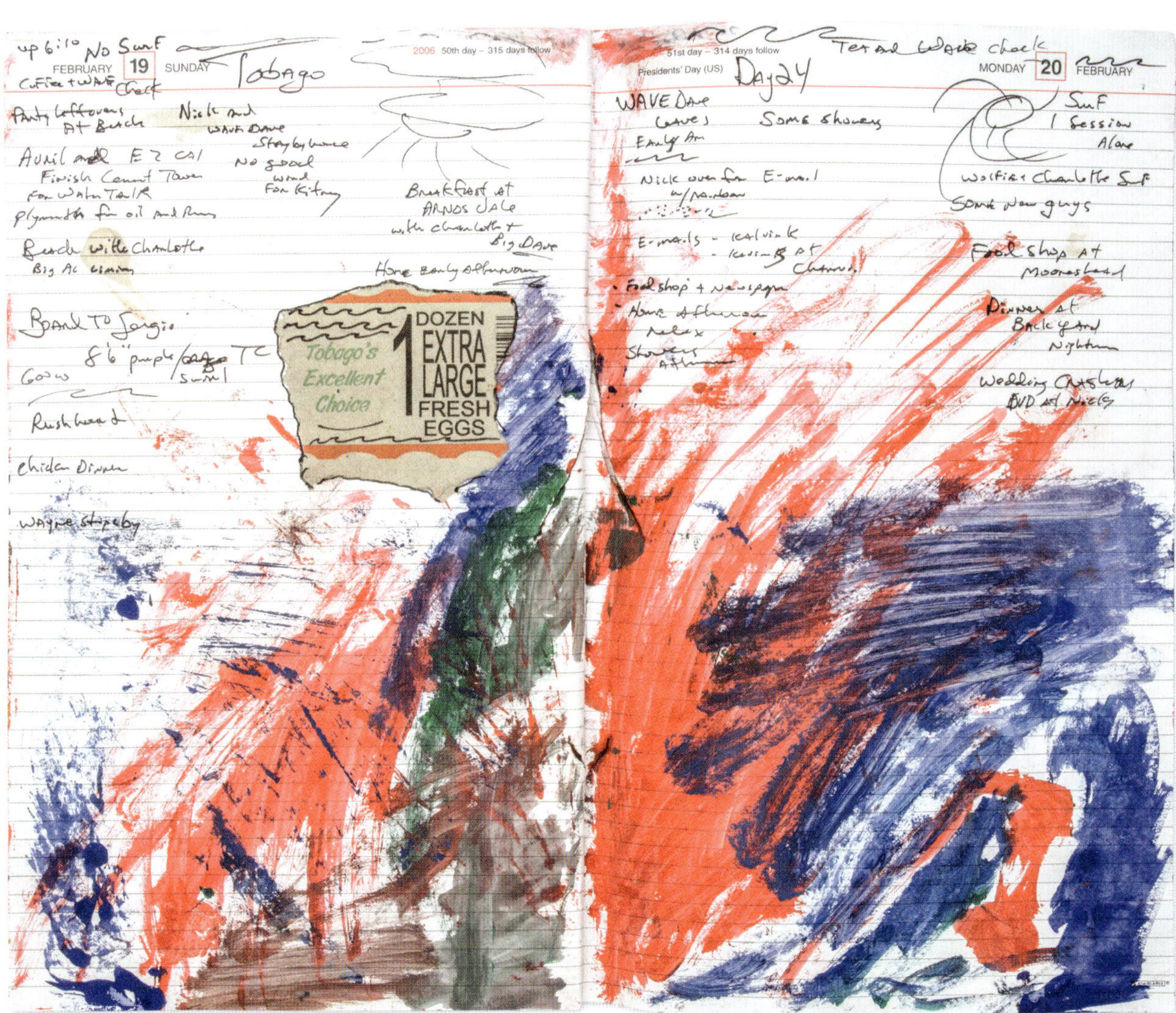
FEBRUARY 19 SUNDAY
2006 50th day – 315 days follow
Tobago
51st day – 314 days follow
Presidents' Day (US)
Day 24
MONDAY 20 FEBRUARY
Tobago's Excellent Choice
1 DOZEN EXTRA LARGE FRESH EGGS

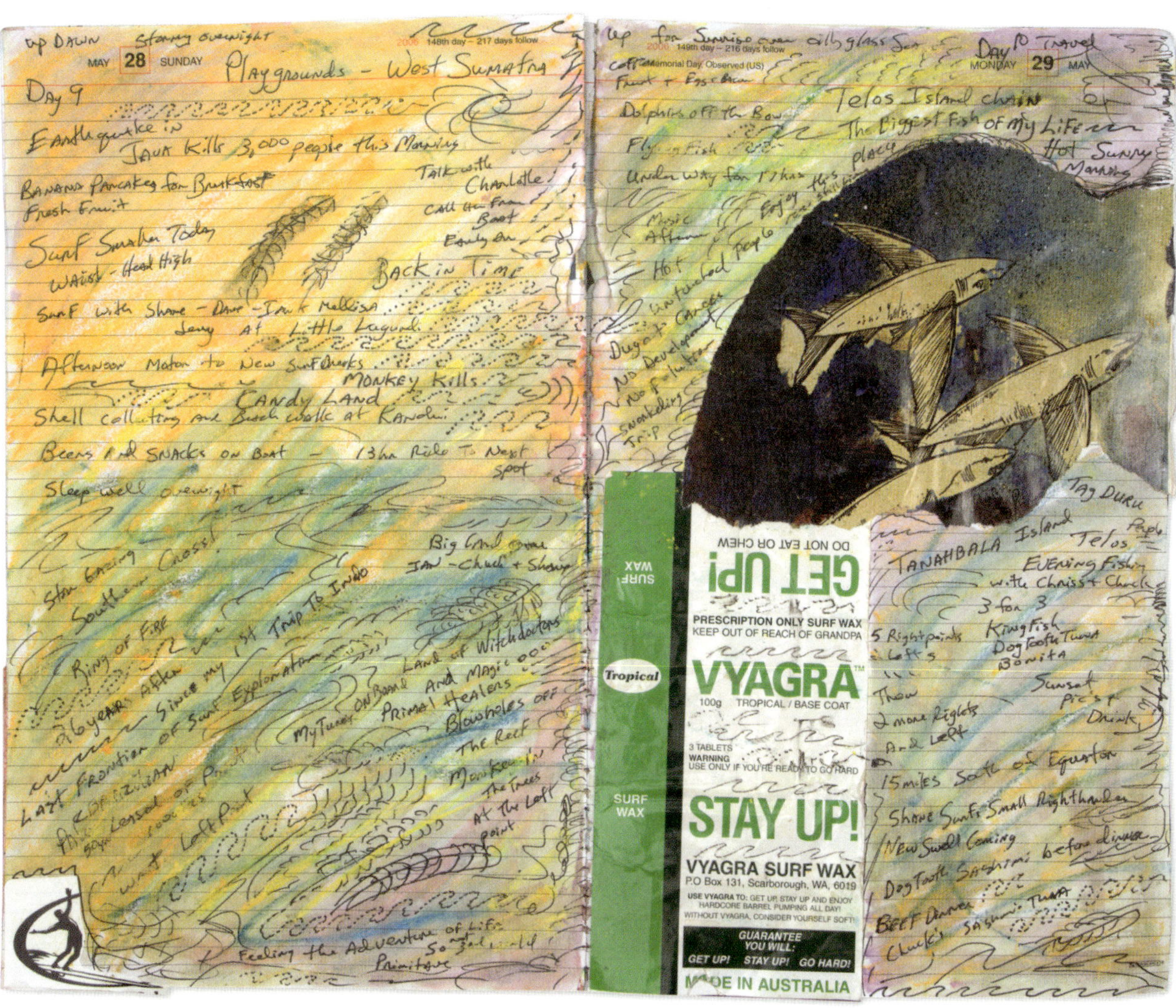

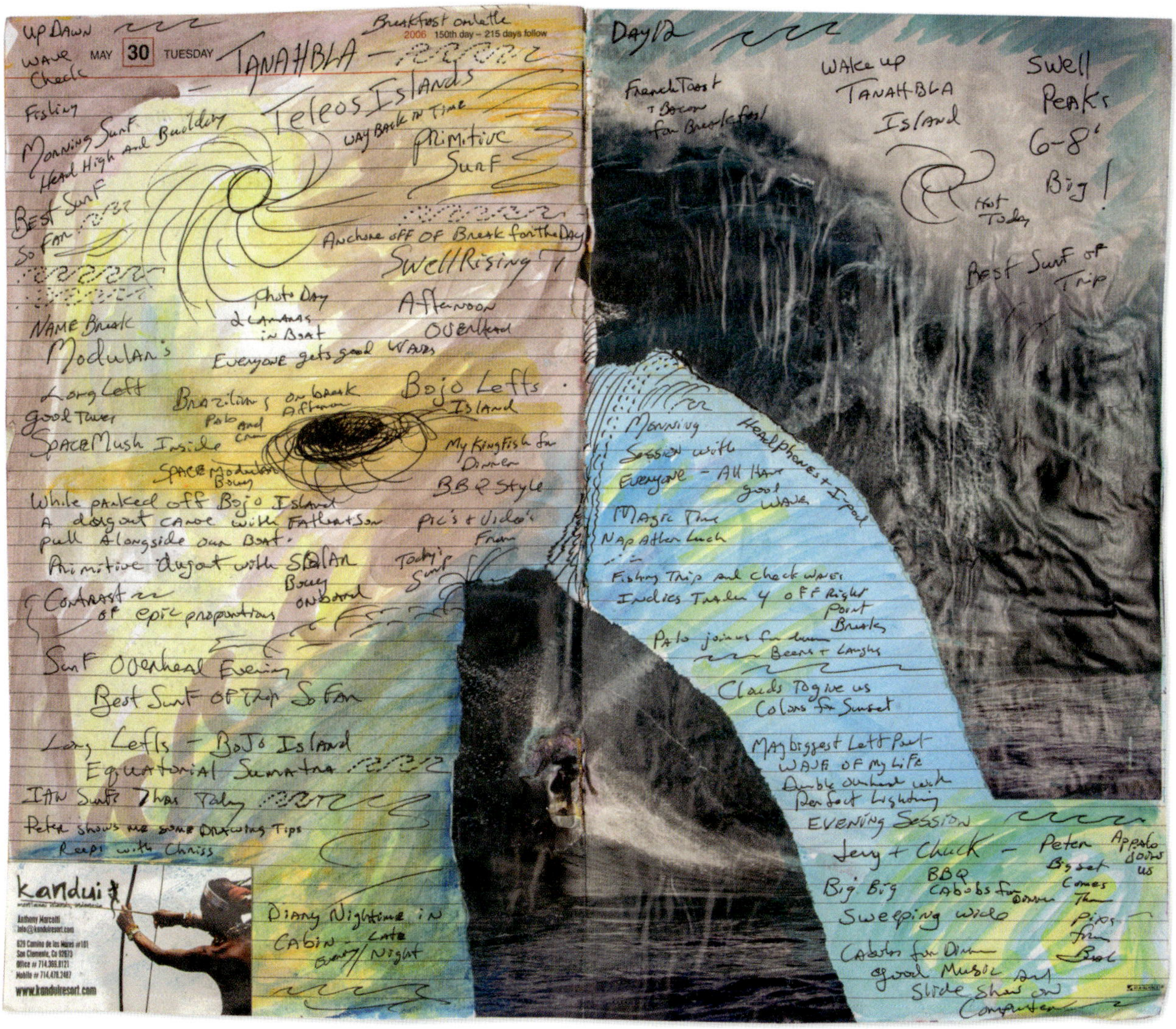

Up Dawn

Wave Check

MAY 30 TUESDAY

2006 150th day – 215 days follow

Breakfast onDeck

TANAHBLA

Teleos Islands

Way Back in Time

Primitive Surf

Fishing

Morning Surf Head High and Building

Best Surf So Far

Anchore off of Break for the Day

Swell Rising

Afternoon Overhead

Name Break Modulan's

Everyone gets good waves

Bojo Lefts Island

Long Left Good Tower

SpaceMush Inside

My Kingfish for Dinner BBQ Style

While parked off Bojo Island a dugout canoe with Father & Son pull alongside our Boat.

Primitive dugout with Solar Buoy onboard

Surf Overhead Evening

Best Surf of Trip So Far

Long Lefts – Bojo Island

Equatorial Sumatra

Diary Nighttime in Cabin – Late Boat/Night

Day 12

French Toast + Bacon for Breakfast

Wake up Tanahbla Island

Swell Peaks 6–8' Big!

Hot Today

Best Surf of Trip

Morning Session with Everyone – All Have good waves

Headphones + I-pod

Nap After Lunch

Clouds To give us Colors for Sunset

My biggest Left Point Wave of my Life

Evening Session

Jerry + Chuck

BBQ Cabobs for Dinner

Sweeping winds

Good Music and Slide Show on Computer

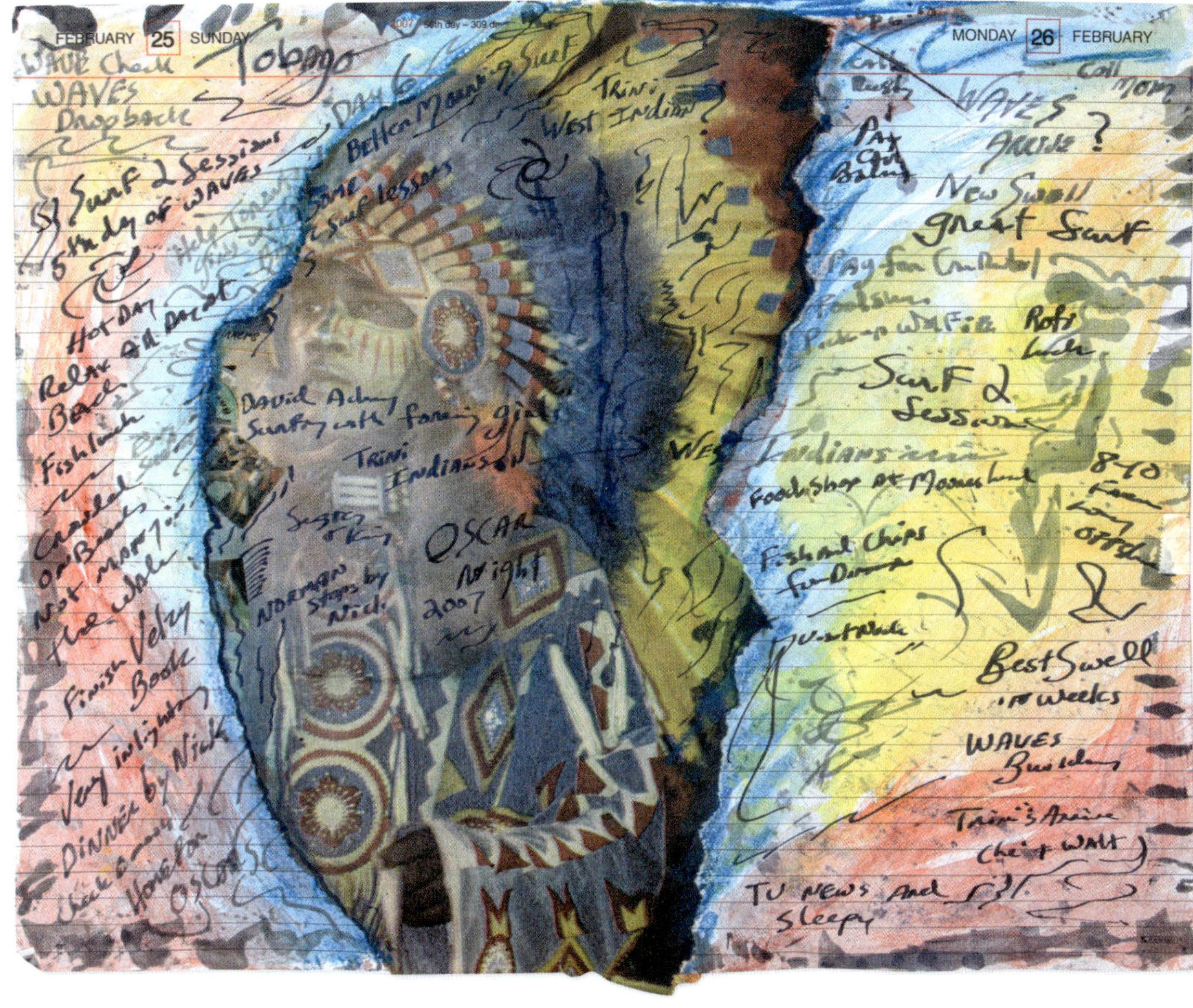
FEBRUARY 25 SUNDAY
MONDAY 26 FEBRUARY
Tobago
WAVES
New Swell
great Surf
Surf 2 Sessions
OSCAR Night 2007
Best Swell
TV NEWS and sleepy

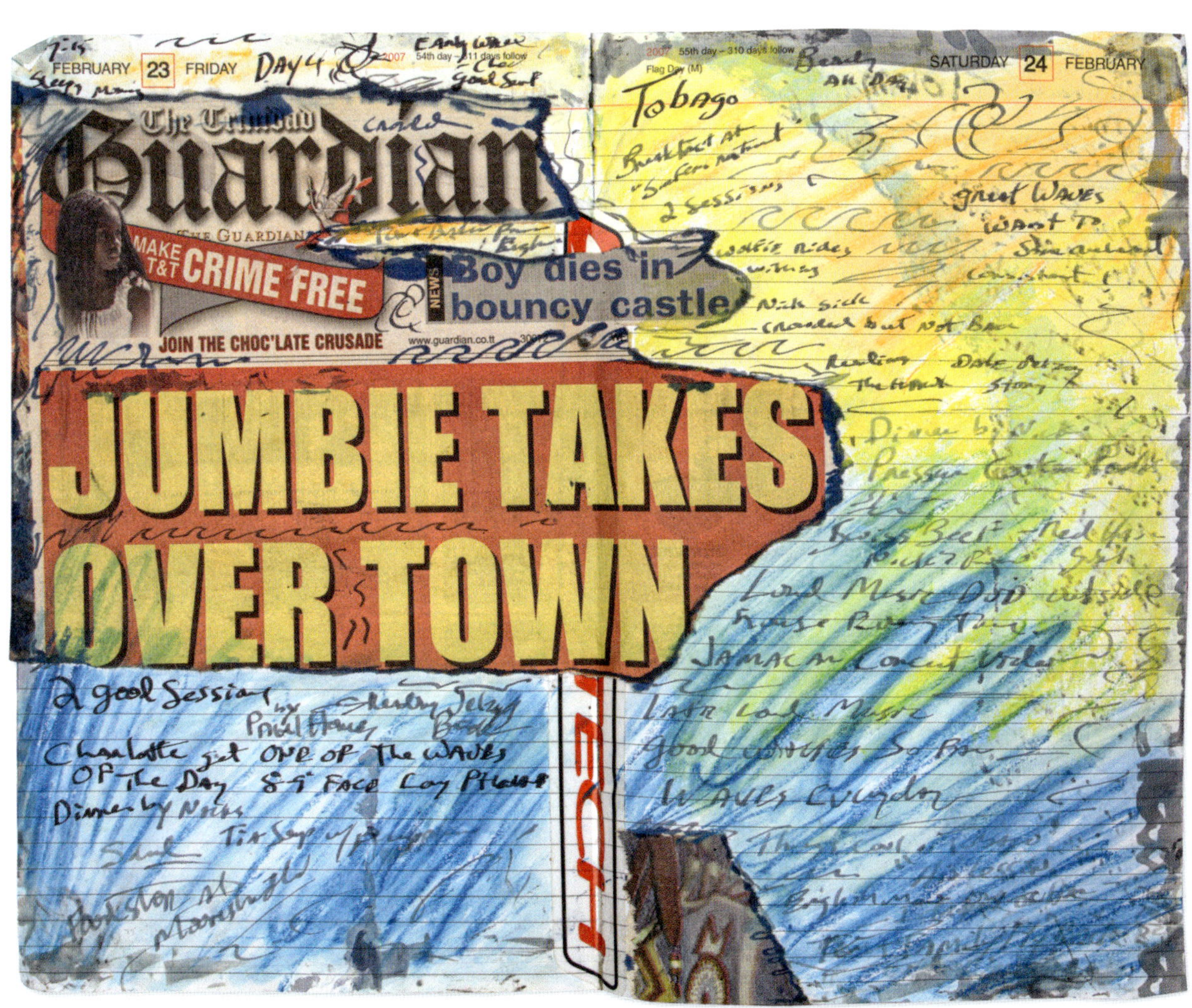
FEBRUARY 23 FRIDAY
54th day – 311 days follow
55th day – 310 days follow
Flag Day (M)
SATURDAY 24 FEBRUARY
Tobago
The Trinidad Guardian
MAKE T&T CRIME FREE
JOIN THE CHOC'LATE CRUSADE
www.guardian.co.tt
NEWS
Boy dies in bouncy castle
JUMBIE TAKES OVER TOWN
TECH

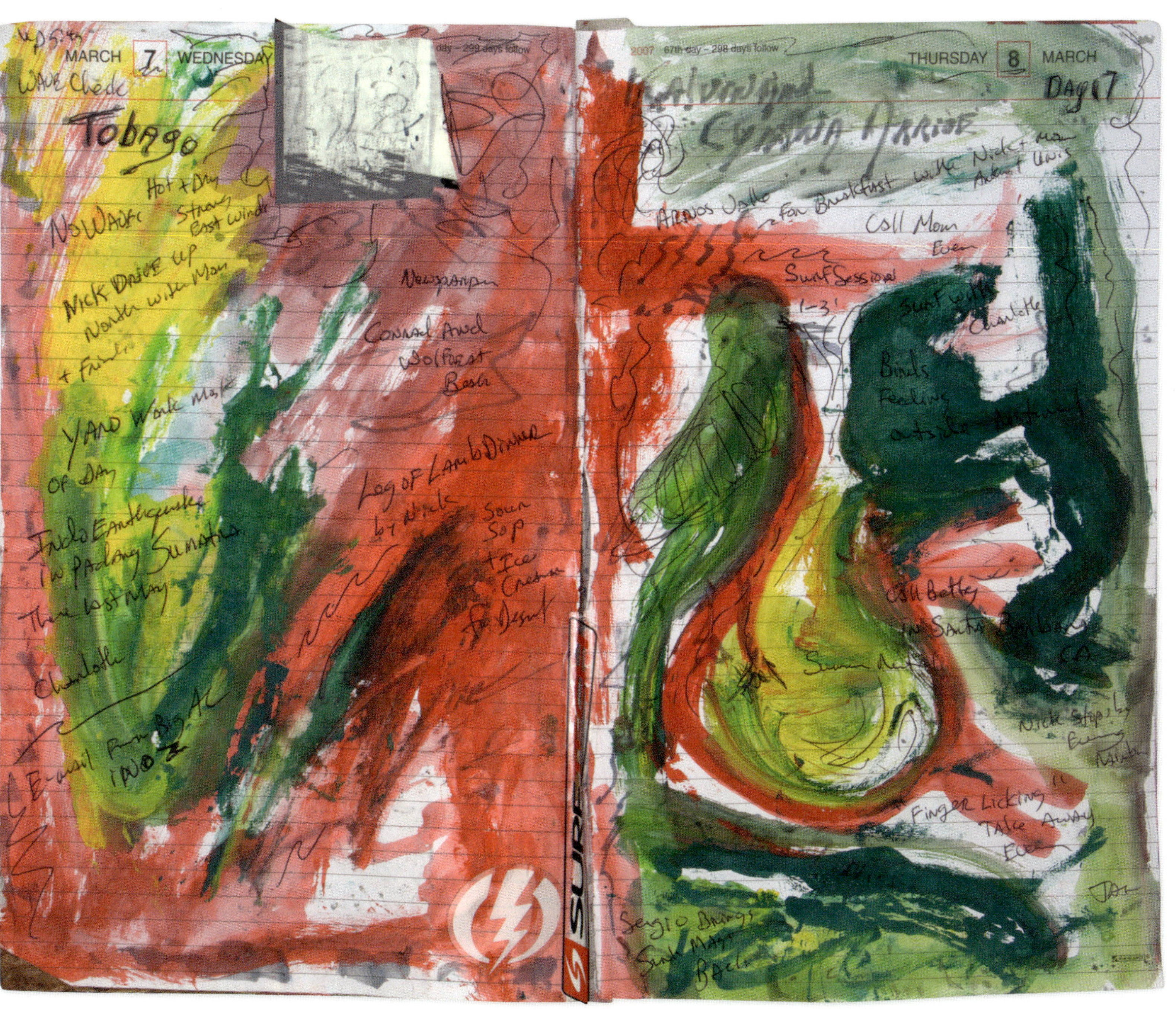
MARCH 7 WEDNESDAY
day – 299 days follow
Tobago
Hot + Dry
Strong East winds
No Waves
Nick Drove up North with Mom + Family
Newspaper
Conrad And Wolforst Bash
Log of Lamb Dinner by Nick
Sour Sop + Ice Cream for Desert
Charlotte
2007 67th day – 298 days follow
THURSDAY 8 MARCH
Day 67
Call Mom Even
Surf Session 1-3'
Surf with Charlotte
Birds Feeding
Call Betty in Santa Barbara CA
Finger Licking Take Away Even
Sergio Brings Surf Mags Back

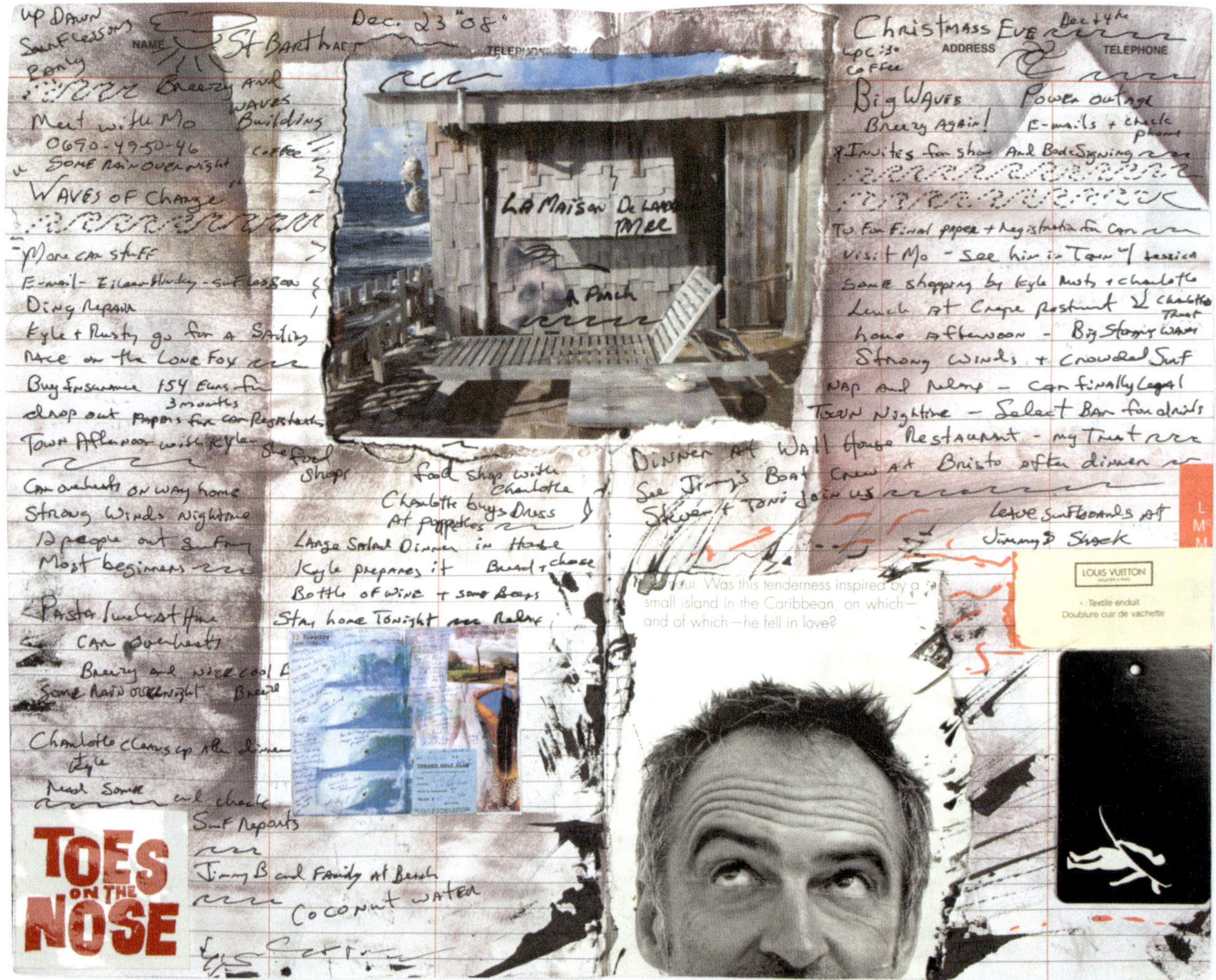
St Barth
Dec. 23 "08"
Christmass Eve
LA Maison De La
A Porch
TOES ON THE NOSE
Was this tenderness inspired by a small island in the Caribbean, on which— and of which—he fell in love?
LOUIS VUITTON
Textile enduit
Doublure cuir de vachette
Coconut water

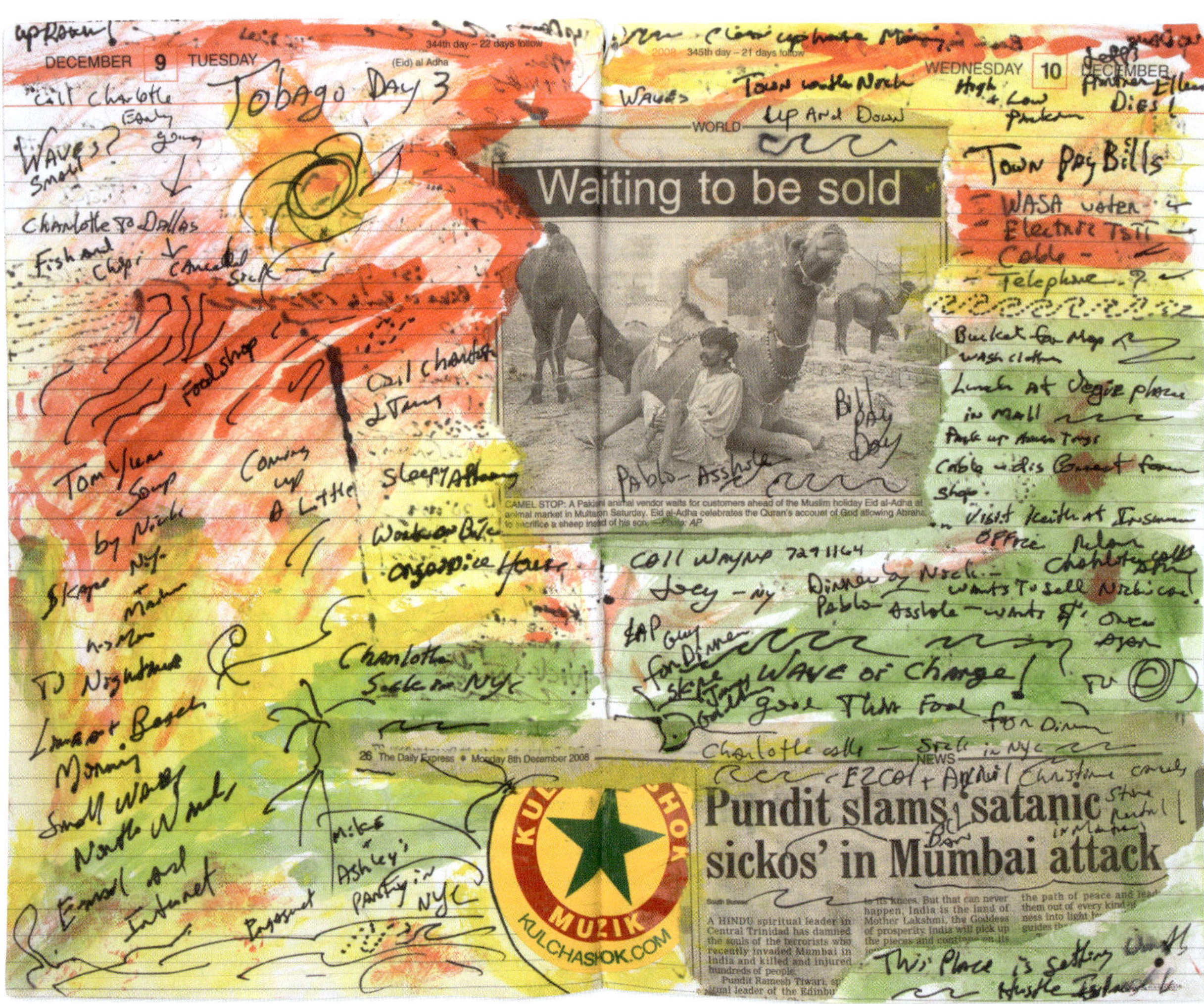
DECEMBER 9 TUESDAY
344th day – 22 days follow
(Eid) al Adha
Tobago Day 3
345th day – 21 days follow
WEDNESDAY 10 DECEMBER
WORLD
Waiting to be sold
CAMEL STOP: A Pakistani animal vendor waits for customers ahead of the Muslim holiday Eid al-Adha at animal market in Multan on Saturday. Eid al-Adha celebrates the Quran's account of God allowing Abraham to sacrifice a sheep instead of his son.—Photo: AP
Town Pay Bills
WAVE of Change
26 The Daily Express • Monday 8th December 2008
NEWS
Pundit slams 'satanic sickos' in Mumbai attack
KULCHASHOK.COM
MUZIK
This Place is Getting Crazy

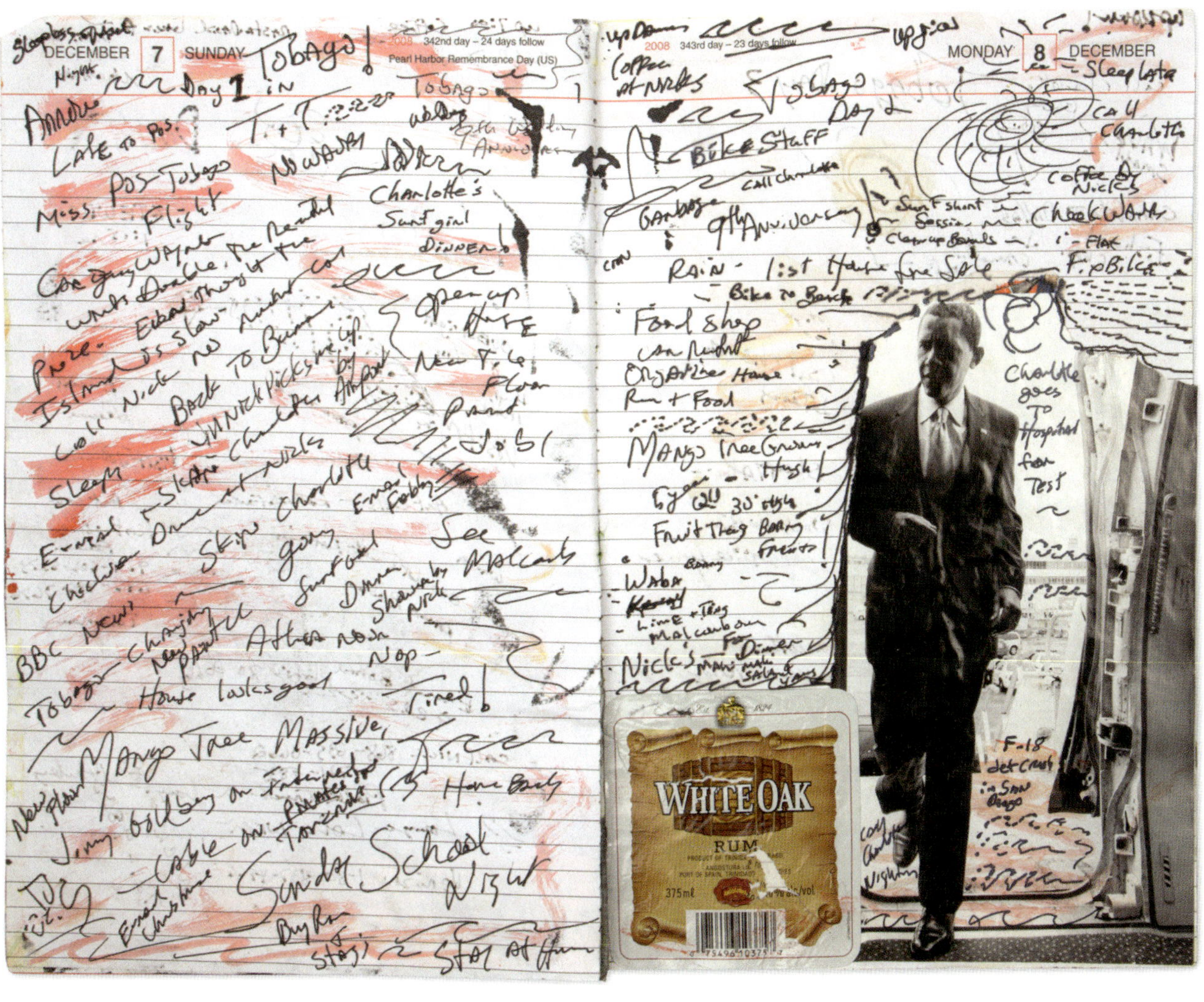
DECEMBER 7 SUNDAY
2008 342nd day – 24 days follow
Pearl Harbor Remembrance Day (US)
Tobago!
Mango Tree Massive
Sunday School Night
2008 343rd day – 23 days follow
MONDAY 8 DECEMBER
WHITE OAK
RUM
375ml

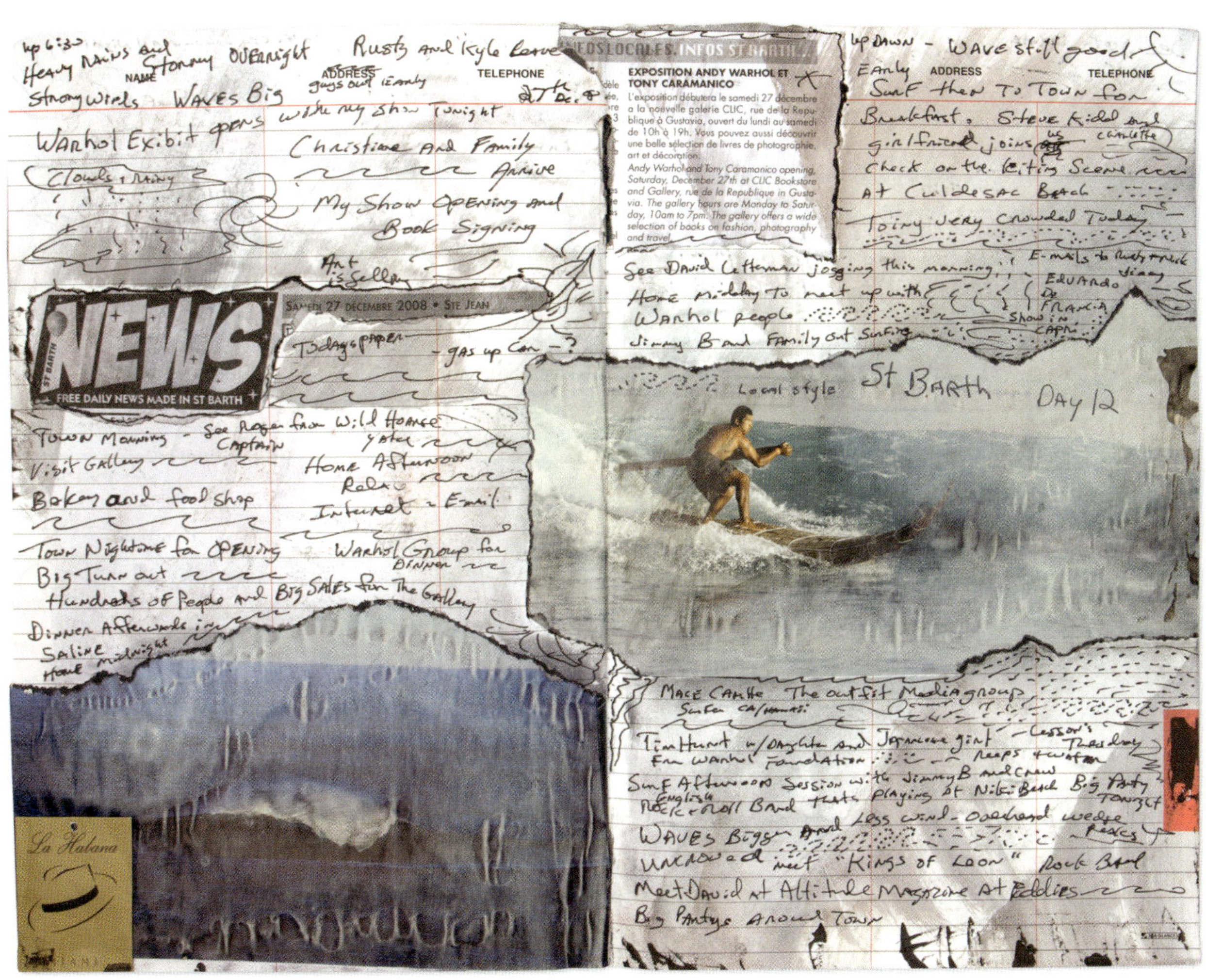
NAME
ADDRESS
TELEPHONE
Warhol Exibit opens
Christine and Family Arrive
My Show Opening and Book Signing
NEWS
SAMEDI 27 DÉCEMBRE 2008 • STE JEAN
FREE DAILY NEWS MADE IN ST BARTH
INFOS ST BARTH
EXPOSITION ANDY WARHOL ET TONY CARAMANICO
L'exposition débutera le samedi 27 décembre a la nouvelle galerie CLIC, rue de la Republique à Gustavia, ouvert du lundi au samedi de 10h à 19h. Vous pouvez aussi découvrir une belle sélection de livres de photographie, art et décoration.
Andy Warhol and Tony Caramanico opening, Saturday, December 27th at CLIC Bookstore and Gallery, rue de la Republique in Gustavia. The gallery hours are Monday to Saturday, 10am to 7pm. The gallery offers a wide selection of books on fashion, photography and travel.
See David Letterman jogging this morning
Warhol people
St Barth Day 12
La Habana

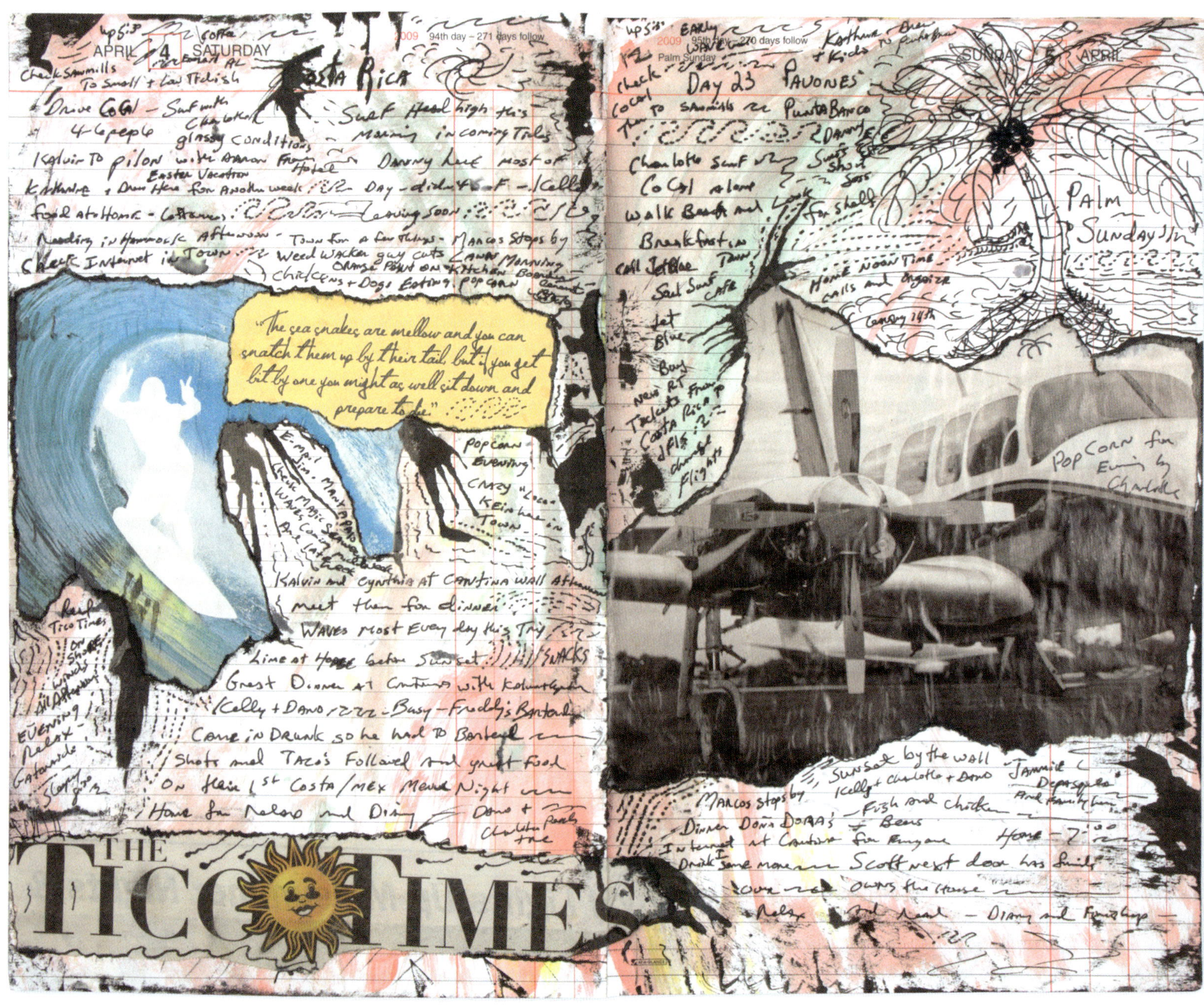
APRIL 4 SATURDAY
2009 94th day – 271 days follow
Costa Rica
"The sea snakes are mellow and you can snatch them up by their tail but if you get bit by one you might as well sit down and prepare to die."
THE TICO TIMES
2009 95th day – 270 days follow
Palm Sunday
SUNDAY 5 APRIL
Day 23 Pavones
Palm Sunday
Popcorn for Evening by Charlotte

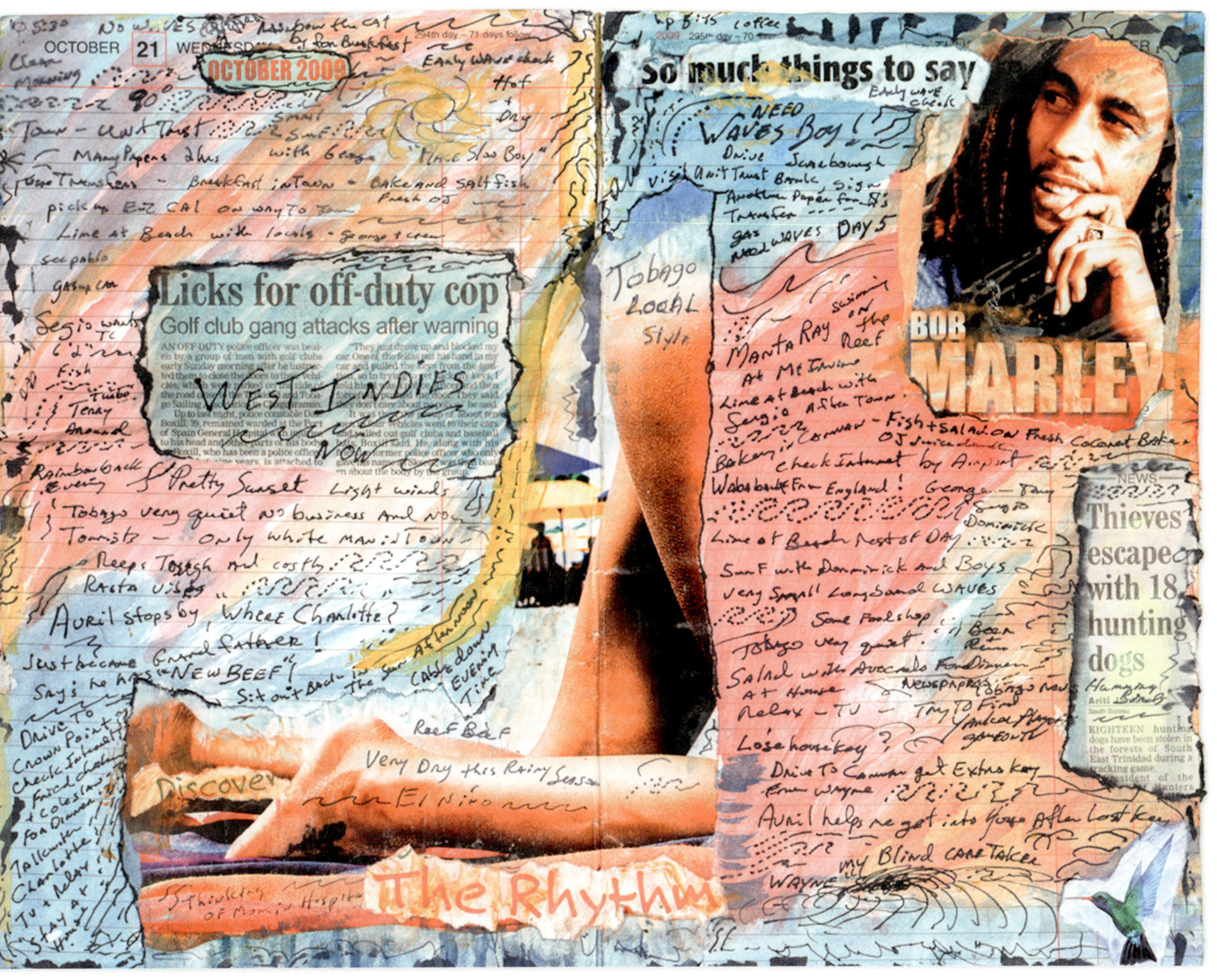
OCTOBER 21 WEDNESDAY
OCTOBER 2009
Licks for off-duty cop
Golf club gang attacks after warning
WEST INDIES
So much things to say
Tobago LOCAL Style
BOB MARLEY
NEWS
Thieves escape with 18 hunting dogs
Discover
The Rhythm

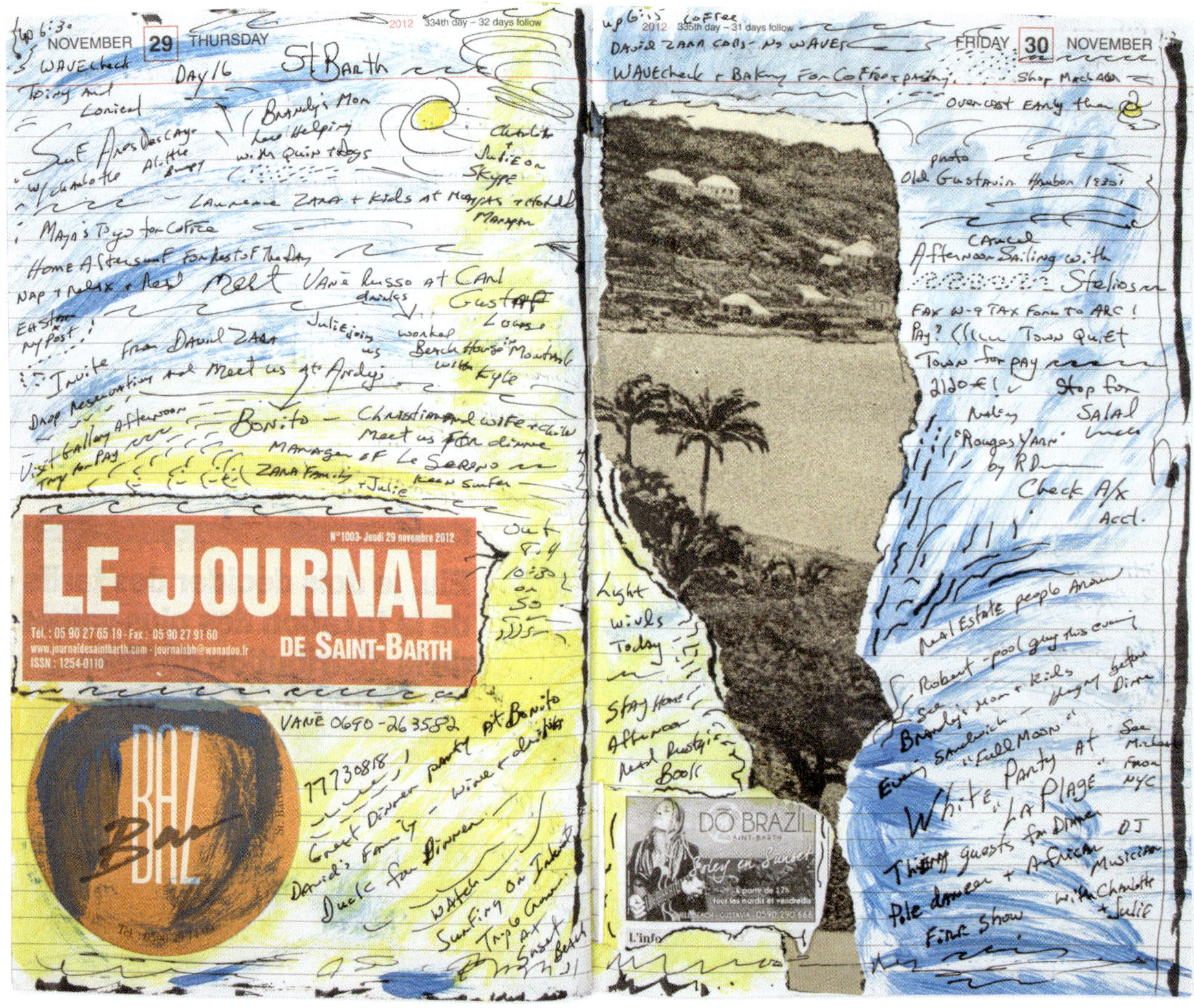
NOVEMBER 29 THURSDAY
FRIDAY 30 NOVEMBER
LE JOURNAL DE SAINT-BARTH
N°1003- Jeudi 29 novembre 2012
ISSN : 1254-0110
DO BRAZIL
SAINT-BARTH

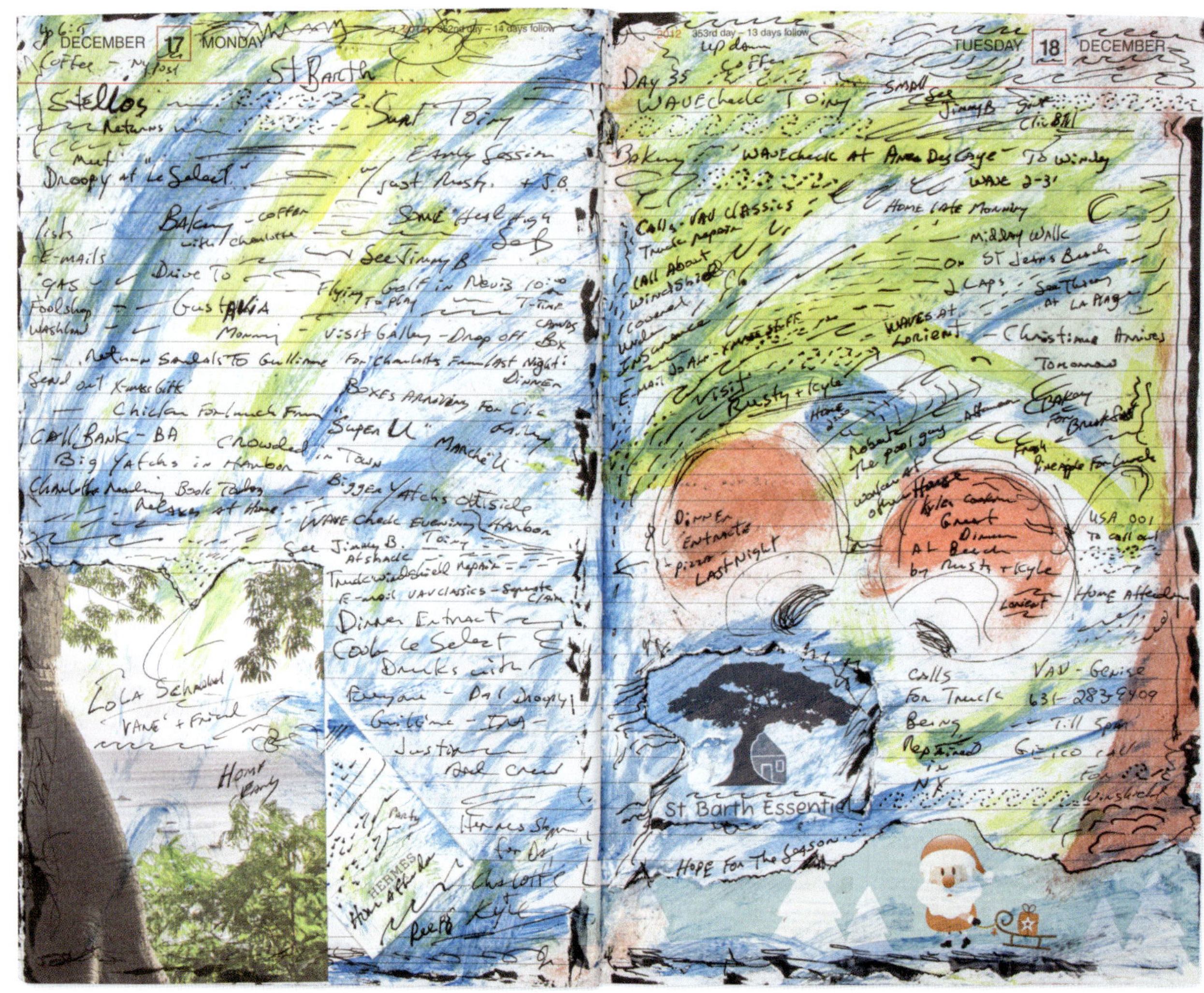
DECEMBER 17 MONDAY
TUESDAY 18 DECEMBER
St Barth Essentiel

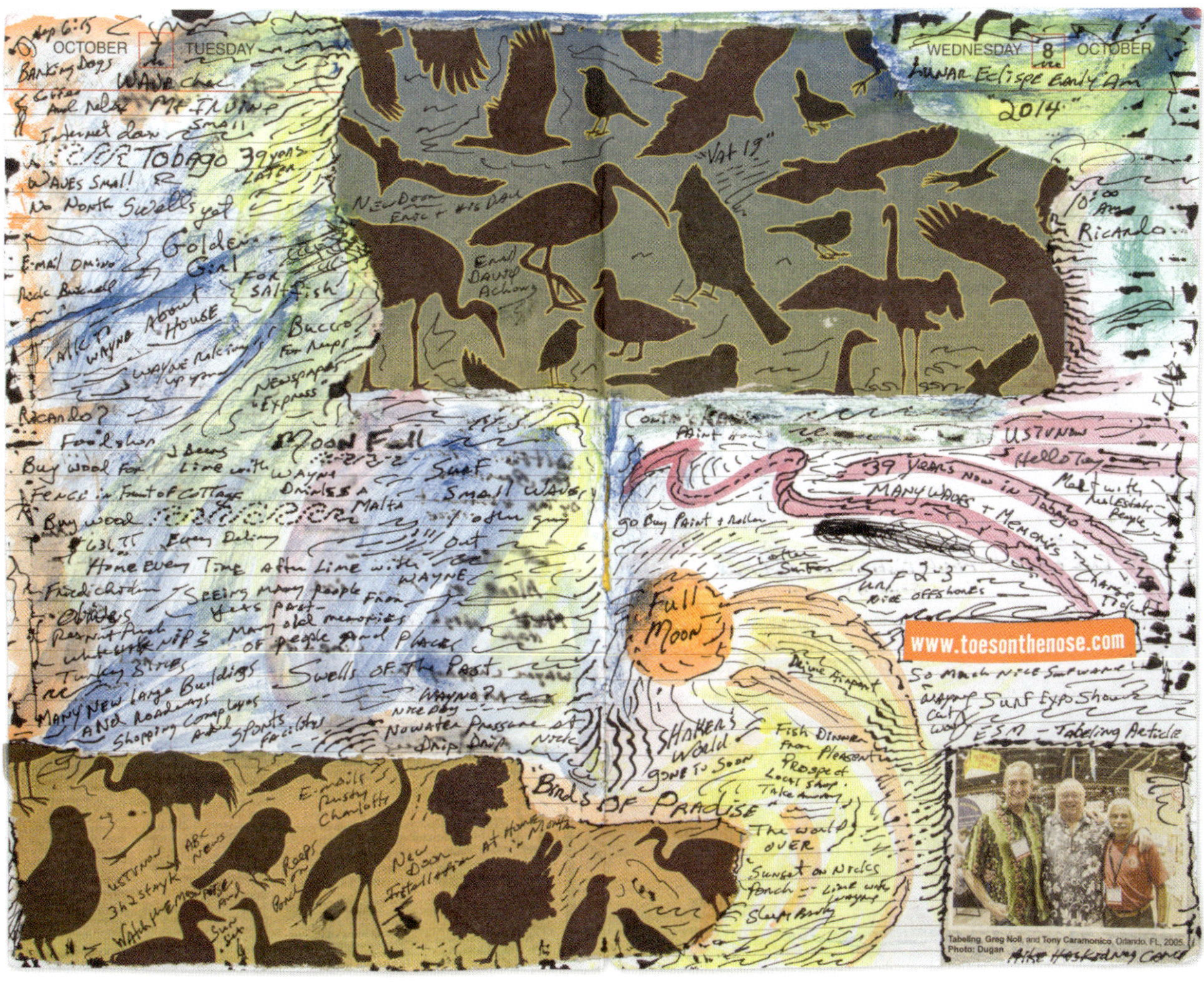
OCTOBER 7 TUESDAY
WEDNESDAY 8 OCTOBER
Lunar Eclipse Early Am
Tobago 39 years Later
Full Moon
Birds of Paradise
www.toesonthenose.com
Tabeling, Greg Noll, and Tony Caramonica, Orlando, FL, 2005. Photo: Dugan

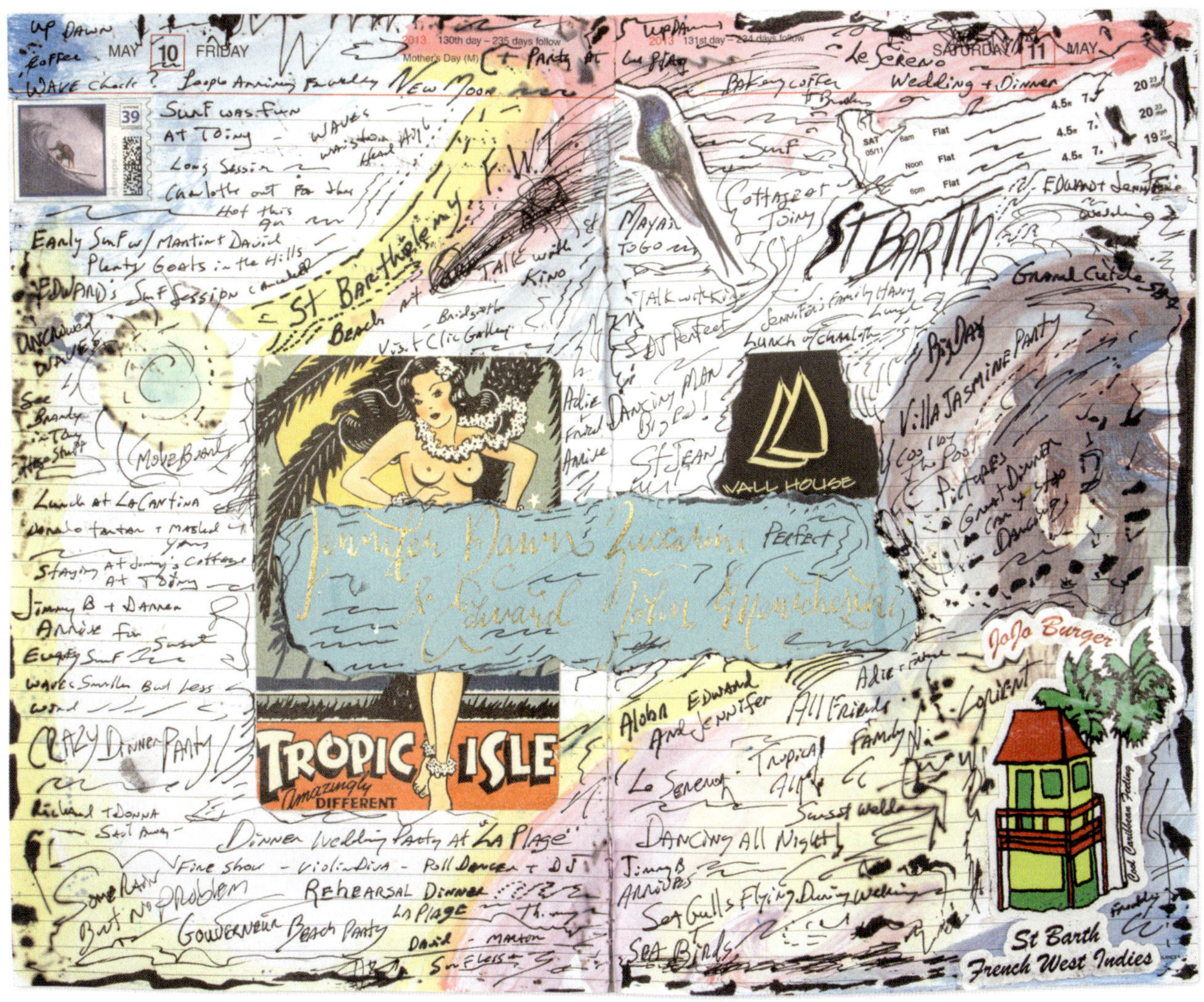
MAY 10 FRIDAY
SATURDAY 11 MAY
New Moon
St Barth
TROPIC ISLE
Amazingly DIFFERENT
JoJo Burger
St Barth
French West Indies

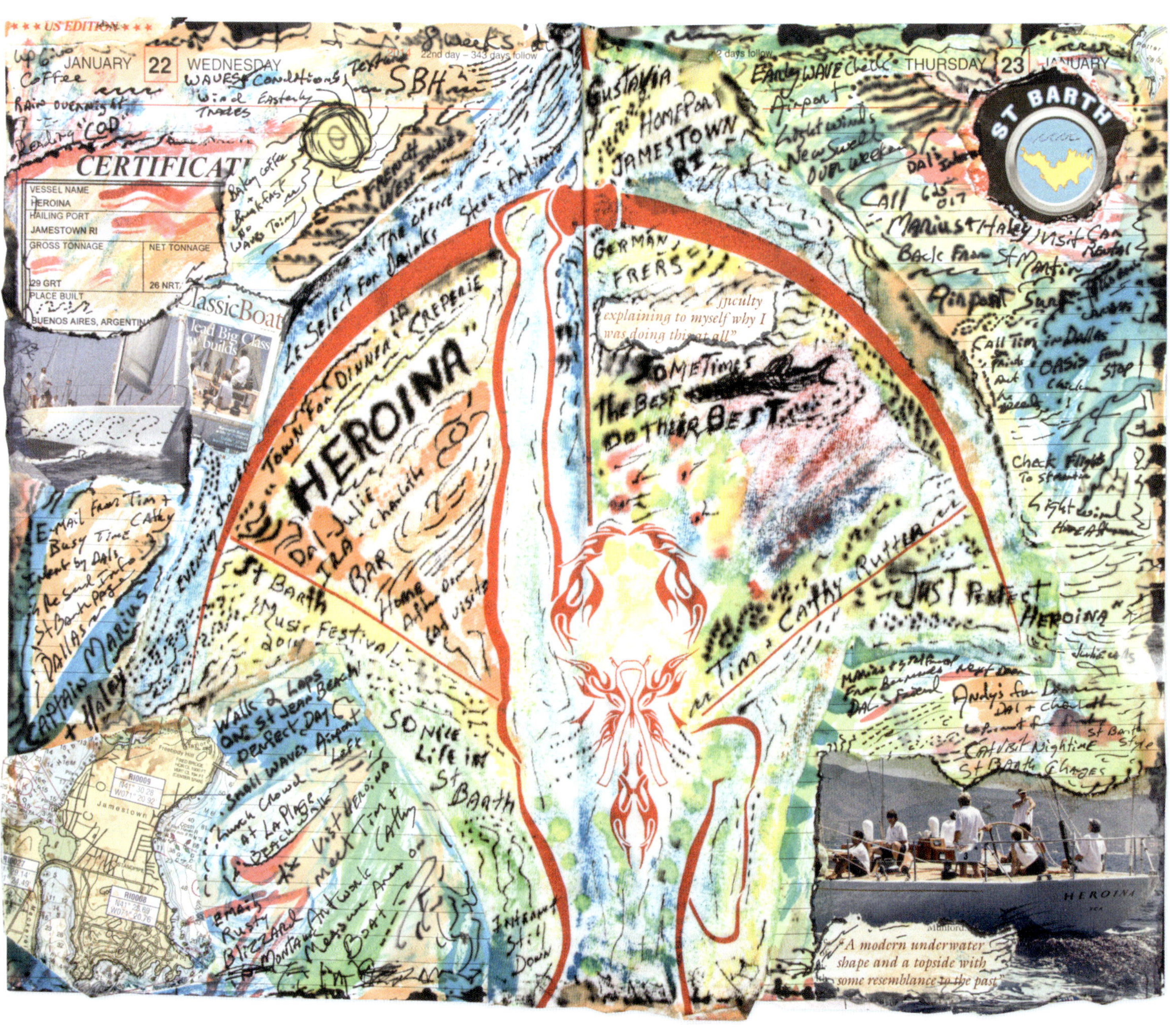
US EDITION
JANUARY 22 WEDNESDAY
22nd day – 343 days follow
THURSDAY 23 JANUARY
CERTIFICATE
VESSEL NAME
HEROINA
HAILING PORT
JAMESTOWN RI
GROSS TONNAGE
NET TONNAGE
29 GRT
26 NRT
PLACE BUILT
BUENOS AIRES, ARGENTINA
ClassicBoat
ST BARTH
HEROINA
SBH
GUSTAVIA
HOMEPORT
JAMESTOWN RI
GERMAN FRERS
explaining to myself why I was doing this at all"
SOMETIMES THE BEST
JUST PERFECT
"A modern underwater shape and a topside with some resemblance to the past"

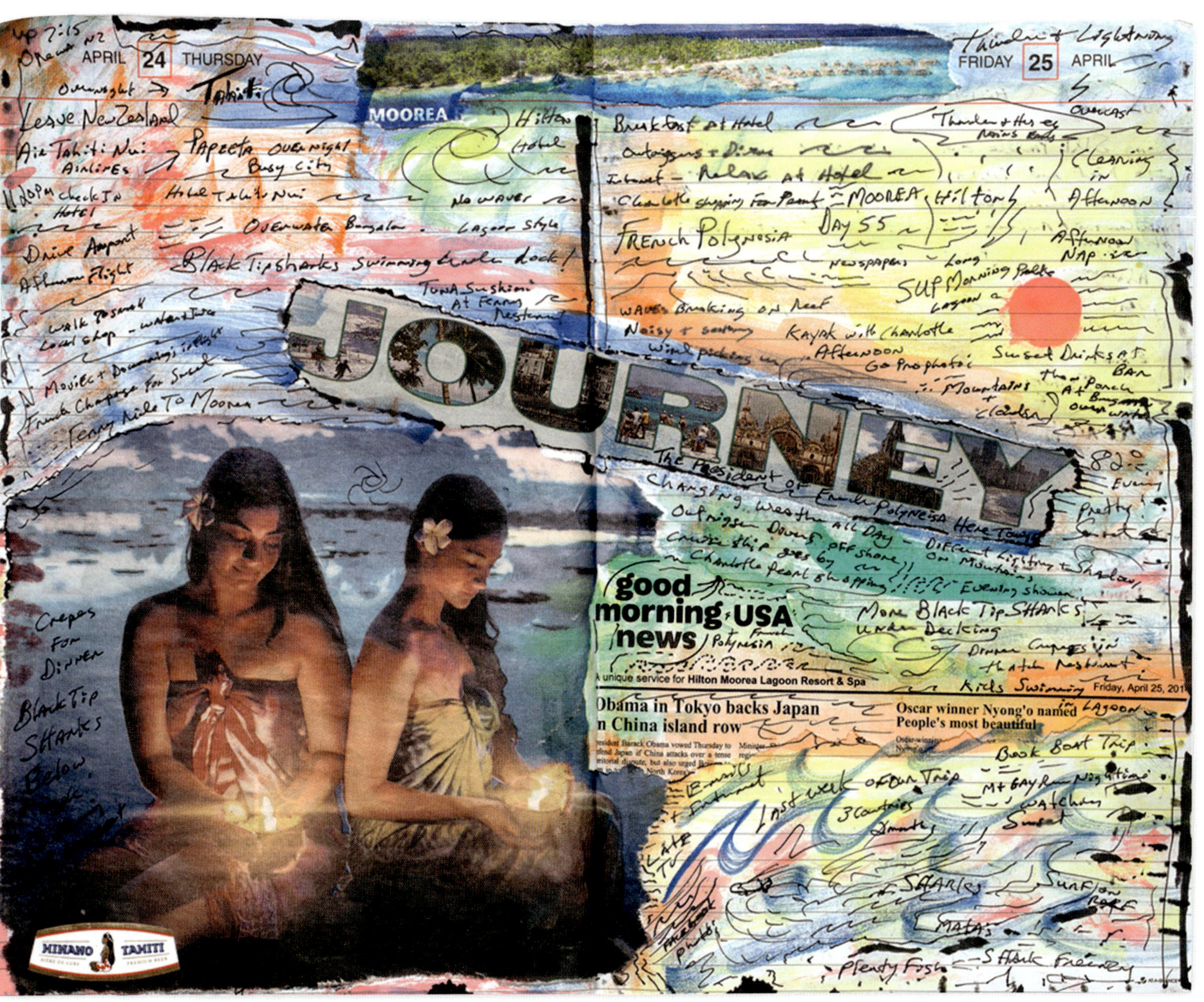
APRIL 24 THURSDAY
FRIDAY 25 APRIL
MOOREA
JOURNEY
good morning USA news
A unique service for Hilton Moorea Lagoon Resort & Spa
Friday, April 25, 201
Obama in Tokyo backs Japan
n China island row
Oscar winner Nyong'o named
People's most beautiful
HINANO
TAHITI

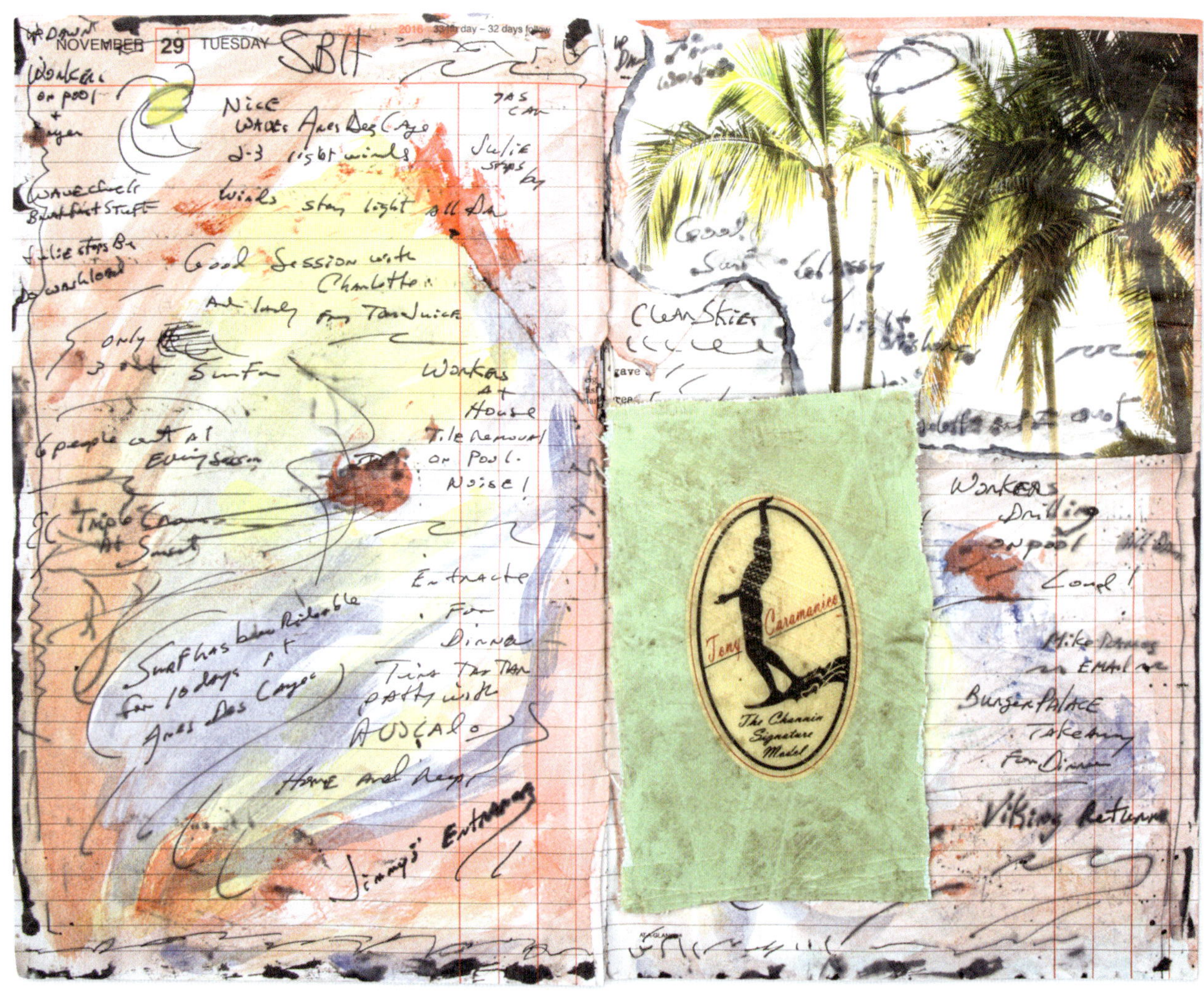
NOVEMBER 29 TUESDAY
SBH
Nice
Waves Anse Des Caye
Good Session with Charlotte
Workers at House
Tile Removal on Pool
Noise!
Entracte
For Dinner
Surf has been Rideable for 10 days at Anse Des Cayes
Home and Nap
Clear Skies
Workers Drilling on pool
Mike
Email
Burger Palace
For Dinner
Viking Returns
Tony Caramanico
The Channin Signature Model

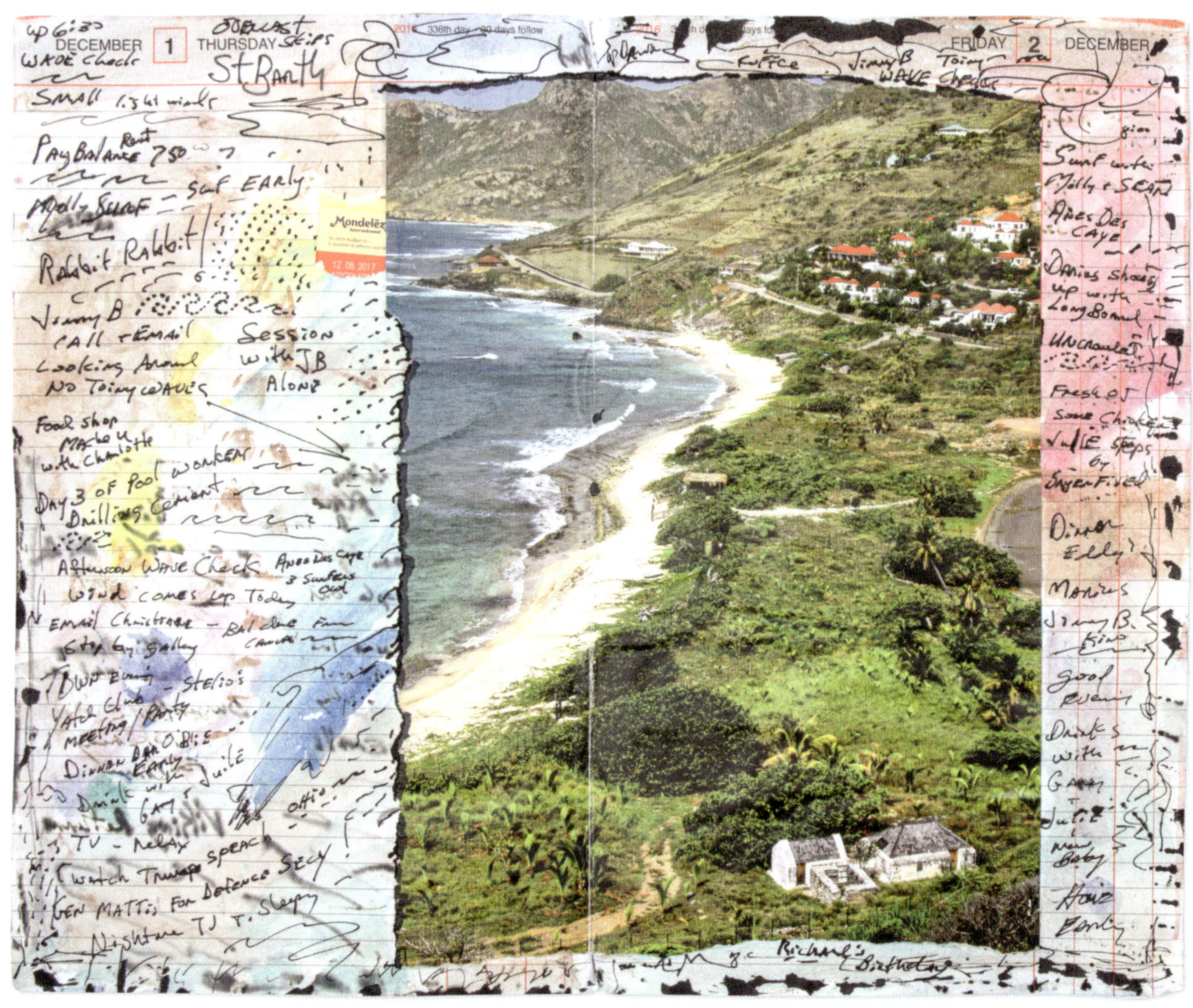
DECEMBER 1 THURSDAY
St Barth
Wave Check
Small
Pay Balance
Surf Early
Rabbit Rabbit
Jimmy B
Session with JB
Alone
Looking Around
No Tiny Waves
Food Shop
Day 3 of Pool Workers
Drilling Cement
Afternoon Wave Check
Wind comes up Today
Email
Dinner
Drink with
TV - Relax
Watch Trumps Speach
Gen Mattis For Defence Secy
Nightime TV + Sleep
FRIDAY 2 DECEMBER
Coffee
Wave Check
Surf with
Molly + Sean
Anse Des Caye
Fresh OJ
Julie Stops by
Dinner
Good Evening
Drinks with
Julie
New Baby
Home Early
Richard's Birthday

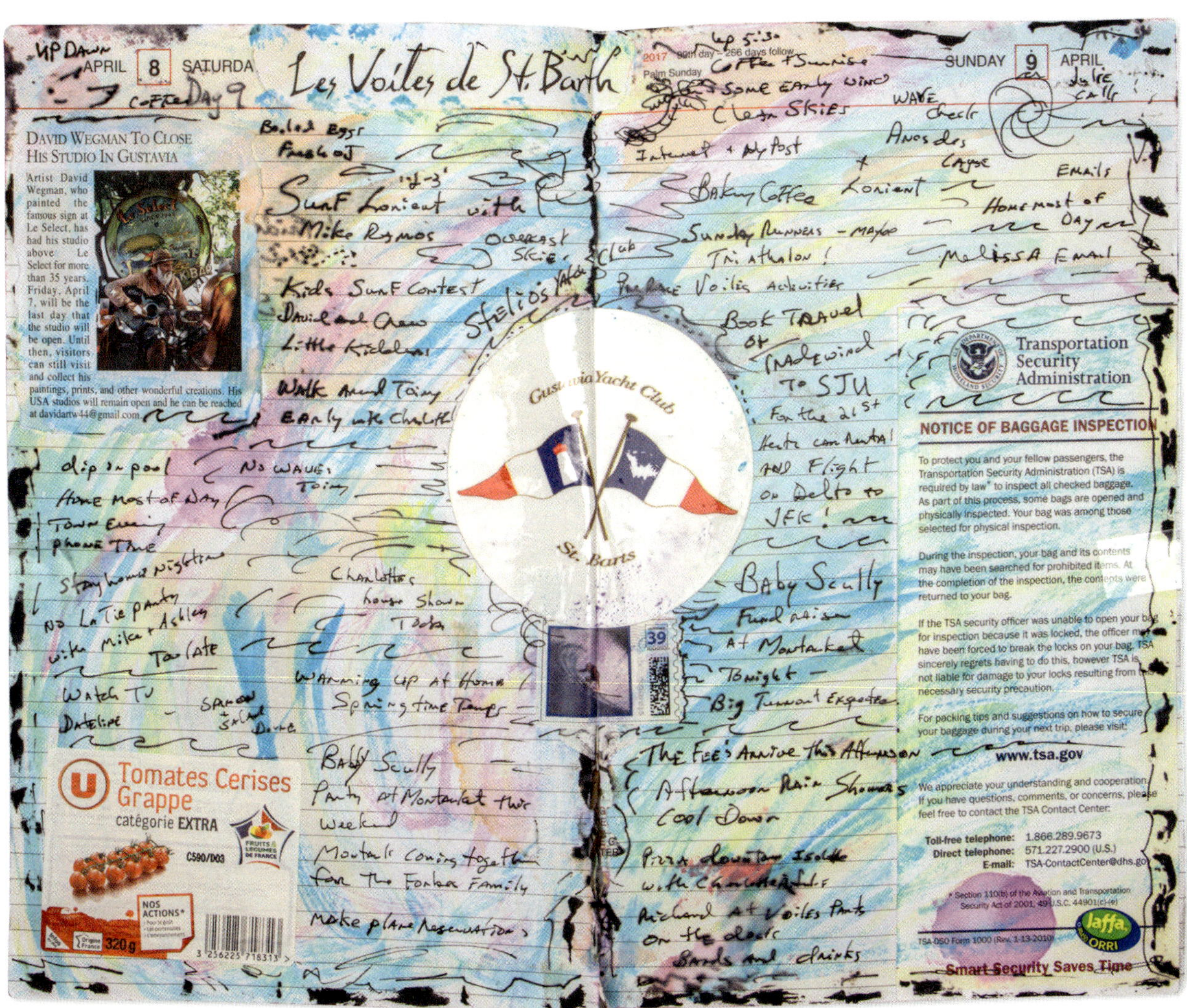
APRIL 8 SATURDAY
Les Voiles de St. Barth
SUNDAY 9 APRIL
DAVID WEGMAN TO CLOSE HIS STUDIO IN GUSTAVIA
Artist David Wegman, who painted the famous sign at Le Select, has had his studio above Le Select for more than 35 years. Friday, April 7, will be the last day that the studio will be open. Until then, visitors can still visit and collect his paintings, prints, and other wonderful creations. His USA studios will remain open and he can be reached at davidartw44@gmail.com
Gustavia Yacht Club
St. Barts
Tomates Cerises Grappe
catégorie EXTRA
320 g
Transportation Security Administration
NOTICE OF BAGGAGE INSPECTION
To protect you and your fellow passengers, the Transportation Security Administration (TSA) is required by law* to inspect all checked baggage. As part of this process, some bags are opened and physically inspected. Your bag was among those selected for physical inspection.
During the inspection, your bag and its contents may have been searched for prohibited items. At the completion of the inspection, the contents were returned to your bag.
For packing tips and suggestions on how to secure your baggage during your next trip, please visit:
www.tsa.gov
We appreciate your understanding and cooperation. If you have questions, comments, or concerns, please feel free to contact the TSA Contact Center:
Toll-free telephone: 1.866.289.9673
Direct telephone: 571.227.2900 (U.S.)
Smart Security Saves Time

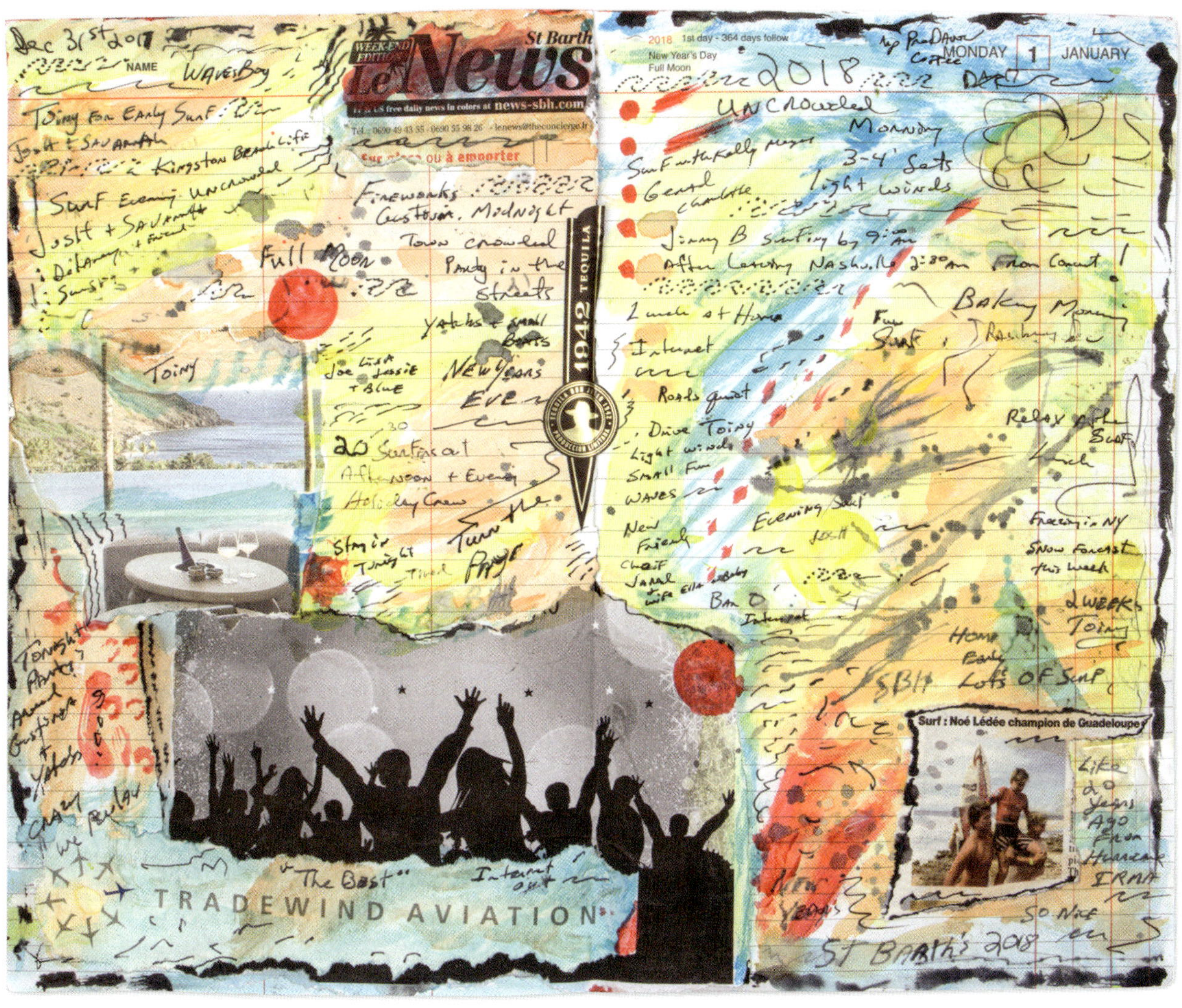
WEEK-END EDITION Le News St Barth
1942 TEQUILA
New Year's Day
MONDAY 1 JANUARY
2018
Surf : Noé Lédée champion de Guadeloupe
TRADEWIND AVIATION
ST BARTH'S 2018

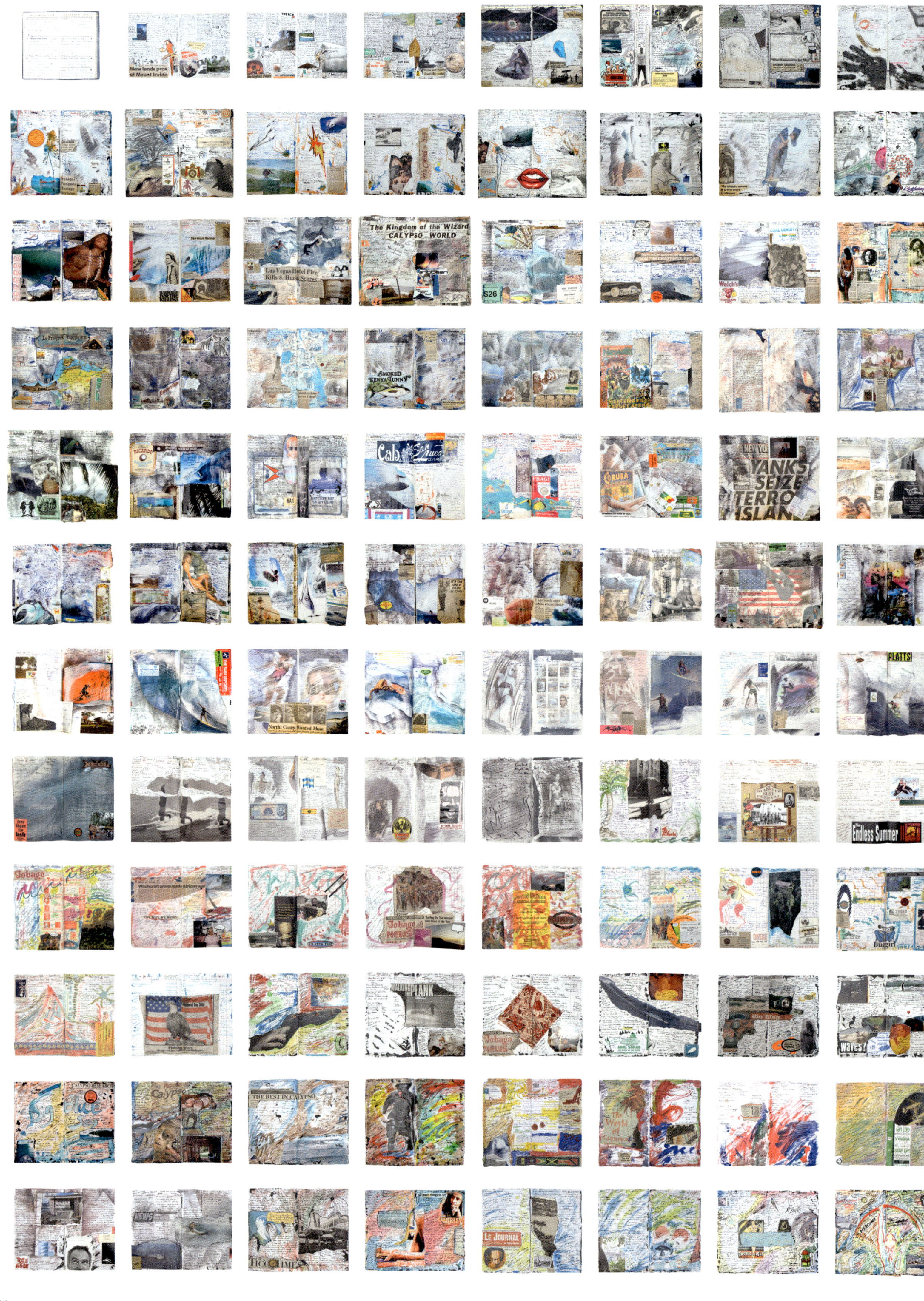

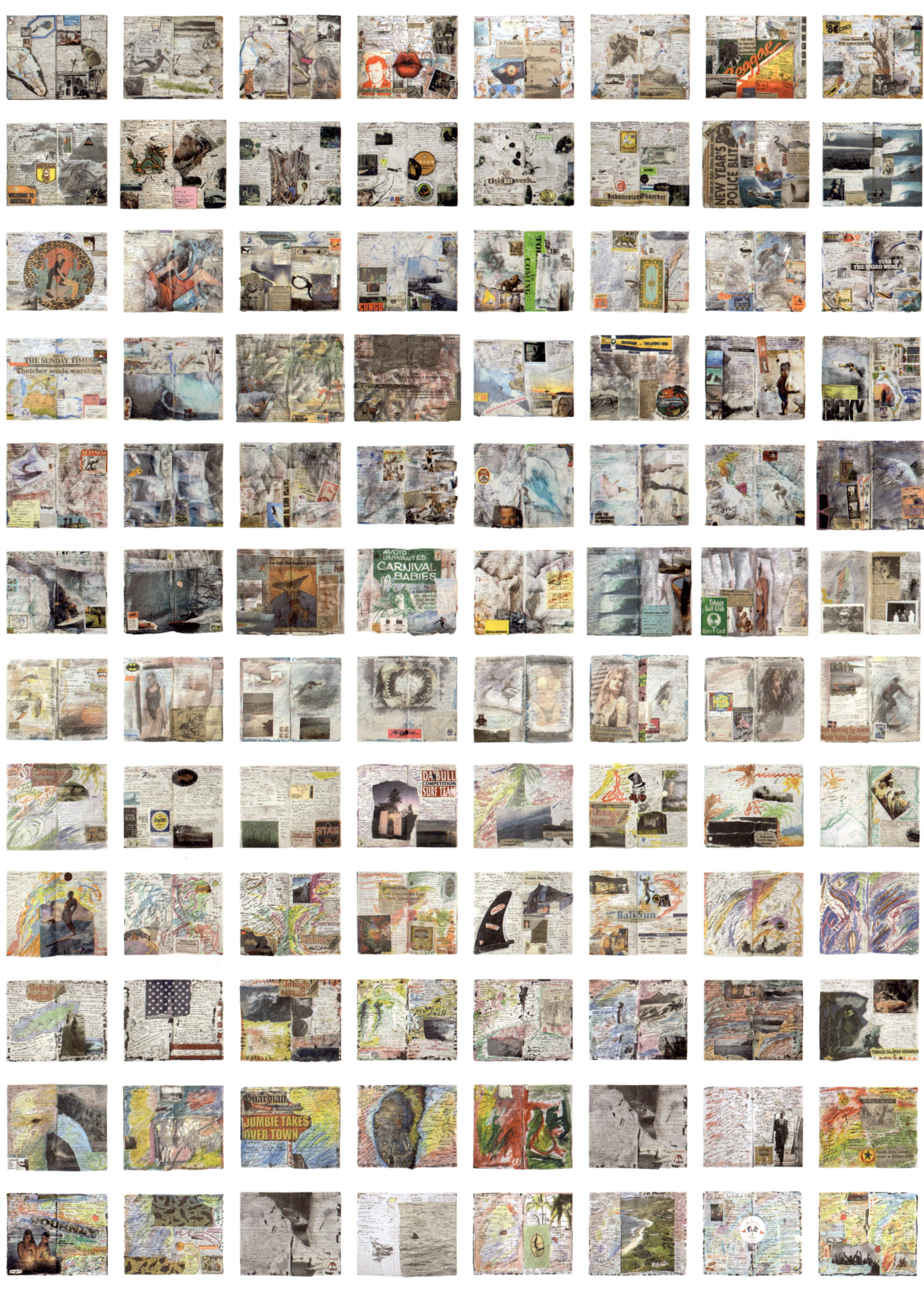

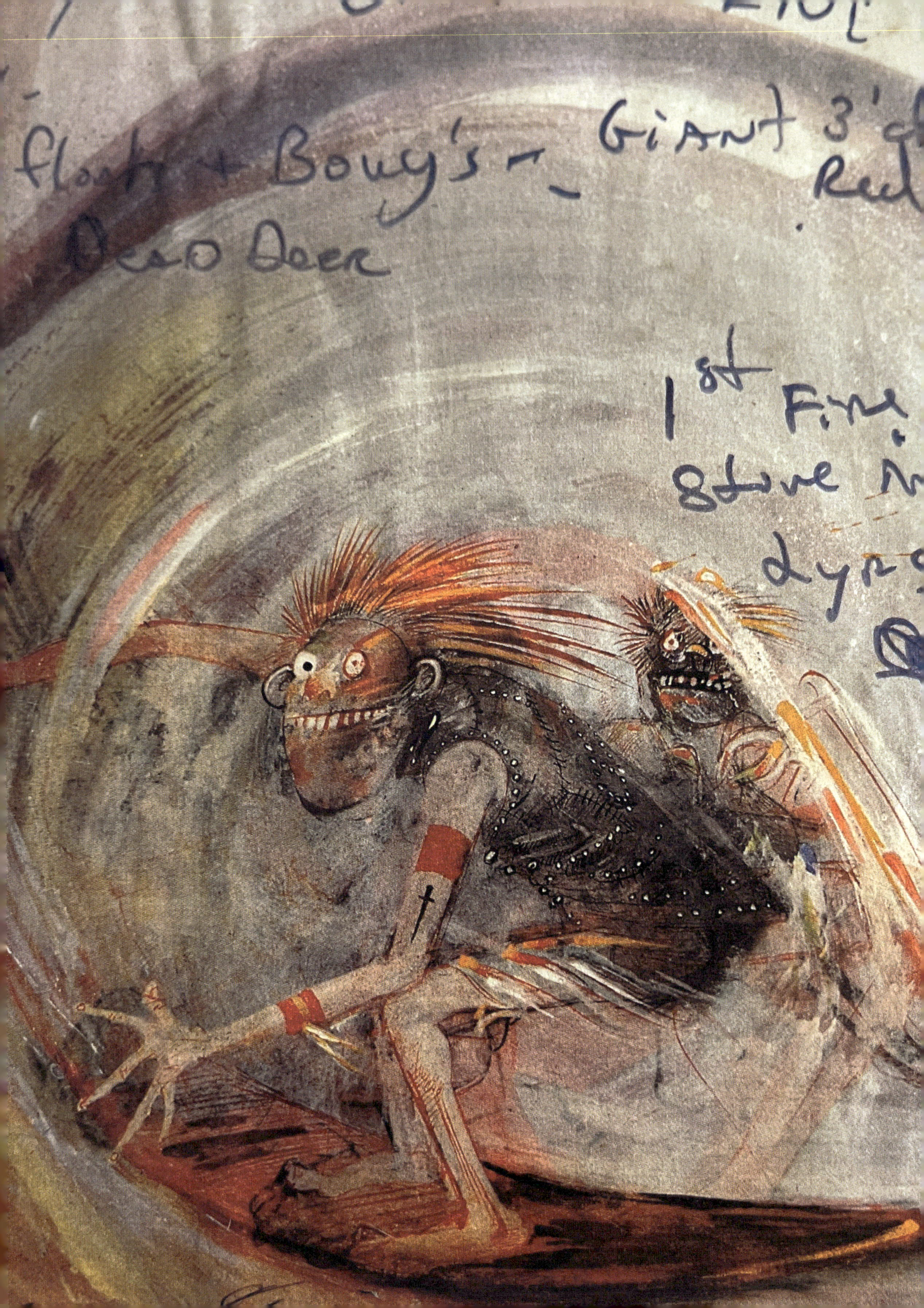

floats + Bouy's — GIANT 3'

Dead Deer

1st Fire